The Operating Systems
Handbook

Other Related Titles

The Operating Systems Handbook

UNIX, OpenVMS, OS/400, VM, and MVS

Bob DuCharme

McGraw-Hill, Inc.

New York   San Francisco   Washington, D.C.   Auckland   Bogotá
Caracas   Lisbon   London   Madrid   Mexico City   Milan
Montreal   New Delhi   San Juan   Singapore
Sydney   Tokyo   Toronto

Library of Congress Cataloging-in-Publication Data

DuCharme, Bob.
    The operating systems handbook : UNIX, OpenVMS, OS/400, VM, and MVS
UNIX / Bob DuCharme.
        p.   cm.
    Includes index.
    ISBN 0-07-017891-7
    1. Operating systems (Computers)   I. Title.
QA76.76.063D83   1994
005.4'44—dc20   94-1538
                                                                    CIP

2 3 4 5 6 7 8 9 0   **DOH   DOH**   9 0 9 8 7 6 5 4

ISBN 0-07-017891-7

The sponsoring editor for this book was Jerry Papke, the editing supervisor was Jim Halston, and the production supervisor was Pamela A. Pelton. It was set in Century Schoolbook by McGraw-Hill's Professional Book composition unit.

Printed and bound by R. R. Donnelley & Sons Company.

Contents

Acknowledgments   xv
Trademarks   **xvii**

Chapter 1. Introduction   1

1.1   Why Should You Learn How to Use Minis and Mainframes?   1
    1.1.1   What This Book Assumes That You Know   3
1.2   Minicomputers   4
1.3   Mainframes   5
1.4   Getting to Know an Operating System   7
    1.4.1   History and Culture   8
    1.4.2   Starting Up: Getting to Use the System   9
    1.4.3   Filenames   9
    1.4.4   How Files Are Organized   10
    1.4.5   On-Line Help   10
    1.4.6   Dealing with Files: The Most Important Commands   10
    1.4.7   The Text Editor   11
    1.4.8   Printing Text Files   12
    1.4.9   Command Files   12
    1.4.10   Sending and Receiving Mail   13
    1.4.11   A Sample Session   13
1.5   General Advice   14
    1.5.1   Filenames   14
        1.5.1.1   Wildcards   15
        1.5.1.2   Wildcards and File Deletion   17
    1.5.2   Mail   18
    1.5.3   The Text Editor   18
        1.5.3.1   Line Editors, Full-Screen Editors   18
        1.5.3.2   The Editing Buffer   19
    1.5.4   Looking at Text Files   20
    1.5.5   "Printing" on the Screen   20
    1.5.6   Reading and Writing   21
    1.5.7   Logging Off (or Out)   21
    1.5.8   Terminal Emulation and File Transfer   22
        1.5.8.1   Emulated Terminals   23
1.6   Syntax Expressions in This Book   23
1.7   Comments and Suggestions   24

Chapter 2. UNIX: An Introduction — 25

2.1   History — 25
   2.1.1   Today — 27
   2.1.2   USENET — 28

Chapter 3. Getting Started with UNIX — 31

3.1   Starting Up — 31
   3.1.1   Finishing Your UNIX Session — 32
3.2   Filenames — 32
   3.2.1   Wildcards — 33
      3.2.1.1   The Asterisk — 33
      3.2.1.2   The Question Mark — 33
3.3   How Files Are Organized — 34
   3.3.1   Relative Pathnames — 35
   3.3.2   Moving Between Directories — 36
3.4   Available On-Line Help — 37

Chapter 4. Using Files in UNIX — 39

4.1   The Eight Most Important Commands — 39
   4.1.1   Command Options: Switches — 40
   4.1.2   Common Error Messages — 40
   4.1.3   Listing Filenames — 41
      4.1.3.1   Listing More Than Filenames — 43
   4.1.4   Displaying a Text File's Contents — 48
      4.1.4.1   Looking at Text Files One Screen at a Time — 48
   4.1.5   Copying Files — 50
   4.1.6   Renaming Files — 52
   4.1.7   Deleting Files — 53
   4.1.8   Controlling Access to a File — 55
   4.1.9   Creating Directories — 57
   4.1.10   Removing Directories — 58

Chapter 5. The UNIX vi Text Editor — 61

5.1   Entering vi — 62
5.2   Inserting Text — 63
5.3   Deleting Text — 63
5.4   Typing Over Existing Text — 64
5.5   Searching for Text — 64
5.6   Saving Your Changes — 64
5.7   Quitting vi — 66
5.8   Other vi Commands — 66

Chapter 6. Using a UNIX System — 69

6.1   Printing Text Files — 69
   6.1.1   Checking the Print Queue — 69
   6.1.2   Canceling Your Print Job — 70
6.2   Command Files — 70
   6.2.1   The Automatic Login Command File — 71
6.3   Communicating with Other Users — 72
   6.3.1   Receiving Mail — 73
6.4   A Sample UNIX Session — 75

Chapter 7. OpenVMS: An Introduction   79

7.1   History   80
    7.1.1   Today   81
        7.1.1.1   Popular VMS Software   82
    7.1.2   VMS, DCL   82

Chapter 8. Getting Started with OpenVMS   85

8.1   Starting Up   85
    8.1.1   Finishing Your VMS Session   86
        8.1.1.1   Reconnecting   86
    8.1.2   Entering Commands   86
        8.1.2.1   Retrieving Previous Commands   87
        8.1.2.2   Aborting Screen Output   87
        8.1.2.3   Command Parameters   87
        8.1.2.4   Case Sensitivity   88
8.2   Filenames   88
    8.2.1   Wildcards   89
        8.2.1.1   The Asterisk   89
        8.2.1.2   The Percent Sign   90
8.3   How Files Are Organized   90
    8.3.1   Moving Between Directories   92
        8.3.1.1   Default Directory? Current Directory?   93
    8.3.2   Querying Available Disk Space   94
8.4   Available On-Line Help   94

Chapter 9. Using Files in OpenVMS   99

9.1   The Eight Most Important Commands   99
    9.1.1   Command Options: Qualifiers   99
    9.1.2   Common Error Messages   100
    9.1.3   Listing Filenames   101
        9.1.3.1   Listing More Than Filenames   102
    9.1.4   Displaying a Text File's Contents   103
        9.1.4.1   Looking at Text Files One Screen at a Time 103
    9.1.5   Copying Files   104
        9.1.5.1   Copying Files to Other Directories   105
    9.1.6   Renaming Files   106
    9.1.7   Deleting Files   107
        9.1.7.1   Purging Old Versions of Your Files   108
    9.1.8   Controlling Access to a File   108
    9.1.9   Creating Directories   110
    9.1.10   Removing Directories   110

Chapter 10. The OpenVMS EVE Text Editor   113

10.1   EVE and Special Keys   113
10.2   Entering EVE   114
10.3   Inserting Text   116
10.4   Deleting Text   116
10.5   Typing Over Existing Text   117
10.6   Searching for Text   117
10.7   Saving Your Changes   117
10.8   Quitting EVE   118
10.9   EVE On-Line Help   118
10.10 Other EVE Features   120

Chapter 11. Using an OpenVMS System   121

11.1   Printing Text Files   121
    11.1.1   Checking the Print Queue   121
    11.1.2   Canceling Your Print Job   122
11.2   Command Files   122
    11.2.1   Symbols   123
    11.2.2   DCL Command Procedures   123
    11.2.3   The Automatic Login Command File   124
11.3   Communicating with Other Users   125
    11.3.1   Sending an Existing File   126
    11.3.2   Receiving Mail   126
        11.3.2.1   Mail Folders   126
        11.3.2.2   Reading Mail   128
        11.3.2.3   Moving a Message to Another Folder   128
        11.3.2.4   Deleting Messages from a Folder   129
        11.3.2.5   Leaving the MAIL Program   129
        11.3.2.6   Saving a Message in a Text File   129
    11.3.3   On-Line Help in the MAIL Program   130
11.4   A Sample OpenVMS Session   130

Chapter 12. OS/400: An Introduction   133

12.1   History   134
    12.1.1   Today   135
        12.1.1.1   Popular OS/400 Software   137

Chapter 13. Getting Started with OS/400   139

13.1   Starting Up   139
    13.1.1   Finishing Your OS/400 Session   141
    13.1.2   Entering Commands   141
        13.1.2.1   Command Parameters   142
        13.1.2.2   Positional Parameters   144
        13.1.2.3   Case Sensitivity   145
        13.1.2.4   The Four Types of Displays   145
        13.1.2.5   Important Special Keys   147
13.2   Filenames   149
    13.2.1   Wildcards   149
13.3   How Files Are Organized   150
    13.3.1   Physical, Source Physical, and Logical Files   152
    13.3.2   The Library List and Your Current Library   152
13.4   Available On-Line Help   153
    13.4.1   The Search Index   154
    13.4.2   Navigating Help Screens   156
        13.4.2.1   Expanding Help Windows   156
        13.4.2.2   The User Support and Education Menu   158
        13.4.2.3   Hypertext Links   160
    13.4.3   The On-Line Tutorial   161
    13.4.4   Other Helpful Features   162

Chapter 14. Using Files in OS/400   165

14.1   The 12 Most Important Commands   165
    14.1.1   Common Error Messages   165
    14.1.2   Listing Filenames   168

14.1.2.1   Listing a File's Members   169
14.1.2.2   Listing a File's Members with the Program
            Development Manager   171
14.1.3   Displaying a Text File's Contents   172
14.1.3.1   Displaying a File's Members with the Program
            Development Manager   174
14.1.4   Copying Files   174
14.1.4.1   Copying Members   176
14.1.4.2   Copying Members with the Program Development
            Manager   176
14.1.5   Renaming Files   177
14.1.5.1   Renaming Members   178
14.1.5.2   Renaming Members with the Program Development
            Manager   179
14.1.6   Deleting Files   179
14.1.6.1   Deleting Members   179
14.1.6.2   Deleting Members with the Program Development
            Manager   179
14.1.7   Editing Your Library List   180
14.1.7.1   Changing Your Current Library   183
14.1.8   Creating and Deleting Libraries   183

Chapter 15. The OS/400 SEU Text Editor   185

15.1   Entering SEU   185
        15.1.1   Entering SEU from the Program Development Manager   187
15.2   Line Commands   187
        15.2.1   Adding New Lines   188
        15.2.2   Moving Your Cursor Around   190
15.3   Inserting, Deleting, and Typing over Words and Characters   191
        15.3.1   Duplicating Lines   191
        15.3.2   Deleting Lines   192
        15.3.3   Copying Lines   193
        15.3.4   Moving Lines   194
15.4   Searching for Text   194
        15.4.1   Case Sensitivity   195
15.5   Saving Your Changes   196
15.6   Quitting SEU   196
15.7   Other SEU Features   196
        15.7.1   SEU On-Line Help   196
        15.7.2   Syntax Prompting   197

Chapter 16. Using an OS/400 System   199

16.1   Printing Text Files   199
        16.1.1   Printing a File Member from the Program Development
                  Manager or SEU   202
        16.1.2   Checking the Print Queue   202
        16.1.3   Canceling Your Print Job   203
16.2   Command Files   203
        16.2.1   The Automatic Signon Command File   208
16.3   Communicating with Other Users   209
        16.3.1   Receiving Mail   211
        16.3.2   Inquiry Messages   212
        16.3.3   Sending an Existing File   215
                  16.3.3.1   Receiving a File   216
16.4   A Sample OS/400 Session   216

Chapter 17. VM/CMS: An Introduction   223

17.1   History   223
          17.1.1   CP: The Control Program   225

Chapter 18. Getting Started with VM/CMS   227

18.1   Starting Up   227
          18.1.1   The Logon Screen   227
          18.1.2   Entering CMS   229
          18.1.3   Entering Commands   230
                      18.1.3.1   MORE...   231
                      18.1.3.2   Aborting Screen Output   232
                      18.1.3.3   Case Sensitivity   233
          18.1.4   Finishing Your CMS Session   234
18.2   Filenames   234
          18.2.1   Wildcards   235
                      18.2.1.1   The Asterisk   236
                      18.2.1.2   The Percent Sign   237
18.3   How Files Are Organized   237
          18.3.1   Free Space on Your Disk   238
18.4   Available On-Line Help   238
          18.4.1   Help Function Keys   240
          18.4.2   Help Menus   241
          18.4.3   Command-Line Help   244
                      18.4.3.1   Command-Line Help and Error Messages   248

Chapter 19. Using Files in VM/CMS   249

19.1   The Five Most Important Commands   249
          19.1.1   Command Options   249
          19.1.2   Common Error Messages   250
          19.1.3   Listing Filenames   251
                      19.1.3.1   Listing More Than Filenames   253
          19.1.4   Displaying a Text File's Contents   255
          19.1.5   Copying Files   255
                      19.1.5.1   Changing a File's Format   257
          19.1.6   Renaming Files   258
          19.1.7   Deleting Files   259
19.2   Sharing Files Between Users   260
          19.2.1   Unlinking the Disk   262
          19.2.2   Other Ways to Link   263

Chapter 20. The VM/CMS XEDIT Text Editor   265

20.1   Entering XEDIT   265
20.2   Customizing Your XEDIT Environment   266
20.3   Prefix Commands   268
          20.3.1   Adding New Lines   269
          20.3.2   Moving Your Cursor Around   269
          20.3.3   Inserting, Deleting, and Typing over Words and Characters   270
          20.3.4   Duplicating Lines   270
          20.3.5   Deleting Lines   272
          20.3.6   Copying Lines   273
          20.3.7   Moving Lines   274
20.4   Searching for Text   274

20.5   Saving Your Changes   275
20.6   Quitting XEDIT   275
20.7   Other Useful XEDIT Features   276
    20.7.1   XEDIT On-Line Help   276
    20.7.2   The Automatic Startup Macro   276
    20.7.3   The Split/Join Key   277

Chapter 21. Using a VM/CMS System   279

21.1   Printing Text Files   279
    21.1.1   Checking the Print Queue   279
    21.1.2   Canceling Your Print Job   280
21.2   Command Files   280
    21.2.1   The Automatic Logon Command File   282
21.3   Communicating with Other Users   282
    21.3.1   Sending Files   283
    21.3.2   Receiving Mail and Files   284
        21.3.2.1   Looking at a File in the Reader   285
        21.3.2.2   Saving a File from the Reader   286
        21.3.2.3   Discard a File from the Reader   288
21.4   The FILELIST Program   288
    21.4.1   Copying Files   289
    21.4.2   Renaming Files   289
    21.4.3   Deleting Files   290
    21.4.4   Displaying a Text File's Contents   290
    21.4.5   Editing a File   290
    21.4.6   Printing a File   290
21.5   A Sample VM/CMS Session   290

Chapter 22. MVS: An Introduction   295

22.1   Batch Jobs   296
22.2   Interacting with MVS   297
    22.2.1   TSO   297
    22.2.2   ISPF   297
    22.2.3   CICS   298
    22.2.4   Other MVS Components   298
22.3   History   299

Chapter 23. Getting Started with MVS   301

23.1   Starting Up   301
    23.1.1   VTAM   301
    23.1.2   Logging On   302
        23.1.2.1   Reconnecting   304
        23.1.3   Entering Commands   304
        23.1.3.1   Aborting Screen Output   306
        23.1.3.2   Command Parameters   306
        23.1.3.3   Long Commands   306
        23.1.3.4   Case Sensitivity   307
        23.1.3.5   Command-Line Options   307
    23.1.4   Finishing Your MVS Session   308
23.2   Filenames   308
    23.2.1   Sequential and Partitioned Data Sets   308
    23.2.2   Line Numbers and Data Sets   309

23.2.3   Naming Data Sets   309
            23.2.3.1   The Members of a Partitioned Data Set   311
23.2.4   Wildcards   311
23.3   How Files Are Organized   312
23.4   Available On-Line Help   312

Chapter 24. Using Files in MVS   315

24.1   The Seven Most Important Commands   315
        24.1.1   Common Error Messages   316
        24.1.2   Listing Data Set Names   317
                    24.1.2.1   Listing a Catalog's Data Sets   318
                    24.1.2.2   Listing a Partitioned Data Set's Members 319
        24.1.3   Looking at Data Sets   320
        24.1.4   Copying Data Sets   321
                    24.1.4.1   Copying and Partitioned Data Sets   321
        24.1.5   Renaming Data Sets   322
        24.1.6   Deleting Data Sets   323
        24.1.7   Allocating Data Sets   324
                    24.1.7.1   Allocating Existing Data Sets   324
                    24.1.7.2   Allocating New Data Sets   326
                    24.1.7.3   Unallocating Data Sets   329
                    24.1.7.4   Finding Out a Data Set's Allocation Status 330
        24.1.8   Adding a Data Set to a Catalog   332

Chapter 25. The MVS ISPF Text Editor   333

25.1   The ISPF Text Editor   333
25.2   Entering the ISPF Editor   333
        25.2.1   Customizing Your Editor's Environment   337
25.3   Line Commands   338
        25.3.1   Adding New Lines   339
        25.3.2   Moving Your Cursor Around   341
25.4   Inserting, Deleting, and Typing over Words and Characters   341
        25.4.1   Duplicating Lines   342
        25.4.2   Deleting Lines   343
        25.4.3   Copying Lines   344
        25.4.4   Moving Lines   345
25.5   Searching for Text   345
25.6   Saving Your Changes   347
25.7   Quitting the ISPF Editor   347
        25.7.1   On-Line Help in the Editor   348
25.8   TSO's EDIT Text Editor   349
        25.8.1   Starting the Editor   349
        25.8.2   Creating a New Data Set   349
        25.8.3   Line Numbering and the EDIT Editor   350
        25.8.4   Input Mode and Edit Mode   350
        25.8.5   Displaying the Data Set's Current Contents   352
        25.8.6   The Current Line   352
        25.8.7   Adding New Lines   353
        25.8.8   Editing Existing Lines   354
        25.8.9   Deleting Lines   355
        25.8.10   Copying Lines   355
        25.8.11   Duplicating Lines   356
        25.8.12   Moving Lines   356

25.8.13   Searching for Text   357
25.8.14   Saving Your Changes   357
25.8.15   Quitting the TSO Editor   357
25.8.16   On-Line Help and the TSO Editor   358

Chapter 26. Using an MVS System   359

26.1   Printing Data Sets   359
26.2   Command Files   360
    26.2.1   The Automatic Logon Command File   361
26.3   Communicating with Other Users   362
    26.3.1   Sending Files   363
    26.3.2   Receiving Mail and Data Sets   365
26.4   ISPF   366
    26.4.1   Allocating Data Sets   368
    26.4.2   Copying Data Sets   370
    26.4.3   Renaming Data Sets   372
    26.4.4   Deleting Data Sets   373
    26.4.5   Displaying A Data Set's Contents   374
    26.4.6   Printing a Data Set   374
26.5   A Sample MVS Session   374

Index   379

Acknowledgments

My thanks to Howard Lune, who explained to me the relationship between VM, CMS, and CP as we killed a bottle of Dewar's at 2 in the morning in a Miami hotel room, and who has since graciously reviewed the mainframe chapters; to Don Bonnice, whom I have never met, but who helped me with the OS/400 chapters through the miracle of e-mail; to Ray Hood, who first taught me UNIX and, more importantly, taught me how to quickly identify and learn the important parts of a software system; to Alex Berson, for taking the time to review the manuscript; to Chet Ensign and Frances Gambino, who taught me how to put a book together; to Madeline—may file allocation be as distant a memory to her generation as magnetic core memory is to ours; and most of all, to my wife Jennifer, who has patiently learned more about minis, mainframes, Elvis Presley, Formula 1, Indy Cars, and electric guitars than she ever planned to before she met me.

Bob DuCharme

Trademarks

All OpenVMS screen images are used by permission of Digital Equipment, Maynard, MA.

All IBM screen images are used courtesy of International Business Machines Corporation.

The following are registered trademarks of International Business Machines Corporation: AIX, AS/400, AT, IBM, OfficeVision. The following are trademarks of International Business Machines Corporation: PC/DOS, RACF, ESA/370, MVS/XA, VM/XA, VM/ESA.

The following are registered trademarks of Digital Equipment Corporation: ALL-IN-ONE, DCL, DEC, PDP, Rdb, RMS, ULTRIX, VAX, VAXcluster, VAXstation, VAX/VMS. The following are trademarks of Digital Equipment Corporation: DECstation, OpenVMS, Pathworks, VMS, VT.

The following are registered trademarks of Novell, Inc.: Novell, NetWare.

The following are registered trademarks of AT&T in the USA and other countries: AT&T, UNIX.

The following are registered trademarks of Sun Microsystems, Inc.: Sun, Sun Microsystems.

The following is a trademark of Sun Microsystems, Inc.: SunOS.

The following are registered trademarks of Microsoft Corporation: Microsoft, MS-DOS, XENIX.

CompuServe is a registered trademark of CompuServe Incorporated.

The following are registered trademarks of Hewlett-Packard company: Apollo, Hewlett-Packard.

The following are registered trademarks of Apple computer: Apple, Macintosh.

The Operating Systems
Handbook

1

Introduction

Today it is fashionable among many personal computer (PC) users to proclaim that minicomputers and mainframes are dinosaurs, and that the meteor that will render them extinct is coming fast. [When I say personal computer, or PC, I mean one that's personal, that you have all to yourself, and that you can afford to have at home or on your desk at work. This includes Macintoshes, Amigas, and the Atari ST, not just Disk Operating System (DOS) machines.] They call the big machines primitive, because you don't use a mouse and icons to start up programs.

These personal computer users probably feel frustrated when they look through the want ads and see the many job openings for people who know UNIX, OpenVMS, OS/400, VM/CMS, and MVS. They don't understand that the big rigs aren't dying out; their roles are being redefined to take advantage of their strengths while PCs take over the jobs that PCs can do better.

The PC's mouse and icons mean that its interface is easier to use and more responsive. Unfortunately, PC snobs judge other operating systems by their interfaces. They see the on-line help in MVS scrolling up the screen in all capital letters and snort, "How very primitive!" They don't realize how many sophisticated features, unrelated to the user interface, have always been integral parts of MVS and other large operating systems—features that many in the PC business are only now trying to shoehorn into their products. Data safety, proper multitasking, and serious multiuser support still have a way to go for networks of personal computers. And minicomputer and mainframe technology is not standing still; a glance at trade papers shows that they become faster and more powerful every year.

1.1 Why Should You Learn How to Use Minis and Mainframes?

For many, the want ads mentioned above provide sufficient impetus to learn about larger systems. The line "Working knowledge of UNIX, OpenVMS, OS/400, VM/CMS, and MVS" looks great on a resume.

1

The recent trend toward downsizing means that some of the development jobs for your favorite operating system involve moving (or "migrating") existing applications from larger systems to smaller ones. Many jobs involve moving only part of an application to a different system. Another big trend is distributed, "client/server" systems, in which the application's user interface runs on the smaller system and its data is stored on a larger system, and the two (or more) systems must communicate and cooperate. If you want any of these jobs, you better know the systems at both ends of the job.

An AS/400 running release V2R2 or later of the OS/400 operating system can store a database of up to 2 billion records taking up 248 gigabytes of space. (And remember—that's a minicomputer, not a mainframe!) It will be quite a while before any personal computer-based system can handle a database that large. The practicality of storing larger databases on larger systems brings up another reason for learning how to use minis and mainframes: just as Willie Sutton said that he robbed banks "because that's where the money is," it's a good idea to get comfortable with large computer systems because that's where the really massive databases are stored. Access to the big systems means access to more information.

Actually, the best reason for learning these systems is this: they're really not that difficult. When people discuss the relative merits of different operating systems, they talk about the advanced features. That's where the difficult parts come in; when it comes to the basics, the tasks that are necessary to get by are remarkably similar from one operating system to another.

BUZZWORD: "Downsize." Minicomputers have provided an alternative to mainframes since 1961 and PCs have provided an alternative to both since 1977. There have always been applications that were too big for PCs, and many that were too big for minis as well. As all classes of computers become more powerful by an estimated 20% a year, minicomputers and PCs can more easily handle applications that were formerly considered too big for them.

The process of moving an application from a mini to a PC (or to a networked group of PCs) or from a mainframe to either is known as "downsizing." Some development environments boast of their availability on multiple platforms, making downsizing easier—in other words, if you know how to use the language or development program that was used to create an application, and it's also available on the target system, then you're halfway there. Still, you must be familiar enough with the basic operating system commands on both ends of the project to be able to log in and to read, copy, edit, and transfer files.

A recent variation on "downsizing" is "rightsizing." It essentially means the same thing, but implies that you're considering options besides moving from a bigger system to a smaller system. Its main advantage over the word "downsizing" is that it is more recent, and therefore sounds more up-to-date—always a big plus with buzzwords.

Show me someone who insists that a certain operating system is superior to all others and I'll show you someone who probably only knows one operating system. (Or else a DOS user who has just learned UNIX—sometimes the added power goes to their heads and they forget why personal computers were invented.) Someone once called it the "baby duck syndrome"—these users behave like baby ducks who think that the first thing they see after being born is their mother.

Sometimes, it's fun to be a snob. It's even better, though, to have a broader background and wider perspective than one particular subset of computer nerds. Once you can log in, create and manipulate files, navigate the file system, and send and receive mail on many different operating systems, you gain a perspective on the strengths and weaknesses of each—a perspective that helps you to appreciate these operating systems individually as well as the roles each can play when they must work together. And, people are impressed by someone who appears comfortable with several large systems. It doesn't matter if you only know how to do ten things on each one, as long as they're the right ten things!

1.1.1 What this book assumes that you know

This book is not a beginner's introduction to computers. Although it sticks to basic topics, it contains a series of crash courses, so it moves quickly through these topics.

Presumably, you already know what an operating system is: the supervisory program that runs on a computer at all times, taking your instructions to run other programs or to manipulate and print files, and carrying out these instructions while it coordinates your actions with those of other users on the system. You know what a file is, and you know that a computer that can store thousands of files needs a way to organize them, so that learning a little about the file system is one of the first steps in learning to use a particular operating system. You also know the basic operations that people do with text editors and word processors: creating new files, adding text to them, deleting and editing text, and saving or aborting the edits made in a given session.

Ideally, you should have some experience with a command-line driven operating system—the kind where you type commands and press Enter (or Return) to get results. Some operating systems, like AmigaDOS and the UNIX found on Sun workstations, offer a mouse-driven graphical user interface to handle files and applications, but also offer a window with a command line. They do this because, contrary to the insistence of Macintosh purists, typing out commands is often a more efficient way to accomplish things. For example, typing the word "erase" followed by a filename and then pressing Enter is a simpler—and, yes, more intuitive—way to erase a file than pushing around a hunk of plastic with a rubber ball inside of it.

As this book shows you, mini and mainframe operating systems either erase files with this command or with a slight variation, like using the word "delete" instead of "erase." Some commands are more complicated than this, but remember, learning the basics of an operating system does not require memorizing complicated commands! The keys are remembering simple commands and remembering how to find out the ways to put together more complicated ones when necessary.

For someone only interested in the basics of using an operating system, the easy-to-remember way to accomplish something is always more important than the most efficient way. If you already know one of the operating systems covered in this book, you will find that it doesn't always explain the most efficient techniques. Again, this is because of the crash course approach. Learning the efficient way to do something usually involves learning why it's more efficient; this undoubtedly takes you into areas that the dabbler would rather avoid.

> BUZZWORD: "Client/Server." This is actually two words, but because it describes a particular relationship between two or more computers, the two are often used together. In a client/server system, smaller computers are hooked up to larger systems, and developers create applications that take advantage of the combination.
>
> Usually, the smaller computer (the "client") presents the user interface and formulates a query or command based on the user's actions. It then sends this query or command to the larger computer, or "server," which carries out the smaller computer's request and returns the results—often a specific subset of the data stored there—to the smaller computer. The user has the advantage of the small computer's better interface, but the data is stored on a system with a large storage capacity, better multi-user support, and built-in safeguards against possible problems ranging from power outages to attempted break-ins by hackers.
>
> In a broader sense, a server is something that provides a service to a client system. It may refer to hardware, as with a file server that stores files for other computers to use. It may refer to software; a database server is a program that mediates requests for data from clients and ensures the integrity of the stored data.
>
> Along with downsizing, increased development of client/server systems is another important reason that mainframe, minicomputer, and microcomputer people must learn more about each others' systems. This way, they can make these different computers work together as efficiently as possible.

1.2 Minicomputers

In 1961, Digital Equipment Corporation (DEC) introduced the "Programmed Data Processor 1" (PDP-1). The PDP-1 is generally considered to be the first commercially available minicomputer. It was a scaled-down, less expensive (only $120,000!) version of the multimillion-dollar behemoths that were synonymous with the word "computer" at the time. To distinguish it from the bigger computers, they called it a "minicomputer." Before the invention of the minicomputer, the word "mainframe" was not even necessary, because people just called them "computers." (Actually, some people called them "IBMs," but that's another story.)

The PDP-1's various successors, especially the $20,000 PDP-8 that DEC introduced in 1965, proved that there was a real market for minicomputers. Other computer makers soon entered the minicomputer market—Hewlett Packard, Wang, Data General, even IBM.

The word "minicomputer," coined in the same era as the word "miniskirt," has become anachronistic. Nowadays, when someone says "computer," they're usually talking about a PC or "microcomputer"—something that costs a few thousand dollars and sits on a desk. A "minicomputer" costs five or six figures and can be as large as a refrigerator.

Considering that modern PCs are much more powerful than the original minicomputers, and that modern minis are much more powerful than the mainframes available when the PDP-1 was first released, what does that make a minicomputer today?

People often use the term "departmental computing" in the same breath as the word "minicomputer." This gives a good clue about the role of minis. If all the people in one department share one computer, it will be bigger than a PC, and smaller than a mainframe. It supports from 10 to 100 people. Maintaining it shouldn't be a full-time job for one person. Of course, the use of minicomputers isn't limited to individual departments of large companies or universities; small companies provide one of the minicomputer's biggest markets.

Of the operating systems described in this book, the AS/400's cleverly named OS/400 operating system is the only one that is unequivocally a minicomputer operating system. Because the smallest VAXes sometimes qualify as personal computers, and the largest ones as mainframes, and because versions of UNIX have been developed for everything from IBM PC/ATs to Cray supercomputers, devotees of these two operating systems insist that their versatility ranges beyond the middle of the computing spectrum designated by the word "minicomputer." However, since the majority of the computers running these two operating systems fit the profile of a mini described above, most people think of OpenVMS and UNIX as minicomputer operating systems.

1.3 Mainframes

Reports of the death of mainframes have been greatly exaggerated. Mainframes can store huge amounts of data and accomplish a lot of work. If the PC of your dreams can be compared to an eight-cylinder

Ferrari, then a mainframe is an 18-wheel truck. They are the big rigs. Some PC snobs claim that a properly networked configuration of PCs can accomplish anything a mainframe can; these people have no idea of the kinds of things that banks, insurance companies, and governments call on mainframes to do: to process *huge* amounts of data, 24 hours a day, in an extremely secure environment.

> BUZZWORD: "Big iron." Refers to mainframe hardware. For example, "The insurance company's main office had one Amdahl, but most of the big iron was IBM."

The fact that many people who've never used mainframes consider them antiquated has hurt their reputation. In order to appear up-to-date, more people try to avoid using the word "mainframe." In late 1990, an important trade magazine called *Mainframe Journal* changed its name to *Enterprise Systems Journal.* The use of the buzzword "enterprise" reflects more than a desire to look current: it shows a change in attitude about mainframes and their role in business computing today.

> BUZZWORD: "Enterprise." Usually used as part of an adjective, as in "Enterprise-Wide Computing." A fancy way to say "the whole company." This sort of phrase comes up more and more as people try to hook up all the computers in a given company into one cooperative system.

Instead of being The Computer, which is what a mainframe represented at most companies for years, people now consider it to be one of the resources in a computing environment. Plenty of former mainframe tasks can now be done better and more cheaply on minicomputers, or even on PCs, but many jobs remain that are more suited to mainframes. Since so many computers are hooked up to other computers, the best possible system is one that distributes the jobs so that each computer does what it's best at. Of course, someone sitting at a terminal—the company president, a secretary, or a consultant pretending to know the system—shouldn't have to worry about which computer is performing which task as long as this user gets what he or she wants.

A system in which PCs and mainframes work together distributes the jobs that each computer does best. For PCs, this means the interface, or "front end": windows, colors, fonts, and the use of a mouse. For mainframes, this means coordinating vast amounts of data that many other users might be trying to use simultaneously. (This role has been cleverly named the "back end" of such a cooperative system.) After the person sitting at the personal computer uses the flashy interface to describe the needed data, the personal computer sends a request to the mainframe, which does the sorting and manipulation necessary to pull out the requested data and send it back to the PC.

Because of this changing role, organizations that develop mainframe systems no longer bother with attempts to make fancy interfaces to their systems. They realize that the mainframe version of a

DOS on a Mainframe?

Computers did not always use disks to store information. When the disk drive was invented, it was considered such a breakthrough that virtually all computers today have at least one disk built in. In 1966, when PCs were only a dream, IBM released the first operating system that took advantage of disk storage and called it the Disk Operating System, or DOS. It went through several versions with names like DOS-2314, DOS MP, DOS/VS, and DOS/VSE. This last one—Disk Operating System/Virtual Storage Extended—is still used on some smaller mainframes today, although its popularity waned in the mid-seventies with the rise of VM/CMS and MVS.

When IBM released a PC operating system that used disks, they called it PC/DOS to distinguish it from the mainframe DOS. Microsoft called their version of PC/DOS "MS-DOS," for "Microsoft Disk Operating System." PC/DOS and MS-DOS are similar enough that people usually don't bother to distinguish between the two; they refer to both as "DOS." Because DOS VSE is the most common version of the mainframe DOS that anyone still uses, people usually refer to the mainframe DOS as "DOS/VSE" to distinguish it from the PC operating system.

Actually, they refer to it less and less with each passing year, because its place in history as a predecessor to MVS and CMS makes it increasingly archaic. What happens to a DOS/VSE installation that's ready to move on? They don't always replace DOS/VSE with a more up-to-date mainframe system. It tends to be used on smaller System/370s, so the increasing power of the AS/400 and its comparative simplicity in use and maintenance make it a popular replacement for DOS/VSE systems.

fancy interface, when used with typical mainframe terminals, pales in comparison to something as common and inexpensive as a hand-held video game. Instead, they concentrate on making the huge data manipulation power of mainframes available to other computers that are connected to mainframes, so that mainframes can play an efficient role in the increasingly popular "distributed systems" made up of various computers connected together.

To sum up, the role of mainframes is changing and evolving faster than it is shrinking. After all, the guys who designed these things came from the generation of engineers who put men on the moon. Give them a little credit.

> BUZZWORD: "DASD." Because it does have a specific technical meaning, it may not count as an official buzzword—it sounds so impressive, though, when you say "dazzdee" instead of "mainframe hard disk." It stands for "Direct Access Storage Device." (By the way, "device" is practically its own buzzword, meaning "hardware thing.") A DASD unit is really a stack of hard disks, but you can think of it as one, since it functions as a single unit of storage.

1.4 Getting to Know an Operating System

Because the most basic, necessary tasks on any operating system are pretty much the same, each part of this book has a similar outline. Each covers the following subjects:

- History
- Starting up
- Filename rules
- The file system
- Important commands for dealing with files
- On-line help
- Using the text editor
- Printing
- Command files
- How to send and receive electronic mail
- A sample session

IBM's 360 Series of Mainframes

In the early days of computers, the question of compatibility, even among machines from the same company, was moot. Different computers were designed to specialize in handling either characters, integers, or decimal numbers. Of the six different computer models offered by IBM in the early 1960s, no two could run the same programs.

It didn't occur to anyone that a program written on one computer should be able to run on another computer. This changed when people started getting new computers and realized how much work would be required to rewrite the programs to work on their new computers.

IBM saw that it would be easier to sell software if it could offer a wide range of hardware to run that software. In 1964, IBM announced the System/360 series. The number came from the number of degrees in a circle, and was supposed to symbolize the computer's ability to be all things to all people. Even better, the different models were compatible, so that a program that ran on one could run unaltered on a more powerful model in the series.

Eight years later, after introducing VM/CMS, IBM brought out the 370 series. Although there have been many upgrades and improvements, just about all IBM mainframes used today are part of the 370 series.

1.4.1 History and culture

Knowing an operating system's history is not particularly important to becoming a comfortable user of that system. Usually, only the experts who have used the system for years seem to know or even care about its origins and development. This is precisely why it's great to know a little of the history: If you want to pretend that you're an expert, it's much easier to learn where an operating system came from and why it became popular than to memorize the syntax and usage of dozens of commands. People discussing UNIX at a party or at work will be impressed when you casually say, "Of course, the fact that the original UNIX license agreement included the source code while excluding any technical support was a complete reversal of standard practice at the time, and a key factor in the eventual priestlike status of the important UNIX gurus." On the other hand, if you know every little switch to the UNIX `ls` command and can make the filenames list out backward, forward, and sideways, they'll just think you're a computer nerd.

The culture, or general attitude of an operating system's typical heavy users, is closely tied to the system's strengths and weaknesses. Familiarity with it helps you fake at least a nominal membership in these cultish groups. It certainly helps you communicate with the real devotees, which is crucial to moving beyond beginner status.

1.4.2 Starting up: getting to use the system

When you turn on a PC, unless some special security hardware or software has been added, you can use it right away. Multiuser systems have some measure of security to prevent the wrong people from using them. The first concern for you, as a user of one of these systems, is to establish that you are a legitimate user of that system by logging in or logging on. This generally involves entering your user ID—a name assigned to you as a user of the system—and a password that you theoretically keep secret so that only you can use that user ID.

1.4.3 Filenames

You and the operating system distinguish one file from another by its name. But while `joememo.txt` and `JOEMEMO.TXT` would both refer to the same file in CMS or OpenVMS, they would refer to two different files in UNIX, because UNIX is case-sensitive. (Like many aspects of UNIX, this is considered both an advantage and a disadvantage, depending on who you ask.)

As you'll see in Section 1.5, "General Advice," we can apply certain guidelines to the naming of files on all computers, but you must learn

---

Logging In/On/Out/Off

Which is more proper, saying that you log in to a computer, then log out, or log on, then log off? The original IBM way was to say "log on." However, when you connect to a UNIX or OpenVMS system, it asks you to "log in," and it's improper to say that you log on to one of these systems. It's interesting to note that AIX, IBM's version of UNIX, asks you to "log in," which acknowledges the influence of the world of UNIX on IBM. Novell networks of personal computers also ask you to "log in." On the other hand, IBM's AS/400 minicomputer skips the whole question by asking you to "sign on."

Before I remotely connect to my UNIX ID on a Sun workstation ID or to my mainframe VM/CMS account, I must first log in to a DEC Server that can route my request to any of several computers. In other words, I must log *in* to the DEC Server before I log *in* to a Sun workstation, but I must log *in* to the DEC Server before I log *on* to an IBM mainframe.

the basic idiosyncrasies of file naming rules on a particular system before you create or rename files on it. How many parts does a filename have, and what are their names? What does each part do? How long can each part be? Are any keyboard characters that taboo in filenames? What tricks are there for dealing with more than one file at a time?

1.4.4 How files are organized

Another crucial aspect of an operating system is the method it uses to organize files. When you issue the command to list filenames, you don't want to see thousands of them; there should be some way to categorize them into groups, just as you can categorize the files in a file cabinet according to project or client. Also, on a multiuser system, you will probably be assigned your own storage area in which to keep your files. This brings up several new questions: What is the relationship between your files, those of other users, and the program files that make up the system software? Is there a way to check out what's stored outside of your own area?

The file organization system is one of the most important features that distinguish one operating system from another. Until you learn it, you can't get around on a computer to see what's there and to find the programs and data you need.

1.4.5 On-line help

If you remember only one thing about any computer or program (in addition to starting up), remember how to access and use any available on-line help. If you know this, you can discover all the other necessary information on your own. You can also get beyond the basics covered by this book and become of a real expert in that system.

1.4.6 Dealing with files: the most important commands

Each operating system's "Most Important Commands" chapter describes the crucial commands for manipulating and organizing files.

Using a computer is ultimately about the manipulation of files. (Some systems may use a different term instead of "file," but the same principles apply.) These are the units in which we group stored data on a computer, regardless of the data's source, destination, or purpose. We take files called programs that are instructions to the computer, run them, and use them to create, look at, alter, delete, and transfer other files.

This section shows you the most important things that you can do to files:

- List their names, with any pertinent information about them (like their size and the last time that they were changed)

- Put a text file's contents on the screen where you can see it
- Copy files
- Rename files
- Delete files

Where applicable, this section also shows how to create and remove subdirectories (subdivisions of the disk space allotted to your user ID) and how to move files in and out of these subdirectories.

Many operating systems provide a way to control other users' access to your files. If not knowing this prevents you from using any of a particular system's essential commands, the "Using Files" chapter for that operating system explains how to control access to your files. For example, an OpenVMS system may not give you permission to remove your own subdirectories, so Chapter 9, "Using Files in OpenVMS," explains how to give yourself permission with the SET PROTECTION command. When you create a command file in UNIX, you may not have permission to execute it, so Chapter 9 explains how to give yourself this permission with the chmod command.

This section also prepares you for an operating system's typical error messages. A beginner will encounter many, and knowing which part of these messages to ignore and which parts can help you will speed the process of discovering what you did wrong.

1.4.7 The text editor

To create your own text files, or to edit existing ones, you need a text editor. Writing your own command files requires one. Composing mail usually requires one (unless the mail program has a text editor built in). Files moved to one computer from another running a different operating system often have extraneous characters that need to be removed. (For example, although a text file is a text file on any system, older DOS programs indicated the end of a text file with a ^Z character, which may show up as an unwanted character at the end of a file that was moved from a DOS PC to another computer.)

This book shows you how to use the text editor that comes with each operating system to do the following:

- Create a new text file
- Edit an existing file
- Insert new text into a file
- Delete existing characters or lines from a file
- Search for an expression within a file
- Save your changes
- Abort your editing session, so that changes are not saved

Text Files, Binary Files

A text file is generally made up of keyboard characters. Because the American National Standard Institute (ANSI) standardized a code that specified which bytes represent which keyboard characters (the American Standard Code for Information Interchange, or ASCII), each letter or number in a text file is represented by the same byte on nearly any computer. For example, the uppercase letter "A" is represented by 01000001, or byte number 65. This system makes it easy to move text files from a computer running one operating system to a computer running another.

Most programs that you run on a computer were originally written as text files, then compiled into binary files. In other words, they were translated by a special program known as a compiler into the computer's own language. These files are just collections of bits and will appear as gibberish if you try to look at them. Compiled programs aren't the only binary files—data files stored by popular word processors, spreadsheets, and graphics programs are also binary. They are full of hidden codes and compressed data stored in whatever data structures the programmers who designed them thought would be most efficient.

To do anything with these binary data files, you usually need a copy of the program that created them. (For instance, to edit a file created with Microsoft Word, you need Microsoft Word.) Text files, however, are more universal; any text editor can edit any text file.

1.4.8 Printing text files

A computer industry analyst once said "The paperless office is about as useful as the paperless bathroom." Today, people are using their screens more often to read the information that they need, but the vast majority of computing that takes place still leads to a hard copy result. People use word processors to write letters that they will print out and mail; they use spreadsheet and database programs to print out data that they will photocopy and distribute to co-workers.

Sending a file to a printer is usually pretty simple. The use of a multiuser system adds a few wrinkles. Because the system may have more than one printer available, you might have to identify the printer you want to use. Since other users may have print jobs waiting to print on that same printer, this section also shows how to list out the waiting print jobs, if possible, to get an idea of how long you must wait. And, if you send something to the printer and then change your mind about printing it, this section shows you how to cancel the print job.

1.4.9 Command files

Any computer that lets you issue commands by typing them at a command line will also allow you to create a text file with a series of commands and to then execute those commands by typing in the name of the file where you stored them. These command files provide a way to automate repetitive tasks. In some cases, they provide a complete programming language.

Command files help you pretend to know more about an operating system than you really do for two reasons:

- Beginners tend to believe that only experts write and use command files.

- If you look up the syntax of complex commands and put them into command files with simple names that are easy to remember, you'll have an easy way to execute complex commands without remembering their syntax.

It's not hard to create simple command files if you are reasonably comfortable with a system's text editor. This section shows you how.

1.4.10 Sending and receiving mail

The ability to communicate through electronic mail, or "e-mail," is one of the greatest advantages of a multiuser system. It cuts down on phone tag. It allows you to ask people questions when you feel like it, not when they're free, and they can answer you when it's convenient for them. If the subject of your discussion is in a file on the computer, you can send it, or embed part of it in your message. If you can log in to the computer over telephone lines, you can communicate remotely, which by itself has several advantages: you can communicate with people whose hours are different from yours, and you can keep current on issues in the office when you are on the road or staying at home. Many people have accounts on multiuser systems solely to use the e-mail program.

Because the mail program that comes with a system often leaves something to be desired, many companies purchase and install a better one. Different mail programs on the same system can usually communicate with each other, so even if your company has purchased a new one, you won't be wasting your time if you learn the basics of the one that's included with the operating system. The following are the crucial tasks for dealing with your mail:

- Checking to see if you have mail
- Reading messages
- Deleting messages
- Saving a received message as a file
- Replying to a message
- Creating a new message
- Sending an existing file to someone

1.4.11 A sample session

Each part of the book ends with a brief scenario that demonstrates a typical session on that operating system. Joe User, our hero, works in an office where he is expected to know the basics of the system described. Usually, he logs in and finds a mail message that asks him to do something. As he sets out to fulfill the request, he may encounter problems, but perseverance and the information in this book enable him to work around them. When you read about someone executing the various commands described for a given operating system, it becomes easier to see how some of the pieces fit together in a typical situation.

You will also find references, in the sample sessions and throughout the book, to a mythical database management program called UpRiteBase. No such program really exists; in describing how an application might fit into a typical installed version of each operating system, I simply chose to make up a sample application program name.

1.5 General Advice

Your life will be easier if you keep certain hints in mind when you attack a new operating system. Trying to distinguish the key differences and similarities between a new one and one that you already know can be very confusing. This section offers some advice on strategies by which you can take advantage of the similarities and minimize the problems caused by the differences.

> BUZZWORD: "String." This isn't really a buzzword, but a technical term describing a sequence of characters. Single or double quotes are often used to show where a string begins and ends; for example, "here is one" and 'here is another'.

1.5.1 Filenames

The rules for naming files on different computers can seem very different. How many parts a name has, how long these parts can be, and which characters you may use vary from computer to computer. I like to use some guidelines that are based on the common denominator of all the rules I know. They allow me to make up a filename on a particular computer while knowing that the same name would cause little, if any, trouble on another. This is particularly important when using a computer that may be attached, through a network, to other computers; it's a shame when all the technical details of file transfer and file sharing are worked out and automated for you but they don't work because of something as simple as one system's inability to recognize a filename on another.

- *Parts in the name:* UNIX, like the Macintosh and the Amiga, has filenames of only one string of characters; the name of a DOS filename has two parts; CMS, MVS, and OpenVMS filenames have three parts. Two is a nice compromise, and systems that use three-part names usually add a default third part if you don't include one. It's a common practice (although not a rule) on UNIX machines to use a period as a filename's second, third, or fourth-to-last character, separating the last few characters so that they can give a clue about the type of file it is. `junememo.txt`, `clean_up.c`, and `budget.wks` would not be unusual filenames. The use of the period on DOS and OpenVMS machines to separate the first two parts of the filenames makes these names just as valid on both of these systems. The use of more than one period in a filename is a good example of something that works on some systems but not on others, and which you should therefore avoid.

- *Length of the parts:* Systems that divide the name up into parts rarely allow any part to be more than eight characters long. A three-character length for the filename's second part is a convention in UNIX and OpenVMS and a rule in DOS, so a maximum of eight for the first part of our two-part compromise and up to three for the second is a guideline that gets you by on many different operating systems.

  The second part of these names usually give a clue about the nature of those files—for instance, `clean_up.c` would be the source code for a program written in the C programming language, `budget.wks` might be a worksheet, and `junememo.txt` is probably a simple text file.

- *Characters to use:* All the operating systems that I know of allow you to use the letters of the alphabet and the 10 numeric digits. All but MVS and OS/400 allow you to use the underscore character (_). If you use some other character from the top row of your keyboard, you may find that it works at first but causes a problem later. Maybe the problem will occur when you move the file to another computer; maybe it will occur on the computer where you created the file. The section below entitled "Wildcards" shows examples of characters that lead to trouble if you try to incorporate them into filenames.

  Filenames on any computer are notorious for torturous abbreviations that completely obscure their meaning. This is where the underscore comes in handy on operating systems that allow its use in filenames—if you use it to separate different abbreviations, the name becomes easier to figure out. `aprschd.txt` is a tough one, but `apr_schd.txt` is a little closer to "april schedule."

1.5.1.1 Wildcards. If you want to carry out an operation on 17 different files, you don't necessarily need to type the command 17 times. Nearly all operating systems let you refer to more than one file at once by using wildcards to take advantage of common characters in the filenames.

A *wildcard* is a special character that does for regular characters what its namesake does for regular cards in poker: it can be treated as any other character—or, sometimes, other characters. For example, to delete the files `april1.txt`, `april8.txt`, `april15.txt`, `april15a.txt`, and `april22.txt`, you don't need to type in five commands that each delete a single file. On most computers, you can simply tell the operating system to delete something like `april*.txt`.

On most systems, an asterisk represents zero or more characters; other special characters are often available to represent other numbers or ranges of characters. (This is why you should stick to letters and numbers when you make up filenames—characters that can represent other characters will cause trouble.)

For example, if one computer's command to list out filenames is the word `list`, then the command

```
list schedule*
```

might list files with the names `schedule.jan`, `schedule.feb`, `schedule.bak`, `schedules`, even a file whose entire name is just `schedule`, because the asterisk can represent zero or more characters. The term `schedule*` is known as the *file specification,* because it is not itself a filename, but a way to specify a file or group of files.

Wildcards are often demonstrated with the command that lists files, but they can usually be used with other commands as well. For example, if the command to copy a file is the word `copy` and the word `accounting` represents a disk, subdirectory, or other location where you store accounting files, then the file specification `budget*` in the command

```
copy budget* accounting
```

could copy the files `budget92`, `budget93`, `budget94`, `budget.bak`, and `budget` to the new location.

Notice how both sample commands have the asterisk at the end of the file specification. On some operating systems, it might be possible to list out `aprbud.94`, `maybud.94`, and `junbud.94` by typing this:

```
list *bud.94
```

Here the asterisk represents any letters at the beginning of a filename. This is not as common as using an asterisk at the end of the name or, on an operating system that allows multi-part filenames, at the end of one part of the name. Check the "Wildcards" section for each operating system to make sure.

The file `litebud.txt` would also be listed by the above command, because of the asterisk's flexibility. What if you don't want to be that flexible and only want to list filenames with exactly three letters before the "bud.txt" part? Most operating systems also offer a wildcard to represent individual characters. If it were a question mark, then the command

```
copy part?cal.txt accounting
```

would copy the files `part1cal.txt`, `part2cal.txt`, `part3cal.txt`, and `part4.cal` to the accounting area, but it would not copy `part12cal.txt` or `partcal.txt`.

This character could be repeated to represent a specific number of characters in a filename. This would solve our problem of listing the 1994 budget files without including `litebud.txt`; if each begins with exactly three letters before the "bud.94" that they share, you could enter this:

```
list ???bud.94
```

This brings us to an important point about naming your files: Files with a similar purpose should have similar names, so that you can deal with them as a group with a minimum of typing. If the 1994 budget files had been called `aprilbud.94`, `bud94.may`, and `june94.bud`, it would take three separate commands to delete, list, or copy them on many operating systems.

And remember, these aren't the only commands for manipulating files. Any command that can do something to a file—whether it prints it, searches through it, or e-mails it to another user—can usually do it to many files at once, if you know how to use wildcards.

1.5.1.2 Wildcards and file deletion.   When you enter any operating system's command to delete files and use a file specification that includes wildcards, it's a good idea to first use the same file specification with the command that lists files. This way, you see a list of which files you're about to erase.

For example, let's say a given operating system's commands for listing and deleting files are LIST and DELETE, and the asterisk is used to represent one or more characters. If you want to delete five files that all begin with the letters "JUNE," you should enter

```
LIST JUNE*
```

before you type this:

```
DELETE JUNE*
```

If LIST JUNE* lists seven files that fit that pattern, then you'll know that your pattern is too general, and that using the same pattern with the DELETE command would have deleted more files than you had intended.

The command that lists file names can be very useful as you learn about other file manipulation commands. Until you are comfortable with a system, always use the file listing command to make sure that the results of your delete, copy, and rename commands had the desired effect.

1.5.2 Mail

The best way to learn about the mail system on any computer is to send mail to your own ID. It's nice if you have a friend willing to put up with messages like

```
Subject:mail^H^Hest?
I ope thethis woks^[^[rks
```

but you'll spare yourself some embarrassment and get a good idea of what your e-mail looks like to recipients if you send your first messages to yourself.

To be comfortable with a mail program, you have to be comfortable with the text editor first. Make sure you understand the basics of creating and editing text files before you try to get too far with your e-mail system.

1.5.3 The text editor

Don't wait until you have to create important files before practicing with the text editor. At that point, you'll want to concentrate on what you're saying, not on the commands and keystrokes necessary to make the file look the way you want. Create some dummy files, or letters to e-mail to yourself for e-mail practice. Just make sure that they're files that will cause you no pain if you ruin them.

A good opportunity to practice with the editor is to use it to take notes about the operating system as you play with it. Save your work often, keep a backup copy of the file, and print it every now and then in case something unplanned happens to it. If you don't use that computer for a while and forget some aspects of using it, your file full of notes will be handy when you have to use the system again.

1.5.3.1 Line editors, full-screen editors. Many operating systems provide you with two different editors: a line editor, which works in TTY mode, and a full-screen editor. The line editor will be the older of the two, and will be provided for the convenience of people who have been using that system for a long time. To use a line editor, you don't move your cursor from line to line as you do with a modern word processor or text editor; you issue commands in terms of line numbers. A typical series of editing commands would tell the editing program to carry out instructions like this: add a new line after line number 5, show me lines 3 to 15, change the phrase "file name" in line 12 to "filename," delete line 11, save the file. Unless this sounds like fun, you'll want to use the full-screen editor provided with each operating system.

> BUZZWORD: "Full screen." The ancestors of modern computer terminals were called teleprinters or teletypewriters. These were essentially printers with typewriter keyboards attached to them. When you typed a command and pressed Return, the terminal printed your command and then, if there were no problems with it, printed the output underneath it.
>
> The first Video Display Terminals (VDTs) to replace these machines substituted the VDT screen for the long roll of paper necessary on teletypewriters. Commands and output still appeared one line at a time, but this time they appeared on the bottom of the screen, and as more data appeared the earlier data scrolled up the screen. If it scrolled off the screen, it was lost forever; to see it again, you entered the command again.
>
> Eventually, engineers figured out how to make characters appear at specific places on a screen, instead of always at the bottom. They also devised ways to display the cursor at a specific location and still have the computer read whatever the user typed there. This enabled them to create input forms, or on-screen versions of paper forms, where the user could move the cursor from place to place on the screen and enter the appropriate data.
>
> This more sophisticated way of dealing with terminals became known as "full-screen mode." The old way, in which the text perpetual scrolled from the bottom of the screen to the top, became known as teletypewriter mode, or more commonly, TTY mode.

Although this book will show you the most common text editor available for each operating system, you should investigate any alternative editors available on your system. Some sites purchase and install a different text editing program if they consider it superior to the one included with the operating system.

People who are familiar with the editor on one system can often find a version of it for another operating system that they may use—the PC/DOS KEDIT editor is a PC version of the mainframe XEDIT program, and various versions of the UNIX vi editor are also available for PC/DOS and OpenVMS. So, when you move to a new operating system, you may not have to learn a new text editor.

1.5.3.2 The editing buffer. On several different platforms, the word "buffer" comes up occasionally in the text editor's status messages and, if available, in its on-line help. It just means "the part of memory set aside for the file you're editing." When you edit a file on any computer, it copies the file from the disk to the computer's memory, and you then edit that copy. Saving your work means copying the edited version in memory back to disk; this is why you lose your work when you lose power in the middle of editing a file on a personal computer.

Sometimes technical talk refers to the copy sitting in memory as the copy in the buffer. For example, when you edit a file with the OpenVMS EVE editor and then quit without first saving your changes, a message tells you "Buffer modifications will not be saved, continue quitting?" This means "The edits that you made to the copy of your file sitting in memory won't be saved, are you sure you want to quit?"

1.5.4 Looking at text files

All command-line operating systems have a command to display a text file's contents on your screen. The command might be TYPE, cat, or LIST. (This last one can be confusing, because it displays a text file in MVS, but lists file names in VM/CMS.) Remember that these commands are for looking at *text* files, not binary files. If you try to display a binary file with one of these commands, the system tries to interpret the binary information as text so that it can put it on the screen. At best, it looks like gibberish; at worst, the system interprets some of the information as special codes telling it that you've changed the settings on your terminal or terminal emulation software. In response to this, it starts sending codes to your terminal that have nothing to do with what your terminal expects. If this happens, your terminal may lock up, forcing you to end your session and start all over again.

Moral: Don't start using this command to try to look at every file whose name shows up when you list filenames. One part of the filename on each system (usually the second part—it might be called the filetype or extension) gives you a clue as to what kind of file each one is. Get to know which ones represent text files and which represent binary files.

1.5.5 "Printing" on the screen

Be careful when you come across the word "print" in a command or a command's description. In the days of teletypewriters, every program that showed you any information literally printed it on the paper that scrolled through the terminal. As VDTs proliferated in the 1970s, they existed side by side with the teletypewriters, and it was understood that text that would have printed on a teletypewriter was displayed on a VDT's screen.

Although VDTs have replaced teletypewriters, the terminology still hadn't changed. This means that today a help message that explains that a given command "prints the names of your files" doesn't mean that it sends filenames to the printer; it means that it "prints" it on your terminal.

1.5.6 Reading and writing

When discussing a computer's operations, the use of the terms "read" and "write" often confuse novices. Reading a file doesn't necessarily involve your seeing it; it's the hardware that reads and writes data. A tape recorder provides the best analogy to understand what computers are doing when they read and write: writing is essentially the act of recording data on your storage medium, and reading is the playback of that data—that is, pulling it off the storage medium so that you can use it.

When you save a file that you created with a word processor or spreadsheet, you are writing it to disk. (Writing it "on" the disk may sound like better English, but we're talking computer talk here—the correct preposition is "to.") When you call up a previously created file into your word processor or spreadsheet, you are reading it from the disk. When you copy a file from one disk to another, your computer reads it from the source disk and writes it to the destination disk; this is like playing a song that has been stored on one tape while you record it on another.

Just as audio cassettes have a little piece of plastic that you can punch out to prevent someone from recording over the information that exists there, floppy disks have either a little plastic switch to move or a notch that you cover with a sticker to prevent anyone from "recording" on that disk, or writing over the information there. This protects the data on that diskette, and is called a "write protect" switch.

One of the most dreaded error messages on any kind of computer is a "read error." This usually means that there's a problem with the disk that the computer is trying to read. Picture an audiocassette that fell into a pond and then, after it was fished out, was left out in the cold so that the moisture inside had a chance to freeze up. Your tape recorder would have a hard time playing this cassette or reading the information stored on its tape. If your hardware can't get the data off the storage medium, the data is lost. The same principle applies to the data on disks. That's why people make backups—with more than one copy of valuable information, they can read from the backup if the primary disk is corrupted (computer talk for "screwed up").

1.5.7 Logging off (or out)

When you type the command to end your session on a computer and press Enter, some computers give you a clear indication that you finished your session—for example, a summary that shows the time of day you quit and the amount of time that you were connected. Others don't. You should always make sure that you have properly ended your session, since some sites bill you according to the amount of time that you are connected.

If you don't see such a message, press Enter a couple of times and see what happens. If you return to a login screen or login prompt, you know that you no longer have an active session. If you're still unsure, type a simple command for that operating system and see if anything happens. If anything does, you're still logged in.

What happens at the end of a session can vary from site to site. Even an expert on a particular operating system would not know exactly what to expect at a particular installation. Don't be afraid to ask.

1.5.8 Terminal emulation and file transfer

All operating systems have communications software available for doing file transfer to and from other computers. It may be part of the operating system, or it may be purchased from a third party. (It is likely that both hold true on a particular system; as with text editors and mail programs, the one included with the operating system may be so limited that a commercial one is purchased anyway.) On a PC or workstation, these programs often must also do terminal emulation, which lets you use your local computer as if it were a terminal for the host computer.

The Kermit file transfer and terminal emulation program is available for virtually all operating systems, and it's free. This is particularly important when doing downsizing work, because downsizing means "moving an application from a larger computer to a smaller one" and you need a program to do the file transfer. Once you learn Kermit's most important commands, you can use it on any operating system where you find it installed.

For PCs, Kermit is available from nearly any bulletin board catering to your computer. CompuServe has it for DOS computers, the Macintosh, the Amiga, and the Atari-ST (use the file finder forums—IBMFF, MACFF, AMIGAFF, and ATARIFF—to locate the latest versions). On minicomputers and mainframes, it takes a system administrator to install Kermit, but if you're using a computer that is part of an academic computing center, you can bet that Kermit is already installed.

To find out, enter

```
kermit
```

at the operating system's command prompt. If the Kermit prompt appears (this will look different on different systems, but probably be some variant of `Kermit>`), you've found it. Enter

```
help
```

at the Kermit prompt to learn more.

1.5.8.1 Emulated terminals. There are two terminals whose names come up often, even though you may never see examples of the actual terminals:

- The *VT100* was one of the original members of DEC's VT ("virtual terminal") series of terminals. Although they have come out with more advanced models since (each designated by a higher number, such as VT220 and VT340), emulation of the VT100 has become a baseline of emulation competence for emulation programs and for the terminals with which a system will work. If the terminals that your system will work with and the terminals that your emulation software can emulate only have one name in common, it will be VT100. If they have other names in common, they will probably be more sophisticated terminals, and more worthwhile for you to use.

- The *3270* was an important IBM terminal, whose descendants (the 3278, 3279, etc.) are also still in use. People refer to the family generically as "3270 terminals." 3270 keyboards have a couple of keys not found on typical PC keyboards (for example, the Reset key, and separate Return and Enter keys) so when you're emulating a 3270 terminal, you must sometimes figure out which PC keys are standing in for the 3270 keys not found on a typical PC keyboard. In this book, you'll find 3270 issues mentioned in the material on the three IBM systems covered: OS/400, VM/CMS, and MVS.

1.6 Syntax Expressions in this Book

This book shows you the syntax for many commands in the various operating systems covered. Some commands have mandatory parts, optional parts, and default settings. The following conventions show what each part of a command's syntax means:

[ ]	Anything in brackets is optional.
/	A slash indicates options from which to choose.
<u>underline</u>	If several options are possible, the default setting is underlined.
Key + Key	When two keys should be pressed simultaneously, they are written with a plus sign between them. For example, to type an uppercase "S," you would press Shift + S.

The following syntax for the mythical `whatgives` command

```
whatgives [today/yesterday/tomorrow]
```

means that you could type the word `whatgives` by itself, because everything else is in square brackets, and therefore optional. If you did include a parameter, it should be either "today," "yesterday," or "tomorrow" because the slash characters show that these are the only options. If you didn't include any parameter, the `whatgives` command would be executed as if you had put "today" after it; this is the default parameter, as indicated by the underline.

1.7 Comments and Suggestions

Comments and suggestions about this book can be sent to me in care of McGraw-Hill Professional Book Group, 11 West 19th Street, 3rd Floor, New York, NY 10011.

To send them more directly to me, you can use e-mail to send them to BOBDUCHARME@ACM.ORG or CompuServe 72441,3003.

2

UNIX: An Introduction

UNIX has been around for over 20 years and many consider it to be the operating system of the future. Why? Because as PCs become cheaper and more powerful, the original operating systems designed for them are less and less adequate; the portability and multitasking ability of UNIX make it a strong candidate for those who want to upgrade from single-user systems. From PC/DOS 2.0 to the Macintosh's System 7, other operating systems have increasingly reflected the UNIX influence as their manufacturers strive to increase their power and capabilities.

UNIX also has a certain mystique, making it a magnet for would-be hackers. Clifford Stoll's bestselling 1988 book *The Cuckoo's Egg* boosted this mystique with the story of a crunchy-granola Berkeley astronomer who tracks down some German spies employed by the KGB. What made this story different from a John LeCarre novel, besides the fact that it was true, was that the bad guys' spying and the good guy's detective work were all done over a worldwide UNIX network. (You don't need to know any UNIX to enjoy the book, but a basic knowledge—the kind provided by this book—definitely enhances your appreciation of the key characters' maneuverings.)

2.1 History

The mystique of UNIX, however, is much older than Stoll's book. To understand its roots, we must go all the way back to the twenties. Before the invention of computers, IBM realized that people would pay good money for solid, reliable support after they bought IBM's time clocks and tabulating machines. They knew that the relationship between business machines and postsales support resembled the relationship that Eastman Kodak had found between cameras and film: Customers may buy the former only once, but they need to purchase the latter over and over. That's where the real money was.

When IBM started making computers and selling software to go with them, the software's source code was naturally a trade secret. Source code is the program as the programmers wrote it; a program called a compiler translates this into the binary file that is the software you buy and run. The binary file is unintelligible to the eye, while the source code shows how the program really works. Hobbyists show each other their source code, and computer science students hand theirs in to be graded, but no IBM source code went beyond IBM.

In 1969, Ken Thompson of Bell Labs developed the first version of UNIX on a DEC PDP-7 for his own use. (The name and several of the concepts were derived from an unfinished joint venture with General Electric and Massachusetts Institute of Technology called MULTICS.) Other Bell Labs programmers liked it, used it, and added to it. It spread rapidly throughout Bell Labs, where it continues to be the dominant operating system today.

Bell Labs' parent company, American Telephone and Telegraph (AT&T), realized that they had something valuable on their hands, but this was before the breakup of AT&T, when government regulations restrained them from getting too far into the computer market. AT&T did license UNIX for inexpensive use by educational institutions, but with some twists to the typical licensing agreements that followed the IBM pattern: instead of selling the operating system and being responsible for supporting it, the deal included the complete source code and the understanding that there would be no support available.

The bargain price of UNIX and its ability to run on many different computers quickly made it popular in universities and small companies that were just acquiring their first computer. The universities turned out computer science students who knew UNIX, and its popularity spread further.

The lack of support remained a problem, however, so users banded together to support each other. Some users formed a user group called /usr/group (a pun on the term "user group" and on a UNIX subdirectory name) in order to pool the knowledge they had gained by studying the source code. This could be considered the original UNIX cult—at least the first beyond Bell Labs. Certain Bell Labs names (Kernighan, Ritchie, Aho, and Weinberg, among others) are still the high priests of this cult.

> BUZZWORD: "The Labs." In addition to UNIX, the C programming language, lasers, communications satellites, and the transistor, Bell Labs is responsible for countless other things that we take for granted in the world of computers and in everyday life. Many consider Bell Labs so important that they don't even need the word "Bell," so you will sometimes hear people refer to "The Labs."

The extreme terseness of UNIX also contributed to its cultiness. Its most important commands are only two or three letters long—for ex-

---

ULTRIX? XENIX? AIX? AUX? POSIX? DYNIX? MACH? SunOS?

AT&T registered "UNIX" as a trademark, so although anyone may create their own version and market it, they may not call it UNIX. As a result, different companies have come up with their own names. We call these slightly different versions "flavors" of UNIX. They often end in the letter "X" so that they sound like the word "UNIX": Digital Equipment Corporation's (DEC's) ULTRIX, which runs on their DECstation workstations; IBM's AIX, which runs on its RS series of workstations; XENIX, developed for computers with Intel processors (usually machines considered to be powerful PCs that otherwise run DOS); Sequent's Dynix, and Apple's AUX. Sun Microsystems calls the operating system for their workstations "SunOS," and the NeXT computer uses an Massachusetts Institute of Technology (MIT)-developed variant of UNIX called Mach.

POSIX is not an actual operating system, but a developing government standard for a version of UNIX that any vendors must conform to if they want to sell their UNIX products to the government.

The differences between these various flavors, from the user's point of view, are usually slight—for example, an error message might be worded differently. It's safe to say that if you're comfortable with one flavor of UNIX, you can fake it on the others.

---

ample, the command to list filenames, `ls`, and the command to copy a file, `cp`. (The real fun comes with commands that are abbreviated to look like completely unrelated words. The command `man` has nothing to do with men; it brings up the on-line manual. The command `cat`, which you will find in Section 4.1 ("The Eight Most Important Commands") has nothing to do with feline domestic pets. The command `tar` is used for tape archiving, and has nothing to do with road surfaces or Brer Rabbit; the `wall` command is used by system administrators to write a message to all terminals, and has nothing to do with the sides of a building.)

These abbreviated commands, along with the use of symbols like the period, the double period, the slash (/), the pipe (|), and the greater-than and less-than symbols (>, <), enable UNIX users to put together flexible, powerful commands with a minimum of typing. People who don't understand these commands and symbols find them intimidating. The combination of terseness, power, and strange symbols in a command like

```
ps -aux | grep ../getty | sort >> gettyproc.txt
```

reminds the uninitiated of the mystical symbols of alchemy, or worse, of assembly language.

2.1.1 Today

When the federal government ordered the breakup of AT&T on January 1, 1984, AT&T did benefit from the deal: Restrictions on many of their potential activities were lifted. Some of these restrictions had prevented them from getting too far into the computer industry. With their removal, UNIX became a marketable product for them.

The power and flexibility of UNIX helped it to grow into a big business, but the cultiness was hurting business. /usr/group, whose very name only made sense to the initiated, changed its name to UNIX International in 1989. Complaints about the cryptic nature of UNIX commands and the success of graphical user interfaces on computers like the Macintosh and the Amiga inspired people to create interfaces for UNIX systems with windows and icons that could be controlled with mice.

Computer science students still study UNIX closely at colleges and universities, because when you study the responsibilities and methods of an operating system, the best way to learn is to look at the source code of a real operating system. Although commercial versions of UNIX are more proprietary these days and often too complex for students to understand the source code, simpler versions of UNIX like MINIX and XINU have been developed specifically for students to dissect and study.

Today, the graphical user interface versions of UNIX always have a window where you can type in old-fashioned UNIX commands. In fact, they let you have several of these windows at once.

These commands are not as difficult as their reputation; they're just very abbreviated. DOS and Amiga users in particular will understand more about their PCs' operating systems when they study UNIX, because so much of DOS and AmigaDOS were modeled on UNIX. (Knowing about the UNIX heritage of DOS has earned me some easy money on two occasions—both times, I earned $60 for sending a single paragraph to the "User-to-User" column in the back of *PC Magazine*. Each one described a common UNIX trick that also worked on the DOS command line.)

2.1.2 USENET

When you know UNIX, you not only have the ability to deal with a wide variety of computers from a wide variety of manufacturers (not to mention the many "flavors" of UNIX—see sidebar); you also have the tools necessary to take advantage of USENET.

Some people call USENET a giant computer bulletin board. From the user's perspective, it bears a strong resemblance to a bulletin board; you can download programs and you can send e-mail and programs to other users. You can read messages from people all over the world and leave them yourself on any topic imaginable. It keeps many scientists and researchers far more up-to-date on news in their fields than any journal published on paper could. In spreading hot stories, USENET has often been known to scoop CNN.

Workstations

Imagine that you had a PC so powerful that no existing PC operating system enabled you to take full advantage of that power and that you used some variant of UNIX instead. This is essentially what a workstation is. Although their multitasking ability allows UNIX computers to be used by more than one person at once, workstations are usually used by one person at a time.

Workstations are also designed to communicate easily with each other. Sun Microsystems, the company that first popularized UNIX workstations, is famous for its slogan "The network is the computer."

Workstations usually have large, high-resolution monitors and graphics capabilities far superior to those of other computers. Because of these abilities, they are popular for scientific visualization and computer animation. This makes them far more glamorous (or in computer industry parlance, "sexy") than computers used for mundane tasks such as processing purchase orders. As a result, workstations have become a popular bandwagon. IBM had Hagar the Horrible selling its RS workstations, Steve Jobs pushed his NeXT machine from the cover of *Newsweek,* Hewlett-Packard bought out the popular workstation manufacturer Apollo to gain an entry, and DEC brought out its DECstation.

Meanwhile, as PC and their operating systems get more and more powerful, computer trade press journalists each write their annual "We have to redefine what we mean when we say workstation" column.

It isn't really a bulletin board, though. USENET is actually much more dynamic than that. Rather than a central computer where people log in to to see what's new, USENET provides a constant flow of information between nodes, or computers designated to receive and send along this information. If your system is hooked into one of these nodes, then your system is itself a node and you have access to whatever portion of USENET is being pulled in to your node.

3

Getting Started with UNIX

3.1 Starting Up

When you turn on a terminal connected to a UNIX system, or successfully connect to such a system over a network or phone line, the first
thing you see is the login prompt:

```
login:
```

As an authorized user of this system, you should have a login name
that represents your identity on the system. Type it in here and press
the Enter key. The next prompt asks for your password:

```
password:
```

Type it in and press the Enter key. If all went well, you will be
logged in.

A couple of things to remember:

- If you make a typing mistake, press Enter until the system asks
you to log in again. Don't try to use your Backspace or cursor movement keys to correct the mistake. Because the computer probably
doesn't know what kind of terminal you are using or emulating yet,
it may not understand the codes sent by these keys. If Joe User enters `job`, then presses the Backspace key to get rid of the `b` and
types `euser`, his screen may show that he has typed `joeuser`, but
when he presses Enter the system may receive something that
looks more like `job^]euser` as a login name. It won't have a
record of such a user and won't give him access to the system regardless of the password that he types with this login name.

- Some systems, if you log in in uppercase letters, assume that you
are using one of the old-fashioned terminals that cannot type low-

ercase letters. They will then display all text for that session in uppercase letters. Make sure you log in in lowercase.

- Just because the system asks you for a password doesn't mean that you entered the login name correctly. It always asks. If it only asked when you entered a valid username, then people trying to break in to the system would have an easy way to determine which login names were valid.

- A login name may have no password. This may be the case the first time you log in. As soon as you enter the login name, the system displays the screen indicating that you have logged in.

Once you log in, the system probably displays some information about the particular system that you are logged in to before it displays the prompt where you enter commands. The prompt usually appears as a dollar sign ($) or a percent sign (%), but can be easily changed.

There are ways to set up a UNIX ID so that, when someone logs in, a certain program automatically runs whether that user wants it to or not. You will often find arrangements like this for IDs that have no password—this way, anyone can log in to run one particular program, but they can't have the run of the system. I was once given a UNIX account just to use the mail program. When I logged in, it automatically started up the mail program; when I quit the mail program, it automatically logged me out.

3.1.1 Finishing your UNIX session

To show that you want to disconnect from the system, type:

```
exit
```

A shortcut available on most systems is to type Ctrl + D.

> BUZZWORD: "Box." Many manufacturers produce computers that can run UNIX, or some flavor of it, and users often identify the brand of hardware being used in a given situation as a "box"—For example, "They're using AT&T UNIX, but running it on an NCR box."

3.2 Filenames

Filenames in UNIX can be up to 14 characters long and can consist of just about any characters. Certain characters have special meanings in UNIX and could lead to trouble if used in filenames; for example, you should avoid <, >, |, -, ?, [,], and *. Most people use letters, numbers, the underscore, and the period. Because spaces are not allowed in filenames, the underscore provides a way to make abbreviated filenames more readable. jul_budget is a more understandable filename than `julbudget`. Also, UNIX is case-sensitive—it would treat `BUDGET.TXT`, `Budget.txt`, and `budget.txt` as three different files. Again, stick to lowercase.

Be careful about using a period for a file's first character, because this makes that file hidden. This means that including its names in a list of files on the screen requires you to use a special option when you use the `ls` command to list filenames. As a rule, UNIX users only begin very specific filenames with a period. Section 6.2, "Command Files," covers two examples: `.profile` and `.login`.

3.2.1 Wildcards

The main wildcards in UNIX are the asterisk and the question mark. Although the examples below demonstrate their use with the `ls` command, remember that you can use them with almost any command that uses a filename as a command line parameter. For more information, see the material on wildcards in Section 1.5, "General Advice."

3.2.1.1 The asterisk. The asterisk at the end of a filename has the same significance in UNIX that it has in most other operating systems. It can represent zero or more characters at that position in the filename or file type.

This is typical of many operating systems. In UNIX, however, the asterisk is much more versatile, because it doesn't have to go at the end of the expression you type. For example

```
ls *may
```

lists all the filenames that end with the letters "may," and

```
ls *may*
```

lists out all filenames with the letters "may" anywhere in them.

```
ls rpt*94
```

would list out all the filenames that began with the letters "rpt" and ended with the digits "94," regardless of how many characters are between them.

3.2.1.2 The question mark. The question mark represents a single character—no more, no less. Several question marks represent that number of characters, so that

```
ls ???94rpt.txt
```

would list out all of the filenames with exactly three characters before the characters "94rpt.txt."

3.3 How Files Are Organized

Like many other aspects of UNIX, its file system has provided a model for many operating systems developed after it, such as PC/DOS and AmigaDOS. We call this system of file organization *tree-structured directories*, which means that the disk is divided into sections called *directories*. A directory can be divided into sub-sections called *subdirectories*, which can also be divided. The terms "directory" and "subdirectory" are used almost interchangeably, since every directory—except the root—is a subdirectory of another.

To understand how the main directory, or *root* directory, leads to subdivisions which lead to subdivisions which lead to subdivisions, think of the branches of a tree. The root is like the tree's trunk, which branches into several main branches. These main branches then divide into smaller and smaller branches.

In a typical UNIX system, one of the main branches usually holds most of the programs that come with the operating system. We call this the /bin directory. Another main branch could hold the software that was purchased for installation on this UNIX system. This branch might be called /usr, and the system administrator would subdivide it into sections to hold each of the software packages. For example, the UpRiteBase database package could be in one of these subdivisions in a directory called /urbase. This subdivision's full name would be /usr/urbase, because it is a subdirectory of the /usr directory and the full name of any directory includes its *pathname*, or the name describing the path up the tree along the various branches it took to get there. Since the UpRiteBase software package consists of quite a few files, it is more efficiently organized if the system administrator divides the /usr/urbase directory into subsections when installing it. The binary files sit in a branch called /usr/urbase/bin, the files associated with the demonstration database that comes with it are in a subdirectory called /usr/urbase/demo, and so forth.

Notice how a slash character separates each component of the pathname. The pathname of the root, or main trunk of the tree, is just a slash by itself. We create a complete pathname by combining the names of the various subdirectories traversed to get to the subdirectory in question, separating each with a slash, and by putting a slash at the very beginning to represent the root.

Figure 3.1 shows a sample UNIX directory tree structure. (Keep in mind that an actual system would have many more branches.) A level of indentation represents a level of the subdirectory structure; for example, the ninth line represents the subdirectory /usr/urbase/sql. The first line shows the root directory.

No two directories can have the same name. Although you may see three subdirectories seemingly named bin in the directory structure in Figure 3.1, keep in mind that their complete pathnames are different: /bin, /usr/bin and /usr/urbase/bin.

```
/
    bin
    usr
        bin
        tmp
        urbase
            bin
            demo
            sql
    usr2
        joeuser
            mail
            networking
        maryjones
            mymail
            payroll
        jimcasey
            inventory.dbs
            letters
```

Figure 3.1   Sample UNIX directory structure.

At any given time, one of these directories is your "current" or "default" directory. (An equivalent expression describes you as being "in" that directory.) This matters to many of the UNIX commands—for example, if you enter the command to erase a file but don't specify the directory where the file is located, the system assumes that you want to erase a file in the current directory. Section 3.3.2, "Moving between directories," shows how to make a new directory the current one.

Each user is assigned his or her own subdirectory known as their *home* directory. The system administrator assigns subdirectories to users as their own disk space in which to keep their personal files. A UNIX system's directory structure has one or more main branches off the root to hold these personal directories for the various users (in Figure 3.1, it's called /usr2), just as main branches exist to hold the software that they use.

In the example, /usr2 leads to the subdirectories /usr2/joeuser, /usr2/maryjones, and /usr2/jimcasey, which would be the home directories for three different users.

These users can create and maintain subdirectories of their home directories in whatever arrangement they like. Mary Jones might keep her correspondence in a subdirectory called /usr2/maryjones/mymail and Joe User might keep his files pertaining to a new networking project in a subdirectory called /usr2/joeuser/networking. Section 4.1.9, "Creating directories," and Section 4.1.10, "Removing directories," show you how to maintain subdivisions of your own home directory.

3.3.1 Relative pathnames

Because you can divide up subdirectories into so many subdivisions, full pathnames can get long. UNIX provides two shortcuts to make it easier to refer to directories:

- You can substitute of two periods (..) where the system expects a pathname. This means that the you are referring to the *parent* of the current directory, or one level closer to the root. The parent of /usr2/maryjones and /usr2/joeuser is /usr2; the parent of /usr/urbase is /usr; and the parent of /usr, /usr2, and /bin is /, the root. Section 3.3.2, "Moving between directories," gives an example of how to use the two dots as a substitute for the parent directory's name.

- Another shortcut makes it easier to refer to the *child* of the current directory (a subdivision of the current directory). Note how all references to directory names up to now begin with the slash (/) character. You don't always need this; if you omit the slash, the system assumes that you are referring to a subdivision of the current directory. For example, if Mary wants to copy some mail messages from the /usr2/maryjones directory into the /usr2/maryjones/mymail directory, she could just enter mymail as the destination of her copy command instead of typing out /usr2/maryjones/mymail. This works as long as she was in the /usr2/maryjones directory at that time. If she was in her /usr2/maryjones/payroll directory and entered mymail as the destination of her copy command, the system would look for a subdirectory called /usr2/maryjones/payroll/mymail and not find it. (Instead of giving you an error message, it would create a file called mymail in the /usr2/maryjones/payroll subdirectory. See Section 4.1.5, "Copying files," for more information on the logic behind this.)

We call these two shortcuts *relative* pathnames, because the system figures out the directory that you are referring to relative to your current directory. If you enter a command to copy files into a directory called bin, without a slash, this would mean the /bin directory if you were currently in the root directory, the /usr/bin directory if you were in the /usr directory, or the /usr/urbase/bin directory if you were currently in the /usr/urbase directory. (In reality, you would not have permission to alter the contents of subdirectories outside of your home directory unless you were the system administrator). Similarly, the directory that you refer to when you type .. completely depends on which directory is current when you type it.

3.3.2 Moving between directories

When you first log in to a UNIX system, your current directory is the one assigned to your login name by the system administrator. If you type ls, the command to list out filenames, the system lists out the files in the current directory. (The first time you log in to a given system and enter this command, there may not be any files to list out.)

The command `cd`, followed by the name of a directory, changes your current location into that directory. For example

```
cd /
```

puts you into the root directory, and

```
cd /bin
```

puts you into the `/bin` directory. If you misspell a directory name so that your command tells the system to change into a nonexistent directory—for example, `blin`—it gives a reply similar to this:

```
blin: bad directory
```

When the command executes successfully, the system does not acknowledge that you have a new working directory, but you can easily find out where you are at any given time with the `pwd`, or "print working directory" command. This "prints" the full name of your current directory on the screen. (See Section 1.5, "General Advice," if the idea of "printing on the screen" doesn't make sense to you.)

Changing the current working directory provides one example of how the use of relative pathnames can save you a great deal of typing. If your current directory is the `/usr/urbase/bin` directory and you want to change into the `/usr/urbase` directory, you could type

```
cd /usr/urbase
```

but it would be much easier to type

```
cd ..
```

because `/usr/urbase` is the parent directory of `/usr/urbase/bin`. To change back to `/usr/urbase/bin`, just type

```
cd bin
```

because the `bin` directory that you want is a child directory of `/usr/urbase`. Remember, when you type `cd bin`, the system looks for a child of your current directory called `bin`. If you had been in the root directory when you typed the same command, you would have ended up in the `/bin` directory, not `/usr/urbase/bin`.

3.4 Available On-Line Help

There are two commands that may give you help after you log in. The first, `help`, is fairly obvious. On many systems, typing `help` by itself starts up a menu-driven program that tells you a great deal about using UNIX. The first screen that it displays explains how to use it.

The `man` command may also assist you. In the great tradition of naming UNIX commands by abbreviating them until they look like completely different words (like `cat tar`, or `wall`) this is an abbreviation of the word "manual." Being more old-fashioned than the `help` command, `man` is used strictly from the command line—there are no menus to help you along. Type in `man` by itself, and it tells you how to use it: you enter `man` followed by the word that you want to look up in the manual. For a start, look up `man` itself by typing:

```
man man
```

(If a screenful of text scrolls up and then stops, press the Enter key each time you want to scroll to a new screen.)

It's possible that nothing happens with either the `help` or `man` commands. Both get the information you request by looking it up in text files stored on the computer's hard disk for this purpose, and some system administrators erase these files from the hard disk to make more room for other files.

> BUZZWORD: "Gen." (pronounced "jen") When PC users think of putting an operating system onto a computer, they think of copying the operating system files onto their hard disk and maybe running a configuration program to tell the operating system more specific information about the hardware they are using. On a UNIX system, the system administrator must run a program that takes various data and code files and actually creates many of the operating system files. This is known as "generating" the operating system, but if you really know your UNIX slang you refer to "genning" the operating system. For example, "I'm looking forward to checking out the new features of the system upgrade, but I don't know when I'll have the time to gen it."

Using Files in UNIX

4.1 The Eight Most Important Commands

The *shell* is the part of UNIX that interprets the commands that you type at the UNIX prompt. It passes the instructions along to the *kernel*, the part of UNIX that does the real operating system work. We call the basic operating system commands that you enter at the UNIX prompt "shell commands." If someone in the middle of running a program talks about "accessing the shell" or "shelling out," they're talking about temporarily gaining access to the main system prompt where they can type shell commands.

If you are using a graphical user interface version of UNIX and don't see a window where you can type in commands, never fear—there's one in there somewhere. Either there will be an icon (on a Sun workstation, it's a little picture of a conch shell) or there's a main menu with "Shell" as a choice. (To bring up such a menu, try clicking on the screen background—that is, with your mouse pointer on the background picture, and not on any window or icon—with any buttons available on your mouse.)

There are two basic versions of the shell, with several variations available. All the UNIX commands described here work with both of the most popular ones, the Bourne shell and the C shell. Many systems can run either one, so it's not a dumb question to ask which shell is the default on a given system.

The eight most important shell commands in UNIX are

ls	Lists file names
cat	Displays the contents of files
cp	Copies files
mv	Renames and moves files
rm	Deletes files
chmod	Grants and revokes access to files

```
mkdir      Creates subdirectories
rmdir      Removes subdirectories
```

4.1.1 Command options: switches

UNIX uses a hyphen (–) to indicate options, or *switches* that give special instructions about how a command should operate. For example, the `ls` command by itself only lists filenames, but with the `l` switch it lists other information about the file, and with the `t` switch it lists out the files in reverse chronological order instead of alphabetical order. You could enter

```
ls
```

by itself, or you could enter

```
ls -l
```

to indicate that you want to see all the information about the files, or you could enter

```
ls -t
```

to see the filenames in reverse chronological order. You can also combine these switches; you could enter

```
ls -lt
```

or even

```
ls -tl
```

to see all the information about the filenames, listed in reverse chronological order. The order in which you put the switches doesn't matter, as long as you remember to include the hyphen, which means "here come the switches," and to avoid putting any spaces between the letters that denote command-line options.

Section 4.1.3, "Listing filenames," gives more information on using switches with the `ls` command. When you use UNIX's on-line help system to inquire about a command, it tells you all about the command's various switches and what they do. Knowing that this information is available in on-line help is the main reason to not worry about memorizing a lot of command line switches.

4.1.2 Common error messages

When you type anything at the UNIX command prompt, it looks for a program with that name and executes it. If you make a typing mistake, for example

```
max man
```

when you meant to type `man  man`, UNIX gives you a message along the lines of

```
max: not found
```

This means that it looked for a program called `max` and couldn't find it.

Many commands expect you to include some information on the command line after the command's name. If you omit any, most UNIX systems display a terse explanation of how much information they expected. For example, to make a copy of a file, you must indicate the file you want to copy and the name you want to give to the new copy. If you type the `cp` command by itself without any filenames, the system responds with something similar to this:

```
Usage: cp [-ip] f1 f2; or: cp [-ipr] f1 ... fn d2
```

This shows you that you had to include at least two filenames (represented by `f1` and `f2`) after the `cp` command. The alternative syntax, after the `or:` part, shows that you could also type one or more filenames followed by the name of a destination directory name, if you want to copy the files to another directory. Remember—you can always type `man  cp` for more detailed help on the `cp` command.

Another common inspiration for error messages is when you instruct the system to do something to a file that doesn't exist. For example, let's say you want to copy a file called `template.txt` and call the copy `may_bud.txt`, but you make a typo when you enter the command:

```
cp tempalte.txt may_bud.txt
```

The UNIX system responds with

```
cp: tempalte.txt: No such file or directory
```

as if to say "There's a problem executing the `cp` command: I can't find any file or directory named `tempalte.txt`."

Remember, the `cp` command is just used as an example here. Similar mistakes with many other commands will elicit similar error messages. For a full explanation of the use of the `cp` command, see Section 4.1.5, "Copying files."

4.1.3 Listing filenames

The `ls` command lists filenames. If you type `ls` by itself, it lists out the names of the files in your current directory in alphabetical order, along with the names of any subdirectories of the current directory. This list might look like the following:

```
061293rr
062093rr.prn
06ifp.txt
082294ts.txt
083194vd.txt
index.txt
mail
notes.txt
prepprn.awk
rptapr94
rptfeb94
rptjan94
rptmar94
rptmay94
s_and_rep.awk
sample.txt
schedule.txt
text.txt
```

You can put two kinds of parameters after the `ls` command:

- A directory name, which shows that you want to list the files in a directory other than the current one.
- A file specification, which shows that you only want to list files whose names follow a certain pattern.

If you type `ls` followed by a directory name, like this

```
ls /bin
```

you will see several screenfuls of filenames from the `/bin` directory scroll by alphabetically, without stopping, until it ends with a screenful of filenames similar to the ones shown in Figure 4.1.

```
uuencode
uulog
uuname
uupick
uusend
uustat
uuto
uux
vax
vplot
wall
who
write
xargs
xget
xsend
yacc
ypcat
ypchfn
ypchsh
ypmatch
yppasswd
ypwhich
```

Figure 4.1 End of the output from the command ls /bin.

If you type `ls` followed by a filename, it only lists that file's name. For example, if you type

```
ls .profile
```

it shows you this

```
.profile
```

This isn't particularly useful unless you include wildcards when you specify the filename. For example, to list all the files that begin with the characters "rpt" and end with the characters "94" you would type

```
ls rpt*94
```

and perhaps see output similar to this:

```
rptapr94
rptfeb94
rptjan94
rptmar94
rptmay94
```

(For more information on using wildcards to specify the filenames you want included in your list, see Section 3.2.1, "Wildcards.")

If you want to see specific files in a specific directory, you can add the directory and filename specification after the command. Don't put any spaces between them. For example, to list all the files in the /bin directory that begin with the letter "l," type this:

```
ls /bin/l*
```

Your output might look like this:

```
/bin/ld
/bin/line
/bin/ln
/bin/login
/bin/lorder
/bin/ls
```

It just so happens that one of the files beginning with "l" in the /bin directory is the "ls" program itself. The /bin directory holds many of the most often-used commands in UNIX.

4.1.3.1. Listing more than filenames.   The `ls` command may have more switches than other UNIX commands: at least 20, depending on the flavor of UNIX that you are using. There is a switch to put slashes next to the directory names that show up with the filenames, a switch to list the filenames in chronological order instead of alphabetical order, and a switch to reverse the order in which the names appear.

Few of these switches are worth memorizing; you can always use the man or `help` command to learn about them.

The most important switch gives you the "long" listing of the files. It's not really longer, but actually wider—if you call it the "long" listing, it's easier to remember that the switch is the letter "l." It tells the `ls` command to give much more information about the files than just their names. If you enter the command

```
ls -l
```

the output would look something like this:

```
-rw-rw-r-- 1 joeuser marketing   520 Jun 12 1993 061293rr
-rw-rw-r-- 1 joeuser marketing  3592 Jun 20 1993 062093rr.prn
-rw-rw-r-- 1 joeuser marketing 22305 Nov  6 1993 06ifp.txt
-rw-rw-r-- 1 joeuser marketing   660 Aug 23 1993 082294ts.txt
-rw-rw-r-- 1 joeuser marketing   542 Aug 31 1993 083194vd.txt
-rw-rw-r-- 1 joeuser marketing   504 Jan  2 1994 index.txt
drw-rw-r-- 1 joeuser marketing   512 Nov 12 1993 mail
-rw-rw-r-- 1 joeuser marketing    66 Mar 22 1993 notes.txt
-rwxrwxrwx 1 joeuser marketing    33 Dec  4 1993 prepprn.awk
-rw-rw-r-- 1 joeuser marketing    47 Nov 28 1993 rptapr94
-rwxrwxrwx 1 joeuser marketing   165 Sep  6 1993 rptfeb94
-rw-rw-r-- 1 joeuser marketing    98 Jan  2 1994 rptjan94
-rw-rw-r-- 1 joeuser marketing    73 Dec  4 1993 rptmar94
-rw-rw-r-- 1 joeuser marketing    44 Nov 28 1993 rptmay94
-rw-rw-r-- 1 joeuser marketing    46 Dec  4 1993 s_and_rep.awk
-rw-rw-r-- 1 joeuser marketing   512 Dec  7 1993 sample.txt
-rw-rw-r-- 1 joeuser marketing   276 Jul  8 1994 schedule.txt
-rw-rw-r-- 1 joeuser marketing   105 Nov 28 1993 text.txt
```

There's a lot of information here. The last column to the right should look familiar; it's the file's name. To the left of that is the date that the file was last modified, and to the left of that is the current size of the file in bytes. The columns that say joeuser and marketing show the file's owner (usually the user who created the file) and the group that the user belongs to.

What is a group? UNIX lets the system administrator assign users to groups because it makes the system administrator's job easier when giving or taking away system privileges. For example, let's say that the system administrator Mary Jones has just installed a new spreadsheet program on the system. To enable the 23 people in the accounting department to use it, she could just give execution rights to the group "accounting" instead of typing 23 commands to individually give access rights to 23 people.

What are execution rights? And what's the cryptic column all the way to the left? (Ignore the column of ones just to the left of the joeuser column—this column shows how many links this file has to substituted names, an advanced UNIX trick.) The first column shows something called the file's mode. The first character in the file's mode is usually either a hyphen (-) or a d. A hyphen means that the line describes a normal file, and a d means that it's a subdirectory of the di-

```
       r   w   x       r   w   x       r   w   x
whose rights:   owner's      owner's group's    everyone else's
```
Figure 4.2 Key to file mode codes.

rectory whose files are being listed. The "r"s, "w"s, "x"s, and other hyphens show who has what rights with that file or directory. Three kinds of rights are available when you access a file:

r   The right to read (look at or make copies of) a file

w   The right to write (make changes) to a file

x   The right to execute a file. If a file is not some kind of program, execution rights are irrelevant.

You can assign one set of rights to the file's owner, another to the other people in the owner's group, and a third set to everybody else. The second through fourth characters (after the one that tells you whether it's a directory) show the owner's rights; the next three, the group's rights; and the last three, everyone else's. Figure 4.2 illustrates this.

If the r, w, or x appears, that right exists for that category of user. A hyphen means that right doesn't exist. For example, the following shows a filemode for a file that its owner can read or write, that the owner's group can read, but not write, and that people outside of the owner's group cannot even read:

```
-rw-r-----
```

A programmer working on a new program might set its filemode to something like this:

```
-rwxr-xr-x
```

This lets the programmer read, write, or execute the program, and lets everyone else look at it or execute it, but not change it.

As mentioned above, a "d" instead of a hyphen in the first character of the first column means that the name listed is a subdirectory of the current directory, not the name of a file in that directory. The rest of the characters in the file's mode mean the same thing that they do when describing a file, only they describe the privileges that users have when using that directory:

r   The right to read (list the files in) the directory

w   The right to write to (create files in) the directory

x   The right to execute the cd command to change into that directory

Try using the -l switch with the ls command to look at some of the files in the /bin directory, like the ones beginning with "c". With the ls command, any switches go before the file specification (the part that shows which files you want to see):

```
ls -l /bin/c*
```

The output looks something like this:

```
-rwxr-xr-x 1 bin bin  28672 Apr 14 1992 /bin/cat
-rwxr-xr-x 1 bin bin  43008 Apr 14 1992 /bin/cc
-rwxr-xr-x 1 bin bin  32768 Apr 14 1992 /bin/chgrp
-rwxr-xr-x 1 bin bin  26624 Apr 14 1992 /bin/chmod
-rwxr-xr-x 1 bin bin  32768 Apr 14 1992 /bin/chown
-rwxr-xr-x 1 bin bin  26624 Apr 14 1992 /bin/cmp
-rwxr-xr-x 3 bin bin  32768 Apr 14 1992 /bin/cp
-rwxr-xr-x 1 bin bin  73728 Apr 14 1992 /bin/cpio
-rwxr-xr-x 1 bin bin  28672 Aug 28 1993 /bin/crypt
-rwxr-xr-x 2 bin bin 110593 Apr 14 1992 /bin/csh
```

It looks like the owner gets to read, write, and execute the files, and everyone else just gets to read them and execute them. Who is the owner? Who is the group? The owner and group columns both say "bin"; this means that the /bin directory itself is a kind of user, and a user in its own group.

To change the read, write, and execute privileges of a file, use the chmod (change mode) command, which is covered in Section 4.1.8, "Controlling access to a file."

Besides -l, the other useful switch for the ls command is -x. Use it to list several filenames across the screen on each line of output. (Another fine example of computer programmers' novel approach to the English language is the way they abbreviate the word "across" with the letter "x.") If you typed

```
ls -x /bin/c*
```

the output would look like this:

```
/bin/cat /bin/cc   /bin/chgrp /bin/chmod /bin/chown /bin/cmp
/bin/cp  /bin/cpio /bin/crypt /bin/csh
```

(The number of filenames on each line varies from system to system.) This is especially useful when you list out more than 25 filenames; otherwise, these filenames won't all fit on the screen at the same time. If you tried the ls /bin command mentioned earlier, you probably saw the names zoom up the screen until it reached the end, at which point you saw the last 25 filenames from the directory. If you added the x switch and typed

```
ls -x /bin
```

you would see output like that shown in Figure 4.3.

Switches can be easily combined. It wouldn't make much sense to combine the x and l switches, because there isn't enough room to list out several filenames to a line along with their sizes and the other in-

```
acctcom      adb          ar           as           att          basename
bs           cat          cc           chgrp        chmod        chown
cmp          cp           cpio         crypt        csh          date
dd           df           diff         dirname      dis          du
echo         ed           env          expr         false        file
find         grep         ipcrm        ipcs         kill         ksh
ld           line         ln           login        lorder       ls
mail         mail.new     mail.newnew  mail.old     make         mesg
mkdir        mv           newgrp       nice         nm           nohup
od           passwd       pdp11        pr           ps           pwd
pyr          red          rm           rmail        rmdir        rsh
sed          sh           sh.new       size         sleep        sort
strip        stty         su           sum          sun          sync
tail         tcsh         tee          telinit      time         touch
true         tty          u370         u3b          u3b10        u3b15
u3b2         u3b5         ucb          uname        universe     vax
wc           who          write
```

Figure 4.3 Sample output of ls -x /bin.

formation that the 1 switch adds to the output. However, you could combine the 1 switch with the t switch, which specifies that you want to see the filenames in reverse chronological order, like this:

```
ls -lt
```

and see output like that in Figure 4.4.

The order of the switches doesn't matter in any UNIX command. If you typed

```
ls -tl
```

you would see the same output.

Switches, like the rest of UNIX, are case-sensitive. For example, -r means "reverse the listed order" while -R means "recursively list subdirectories" (list the contents of any subdirectories along with the

```
-rw-rw-r--   1 joeuser   marketing     276 Jul  8  1994 schedule.txt
-rw-rw-r--   1 joeuser   marketing      98 Jan  2  1994 rptjan94
-rw-rw-r--   1 joeuser   marketing     504 Jan  2  1994 index.txt
-rw-rw-r--   1 joeuser   marketing     512 Dec  7  1993 sample.txt
-rw-rw-r--   1 joeuser   marketing      73 Dec  4  1993 rptmar94
-rwxrwxrwx   1 joeuser   marketing      33 Dec  4  1993 prepprn.awk
-rw-rw-r--   1 joeuser   marketing      46 Dec  4  1993 s_and_rep.awk
-rw-rw-r--   1 joeuser   marketing      44 Nov 28  1993 rptmay94
-rw-rw-r--   1 joeuser   marketing     105 Nov 28  1993 text.txt
-rw-rw-r--   1 joeuser   marketing      47 Nov 28  1993 rptapr94
-rw-rw-r--   1 joeuser   marketing   22305 Nov  6  1993 06ifp.txt
-rwxrwxrwx   1 joeuser   marketing     165 Sep  6  1993 rptfeb94
-rw-rw-r--   1 joeuser   marketing     542 Aug 31  1993 083194vd.txt
-rw-rw-r--   1 joeuser   marketing     660 Aug 23  1993 082294ts.txt
-rw-rw-r--   1 joeuser   marketing    3590 Jun 20  1993 062093rr.prn
-rw-rw-r--   1 joeuser   marketing     520 Jun 12  1993 061293rr
-rw-rw-r--   1 joeuser   marketing      66 Mar 22  1993 notes.txt
```

Figure 4.4 Sample output of ls -lt.

names of the files and subdirectories). Because of this, you need to be careful about whether you type switches in upper- or lowercase. Most of them are in lowercase.

Try using `man` or `help` to learn about the other switches to the `ls` command.

4.1.4 Displaying a text file's contents

Another source of confusion for beginning UNIX users is the fact that commands used for more than one purpose are not always named after their most popular purpose. The `cat` command, which displays text files on the screen, is also used to combine or "concatenate" files. `cat` is an abbreviation of the word "concatenate," even though it's used far more often to put the contents of a text file on the screen. If you had a file called `schedule.txt` and typed

```
cat schedule.txt
```

the contents of the file would then appear on the screen:

```
October 10
10:30 meet Dave C., Laurie. call Laurie first—should I bring new
diskettes?
12:30 lunch with Benny
2:00 expecting call from Chicago office. Have page counts ready.
2:30 Anita's presentation—can I get out of going?
4:00 first draft of outline MUST be ready
```

4.1.4.1 Looking at text files one screen at a time.   One of UNIX's greatest strengths is its ability to make several programs work together, all by issuing one command. Although this is usually an advanced technique, combining the `cat` command with the `more` command is so useful that you should learn it as soon as you learn `cat`.

When you display certain files with the `cat` command, you may notice that any files longer than 24 lines scroll up and off the screen until the end of the file, at which point you are only looking at the last 24 lines.

The `more` command remedies this. (Many systems offer a similar alternative called `pg`. If `more` doesn't work on your system, try `pg`.) It takes what you send it and gives it back to you a screenful at a time (`more` has its own command-line switches that adjust, among other things, how much it outputs at once when you send text to it, but the default value of 24 or 25 lines is just fine for most uses).

How do you send text to it? UNIX has a special symbol called the pipe (|) that means "take the output of the preceding command and send it to be used as input by the following command." (I told you that UNIX was cryptic—it uses only one symbol to say all that.) Sometimes the pipe symbol appears on screen, on paper, or on a keyboard key as an unbroken vertical line. It may also appear as a vertical line with a gap in the middle.

If the `schedule.txt` file was 100 lines long, you could look at one screenful at a time with this command:

```
cat schedule | more
```

By doing this, you are "piping" the output of the `cat` command to be used as input for the `more` command. After the first screenful appears, the message `--More--` appears at the bottom of the screen, as shown in Figure 4.5.

Press the space bar (or, if you piped your output to `pg`, the Enter key) and another screenful appears. Continue this, and you can look at the file at your own pace—unless you want to quit, in which case you type "q" instead of pressing the space bar.

The `more` command isn't limited to use with the `cat` command; you can also use it with the `ls` command. Typing this

```
ls -l bin | more
```

displays a screen similar to the one shown in Figure 4.6.

Any command that sends text to the screen can also send it to `more`. This is a good example of the real beauty of UNIX: instead of giving you a couple of big utilities that claim to do everything you need, UNIX gives you many small ones that you can combine any way you like. If you like a particular combination so much that you'll want to use it repeatedly, you can store those commands in a shell script file and give this file any name you like. When you want to use your shell script, you only need to remember the name you made up rather

```
October 9

9:00 Ed may have Knicks tickets for me; bug him when he gets back from Toronto

10:30 office supplies sales rep coming

12:00 lunch with Benny postponed until the 10th

2:30 getting teeth cleaned--call 687-2300 first for address

4:00 Fed Ex new diskettes to Chicago


October 10

10:30 meet Dave C., Laurie.  call Laurie first--should I bring new diskettes?

12:30 lunch with Benny

2:00 expecting call from Chicago office.  Have page counts ready.

2:30 Anita's presentation--can I get out of going?
--More--
```

Figure 4.5 Output from piping schedule file through the more command.

```
-rwxr-xr-x   1 bin      bin          63488 Jun 23  1992 acctcom
-rwxr-xr-x   2 bin      bin          73728 May 11  1989 adb
-rwxr-xr-x   1 bin      bin          49252 Apr 14  1992 ar
-rwxr-xr-x   2 bin      bin         110593 Apr 13  1992 as
-rwxr-xr-x   2 bin      bin          30720 Apr 14  1992 att
-rwxr-xr-x   1 bin      bin            147 Apr 14  1992 basename
-rwxr-xr-x   1 bin      bin          77824 Apr 14  1992 bs
-rwxr-xr-x   1 bin      bin          28672 Apr 14  1992 cat
-rwxr-xr-x   1 bin      bin          43008 Apr 14  1992 cc
-rwxr-xr-x   1 bin      bin          32768 Apr 14  1992 chgrp
-rwxr-xr-x   1 bin      bin          26624 Apr 14  1992 chmod
-rwxr-xr-x   1 bin      bin          32768 Apr 14  1992 chown
-rwxr-xr-x   1 bin      bin          26624 Apr 14  1992 cmp
-rwxr-xr-x   3 bin      bin          32768 Apr 14  1992 cp
-rwxr-xr-x   1 bin      bin          73728 Apr 14  1992 cpio
-rwxr-xr-x   1 bin      bin          28672 Aug 28  1993 crypt
-rwxr-xr-x   2 bin      bin         110593 Apr 14  1992 csh
-rwxr-xr-x   1 bin      bin          32768 Apr 14  1992 date
-rwxr-xr-x   1 bin      bin          32768 Apr 14  1992 dd
-rwsr-xr-x   1 root     bin          34816 Apr 14  1992 df
-rwxr-xr-x   1 bin      bin          34816 Apr 14  1992 diff
--More--
```
Figure 4.6 Output from piping ls -l bin through more command.

than the spelling and syntax of the combination of commands. Section 6.2, "Command Files," shows you how to do this.

4.1.5 Copying files

Copying files in UNIX is simple. The command is clearly an abbreviation of the word "copy": cp. To make a copy of your file with a different name, type

```
cp sourcefile destfile
```

where sourcefile is the file that you are copying and destfile is the name of the copy that you are making. (See Section 3.2, "Filenames," for information on valid filenames.) For example, if you plan to edit a file called proposal and you're going to make so many edits that you want a backup of your original before you start changing it around, you would type:

```
cp proposal proposal.bak
```

This is the simplest form of the cp command. It assumes that the file you want to copy is in your current directory and that you want to put the copy in the same directory. To get fancier, you can use the syntax

```
cp /pathname/sourcefile /pathname/destfile
```

where /pathname specifies the pathname, or full directory name, of the source and destination files. Let's say Mary Jones tells Joe User that Herb sent her some e-mail that he should look at and add comments to. She says, "I saved it in the subdirectory of my home directory called `mymail` in a file called `aug20.herb`. I'll see you later. I'm flying to Phoenix in an hour, and I want your comments when I get back." Joe calmly sits at his terminal and types

```
cp /usr2/maryjones/mymail/aug20.herb /usr2/joeuser
```

Notice that he included the source file's directory, the name of the source file, and the destination file's directory, but not a new name for the destination file. If you omit the name of the destination file, UNIX gives it the same name as the source file—in this case, `aug20.herb`. (When making a copy of a file in the same directory as the source file, you must specify a new name—you can't have two files in the same directory with the same name.)

In Section 3.3, "How Files Are Organized," we saw that you can use two periods (..) as shorthand to refer to the parent of the current directory. You can also use a single period to refer to the current directory. This doesn't come up when using the `cd` command, because typing

```
cd .
```

would be useless; it means "change my current directory to the one that I'm currently in." The single period does come in handy, however, with the copy command. If Joe is in the `/usr2/joeuser` directory and wants to copy the `aug20.herb` file from the `/usr2/maryjones/mymail` directory into his current directory, he types:

```
cp /usr2/maryjones/mymail/aug20.herb .
```

One more comment about copying that file from Mary's directory: Joe needs read privileges to make a copy of it. If he got a message along the lines of "cannot unlink" or the slightly more comprehensible "permission denied," then he would use the `ls` command with the `-l` switch, as described in Section 4.1.3.1, "Listing more than file names," to see what kind of privileges were assigned to that file. He doesn't need to look at all the filenames in Mary's `mymail` subdirectory, so he types:

```
ls -l /usr2/maryjones/mymail/aug20.herb
```

If he saw something like this

```
-rw------- 1 maryjones marketing 147 Aug 20 1994 aug20.herb
```

he would see that the mode of that file was set so that Mary, its owner, could read it or write to it, but no one else could read it, not even other people in her group (like Joe). Secure in the knowledge that it's Mary's fault that he can't add the comments she's expecting, he sends her e-mail tactfully explaining why he couldn't do as she had asked.

If he could read the file and make a copy of it, he would then own the copy and be able to do anything he wanted to it.

What happens if you name your new copy after an existing file? There may or may not be a warning, depending on the UNIX system that you are using. The copy operation might take place as if the existing file didn't exist, making a new copy over the existing file. Try copying over an unimportant file on your system to see what happens. If there is no warning, you'll have to be careful about destination filenames when using the cp command on your system.

What happens if you try to make a copy of a file that doesn't exist? For example, if you misspell the filename of the source file:

```
cp /usr2/maryjones/mymail/aug20.hreb /usr2/joeuser
```

UNIX would display a message telling you that it "cannot access (the source file)," which implies that the file was there, but it couldn't get to it. In reality, it means that no such file exists.

4.1.6 Renaming files

Like the command to look at a text file, the command to rename a file is named after one of its less common uses. Since it's used to move files from one directory to another, the command is mv. Just as the copy command can make a new copy of a file in the same directory as the original file, but with a new name, the mv command can "move" a file within its current directory, but with a new name—in other words, rename it. For example, if you typed

```
mv aug20.herb herbfile.txt
```

you would take the file called aug20.herb in the current directory and give it a new name: herbfile.txt. If you did want to move the file to another directory, perhaps from your home directory to your /usr2/joeuser/networking directory, the syntax is similar to copying a file from one directory to another:

```
mv aug20.herb /usr2/joeuser/networking
```

Unlike copying, after this command executes, the original aug20.herb file will no longer be in your home directory. You will find it in its new home, /usr2/joeuser/networking. If you want to move it and give it a new name at the same time, it's easy:

```
mv aug20.herb /usr2/joeuser/networking/herbfile.txt
```

When you refer to a file but don't specify its directory location, UNIX assumes that it's in the current directory. If you want to do something with a file that isn't in the current directory, insert its pathname in front of the filename. For example, if Mary had told you to move aug20.herb out of her directory, instead of just making a copy, you would use syntax similar to when you copied it out of her directory into your own:

```
mv /usr2/maryjones/mymail/aug20.herb /usr2/joeuser
```

Of course, you could have assigned a new name to it when you specified where it should end up.

Just as you can use the single period to specify the destination directory when you copy a file to your current directory, you can also use the single period to specify the destination when you move a file to the current directory:

```
mv /usr2/maryjones/mymail/aug20.herb .
```

Section 3.3, "How Files Are Organized," shows you other ways to avoid typing out complete pathnames.

A file's mode has no effect on your permission to rename a file, as it does with the cp command. Regardless of the privileges assigned to a file, only the owner (the user who created the file) may rename it. And remember: if you make a copy of someone else's file, you become the owner of the copy. How do you find out who owns a file? You use the ls command with the -l switch to list out that file's name and then look at the third column of information listed with the filename.

If you rename a file with a name that already applies to an existing file, the renaming takes place with no problem. Or rather, it takes place with no problem for your renamed file—the previously existing file with the same name is lost. For example, if you have files called schedule.txt and dec13.txt and rename dec13.txt to be called schedule.txt, your original schedule.txt will be lost.

If you try to rename a file that doesn't exist, UNIX gives you the same error message as when you try to copy a file that didn't exist: "Cannot access (filename)."

4.1.7 Deleting files

Think of deleting files as removing them, because that helps you to remember the command: rm. The syntax is simple; rm followed by the filename or filenames that you wish to remove. For example

```
rm schedule.txt
```

removes the file called `schedule.txt`. Typing

```
rm schedule.txt junememo.txt
```

removes `schedule.txt` and `junememo.txt`.

To remove a file, you need write permission in the directory in which the file is located. If you do not have write permission for the specific file you want to erase, UNIX displays a cryptic message:

```
(filename): 444 mode?
```

This means "Are you sure you want to remove this file, which has a mode of 444?" Sometimes a numbering system is used as a shorthand for the -rwxrwxrwx notation to describe the permissions that make up a file's mode. Without explaining which numbers mean what, it's enough to say that if you have write permission on a file that you're trying to erase, the system won't give you the warning message. Answer the warning message with either a "y" for "yes" or an "n" for "no," and press the Enter key. To be on the safe side, "n" is probably a better idea; you can then use the `ls -l` command to double-check the file's mode and then enter the `rm` command again if you're sure that you want to erase that file.

Why would someone not have write permission of a file that they own? You might use the `chmod` command to take away write permission from yourself for an important file to protect yourself from accidentally erasing it. You'll still own that file, so you can always grant yourself write permission for it with the `chmod` command. (For more on the `chmod` command, see Section 4.1.8, "Controlling access to a file.")

The `rm` command accepts wildcard characters in its argument. Be careful, though, because this ability to remove more than one file at a time can lead to big mistakes. If you wanted to remove all of the files that ended with ".bak" you would type this:

```
rm *.bak
```

Imagine that you made the simple typing mistake of adding a space after the asterisk:

```
rm * .bak
```

Just as the command `rm schedule.txt junememo.txt` removed the `schedule.txt` and the `junememo.txt` files, this command also specifies two things to remove: first, all the files that match * and second, the file named `.bak`, if it exists. All the files that match * would be all the files in the current directory, so you could get yourself into big trouble.

What if you typed

```
rm maymemos
```

and received the following message:

```
rm: maymemos directory
```

Sometimes UNIX is not much more eloquent than Tarzan. "Me UNIX, maymemos directory." maymemos is a directory, and you can't remove it with the command that removes files. Section 4.1.10, "Removing directories," explains how to use the rmdir command for this.

4.1.8 Controlling access to a file

Use the chmod command to change a file's mode. There are two possible ways to specify the access rights to your file: first, by a three-digit "octal" number (which means that each digit is lower than 8, because the number is written in "base 8" notation); second, by initials representing whose rights are being controlled, whether those rights are being added or removed, and what the rights are. The latter way is easier to remember, so that's the best one for beginners to start with.

Use these initials to specify whose rights are being controlled:

u   You, the file's owner, the **u**ser

g   Other users in your **g**roup

o   **O**thers outside of your group

As you saw in Section 4.1.3.1, "Listing more than file names," the letters r, w, and x indicate read, write, and execute permission, respectively.

To show that you want to add or take away permission, use the plus (+) and minus (-) characters.

The complete format of the chmod command is:

```
chmod [ugo]+/-rwx filename
```

This command has the following parts:

- The [ugo] is where you put the combination of the letters u, g, and o showing whose permissions you are specifying. The square braces mean that you can leave this out. If you do, the system assumes that you mean ugo—in other words, everybody.

- Next, you put a plus sign when adding permission or a minus sign when removing it.

- After the plus or minus symbol, you put the combination of the letters r, w, and x that indicate the permission or permissions being added or taken away.

- Finally, after a space, you type the name of the file for which you are specifying permissions.

You can use wildcards if you want to change the mode of several files at once.

Make sure that the string of characters showing the users, action, and permissions have no spaces. The only spaces in the whole command should be right after the word chmod and just before the filename.

For example, let's say you created a file with your resume in it. You cleverly give the file a boring name that won't attract attention, like "budget.old." You then realize, however, that maybe a clever name isn't enough; maybe your file needs more protection than that, so you check on its permissions with the ls -l command, and see the following:

```
-rw-rw-r-- 1 joeuser marketing 3590 Jun 17 1994 budget.old
```

You and the people in your group may change it, and everyone may read it. This is not good, so you first take away your group's permission to write to your file. To specify rights, you enter "gw" for "group-remove-write privileges":

```
chmod g-w budget.old
```

When you type "ls -l" to see if it worked, you should see this:

```
-rw-r--r-- 1 joeuser marketing 3590 Jun 17 1994 budget.old
```

Next, you want to take away the permission of your group and the others outside of your group to read the file. Instead of doing this in two separate commands, you can combine the g and the o with the following command:

```
chmod go-r budget.old
```

You can also combine the permissions being given or taken away. In fact, the two preceding commands could have been combined with the following command:

```
chmod go-rw budget.old
```

Until you feel comfortable with the chmod command, always use the ls -l command afterward to make sure that you did exactly what you intended to the file's mode.

You can also grant or revoke permissions from more than one file at a time by using wildcards in the filename. For example

```
chmod go+rw *.txt
```

would set the mode of all the files that end with ".txt" so that your group and everyone else could read them and write to them.

Try taking permissions away from yourself by entering u as the user whose rights are being controlled. Then, try to read or write the file with the cat command or the vi editor. Then try giving permission back to yourself. (When fooling around with a new command like this, make sure to use a file that means nothing to you!)

In Section 6.2, "Command Files," you'll see an example of execution permission being added to a file.

4.1.9 Creating directories

The commands to create and remove directories are both simple: mkdir (make directory) followed by a directory name creates a new directory and rmdir followed by a directory name removes a directory.

The rules governing valid subdirectory names are the same as those that govern valid filenames. To create a subdirectory of /usr2/maryjones/mail called oldmail, Mary could type the following:

```
mkdir /usr2/maryjones/mail/oldmail
```

Relative pathnames also work; if Mary is already in the usr2/maryjones/mail directory (and she can always use the pwd command to check which directory she's in) then she only needs to type this:

```
mkdir oldmail
```

If she tried to create a subdirectory of one that she didn't own, like /bin, the system wouldn't allow her to. Typing

```
mkdir /bin/wahoo
```

would cause an error message similar to the following:

```
mkdir: cannot access /bin
```

which means that she doesn't have enough access to the /bin directory to allow her to create something new there. (In other words, she doesn't have "write" access, which would allow her to create something in that directory.) The system administrator can create directories anywhere.

In fact, that's an important part of the system administrator's job—to create and maintain directories to hold the system and application files.

One other word of caution: because of the similarities between names of files and names of child directories, it's possible to try to create one of these when you already have used the same name for the other. For example, if Mary had a file called `oldmail` and entered the command

```
mkdir /usr2/maryjones/oldmail
```

she would get a message similar to this:

```
mkdir: cannot make directory /usr2/maryjones/oldmail
```

Since the error message doesn't tell you why it couldn't make the directory, you'll have to watch out for this yourself.

4.1.10 Removing directories

The syntax and restrictions on removing subdirectories is similar to that of creating them. If Mary had successfully created her `oldmail` subdirectory and she wanted to get rid of it, she could type:

```
rmdir /usr2/maryjones/mail/oldmail
```

If she was already in the `usr2/maryjones/mail` directory then she can use the relative pathname:

```
rmdir oldmail
```

Just as she cannot create subdirectories of directories that she does not own, she cannot remove directories that she does not own. Only the system administrator can remove any subdirectory on the system.

One other obstacle could prevent someone from removing a directory: if it has either files or subdirectories in it, UNIX won't let you remove it. This is really a safety feature to protect you from yourself. If Mary had gotten the message

```
rmdir: oldmail not empty
```

then she would use the `cd` command to change into `oldmail` to see what was there and either erase what she found, move it somewhere else, or change her mind about deleting `oldmail`.

We saw what happens when you mistake a subdirectory name for a filename and try to remove it with the `rm` command, which we normally use to remove files. The reverse is also a common mistake; look what happens when you use the `rmdir` command to try to remove a file. After typing

```
rmdir schedule.txt
```

the system responds with

```
schedule.txt: not a directory
```

to let you know that you can't use this command with `schedule.txt`, because it is a file and not a directory.

5

The UNIX vi Text Editor

There are two commonly used editors on UNIX systems. The older one, known as ed, is a line editor. (Most systems also have a more advanced version of ed called ex.)

The most popular editor on UNIX is a full-screen editor called vi. (Some people pronounce it as a one-syllable word rhyming with "eye" and others pronounce it as the two letters that spell it—"vee eye." I couldn't even find a consensus when I asked a roomful of Bell Labs employees.) The name is an abbreviation of "visual editor." vi has much more in common with modern word processors than it does with ed. You can move your cursor anywhere on the screen and correct the text under the cursor. You can scroll the text and search for specific strings of text. You can use vi to create a new text file, as well as to edit an existing text file.

vi is a command-driven editor. You don't use function keys and menus to tell it what you want, as with other text editors and word processors; you type in commands, many of which are only one letter long, and it carries them out. The advantage to this arrangement is that you can do a lot of different things with very little typing. The disadvantage is that many systems do not indicate when you are in command mode and when you are entering text in insert or replace mode. This leads to two common mistakes:

- You might accidentally enter a command when the system thinks that you are entering text, so that you enter d3w to delete three words and the characters "d3w" show up in the middle of your memo, program, or whatever you are writing.

- The opposite problem also occurs: you type a word onto you document, such as "Hello," and the system thinks that you are doing whatever the H command means, followed by the e command, followed by the l command twice, and so on.

The best way to avoid this problem is to double-check your current mode when you are unsure by pressing the Escape key. The Escape key puts you into command mode, and if you press Escape when you are already in command mode, the terminal beeps at you, as if to tell you, "Enter command mode? We're already in command mode."

Because many programs and operating systems require you to press the Enter key after you enter a command, it is tempting to do so with vi, but unnecessary with most commands. In fact, if you enter an i command (which puts you into insert mode) and then press Enter, you insert a carriage return into your document. If you press Enter in command mode when it didn't make sense in the context of what vi thought you were doing, it would just beep at you. As a vi beginner, get used to those beeps!

5.1 Entering vi

To enter vi, type vi followed by the name of the file that you want to edit at the UNIX shell prompt. If a file with that name does not exist, vi creates an empty, new file with that name. If it does exist, vi displays that file on your screen and waits for you to edit it. If you do not include a filename, you will still enter vi, but you must assign a filename later. See Section 5.6, "Saving Your Changes."

When you first enter vi, you are in command mode. You can use your cursor keys to move your cursor around the screen to any place with text at any time in command mode. (Sometimes you can move your cursor like this in insert mode, but there's a greater chance that vi will act flaky, particularly if you use a PC running a terminal emulation program and not a real terminal.) If a file is too long to fit completely on the screen at once, move your cursor to the bottom of the screen and then continue to press the Cursor Down key to scroll the file up, revealing more text. If there are more lines above the one visible at the top of your screen, move the cursor to the top of the screen and continue to press the Cursor Up key to scroll the file down, revealing the text above the line that was at the top of your screen.

If your file is not long enough to fill up a screen, vi represents lines that have no text with a tilde symbol (~). If you enter

```
vi johngay.txt
```

and that file has only seven lines, you will see a screen like the one in Figure 5.1.

Note also that it tells you at the bottom of the screen the name of the file you are editing and how many lines (including blank ones) and characters it has. If you had created a new file with the vi command, it would say "New File" at the bottom.

```
Thy Younglings, Cuddy, are but just awake,
No Thrustles shrill the Bramble-Bush forsake,
No chirping Lark the Welken sheen invokes,
No Damsel yet the swelling Udder strokes;

O'er yonder Hill does scant the Dawn appear,
Then why does Cuddy leave his Cott, so rear?
~
~
~
~
~
~
~
~
~
~
~
~
~
~
~
"johngay.txt" 7 lines, 265 characters
```

Figure 5.1 Opening vi screen when editing a seven-line file.

5.2 Inserting Text

To insert text, first move your cursor to the place where you want the new text to begin. Make sure you are in command mode (as mentioned above, if you're not sure whether you're in command mode, press the Escape key first). Type a lowercase i to put vi into insert mode. If you are lucky (if you are using or emulating a more sophisticated terminal), the word "INSERT" or something similar appears somewhere on your screen to indicate that you are in insert mode. If not, you won't see anything happen, but all the text you type until the next time you press Escape appears at the cursor as part of your file.

If you type to the end of the line, the cursor jumps to the next line, but only as an alternative to running off the right of the screen—it didn't really insert a carriage return character at that position in your file, so make sure to press Enter when you are inserting text and your cursor nears the right side of your screen. When you finish entering new text, press Escape to return to command mode.

5.3 Deleting Text

The lowercase x has the same effect in vi as the delete key on many keyboards: it deletes the character at the cursor. Press it as many times as you like to get rid of more than one character.

To delete more than one character, it is often easier to use the d command. Pressing d by itself does nothing; vi waits to find out what to delete. The d is used in combination with other letters and numbers to delete words, lines, the rest of a sentence, or the rest of a paragraph. The most important of these for a beginner is the dw command, which deletes from the cursor to the beginning of the next word. You can stick a number in there to delete more than one word; for example, d4w deletes the next four words.

The dw command can also delete a blank line, like the one between "No Damsel yet" and "O'er yonder Hill" in Figure 5.1.

When you use vi commands that consist of more than one character, you may occasionally enter a character or two without being sure of how many you just entered. Again, the Escape key always puts you back to a fresh start in command mode. If you're unsure whether you typed d or d4, press Escape and type d4 again. (If you accidentally typed an extra "4" after your d4, you could end up deleting 44 words!)

5.4 Typing Over Existing Text

All the vi commands that we have seen so far have been lowercase letters. To enter overstrike mode, you'll use your first uppercase vi command. Type R to enter Replace mode, and everything you type writes over the characters at the cursor until the next time you press Escape. (A lowercase r has a related function: it means you only want to type over one character, so the next character you type appears at your cursor, but vi then puts you right back into command mode. This is useful for making minor corrections.)

If you reach the end of a line while typing in replace mode, can continuing to type. vi will add your new text to the end of the line at the cursor position.

5.5 Searching for Text

To search for a string of characters in your document, first press the slash (/) key while in command mode. The slash appears in the lower left-hand corner of your screen, waiting for you to type in the characters to search for. After you type them and press Enter, vi will search for the characters and display that part of the document if the string is found. The search is case-sensitive, so make sure you type the letters in uppercase and lowercase exactly as you want to search for them.

5.6 Saving Your Changes

vi inherited many commands from older UNIX text editors such as ed and ex. High on the list of these commands are those that save your work, indicate another file to edit, and exit from the editor.

This category of commands has its own prompt. To display it, type a colon (:) while in command mode. The prompt, which is also a colon, appears in the lower left-hand corner of your screen. If you type a command at this prompt that vi does not understand (which includes uppercase versions of commands that should be in lowercase), it displays an error message telling you that it doesn't recognize the command. For example, if you enter "potrzebie" at the colon prompt, vi responds with "potrzebie: Not an editor command" or "potrzebie: No such command from open/visual."

To save your work, type a w for "write" at this prompt. If you put a filename after the w, vi saves the file with that name. If you type w alone, vi saves your file with its current name and displays a message telling you the file's name, the number of lines in it, and the number of characters. The first time you save a particular file, it also says "[New file]."

If you've created a new file but try to save it with the name of an existing file, vi displays a message like this:

```
File exists - use "w! filename.txt" to overwrite
```

This means that you tried to save a file with a name that already exists and that you must put an exclamation point (a "bang") after the "w" to override the warning. Although the warning message shows the filename in the syntax, you don't need to include it if the file already has a name; just type w! at the colon prompt.

> BUZZWORD: "Bang." The exclamation point comes up a lot in UNIX. In addition to its use in vi, it's sometimes used to distinguish the components of an electronic mail address when sending mail through a big network to another UNIX machine. Because "exclamation point" can be a real mouthful if you have to say it often, the term "bang" is often used. (Another cute one is "Ballbat.") If someone tells you to "type w bang space filename dot txt," they're telling you to type w! filename.txt.

If you entered vi by merely typing vi at the UNIX shell prompt and then created a new file from scratch, it won't have a name yet, so entering w by itself at the colon prompt causes vi to display the message "No current filename." In other words, type the w command again, but include a filename this time.

You can't edit just any file, or create a new one in just any directory. If you only have read permission for a file, you can still bring it up into vi; when you do, the editor displays the message "[Read only]" at the bottom of your screen. You can make all the changes you like, but when you type the w command at the colon prompt and press Enter, vi doesn't save the file; it displays the message "File is read only" instead. You may save the changed file with a new name by adding a filename after the w command. This is based on the same principle as copying a file that you only have permission to read—if you make a copy, you own the copy, and you can do anything you want to that copy, but you aren't allowed to make any changes to the original.

If you don't even have read permission for a file, vi starts up but displays a message that says "Permission denied." It shows you an empty file, just as if you had typed vi by itself at the command line.

5.7 Quitting vi

To quit vi and return to the UNIX shell prompt, type "q" at the colon prompt. If you made any changes without saving them, vi gives you the message

```
No write since last change (:quit! overrides)
```

instead of quitting. This serves as a reminder that you might want to save your file before you quit, and it also reminds you that if you really want to quit without saving your changes, put an exclamation point after the "q." (It really suggests that you spell out the word "quit" and then put an exclamation point, but spelling out an entire English word would be very un-UNIX, so just enter a "q.")

You can combine commands at the colon prompt. To save your file and quit vi in one command, type "wq" at the colon. vi displays a message telling you that it is writing the file to the disk, and it then returns you to the UNIX shell prompt.

5.8 Other vi Commands

The commands described here are the bare minimum that you need to get by in vi. There are many, many more; they are powerful and often confusing. vi has a reputation among people accustomed to normal word processors as being more cryptic and confusing than UNIX itself. This often stems from the fact that someone once tried to teach them all of vi at once, instead of showing them the basics, letting them get comfortable, and then showing them a little more.

To learn more about vi, check the quick reference cards that are available. Also, nearly every book on UNIX devotes a chapter to it.

There are two more tricks that you should know in case you find vi acting flaky. Usually it's not vi itself that's causing the trouble, but a lack of cooperation between a terminal emulation program on a PC and the system running vi.

The first trick sometimes makes cursor control easier. Before computer users took it for granted that every keyboard had special keys devoted to cursor movement (yes kids, there was such a time), the h, j, k, and l keys were used as the vi commands to move the cursor left, up, down, and right, respectively. If you can remember which four letters are used (they're lined up next to each other on the keyboard), then you can easily remember the purpose of the h and the l because they sit at the left and right of these four keys. j for up and k for down are a little more difficult to remember, and I always need to press them a couple of times to remember which does what. As with any vi command, make sure that you're in command mode when you press these four keys, or you'll add their letters to your file in places where you don't want them.

Many touch typists with cursor keys on their keyboard actually prefer the use of these four letter keys over the cursor keys when they move their cursor around, because they can find them without looking down and moving their hands away from the middle of the keyboard. If this doesn't apply to you, but your cursor keys don't behave correctly when you edit a file with vi, try using these alternate keys for cursor movement.

The other trick for people who find that vi does not cooperate with their terminal emulation program as much as they would like is the redraw command. If you delete characters without seeing them deleted from the screen, or come across other situations where the words on the screen don't reflect the commands you just entered, press Ctrl +L to tell vi to resend the whole screen to your terminal. Your terminal emulation program may have retained or deleted a couple more characters on the screen than it was supposed to. Although the wrong characters may be on the screen, this doesn't necessarily reflect what's in the copy of the file being edited. Ctrl + L straightens out your terminal emulation program by redisplaying the true contents of that portion of the file that you are editing.

Don't worry about the need for this unless you notice vi acting strangely. It's still a good idea to use the cat command to look over any file created or edited with vi after you've saved the file to disk, just to make sure that your terminal emulation program didn't play any tricks on you.

Using a UNIX System

6.1 Printing Text Files

The original term for the machine that printed your file on hard copy was "line printer," because it printed text a line at a time. The command to send text to the printer is an abbreviation of "line printer": lp, pronounced "el-pee." Don't worry if you're attached to a laser printer, which is actually a page printer; it's still the same command.

To print a file, just type:

```
lp filename
```

It's that simple. If the file exists, the system sends it to the printer and UNIX displays a message similar to this:

```
request id is hp1-1151 (1 file)
```

The *request id* is the name by which the system remembers your file. It comes in handy when you want to list out the jobs that are waiting to print and when you want to cancel a print job. If you get an error message (other than the kind indicating that the system didn't understand the filename you typed) contact your system administrator. Various details about printing can be specific to each UNIX system (like the name the system uses to refer to each printer) and you can't be expected to know them on a strange system.

6.1.1 Checking the print queue

To find out the status of jobs waiting to print on the "line printer," the command is lpstat. If Joe User just printed a very short job and no other jobs were waiting to print, it may be too late, so lpstat may display no information. This means that the system has already sent his file to the printer. On the other hand, he may see something like this:

```
$ hp1-1151     maryjones     5,232     Jul 19 09:50 on hp1
$ hp1-1158     joeuser       1,491     Jul 19 09:53 on hp1
$ hp1-1159     jimcasey      2,781     Jul 19 09:53 on hp1
```

This means that three print jobs are waiting to print on the printer that the system administrator named "hp1"—a 5232-byte job that Mary Jones sent at 9:50 AM, then your job, and finally Jim Casey's job.

6.1.2 Canceling your print job

Perhaps Joe realizes, looking at the print queue, that he accidentally sent a draft of a memo about why he can't stand Jim Casey. Since he doesn't want it to pop out of the printer while Jim stands there waiting for his 2781-byte job, he cancels his with the `cancel` command followed by the request ID:

```
cancel hp1-1158
```

Only you and the system administrator are allowed to cancel your jobs.

6.2 Command Files

In UNIX, a file full of commands that you can execute as a program is called a *shell script*, because it's a script of commands for the shell to execute one after the other. Shell scripts can be complex, but simple ones can also be useful—especially for users who have trouble remembering a lot of UNIX syntax.

We saw in Section 4.1.2 ("Common error messages") that when you type anything at the shell prompt, UNIX looks for a program to execute with that name. When you create a shell script, you are essentially adding a new command to your UNIX environment. If you write a shell script that contains valid shell commands and store them in a file called "wahoo," then typing "wahoo" starts up your new program.

For example, let's say you're a DOS or a VAX/VMS user and accustomed to typing `dir` to see a list of filenames. You're also used to seeing the size and age of files along with their names, and you don't want them to zoom off your screen if there are more than 24 of them. The following UNIX command lists files this way:

```
ls -l | more
```

This is kind of a pain for the new user to remember. So, to make things easier for yourself, you use `vi` to create a file called "dir" which only has one line in it:

```
ls -l | more
```

After you save your one-line text file and return to the shell prompt, you can't wait to try your new program, so you type

```
dir
```

and UNIX displays a message telling you "execute permission denied" or worse, "not found." No execute permission? Not found? But you own it! You just created it! Check out the mode of your `dir` file by using `ls -l`, the very command that you planned to avoid by creating the `dir` shell script:

```
ls -l dir
```

You'll see that it has a mode of something like `-rw-r--r--`. (You don't need the `| more` when you check out the `dir` file's mode because you only want to list one filename, so there's no need to use the `more` program to make the `ls` output appear a page at a time.) The system administrator sets the default file mode for everyone's new files. This default usually doesn't include execute permission, because system administrators assume that most of the files you create will not be shell scripts.

As you saw in Section 4.1.8, "Controlling access to a file," we use the `chmod` command to add privileges to a file. In this case, you want to give yourself execution privileges for your `dir` program:

```
chmod u+x dir
```

Now when you type `dir`, it should have the same effect as typing `ls -l | more`. You've written your first useful, working shell script!

At this point, your shell script only works for you if you are in the same directory as the shell script file. Ask your system administrator for help modify your *search path*, which determines where UNIX looks for programs to execute when you type a command name at the shell prompt. If you store your shell scripts in their own subdirectory of your home directory and add the name of that directory to your path, you can use your scripts no matter which directory you are in.

6.2.1 The automatic login command file

If you type

```
ls -al
```

you may see one or more files that you didn't see before in the list of files in your home directory. The a means "all," and tells `ls` to include the "hidden" files from that directory in the list. As you can see, they're not hidden very well; they all have a period (.) as the first character in their filename. Typing

```
ls -l .*
```

is another way to list these files—you're telling UNIX to list the files whose names begin with a period.

One of these files is called either .profile or .login (pronounced "dot profile" and "dot login"). Both are shell scripts; whenever you log in, the system looks for .profile if you are using the Bourne shell or .login if you are using the C shell and executes it automatically. This means that, if there's any commands that you want executed every time you log in, you only need to add them to that file. (If you don't have one, you can create it the same way you create any other shell script. Just remember to store it in your home directory and to give yourself permission to execute it with the chmod command.)

For example, you could add the lines

```
mail
cat schedule.txt | more
```

to your .profile or .login file. The first line, as you will see in the next section, checks to see if you have mail (although some systems automatically check for this when you log in anyway) and the next displays a file called schedule.txt one page at a time. If you keep your appointments in this file, it's handy to have them listed like this whenever you log in.

Some systems automatically create a .profile or .login file when the system administrator creates a new user ID. If this happens with your ID, the shell script probably has some strange-looking commands in it. Try looking these up with the man or help commands.

When you add new commands, add them at the end of the file. To test your revised automatic login script to see if it works, you don't have to log off and log back in again; as with any shell script, you can just type its name to start it up.

6.3 Communicating with Other Users

You can send mail to someone by merely typing the word mail followed by the login name of the person getting the mail. For example

```
mail maryjones
```

indicates that you want to send mail to Mary Jones. The mail program then waits for you to type in your message, but it doesn't give you any proper editing capabilities. It's better to use the vi editor to create a text file with the message that you want to send, and then "send" that file to the mail program the same way that you sent a file to the `more` command when you wanted to see the file's text one screen at a time: with the pipe (|) symbol. The following command sends the file `072194mj.txt` to Mary Jones' mailbox:

```
cat 072194mj.txt | mail maryjones
```

You can send any text file to someone with this trick, not just one that you created yourself for this purpose.

6.3.1 Receiving mail

To check whether you have any mail, simply type

```
mail
```

all by itself at the UNIX prompt. If you have no mail waiting for you, it tells you something like

```
No mail.
```

and returns you to the UNIX prompt.

If you do have mail, this enters the mail program. It first shows you either the message most recently sent to you or a list of headers that describe who sent the messages in your mailbox and when they sent them. Then, the mail program's prompt—usually either a question mark or an ampersand—appears. The mail program has at least 20 commands that you can type at this prompt, but you only need a couple to get by. As with most programs, the most important command is the one that tells you about the others: the question mark.

The system numbers your messages and shows these numbers in the list of mail headers. You can refer to these messages by number; for example, entering d 3 at the mail program's prompt means "delete message number 3."

You don't have to use the numbers, especially if you're a beginner. Keep in mind that when you don't include a number in a command entered at the mail program prompt, the system treats the command as if you're referring to the "current" message. The simplest way to see which message is current is to enter the p command without any number. This displays ("prints") the current message. It's a good idea to do this before you delete a message with the d command, to make sure that you're deleting the right one.

Among the available commands, here are the important ones:

?   List the available commands in the mail program with a brief description of each.

p   Print the current message on the screen. The message will have a header describing, at the very least, the date and time that it was sent and the sender's login ID. It may also include other information with lots of numbers, initials, and punctuation. This is information that the mail program uses to route the message; it may be useful to your system administrator if you have any problems sending or receiving mail.

+   Move forward to the next message and print it. If there is no next message, this may return you to the UNIX prompt. The letter n, for "next," also works.

–   Print the message before the current one.

1   (Or any other number) When you enter a number without any other characters, you're telling the mail program to print the message with that number. See the h command to find out how to see the messages' numbers.

s [filename]   Save the current message with the filename shown. The filename is optional; if you don't include it, the mail program saves the message in your current directory with the name mbox. (If mbox already exists, the mail program will add the message to the end of the file.) Saving a message deletes it from your mailbox, which makes sense, because once you save it in a file, you don't need it in your mailbox anymore.

d [1]   Delete the current message. If you specify a number after the d command, the mail program deletes the message with that number. After you enter this command, the mail program shows you the message in question. The system doesn't actually delete it until you leave the mail program; the u command unmarks a message that you've marked for deletion.

h   Print out active message headers. (Not all mail programs provide this command.) The message headers show one line of information about each message in your mailbox. This line includes the login name of the person who sent you the message, the date and time it was sent, and the size of the message in bytes. (If the size appears as two numbers with a slash, like 11/266, these numbers represent the number of lines in the message and the number of bytes.) A greater-than symbol (>) on the left of the screen shows which message is current; many mail programs also have a column with a one-letter code that tells you more about the status of each message: "u" for unread, "s" for saved, "d" if it was marked for deletion, or "n" for new.

r   Reply to the current message. After you enter r and press Enter, the mail program may prompt you for the subject of your message, and then you will have a seemingly blank line. Enter the first line of your message, press Enter, and continue to type in your reply. Type it carefully, because each time you press Enter there's no going back to edit that line. When you are done, type a period (.) as the first character of a new line and press Enter.

If this sounds like a pain, it is. If you want to send a reply of more than two or three lines, jot down the login ID of the person that sent you this message, quit out of the mail program, and send them mail the normal way by first composing it in a text file with `vi` and then sending it to the mail program with the pipe symbol.

q   Quit out of the mail program and return to the UNIX prompt.

6.4 A Sample UNIX Session

You just received the following fax from your boss Mary in Phoenix:

```
Joe - I just remembered that there's some confidential stuff in the
aug20.herb file, so I may have set it so that only I could read it.
If you had any trouble, most of the info from it is in another file
in my home directory called seppromo.txt. Everyone else has made
copies of that, so you can't have any problems copying it to your own
directory. Look it over, and then give me a status report on your
responsibilities in the special promotion we're doing in September.
Just e-mail me your status report; I'll log in from Phoenix to read it.
Make sure it's there by Wednesday at 9AM, Arizona time.
-MJ
```

No problem, except that you haven't done half the work that you're supposed to on the September promotion. First step: you'll print out your own notes on the promotion, which you've stored in a file called `promo1.txt`. You type the following command:

```
lp porno1.txt
```

The system responds with the message

```
request id is hp1-1343 (1 file)
```

so you know that your file is queued for the laser printer. But wait! You mistyped "promo1.txt" as "porno1.txt," accidentally sending the first chapter of your erotic work-in-progress to the printer! Not only is your eventual masterpiece not ready for a publisher yet, it's definitely not ready for the secretaries who hang around the laser printer waiting for their memos to come out.

You don't panic. Instead, you type

```
lpstat
```

to see the print queue, and you see the following:

```
$ hp1-1318      mlopez        3,275     Aug 22 11:31 on hp1
$ hp1-1325      jimcasey      1,381     Aug 22 11:33 on hp1
$ hp1-1343      joeuser       6,923     Aug 22 11:34 on hp1
```

It's not too late; you type

```
cancel hp1-1434
```

and see the message

```
cancel: request hp1-1434 non-existent
```

Your palms start to sweat. You look back at the list of waiting print jobs, and realize that you typed the wrong request ID number. You try again:

```
cancel hp1-1343
```

and press Enter. This time you type it very carefully. No error message appears. To make sure that it worked, you type

```
lpstat
```

again, and this time you see this:

```
$ hp1-1325      jimcasey      1,381      Aug 22 11:33 on hp1
```

It looks like you were just in time. Maria Lopez's job finished printing, and Jim's is about to start. The important thing is, yours will not print. Now you try printing promo1.txt again, typing more carefully this time:

```
lp promo1.txt
```

Next, you check the print queue with the lpstat command. This time, you see

```
$ hp1-1325      jimcasey      1,381      Aug 22 11:33 on hp1
$ hp1-1348      joeuser       2,348      Aug 22 11:36 on hp1
```

so you know that you'll have it soon.

While you wait for it, you copy the file Mary told you about into your own directory. She said that it was in her home directory, not her mail directory, so you copy seppromo.txt into your home directory with the following command:

```
cp /usr2/maryjones/seppromo.txt /usr2/joeuser
```

After printing it, you check to make sure that it's there. You could type ls and list every file in the current directory, but you only want to check this single file. On the other hand, you're too lazy to type out ls seppromo.txt, so you take advantage of UNIX's wildcards and type:

```
ls -l sep*
```

You include the `-l` because you're curious about the file's size. The system responds with the following:

```
-rw-rw-r-- 1 maryjones marketing 19853 Sep 18 1994 seppromo.txt
```

Almost 20 kilobytes, which is about 10 pages. You hope it's useful.

After you pick up your `promo1.txt` printout from the printer, you look it over and it's not too bad. If you trim it down and add some stuff from `seppromo.txt`, it should keep Mary happy. To be safe, you want to keep the original file, so you make a copy of it and work on the copy. This copy will end up as a summary of your work on the September promotion, so you enter the following copy command:

```
cp promo1.txt seppromo.txt
```

After you press the Enter key, you realize: Mary's file was called `seppromo.txt`, and you just copied over it. Dumb, but not a disaster—you can copy her original file into your directory again. This time, when you copy it, you give the copy a new name:

```
cp /usr2/maryjones/seppromo.txt /usr2/joeuser/mjpromo.txt
```

Then you print it out with the command

```
lp mjpromo.txt
```

You read through your printouts of `promo1.txt` and `mjpromo.txt` and mark them up with ideas for your own `seppromo.txt` file. After bringing up `seppromo.txt` into the `vi` text editor, you delete a bit, turn some phrases into complete sentences, and add some quotes from `mjpromo.txt`. You also use the `vi` `:w` command to save your work every few minutes while you're editing. When you're done, you use the `:wq` to save your final changes and quit out of `vi`.

After printing out your edited file with the lp command and proofreading it, it looks good enough to send to Mary. You mail it to her with the following command:

```
cat seppromo.txt | mail mjones
```

You receive this message:

```
mjones[ell] User unknown
```

Because you entered Mary's login name incorrectly, the system didn't recognize it. You try again:

```
cat seppromo.txt | mail maryjones
```

This time there's no error message, so you know it worked.

That's enough work for the morning, and lunch calls. Because you don't want to leave your desk with your terminal logged in, you type

```
exit
```

to log out.

OpenVMS: An Introduction

VMS has traditionally been the operating system used on DEC's VAX line of computers. OpenVMS is the latest version of VMS, designed to spread its availability beyond the VAX. (The OpenVMS interface has remained similar enough to that of VMS that everything described in these chapters works the same way with recent versions of OpenVMS as it works with VMS. When I refer to "VMS," take it to mean VMS and OpenVMS together.) Today, the VAX is still the primary platform on which OpenVMS runs, and because of the close connection between VMS and the VAX for over 15 years, understanding the advantages of the VAX makes it easier to understand OpenVMS.

While VAX models range from the VAXstation VLC, which is inexpensive enough to compete in the marketplace with PCs, to the VAX 9000, which has enough power to compete with mainframes, all VAXes (or "VAXen"—see the buzzword sidebar on this) are generally considered to be minicomputers.

One of the VAX's major selling points has always been that, despite the wide range in the size and power of the different models, all models have the same architecture (the hardware design, as it appears to the system software) and all can run the same operating system: VMS. The saying "one architecture, one operating system" often comes up when DEC people discuss VAXes. This means that you can more easily port your applications and data if you outgrow one VAX and get a bigger one. It also makes communication between VAXes easier; if you outgrow one, you don't necessarily have to trade up—you can get a new one and hook it up to the old one, setting them up to work together.

VAXes work well together because they can operate in a "peer-to-peer" relationship. This goes a step beyond client/server computing: in a peer-to-peer system, any computer can be a client and any can be a server. This allows greater flexibility when multiple computers carry out tasks in cooperation. (For more on client/server systems, see the Introduction at the beginning of this book.)

It's not difficult to connect several VAXes together so that they work as a cooperating unit called a "VAXcluster." In fact, the "one architecture, one operating system" approach to the design of the VAX line makes this easier with VAXes than with just about any other computer. (Following the VAX's lead, most mini and PC manufacturers are working hard to catch up.) This cooperation is another of the VAX's advantages: it makes it easier to share resources like printers and disk drives and it reduces the chance of problems if part of the system malfunctions. So the VAX you use—especially if it's located at a university or company large enough to own several—may well be part of a VAXcluster.

DEC developed VMS and the VAX together. One benefit of this combination is the idea of "balanced architecture," or how well the designers balanced the tradeoffs between work done by the hardware and work done by the operating system. For computers running an operating system like UNIX, where programs are supposed to be portable from one company's UNIX machine to another's, designers must engineer the hardware to accommodate the lowest common denominator of the various operating system versions. This shifts much of the burden of management in a complex system to the operating system software. Because VMS and the VAX architecture were designed together, DEC engineers could make tradeoffs with fewer compromises. VMS fans assert that this cooperation between the hardware and the system software makes for a much more efficient computer.

Perhaps the greatest reason for the popularity of VMS is its ease of use. The commands are English words that are easy to remember, and the on-line help, while extensive, is simple to figure out. Utilities included with the system, like the mail program and text editors, are also powerful without intimidating beginners, and feature their own very good on-line help.

7.1 History

DEC released the first VAX, the VAX-11/780, in 1977. Its power and quality sent shock waves through the minicomputer industry. (Tracy Kidder's 1981 book *The Soul of a New Machine* describes Data General's feverish response to the VAX, as they built a new mini to compete with it. I highly recommend this classic, the only book on computers that I know of to win a Pulitzer Prize.)

In 1977, the only computer company bigger than DEC was IBM. If you outgrew a smaller IBM system, a lot of work, time, and expense was necessary to move your programs and data to one of their bigger systems. This made the VAX's flexibility a strong selling point to organizations that needed a minicomputer and aspired to more power further down the road. Academic institutions found them particularly appealing, and today VAXes are common at many universities.

VMS versus UNIX

Even if no one had developed versions of UNIX to run on VAXes, proponents of UNIX and VMS would still be engaged in a long, loud debate over the relative merits of the two operating systems. (The VAX was actually the target for one of Bell Labs' first ports of UNIX. Because this version didn't take advantage of the VAX's virtual memory capability—the "VM" in "VMS"—developers at the University of California at Berkeley developed a new version of UNIX that did. The success of Berkeley UNIX made it the primary alternative to AT&T's UNIX, and it became the standard in academic environments.) In Clifford Stoll's book *The Cuckoo's Egg*, he describes how the VMS and UNIX system administrators at the computer center where he worked loved to disparage each other's operating systems. Their accusations and jibes reveal much about how the two main camps in the minicomputer world view each other.

The rivalry between UNIX and VMS can be intense because they compete for much of the same turf. Small companies looking for something to keep track of their inventories and payrolls might use an IBM minicomputer, but academic, medical, scientific, and engineering organizations often have little interest in a "business machine" (the "BM" in "IBM"). They want a computer that gives them power without much cost and the flexibility to let them design their own software.

VMS and UNIX both offer this, but with different approaches. Proponents of VMS claim that UNIX is difficult because its abbreviated commands are cryptic and difficult to learn. They view the UNIX approach of offering you tools and ways to combine them as a disadvantage, because assembling a collection of pieces—especially when they come from different companies—can frustrate all but experienced experts. Compared to UNIX, VMS is easy to learn, and it's easier to coordinate a large amount of VAX hardware and software.

Proponents of UNIX sometimes accuse VMS of being slow, but the wide range of VAXes available mean that there's always a faster or slower model available. They also turn around some of UNIX's alleged disadvantages and call them advantages: they claim that the tools approach gives greater flexibility in putting together the system that they really need, and the wide variety of vendors involved eliminates dependence on the whims and fortunes of a single large corporation—in this case, DEC.

Regardless of individual opinions, VMS and UNIX coexist at many companies and universities. Being comfortable with both is always better than familiarity with one and contempt for the other, because the increasing ease of communication between the two operating systems means that more and more sites are hooking them up into one big cooperating network.

7.1.1 Today

A 1992 estimate put the number of VAX/VMS systems in the field at 500,000 and the number of users at 10 million. OpenVMS may outlive the VAX, or at least the VAX as we know it; DEC's new Alpha processor, a significant jump from the VAX, lies at the heart of their next round of technology. It's based on RISC (Reduced Instruction Set Computing) technology, a new method for designing processors that is playing an increasingly larger role in many companies' new hardware. Although DEC designed the Alpha chip to accommodate several different operating systems, they made sure that OpenVMS would run well on it. Rest assured that OpenVMS will be with us for a long time.

7.1.1.1 Popular VMS software.   You can choose from a wide variety of complete software packages available to run under VMS. By "complete," I mean to distinguish it from UNIX—the UNIX philosophy encourages a wide choice of specialized tools that one can piece together into customized applications more than it encourages the kind of complete software packages familiar to PC users. If you have to take an office full of people, set them up with a multiuser computer, and train them in the operating system and the applications they need as quickly as possible, you will probably want to give them either a system running VMS or an AS/400. Of these two, VMS's seniority means that you have a greater range of complete software packages to choose from, so there's a better chance that the software you need already exists and is optimized to take advantage of the VAX. (AS/400s can run programs from IBM's System/36 and System/38 lines, but these don't take advantage of the AS/400's architecture as well as custom-written applications do.)

One big-selling VMS package is DEC's ALL-IN-1 office management system. It provides word processing, e-mail, meeting and appointment scheduling, and other features that make it popular at many VMS sites.

Another DEC software product closely associated with VMS is Rdb, a relational database system. Although relational, Rdb does not use SQL (Structured Query Language) to manipulate data; to avoid this IBM creation DEC came up with their own system, called Digital Standard Relational Interface (DSRI—the "Standard" part is somewhat ironic). To develop Rdb applications, you must purchase software from DEC, but to run them, you only need Relational Database Operator (RDO), which is included with VMS. This policy has made Rdb popular in the VMS world, and other database systems must coexist efficiently with it in order to compete in the VMS marketplace.

Pathworks consists of a series of programs from DEC that allow, among other things, a system running VMS to act as a file and print server on a network with DOS, OS/2, or Macintosh microcomputers as clients. As the minicomputer's role changes from being *the* computer in a particular company or department to *a* computer cooperating with smaller ones, Pathworks and Novell products like NetWare for VMS make VMS systems better suited to taking on file and print server roles than any other popular minicomputer.

7.1.2 VMS, DCL

VMS stands for "Virtual Memory System." The name derives from the technique it uses to manage memory: the use of virtual memory is the ability to give programs access to more memory than the computer actually has.

VMS users refer to commands as "DCL commands" rather than "VMS commands." "Digital Command Language," or DCL, is the language developed by DEC to tell VMS what to do.

Every command-line driven operating system has a language (really, just a collection of commands) for us to tell it what to do; VMS is the only operating system that I know of that has a separate name for that language. DCL commands are not that different from the commands on other major operating systems (e.g., `COPY`, `RENAME`, and `DELETE`). What confuses beginners is the existence of a separate name to refer to the command language. To some, it implies the existence of special commands above and beyond the "normal" commands used to communicate with the operating system, like the relationship of REXX to the EXEC language on IBM mainframes.

We refer to VMS command files as "DCL command procedures" because, like the command files in other operating systems, they let you string together operating system commands in a text file and then run the series of commands by typing that file's name at the command prompt. Section 11.2, "Command Files," covers this in greater detail.

> BUZZWORD: "Vaxen." The official DEC plural for VAX computers is just that: VAX computers. "VAX," a trademarked brand name, is an adjective that modifies "computer" the same way that "Xerox" is legally a trademark to be used as an adjective modifying the word "photocopier." So just as you're not supposed to say "make some copies with the Xerox," you're not supposed to refer to the computer as a "VAX" or the plural as "VAXes."
>
> People say "VAXes" anyway. But another plural form has arisen: "VAXen." It seems to be preferred in more academic, less corporate environments. It's difficult to trace its etymology. The resemblance to the word "oxen" brings to mind a popular story that compares DEC's computer to the animal. DEC people like to point out that when a farmer realizes that his holdings have grown to the point where his one ox is no longer enough to plow the fields, he does not look for a bigger ox to replace his original one; instead he purchases an additional ox—or maybe several—and yokes them together to combine their power. The farmer increases his plowing power without giving up his original source of power. The connectivity (to use an overly popular industry buzzword) of VAX computers makes oxen a good metaphor for their strengths.
>
> In any case, "VAXes" and "VAXen" mean the same thing. The latter is, at most, probably considered slightly hipper.

8

Getting Started with OpenVMS

8.1 Starting Up

When you turn on a terminal connected to a VMS system, or success-fully connect to such a system over a network or phone line, the first thing you see is a message that asks for your user ID (or your "user-name"). This might be preceded by a message telling you the system you've connected to:

```
        WELCOME TO THE NEPTUNE VAX SYSTEM
           UNAUTHORIZED USE PROHIBITED
               O'ROURKE ENTERPRISES
    Username:
```

As an authorized user of this system you should have a login name that represents your identity on the system. Type it at the Username: prompt and press the Return key. If you make a typing mistake, use your Delete key to back up your cursor and erase the previous character. (The use of the Delete key to perform what many regard as the Backspace key's function can be confusing; see Section 8.1.2, "Entering commands," for more on this.)

VMS is not case-sensitive about your username or password. Whether you enter your username in upper- or lowercase, it appears in uppercase. The next prompt asks you for your password:

```
    Password:
```

Type it in and press the Return key. The characters of your password should not show up as you type them.

If all went well, you are logged in. The system may display some messages from the system administrator before it gets to the DCL command prompt, which is usually a dollar sign.

8.1.1 Finishing your VMS session

To log out, type the `logout` command at the DCL $ prompt. The following shows the system's response when Joe User enters this command:

```
$ logout
JOEUSER logged out at 12-JUL-1994 14:01:58.30
```

8.1.1.1 Reconnecting. If you are ever accidentally disconnected from your session without properly logging out, log back in as you normally do. Some systems display a message like this:

```
You have the following disconnected process:
Terminal     Process name    Image name
VTA1411:     JOE USER        $1NEPDISK:[SYS4.SYSCOMMON.]
                             [SYSCBI]VMS$INT.EXE;2
Connect to above listed process [YES]:
```

This tells you that you left off in the middle of something the last time you were connected, and it asks if you want to resume where you left off. The square braces around the word "YES" show that it is the default; if you press Return, it assumes that you mean "YES" and the system resumes whatever you were doing just before you were disconnected. A response of "NO" tells the system to put you at the DCL $ prompt.

Not all VMS systems have this feature; some display the $ prompt as if you were logging in normally when you reconnect after an aborted session.

8.1.2 Entering commands

When you enter a command at the DCL $ prompt and press Return, the output appears under it and the screen scrolls up if necessary to show the output. You only need to type the first four letters of any DCL command, because no two DCL commands begin with the same first four letters. If a command does not have the same first three letters as any other DCL command, which is often the case, you can get away with only using the first three letters.

When using a microcomputer to emulate a terminal, the most popular terminals to emulate are those of DEC's VT (for "Virtual Terminal") series. Nearly all telecommunications programs can emulate the VT100, one of the original models in this series, and nearly all minicomputers and mainframes can work with a VT100. Most telecommunications programs and computers can also work with more advanced VT terminals, which are named with higher numbers like VT220 or VT340.

Users of some keyboards on other computers, especially IBM-based ones, are accustomed to a Delete key that deletes the character at the cursor and a Backspace key that deletes the character to the left of the cursor. VT keyboards are more like the Macintosh's (actually, the

Mac keyboard is more like the VT's): the key known as the "Delete" key (in the upper right of the keyboard, with a pentagon pointing to the left and an "X" inside the pentagon) deletes the character just before the cursor position. The VT keyboard has no specific key for deleting the character at the cursor position. Terminal emulation programs often assign a PC's Delete key to "delete" in the VT sense of the word, so PC users must get used to using their Delete key to perform a function that they are accustomed to doing with their Backspace key.

To sum up, PC users who want to correct a typing mistake when connected to a VMS system must get used to pressing their Delete key to get their cursor back to the place where they made a mistake. (To confuse things a little more, note that I said "when connected to a VMS system"—when emulating a VT terminal while connected to an IBM or UNIX machine, Delete usually deletes the character at the cursor and Backspace deletes the character on the cursor's left.)

One more thing about a very important key: although certain IBM mainframe keyboards have separate Enter and Return keys, on most other computer keyboards one or the other serves the purpose of both. VT keyboards only have a Return key, which is what you press when you've finished typing a command and want to execute it. On a PC emulating a VT terminal, the Enter key stands in for the Return key. Either way, it's the big one above your right shift key.

8.1.2.1 Retrieving previous commands.   Pressing Ctrl + B retrieves previously entered commands, one at a time, to the command line. If you receive an error message because of a typo in a command you just entered, this saves you some typing, because you can retrieve the command in one keystroke and fix your mistake instead of retyping the whole command. (With some terminal emulation setups, the Cursor Up key also does this.)

8.1.2.2 Aborting screen output.   Ctrl + Y is known as the "Interrupt" key. If a command is displaying screens and screens of output and you don't want to see any more, press Ctrl + Y. VMS displays the word "Interrupt" to show where you stopped the output and it puts the DCL command prompt underneath it, ready for your next command.

Ctrl + Y can interrupt more than just screen output. If things get out of hand with just about any VMS program, it's one of the first things to try if you want to abort your session's current activity.

If you press Ctrl + Y by mistake, enter CONTINUE at the DCL command prompt to resume the running process.

8.1.2.3 Command parameters.   Many commands need some information from you to do their job. For instance, when you type the COPY command, the system needs to know the name of the file you want to copy and the name you want to assign to your new copy. As you'll see in the section on the COPY command, you could type this:

```
copy filename.old filename.new
```

If you type

```
copy
```

by itself, VMS responds in a fairly user-friendly way to this abbreviated syntax—it prompts you for the information it needs. At the _From: and _To: prompts that appear, you indicate the names of your source and destination files. For example:

```
$ copy
_From: inven.c
_To: inven_c.bkp
$
```

8.1.2.4 Case sensitivity.   VMS is not case-sensitive. Whether you enter your commands in upper- or lowercase, they still have the same effect. The same applies to filenames: when you create or refer to a file, whether you write out its name in upper- or lowercase, VMS translates it to uppercase.

8.2 Filenames

VMS users loosely use the term "filename" to refer to the two-part name that identifies a specific file in a directory. I say "loosely" because, more formally, it refers to the first of these two parts, with the second part being the file type. Both the filename and file type can be up to 39 characters long, but the most commonly used file types are three letters long.

Like its counterparts on other operating systems, the file type is like a person's last name. It identifies the family to which the file belongs. For example, the following file types indicate that a file is a member of the following families:

EXE   An executable program.

BAS   A program written in the BASIC programming language.

LIS   A plain text file.

DIR   A special file type: a DIR, for all practical purposes, is a subdirectory, or subdivision, of the current default directory. Technically, it too is a file, but a file that keeps track of the files in the subdirectory that it names. If you try to look at this file, it will mostly look like gibberish. For more on subdirectories, see Section 8.3, "How Files Are Organized."

You can use letters of the alphabet, numbers, and underscores in filenames and file types. Spaces are not allowed. You'll be pushing your luck if you use any other characters—if a command doesn't work and VMS gives you a message like "check use of special characters," you may have tried to create a file with a carat (^), a pound sign (#), or one of the keyboard's other nonalphanumeric characters.

VMS keeps multiple versions of each of your files. The three versions of `memos.lis` might be called `memos.lis;1`, `memos.lis;2`, and `memos.lis;3`. The one with the highest number is the most recent version. If you refer to a file but don't include its version number, many commands assume that you're referring to the most recent one, but some commands (like `DELETE`) force you to include the version number when you tell it which file or files to act on. Section 8.3, "How Files Are Organized," covers version numbers in more detail.

8.2.1 Wildcards

The main wildcards in VMS are the asterisk and the percent sign. Although the examples below demonstrate their use with the `DIRECTORY` command, which lists filenames, remember that you can use them with almost any command that uses file names as command-line parameters. For more information, see the material on wildcards in Section 1.5, "General Advice."

8.2.1.1 The asterisk.   An asterisk at the end of a file name means the same thing in VMS that it means in most other operating systems. It can represent zero or more characters at that position in the filename or file type.

In VMS, you're not restricted to putting the asterisk at the end of the filename or file type; if you use the `DIRECTORY` command to list filenames and enter the following

```
DIRECTORY *MAY.LIS
```

the system lists the names of files with a file type of `LIS` and a filename that ends with the letters "MAY." (Because the asterisk represents zero or more characters, the file `MAY.LIS` fits that pattern as well as `CAMAY.LIS` would.)

Entering this

```
DIRECTORY MAY*94.LIS
```

lists files with "LIS" as a file type and a filename that begins with "MAY" and ends with "94" whether there are 0 or 34 characters between the "MAY" and the "94." (Remember, the filename and file type can each consist of a total of 39 characters, and "MAY" and "94" make five.)

To list filenames that have "MAY" anywhere in the filename, regardless of the file type, enter

```
DIRECTORY *MAY*.*
```

If you don't include any characters or wildcards to indicate a pattern for the file type, VMS assumes a default of *. In other words, it includes files with filenames that fit the entered pattern regardless of the file type. For example, entering

```
DIRECTORY *MAY
```

lists all files with a filename that ends with "MAY," no matter what their file type.

8.2.1.2 The percent sign.   The percent sign represents a single character in a filename—no more, no less. Several percent signs represent that number of characters, so that

```
DIRECTORY %%%93RPT.TXT
```

would list out the filenames with exactly three characters before the characters "93rpt.txt."

8.3 How Files Are Organized

As with several other operating systems, files on a VMS system are organized in divisions and subdivisions of hard disk space called directories, and a file's full name (called its "file specification," or "filespec") includes the directory name. Unlike other operating systems, the complete filespec includes more than the directory name: it also includes the names of the computer and hard disk on which the file is stored.

The following shows a possible complete filespec for Joe User's file `FOR_MARY.LIS`:

```
NEPTUNE::NEPDISK:[JOEUSER.MEMOS.JUNE]FOR_MARY.LIS;3
```

The filespec consists of the following parts:

node   The name of the computer on which the file is stored. This is not a brand name or model name, but more of a nickname that system administrators assign when they install a computer. If you send e-mail to someone using a VMS system other than your own, you need to know their node name. In the example, Joe User's system administrator named their node NEPTUNE. Note the use of the two colons to separate the node name from the rest of the filespec.

device   A given VMS system may store files on several hard disks; the device name is the specific hard disk where a file is stored. NEPDISK is the device name in the example. A single colon separates the device name from the rest of the filename. (DOS users will find this use of the colon to separate a disk name from a file and directory name familiar—for example, in `c:command.com` the disk name is `c` and the filename is `command.com`.)

directory

A hard disk is divided into sections called directories. The system administrator assigns each user ID its own directory, and the user can create subdivisions of this directory known as subdirectories. (These too may be subdivided, and the subdivisions may be subdivided, and so forth to seven levels below the user ID's directory.) A directory's full name consists of the names of the various levels separated by periods with square braces around the whole thing.

We call a user ID's main directory—in the example above, `[JOEUSER]`—that user's "root directory." DOS and UNIX users should keep in mind that in VMS "root directory" means the root of a particular user's arrangement of subdirectories (like a UNIX user's home directory), rather than the root of the whole hard disk.

Joe User might divide his `JOEUSER` directory into several subdirectories and name one of them `MEMOS`. This subdirectory's full name would be `[JOEUSER.MEMOS]`. If he divided his `MEMOS` subdirectory into subsections for each month of the year, the full name of the subdirectory that holds his June memos would be `[JOEUSER.MEMOS.JUNE]`, as in the example.

filename

This means just what it says. See Section 8.2, "Filenames," for information on the two parts of a filename. In the example, the filename is `FOR_MARY.LIS`.

version number

When you first create a file, VMS assigns it a version number of 1. If you edit the file, the text editor saves the edited version with a version number of 2 and the old one remains in the same directory with a version number of 1. The version number is appended onto the filename, separated from it by a semicolon. In the example, the `;3` after the filename `FOR_MARY.LIS` shows that the filespec represents the third version of the file.

You will undoubtedly find that your directories gradually fill up with unnecessary old versions of your files. Section 9.1.7.1, "Purging old versions of your files," explains how to delete all but the most recent version or versions of a file.

The system administrator assigns your user ID to a particular disk of a particular computer. If you don't include a node or device name when you refer to a file, VMS assumes that you're talking about a file on the same node and disk that you're already using.

Why does VMS give you the option of including the computer and hard disk name in a file's complete name, when few other operating systems do? As I mentioned earlier, VAXes are often grouped together into a network called a VAXcluster. The ability to be so specific about a file's location makes it much easier to access a file on other VAXes in your cluster.

8.3.1 Moving between directories

The command SHOW DEFAULT displays the name of your "default" directory. If Joe User types this while his root directory is the default, the system displays the following:

```
NEPDISK:[JOEUSER]
```

While you get used to the various syntax possibilities for changing your default directory, this command is handy, because you can use it to check the success of each attempt to make a new directory the default one.

The SET DEFAULT command changes your default directory. Because this command and SHOW DEFAULT come up so often, it saves you some typing to remember that you only need the first three letters of any DCL keywords. This makes these commands SET DEF and SHOW DEF—or even SHO DEF.

For Joe User to set his default directory to the MEMOS subdirectory of his root directory, he could type this:

```
SET DEFAULT [JOEUSER.MEMOS]
```

Fortunately, there are other shortcuts besides abbreviating the keywords. If you begin the directory name with a period, you tell VMS that the following directory name is a subdirectory of the current default one. For example, if Joe is already in the [JOEUSER] directory and wants to go one level down to the MEMOS directory, he can type this:

```
SET DEFAULT [.MEMOS]
```

If he wanted to go from [JOEUSER] to [JOEUSER.MEMOS.JUNE] in one command without typing the entire name of his destination, he could enter this:

```
SET DEFAULT [.MEMOS.JUNE]
```

When moving back one or more levels, a hyphen represents the directory one level closer to the root. For example, Joe could go from [JOEUSER.MEMOS.JUNE] to [JOEUSER.MEMOS] by entering this:

```
SET DEFAULT [-]
```

To go back multiple levels, you can use multiple hyphens, as long as you separate them with periods. For example, Joe can go from

[JOEUSER.MEMOS.JUNE] to his [JOEUSER] root directory by entering this:

```
SET DEFAULT [-.-]
```

As you'll see in Section 9.1.5, "Copying files," these tricks for abbreviating directory names also work when you specify a directory other than the current default one as the destination for a file that you are copying.

8.3.1.1 Default directory? Current directory?   There is a subtle difference between the VMS concept of a default directory and the DOS or UNIX concept of a "current" directory. When you make a new directory current while using one of the latter two operating systems, you can think of it as moving to a new part of the disk to work. When you set a default directory in VMS, you indicate a directory (or disk) name to use with any files for which you don't explicitly include the directory or disk name. Misunderstanding this difference can lead to aggravation when you get certain error messages.

For example, this happens when you specify a nonexistent directory as your new default directory. In UNIX and DOS, when you issue the cd (change directory) command with a nonexistent directory as its parameter, the system gives you an error message right away. On the other hand, when you use the SET DEFAULT command to tell VMS to "apply this directory name to files that I refer to in future commands," the system takes it on faith that the name is a good one. When you try it with a nonexistent directory name, the system responds with the DCL prompt, and no error message:

```
$ set default [.febyooary]
$
```

If Joe User tries to do anything with this nonexistent directory, he gets an error message or two:

```
$ dir
%DIRECT-E-OPENIN, error opening NEPDISK:[JOEUSER.FEBYOOARY]*.*;* as
input
-RMS-E-DNF, directory not found
-SYSTEM-W-NOSUCHFILE, no such file
```

(See Section 9.1.2, "Common error messages" for more on the format of error messages.) This problem will continue until you fix it, so Joe types

```
set default [joeuser.february]
```

to correct his mistake.

8.3.2 Querying available disk space

A VMS system administrator allocates a certain amount of disk space to each ID. To see how much of yours you have used and how much free space remains, enter the following command:

```
SHOW QUOTA
```

VMS displays a message similar to this:

```
User [207,JOEUSER] has 356 blocks used, 9644 available,
of 10000 authorized and permitted overdraft of 100 blocks on
NEPDISK
```

The [207,JOEUSER] is the User Identification Code (UIC), a unique code that the system uses to keep track of users. A block represents 512 bytes, so to picture a given number of blocks in kilobytes, cut it in half. The preceding example shows that the files in Joe User's ID space take up about 178 kilobytes, and he has about 4822 kilobytes of free space. Section 9.1.3, "Listing filenames," shows how adding the /SIZE qualifier to the DIRECTORY command displays the size, in blocks, of individual files.

8.4 Available On-Line Help

VMS probably has the best on-line help of any operating system that uses character-based screens. In fact, it outshines the help included with many operating systems that use a graphical user interface. Its greatest strength is the ease with which you can move to a greater or lesser level of detail and from topic to topic.

If you type HELP by itself at the DCL prompt, VMS displays an introductory help screen similar to the one in Figure 8.1. This first help screen tells you how to use help. Press Return, and the next help screen looks similar to the one shown in Figure 8.2.

This shows you the beginning of the list of available help topics. (Note that Hints is on the list. The first help screen already indicated that this is a valid help topic.)

Your screen probably won't look exactly like this; part of the beauty of VMS on-line help is the ease with which system administrators can add new help topics, so that users can learn about issues that pertain to their particular system just as easily as they can learn about VMS commands.

When you press Return again, VMS displays the rest of the list, and then a prompt that asks you which topic you want to learn more about:

```
Topic?
```

```
HELP

    The   HELP   command   invokes   the   VMS   HELP   Facility   to   display
    information about a VMS command or topic.  In response to the "Topic?"
    prompt, you can:

        o Type   the   name of the command  or topic for which you need help.

        o Type  INSTRUCTIONS  for more detailed  instructions on how to use
          HELP.

        o Type  HINTS  if you are not  sure of the  name  of the command or
          topic for which you need help.

        o Type a question mark (?) to redisplay the most recently requested
          text.

        o Press the RETURN key one or more times to exit from HELP.



Press RETURN to continue ...
```

Figure 8.1 Screen 1 of the VMS introductory help screen.

```
    You  can  abbreviate any  topic name, although ambiguous abbreviations
    result in all matches being displayed.


    Additional information available:

    :=              =              @              ACCOUNTING ALLIN1     ALLOCATE   ANALYZE
    APPEND          ASSIGN         ASU            ATTACH     AUTHORIZE  AUTOGEN    BACKUP
    BASIC           BTEQ           CACHE          CALL       CANCEL     CC         CDD
    CDDL            CDDV           CDD_PLUS       CDO        CLOSE      CMS        COBOL
    COLLECT         CONNECT        CONTINUE       CONVERT    COPY       CREATE     DATATRIEVE
    DBCCP           DBC_1012       DBMS           DBO        DBO40      DDL        DDL40
    DEALLOCATE      DEASSIGN       DEBUG          DECK       DECtrace   DEFINE     DELETE
    DEPOSIT         DICTIONARY     DIFFERENCES               DIRECTORY  DISCONNECT DISKQUOTA
    DISMOUNT        DML            DML40          DMU        DOCUMENT   DSM        DTM
    DUMP            EDIT           ENCRYPT        EOD        EOJ        EXAMINE    EXCHANGE
    EXIT            FDL            FileChief      FINGER     FMS        FONT       FORTRAN
    FTP             GOSUB          GOTO           GRAPH      HELP       Hints      IDL
    IDMCOPY         IDMDATE        IDMDUMP        IDMFCOPY   IDMLOAD    INITIALIZE INQUIRE

Press RETURN to continue ...
```

Figure 8.2 Screen 2 of the VMS introductory help screen.

If you respond by merely pressing the Return key, VMS returns you to the DCL prompt. If you want to know more about one of the listed topics, enter its name. For example, if you respond to the Topic? prompt by entering EDIT, the help program displays a screen similar to the one shown in Figure 8.3.

Pressing Return another time displays the second and final general help screen for the EDIT command, as shown in Figure 8.4.

```
EDIT


    The EDIT commands perform the following functions:

    o  Invoke the Access Control List Editor  to  create  or  modify  an
       access control list for an object (see /ACL).

    o  Invoke the EDT screen-oriented editor (see /EDT).

    o  Invoke the FDL  editor  to  create  and  modify  File  Definition
       Language files (see /FDL).

    o  Invoke the SUMSLP batch-oriented editor to update a single  input
       file with multiple files of edit commands (see /SUM).

    o  Invoke the TECO editor (see /TECO).

    o  Invoke the TPU editor (see /TPU).


Press RETURN to continue ...
```

Figure 8.3 VMS help screen 1 for the EDIT topic.

```
    Additional information available:

    /ACL        /EDT        /FDL        /SUM        /TECO       /TPU

EDIT Subtopic?
```

Figure 8.4 Additional information available on the EDIT command.

```
    Additional information available:

    EVE_Editor Examples   Logicals   Parameter  Qualifiers /COMMAND    /CREATE
    /DEBUG     /DISPLAY   /INITIALIZATION        /INTERFACE /JOURNAL    /MODIFY
    /OUTPUT    /READ_ONLY /RECOVER   /SECTION    /START_POSITION        /WORK
    /WRITE

EDIT /TPU Subtopic?
```

Figure 8.5 VMS help screen 2 for the EDIT topic.

Note how EDIT, as a topic, has subtopics that you can learn more about. Some subtopics have their own subtopics; if you enter /TPU in response to the EDIT Subtopic? prompt, VMS displays introductory information about the Text Processing Utility (TPU), and then another subtopic menu to select from, as shown in Figure 8.5.

If you respond to any help prompt by pressing Return without first entering anything, the help program takes you back to the previous help level's prompt. In the following, note what happens when a user looking at the EDIT /TPU Subtopic? prompt repeatedly presses Return until the system returns to the DCL prompt:

```
EDIT /TPU Subtopic?
EDIT Subtopic?
Topic?
$
```

When you reach the deepest level of help available on a particular topic (that is, when the currently displayed topic has no subtopics), the help program redisplays the most recent help prompt. For example, if EDIT /TPU has no subtopics of its own, the system displays the EDIT Subtopic? prompt after it displays the help information on EDIT /TPU.

What if you respond to a help prompt with something that the help program doesn't recognize, like POTRZEBIE? The help program responds with a polite message like this:

```
Sorry, no documentation on POTRZEBIE
```

Note that one of the EDIT /TPU subtopics is EVE_Editor. Topic and subtopic names cannot have spaces in them, so they use underscores instead. For example, one subtopic of the HINTS screen is called Batch_and_print_jobs. Don't forget to include the underscores when you enter one of these topic names, or you'll get the "Sorry, no documentation" message.

You don't always have to go through the various menus and screens to get help. If you need help with a specific command, enter HELP followed by the command name at the DCL prompt. For example, to go right from the DCL prompt to the main help screen for the EDIT command, enter this:

```
HELP EDIT
```

For even more specific help, you can add one of a command's qualifiers to go to the help screen for that qualifier. For example, entering

```
HELP EDIT/TPU
```

takes you right to the screen that describes the TPU editor.

As you can see, the VMS help system is easy to get into, easy to navigate, and easy to get out of. Also, as the very first screen shows, you can easily find out more about the help program from the help program itself.

9

Using Files in OpenVMS

9.1 The Eight Most Important Commands

The eight most important commands in VMS are:

DIRECTORY	Lists file names
TYPE	Displays the contents of files
COPY	Copies files
RENAME	Renames files
DELETE	Deletes files and directories
PURGE	Erases old versions of your files and keeps recent ones
SET PROTECTION	Grants and revokes access to files
CREATE/DIRECTORY	Creates directories

9.1.1 Command options: qualifiers

A command option, known as a "qualifier" in VMS, is separated from the command by a slash. Although any spaces before or after the slash don't affect the command's execution, you usually see examples written with no spaces before or after the slash. VMS users usually consider the slash to be part of the qualifier, not a separator between qualifiers. For example, when you're viewing the on-line help's basic description of the EDIT command and want to see subtopic information on its /TPU qualifier, entering just "TPU" as the subtopic name displays an error message. You must include the slash for VMS to recognize what you want.

The DIRECTORY command entered by itself only lists filenames. Various qualifiers allow you to list more information with these filenames. For example, the /SIZE qualifier lists each file's size, in blocks, next to its name, regardless of whether you enter

```
DIRECTORY/SIZE
```

or

```
DIRECTORY /SIZE
```

or this:

```
DIRECTORY/ SIZE
```

This latitude with spaces still applies when you add more than one qualifier to your command. For example, adding the /DATE qualifier tells the DIRECTORY command to list the date of the file's creation, along with the file's name. To list each file's size and creation date, you could enter

```
DIRECTORY/DATE/SIZE
```

or

```
DIRECTORY / DATE / SIZE
```

without any problem.

9.1.2 Common error messages

VMS error messages take the following form:

```
%component-c-abbrev, message
```

This consists of the following parts (don't worry about the first four—the message part is the important one):

%   Marks the beginning of the error message. If the message includes more than one line, the additional lines give details about the main error message. These have the same format as the first, but begin with a hyphen (–) instead of a percent sign.

component   Is the component of VMS that choked on the command that caused the error. This will probably appear as some initials.

c   Is the code that tells you the severity of the error:
            I Informational
            E Error
            S Success
            F Fatal error
            W Warning

abbrev   Is a unique error code abbreviation.

message   Is the actual error message. With luck it will be a whole sentence that explains what went wrong.

The most classic error is to misspell a command name so that the system doesn't recognize the entered command. In the following example, Joe User adds an extra "d" to the DIRECTORY command:

```
$ ddirectory
%DCL-W-IVVERB, unrecognized command verb - check validity and
spelling
\DDIRECTORY\
```

VMS first tells him that it doesn't recognize the command he entered. It then repeats, between the slashes, the command that it didn't recognize. This is handy if the system rejects a complicated command and you don't know which part of it caused the error message.

The other classic error is to misspell a filename so that you enter a command to do something to a nonexistent file. For example, let's say Joe User wants to delete the file SUMRPT.LIS;1 but makes a typo when he enters the filename:

```
DELETE SLUMRPT.LIS;1
```

VMS responds with these messages:

```
%DELETE-W-SEARCHFAIL, error searching for
NEPDISK:[JOEUSER]SLUMRPT.LIS;1
-RMS-E-FNF, file not found
```

The message on the first line indicates that there was a problem searching for the SLUMRPT.LIS file. The second line elaborates on the problem: it couldn't find the file. (Another possible problem that might cause a searching error would be a hardware problem on the hard drive's disk.)

9.1.3 Listing filenames

The VMS command to list out the files in a directory is DIRECTORY. Because this command is used so often, its first three letters are more popular than the final six, especially among DOS users who are used to entering "DIR" on their PCs to list filenames.

Entering this command with no qualifiers displays the directory's full name, the filenames and version numbers arranged alphabetically in several columns across the screen, and the total count of the filenames listed at the bottom, as shown in Figure 9.1.

If you enter DIR without specifying the directory in which to list the files, it lists the files in the default directory. To list the files in another directory, add its name (all shortcuts for directory names are allowed) after the DIR command, like this:

```
dir [.memos.june]
```

```
Directory NEPDISK:[JOEUSER]

INVEN.C;6          INVEN.C;5          INVEN.C;4          INVEN.EXE;3
INVEN.HLP;1        INVEN.JOU;2        INVEN.JOU;1        INVEN.OBJ;3
L543.TMP;1         L544.TMP;1         L545.TMP;1         MEMOS.DIR;1
MENU.C;4           MENU.C;3           MENU.EXE;2         MENU.EXE;4
MENU.HLP;1         MENU.OBJ;3         SETUP.COM;1        SETUP.DAT;2
SUMRPT.C;2         SUMRPT.C;1         SUMRPT.EXE;2       SUMRPT.EXE;1
SUMRPT.HLP;1       SUMRPT.LIS;1       SUMRPT.OBJ;2       SUMRPT.OBJ;1
TEST.C;1           TEST.EXE;4         TEST.HLP;1         TEST.OBJ;1
TESTPAS.EXE;1      TESTPAS.PAS;1      TODO.TXT;8         TODO.TXT;7
TODO.TXT;6         TODO.TXT;5         UR.COM;1           URBASE_TEST.DIR;1

Total of 40 files.
```

Figure 9.1 Sample output of DIR (DIRECTORY) command.

If you don't indicate a file specification, the `dir` command lists all the files in the directory. If you enter a filename, it only lists versions of that one file. (Note that I said "versions of"; if you include a file-name without a semicolon or number after that semicolon, VMS assumes that you want to list all versions of that file.)

It's more common to enter a file specification with wildcards, so that VMS lists a subset of the directory's files. For example, entering the following

```
dir *.c
```

produces output like this:

```
Directory NEPDISK:[JOEUSER]
INVEN.C;6          INVEN.C;5          INVEN.C;4          MENU.C;4
MENU.C;3           SUMRPT.C;2         SUMRPT.C;1         TEST.C;1
Total of 8 files.
```

Adding a file specification to a directory name lists the files in that directory that meet that wildcard pattern. For example, entering

```
dir [joeuser.memos.june]mary*.*
```

lists all the files that begin with the letters "mary" in the [joeuser. memos.june] directory.

9.1.3.1 Listing more than filenames. The DIR command has many qual-ifiers; the most useful are /SIZE, /DATE, and VERSION = n. To learn about the others, enter HELP DIRECTORY at the command prompt.

Enter DIR/SIZE to list the filenames with their individual sizes, in blocks:

```
INVEN.JOU;2        1
INVEN.JOU;1        1
INVEN.OBJ;1        4
L543.TMP;1         2
```

```
L544.TMP;1        3
L545.TMP;1        3
MEMOS.DIR;1       1
MENU.C;4          5
MENU.C;3          5
MENU.EXE;2        3
```

As explained in Section 8.3.2, "Querying available disk space," a block represents 512 bytes, or half a kilobyte. There are no partial blocks; a 513-byte file and a 1024-byte file both take up two blocks of space on a VMS system.

The /DATE parameter adds the creation date and time, in military format, to each filename. If you are more interested in when a file was last modified than in when it was created, just look at the creation date of the copy of the file with the highest version number. For example, if you enter

```
dir/date inven.c
```

and see this as output

```
INVEN.C;7 1-AUG-1994  15:20:49.74
INVEN.C;6 30-JUL-1994 16:42:45.85
INVEN.C;5 30-JUL-1994 16:36:35.59
INVEN.C;4 30-JUL-1994 16:24:28.32
```

you can tell that INVEN.C was last edited at 3:20 PM on August 1.

If the DIR command's output clutters your screen too much, you can instruct it to only list each file's most recent version by adding /VERSION = 1 to the DIR command. (/VERSION = 2 tells it to list the most recent two versions, and so forth.) Section 9.1.7.1, "Purging old versions of your files," shows how to delete older unwanted versions of your files while keeping a specified number of the recent versions.

9.1.4 Displaying a text file's contents

To display a text file on your screen, use the VMS TYPE command. Followed by a filename, it displays that file's contents. For example, the command

```
type test.c
```

puts the contents of the test.c file on the screen:

```
#include <stdio.h>
main() {
   printf("I hope I can get the C compiler to work.");
}
```

9.1.4.1 Looking at text files one screen at a time.   Many files are too long to fit on your screen, and the TYPE command scrolls them up your screen too quickly to read. The TYPE command's /PAGE qualifier tells

```
October 9

9:00 Ed may have Knicks tickets for me; bug him when he gets back from Toronto

10:30 office supplies sales rep coming

12:00 lunch with Benny postponed until the 10th

2:30 getting teeth cleaned--call 687-2300 first for address

4:00 Fed Ex new diskettes to Chicago


October 10

10:30 meet Dave C., Laurie.  call Laurie first--should I bring new diskettes?

12:30 lunch with Benny

2:00 expecting call from Chicago office.  Have page counts ready.

2:30 Anita's presentation--can I get out of going?
```

                         Press RETURN to continue

Figure 9.2 Sample output of TYPE command with the /PAGE qualifier.

the system to show the file one page at a time. For example, after Joe User enters the following

```
type/page schedule.txt
```

and presses Return, VMS displays the first page of the schedule.txt file, as shown in Figure 9.2.

The message Press RETURN to continue tells you to press the Return key when you're ready to see the next page. If you find yourself pressing Return over and over and regretting that you issued the TYPE command with such a large file, press Ctrl + Y to abort the display and return to the DCL prompt. (For more on using Ctrl + Y, see Section 8.1.2.2, "Aborting screen output.")

9.1.5 Copying files

Copying a file is simple. Enter the COPY command followed by the name of the file to copy and the name to assign to the copy. For example, entering the following creates a copy of inven.c called inven_c.bkp:

```
copy inven.c inven_c.bkp
```

After you press Return, if the system returns you to the DCL prompt with no error message, then you know that VMS copied the file without any problems.

If you enter COPY without any parameters, VMS is very forgiving. It prompts you with individual prompts for the information that it needs:

```
$ copy
_From: inven.c
_To: inven_c.bkp
$
```

If you don't include the source file's version number, VMS assumes that you want to copy the most recent version of that file. If you don't include the destination file's version number, VMS starts it at 1 if no file with that name exists. Otherwise, its version number will be one higher than the current highest number assigned to a file of that name.

If you include the destination file's version number, VMS creates the new file with that number. If a file with that name and number already exists, VMS responds with an error message telling you that it couldn't open the destination file for output because it already exists.

You can use wildcards to copy multiple files at once. The following command copies the most recent version of all files with a filename of mainmenu to files with a filename of submenu1:

```
copy mainmenu.* submenu1.*
```

9.1.5.1 Copying files to other directories.   To copy a file to another directory, specify the directory name as the destination of the copy operation. For example, entering

```
copy mainmenu.c [joeuser.inven.old_code]
```

copies the most recent version of the mainmenu.c file into the [joeuser.inven.old_code] subdirectory. The copy in the destination directory will have the same version number as the source version of the file, even if there are no other files in the destination directory with that file's name.

When you include directory names in the copy command's parameters, you can use the same shortcuts to refer to directory names that you can use with the SET DEFAULT command to change the default directory. For example, if [joeuser.inven.old_code] is Joe User's default directory, and he wants to copy the mainmenu.c program to his root directory—which happens to be the parent of the parent of his default directory—he could type this:

```
copy mainmenu.c [-.-]
```

See Section 8.3.1, "Moving between directories," for more on abbreviating directory names.

When you copy a file to another directory, the copy will have the same name unless you specify otherwise. Specifying otherwise is easy; just put the new name immediately after the destination directory's name:

```
copy mainmenu.c [-.-]oldmenu.c
```

Be careful to include the brackets when you specify a directory as the destination of your copy operation. For example, if Joe wants to copy the file 080494mj.txt from his [JOEUSER] directory, which is currently his default, to his [JOEUSER.MEMOS] directory, he enters this:

```
copy 080494mj.txt [.memos]
```

If he makes the mistake of typing

```
copy 080494mj.txt memos
```

then he creates a new file in his [JOEUSER] directory with the name memos.txt. (The system assumes that because he did not specify a file type for his new file, he wants it to have the same file type as the source file.)

Here's a trick that won't make sense on other operating systems, but fits right in to the VMS scheme of things. The following is a perfectly valid, almost useful VMS command:

```
copy todo.txt todo.txt
```

In other operating systems, this would mean "make a copy of the todo.txt file and call it todo.txt"—a command that wouldn't say much. But because of the default version numbers that VMS assigns to the destination of the COPY command, VMS reacts to this command by taking the most recent version of the todo.txt file and making a copy with the next highest version number.

9.1.6 Renaming files

To rename a file, enter the RENAME command followed by the name of the file to rename and the new name to give it. If you do not include the source file's version number, the most recent version of the file will be renamed. For example, to rename the inven.c file as inven_c.bkp, enter

```
rename inven.c inven_c.bkp
```

As with the COPY command, VMS prompts you for any parameters that you omit.

As we saw in Section 8.2, "Filenames," directories are really special files, so renaming a directory is as easy as renaming a file if you remember to include the DIR file type. For example, if Joe User's current default directory is [JOEUSER] and he wants to rename his [JOEUSER.MEMOS] subdirectory as [JOEUSER.LETTERS], he enters this:

```
rename memos.dir letters.dir
```

You can also use the RENAME command to move a file from one directory to another. For example, entering

```
rename [joeuser.memos]052394js.txt [joeuser.letters]052394js.txt
```

moves the file 052394JS.TXT from the [JOEUSER.MEMOS] directory to the [JOEUSER.LETTERS] directory. (In the above example, the second 052394js.txt is actually unnecessary. Unless you're giving the file a new name in its new location, you don't need to specify its name with the destination directory.)

9.1.7 Deleting files

To delete a file, enter the DELETE command followed by the filename. Unlike other commands, DELETE assumes nothing about version numbers when you enter a filename without a version number. Entering delete without one, like this

```
delete inven_c.bkp
```

gives you a message similar to the following:

```
%DELETE-E-DELVER, explicit version number or wild card required
```

The "wild card" part means that if you really want to delete all the versions of inven_c.bkp, you can simply enter this:

```
delete inven_c.bkp;*
```

Otherwise, enter a specific version number after the semicolon.

If you are accustomed to another operating system, you'll probably forget to include the version number pretty often when you try to delete a file. This is a great example of how handy the Ctrl + B or Cursor Up keys can be: if you make a simple mistake with your command and get an error message, you can use one of these keystrokes to retrieve the command that you just typed, make the minor correction necessary (in this case, by adding the semicolon and version number), and press Return. See Section 8.1.2.1, "Retrieving previous commands" for more on this feature.

9.1.7.1 Purging old versions of your files. The VMS practice of keeping multiple versions of your files can quickly clutter up the disk space allocated to your user ID. VMS has a special command to ease the cleanup of old versions of your files: PURGE. Entering PURGE with only a filename as a parameter tells VMS to delete all versions of that file except for the most recent one.

To tell VMS to keep more than one version of the file, use the /KEEP = n qualifier. For example, if you have seven versions of todo.txt and enter

```
purge/keep = 3 todo.txt
```

VMS deletes the four oldest versions of todo.txt and keeps the three newest ones.

9.1.8 Controlling access to a file

The SET PROTECTION command lets you control who can read, write, execute, and delete your files and directories. There are four categories of users whose privileges you can set when you set the protection level for a file or files:

System   The system administrators, who have special privileges in order to maintain the system.

Owner   You, because you own the file. (You can't use SET PROTECTION on files that belong to other users.)

Group   For easier system maintenance, system administrators classify users into groups. They might base these groupings on the users' departments or job titles—for example, people in accounting could be one group, and programmers another. When you set a file's protection level, the Group category lets you give your group's members greater access than everyone else on the system.

World   Everyone on the system.

Owners are considered to be members of their own groups, and the owner's group is considered to be part of "World," so if you try to give the group more privileges than the owner, or the world more privileges than the group, it won't work. (It wouldn't make too much sense to try this anyway.)

To find out the protection levels assigned to existing files, add the /PROTECTION qualifier to the DIR command:

```
$ dir/protection ur.com
UR.COM;1          (RWED,RWED,RE,)
```

The commas separate the privilege lists for the System administrators, Owner, Group, and World, in that order. The letters that show the privileges each stand for Read, Write, Edit, and Delete. In the example, the system administrators and owner can perform any of these operations on the ur.com file. Others in the owner's group can read or edit it; the lack of any initials after the final comma shows that people outside the group cannot do anything with it.

To find out the default protection levels assigned to files that you create, enter the command SHOW PROTECTION, like this:

```
$ show protection
SYSTEM = RWED, OWNER = RWED, GROUP = RE, WORLD = NO ACCESS
```

This makes it pretty clear who has what kind of access to your files, or at least the files to which you don't explicitly assign other access levels.

Use the SET PROTECTION command to assign specific access levels. Its parameters, in parentheses, are the relevant user categories and the access that each should have. To assign ur.com the access levels shown above, use this command:

```
set protection = (system:rwed,owner:rwed,group:re,world) ur.com
```

Note that world is listed with no privileges at all. If you didn't include world in the parentheses, you would assign world the default access levels shown by the SHOW PROTECTION command. In fact, to assign all the default access levels shown by SHOW PROTECTION, you only need type this:

```
set protection ur.com
```

When you assign the different access types that each user category has, you must abbreviate the words Read, Write, Edit, and Delete to their first letters. (No great loss—would you really want to type them out every time?) If you want, you can also abbreviate the user categories to their first letters. This makes the command shown above a bit shorter:

```
set protection = (s:rwed,o:rwed,g:re,w) ur.com
```

It's perfectly OK to use wildcards to specify the files whose access levels you are setting. For example, to make sure that everyone in your group can read but not edit the source code of your existing C programs (which all have a filetype of "c"), and that people outside of your group can't even do that, enter this:

```
set protection = (g:r,w) *.c;*
```

Notice the semicolon and second asterisk after the c file type. As with many other commands, if you don't indicate a specific version number of the file that you want SET PROTECTION to act on, it only affects the latest revision of the specified file or files. To make sure that it sets the protection level of every single file with a particular file type, remember to add an asterisk as a version number.

9.1.9 Creating directories

The VMS CREATE command can be used to create various kinds of files. Usually, you use the text editor or an application program to create a file, but you need the CREATE command with its /DIRECTORY qualifier to create subdirectories of your root directory. (Only system administrators can create subdirectories of directories that aren't their own.)

Enter CREATE with the /DIRECTORY qualifier followed by the name of the new directory to create, like this:

```
create/directory [joeuser.memos.july]
```

After you create a new subdirectory, the DIR command will not show any files in it. You still may want to use it to check whether the directory was successfully created. If you use DIR to inquire about the files in a nonexistent directory, like this,

```
dir [.potrzebie]
```

VMS responds like this:

```
%DIRECT-E-OPENIN, error opening NEPDISK:[JOEUSER.POTRZEBIE]*.*;* as
input
-RMS-E-DNF, directory not found
-SYSTEM-W-NOSUCHFILE, no such file
```

In other words, it couldn't find a potrzebie.dir file in the [JOEUSER] directory to represent a subdirectory of [JOEUSER].

Your subdirectories can have subdirectories and they too can have subdirectories, down to seven levels below your root directory. For example, Joe could create a subdirectory called [JOEUSER.LEV1. LEV2.LEV3.LEV4.LEV5.LEV6.LEV7], but he couldn't create any subdirectories of his LEV7 subdirectory.

9.1.10 Removing directories

If you know that you can treat a directory called [.whatever] as a file called whatever.dir and you know that you delete files with the DELETE command, then you already know how to delete directories. For example, if Joe User's default directory is [JOEUSER] and he wants to delete the [JOEUSER.URBASE_TEST] directory, he just types this:

```
delete urbase_test.dir;1
```

There is a fairly common problem, however. VMS may respond with this message:

```
%DELETE-W-FILNOTDEL, error deleting
NEPDISK:[JOEUSER]URBASE_TEST.DIR;1
-RMS-E-PRV, insufficient privilege or file protection violation
```

This means that Joe lacks the proper access to delete this subdirectory. This is not a big problem; because it's a subdirectory of [JOEUSER], his personal root directory, he can give himself the necessary permission with the SET PROTECTION command. Section 9.1.8, "Controlling access to a file," explains this more fully; for now, it's enough to know that Joe only needs to type the following to give himself permission to delete the URBASE_TEST.DIR "file":

```
set protection = (o:d) urbase_test.dir;1
```

The "o" stands for "owner," and the "d" for "delete." Although there are other categories of users and other categories of access to files, at this point Joe only cares about giving the owner (himself) permission to delete it. All other privileges for all other users are irrelevant, because soon URBASE_TEST.DIR will no longer exist.

After he resets the protection level, he can delete the file without any trouble.

If you try to delete a subdirectory that has any files in it, VMS responds like this:

```
%DELETE-W-FILNOTDEL, error deleting
NEPDISK:[JOEUSER]URBASE_TEST.DIR;1
-RMS-E-MKD, ACP could not mark file for deletion
-SYSTEM-F-DIRNOTEMPTY, directory file is not empty
```

The solution is simple enough: delete anything in the subdirectory, and enter the DELETE command again.

The OpenVMS EVE Text Editor

VMS offers several built-in text editors. Entering EDIT at the DCL prompt, with no qualifiers, invokes the EDT line editor. This was the most popular VMS text editor for a long time. Because it's a line editor, using it means entering commands to go in and out of command, edit, and insert modes. When you edit with the EDT editor, you edit one line at a time. Although it does have a full-screen mode, where you display your file and move your cursor around to edit wherever you want, you don't need to bother with EDT because of the superior full-screen editing offered by a more recent VMS editor called the Extensible VAX Editor, or EVE.

EVE could very well be the easiest text editor to learn and use on any minicomputer or mainframe. The commands are simple without limiting you too much, and EVE provides its own command language that makes it easy to customize and add features to the editor.

The vi Text Editor on VMS

Some VMS systems have the UNIX vi editor installed, so many UNIX users don't need to learn any of the VMS editors. (Unless you're a real vi expert, you should at least check out EVE—a vi beginner will almost certainly prefer it.) If you do look for vi on a VMS system, be aware of a VMS utility called VIEW used for looking at certain kinds of documents. If you try to start up vi and it's not on the system, you may start up VIEW instead. It will probably just give you an error message and return you to the DCL prompt, because VIEW expects very specific types of files as input.

10.1 EVE and Special Keys

On the DEC VT220 terminal and its more advanced successors, you perform many of the most important editing functions by using special keys with their names written right on them. Examples include the Help, Do, and Find keys. If you use a PC running a program to emulate one of these terminals, chances are that certain function keys will do the job of these specialized keys.

You can also use the numeric keypad on the right of your keyboard to accomplish many of EVE's more advanced tricks. In certain situations, you can use a key known as the "Gold" key (usually the key in the numeric keypad's upper-left corner—PF1 on a VT terminal, or the NumLock key on a PC emulating one) in combination with others, similar to the way you use the Control key in combination with letter, number, and function keys.

You don't need these keys, in their Gold version or otherwise, to accomplish the most basic editing tasks; a couple of the specialized keys mentioned above (or their surrogate function keys) provide all you need.

On a PC, the only function key that you have to make sure to remember is F2— the Help key. As you'll see in Section 10.9, "EVE On-Line Help," the Help key shows you what the other keys do. After you've used EVE a little, you'll no longer need F2 to remind you about F4, because you'll use it often: it's the PC's substitute for the "Do" key, the key that displays the Command: prompt below the EVE status line. Commands at this prompt enable you to accomplish basic tasks such as saving your work and quitting EVE.

10.2 Entering EVE

The EDIT command can start up several different VMS editors; you indicate which you want by the qualifier you use. Because /EDT is the default, entering EDIT without any qualifier enters the line editor. (If you accidentally enter the EDIT/EDT editor, enter QUIT at the * prompt to get out of it.)

Unfortunately, you don't enter EVE by entering EVE or EDIT/EVE, so you must remember its other name: the Text Processing Utility, or TPU. (Theoretically, the TPU could be configured to run other editors besides EVE, so I don't mean to make it sound as if TPU and EVE mean the same thing.) When you enter EDIT/TPU at the DCL command prompt followed by a filename, the editor displays that file for you to edit if it exists or creates a new file with that name if it doesn't. For example, when Joe User enters

```
edit/tpu rochester.txt
```

and presses Return, the TPU starts up EVE, and—assuming that Joe has no file called rochester.txt—displays a message (see the bottom of Figure 10.1) informing him that because none exists, it is creating rochester.txt.

If the file had existed, and been six lines long, the message at the bottom would have read:

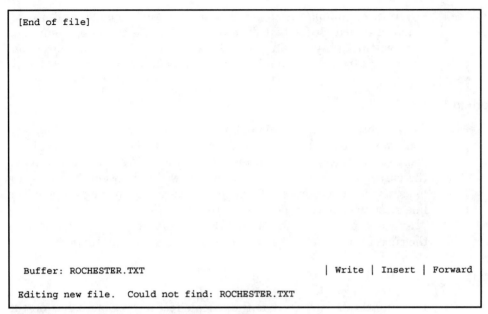

```
[End of file]
```

```
Buffer: ROCHESTER.TXT                        | Write | Insert | Forward

Editing new file.   Could not find: ROCHESTER.TXT
```

Figure 10.1 Opening EVE screen when editing a new file.

```
6 lines read from file NEPDISK:[JOEUSER]ROCHESTER.TXT;1
```

Because the new file is empty before you enter anything, the editor's "End of file" message appears at the top of the screen. The status line at the screen's bottom tells you three things:

- You can write to this file. In other words, you can make changes to it and save those changes. Sometimes people use EVE to just look at a file with no intention of changing it; adding the /NOWRITE qualifier to EDIT/TPU brings up the file with a status line similar to this:

  ```
  Buffer: ROCHESTER.TXT|Read-only|Unmodifiable|Forward
  ```

  When doing this, you can only read the file, and the Insert part of the status line becomes irrelevant, because the file is "Unmodifiable."

- When you are in "Write" mode, the "Insert" part shows that EVE will insert newly entered text at the cursor's position instead of overlaying existing text. As you'll see in Section 10.5, "Typing Over Existing Text," Ctrl + A toggles between Insert and Overstrike mode.

- The final message on the status line shows that the default direction for commands that scroll the text is Forward. EVE doesn't give you separate commands to move or search backward and forward;

you have commands to scroll text a certain amount, and a command to search for text. The direction in which these commands move through your file depends on the current default direction. Section 10.6, "Searching for Text," shows how to change direction.

10.3 Inserting Text

As the bottom of the screen shows, you begin in Insert mode. You don't have to enter or press any special keys to let EVE know that you want to insert text; you can just start typing. Press Return to move the cursor to a new line. To insert a new line between two existing lines, use your cursor keys to move your cursor to the beginning of the line after the insertion point and press Return.

As you type in text, the "End of File" message moves down to show the current position of the end of the file, as shown in Figure 10.2.

10.4 Deleting Text

Pressing the Delete key has the same effect in EVE as it has on the DCL command line: it deletes the character immediately to the left of the cursor's current location. In Insert mode, it shifts all characters on the right of the deleted character to the left when it deletes it. In Overstrike mode, it acts more like a space bar that sends your cursor to the left: it replaces the deleted character with a space and leaves the other characters on that line alone.

To delete a blank line, make sure you're in Insert mode (see Section 10.5, "Typing Over Existing Text," for more on the Insert and

```
Bursting with pride, the loathed impostume swells;
Prick him, he sheds his venom straight, and smells.
But 'tis so lewd a scribbler, that he writes
With as much force to nature as he fights;
Hardened in shame, 'tis such a baffled fop
That every schoolboy whips him like a top.
[End of file]




Buffer: ROCHESTER.TXT                        | Write | Insert | Forward
```

Figure 10.2 The EVE text editor with entered text.

Overstrike modes), move to the beginning of the following line and press the Delete key.

10.5 Typing Over Existing Text

The status line at the bottom of the screen shows whether you are in Insert or Overstrike mode. To change from one to the other, press Ctrl + A. In Insert mode, any new characters typed at the cursor's location move the existing characters on the cursor's right one character further to the right. In Overstrike mode, new characters appear in place of the existing characters at the cursor.

10.6 Searching for Text

Pressing the Find key (on a PC, the F1 key) displays this prompt just below the EVE status line:

```
Forward Find:
```

(It might say "Reverse Find," depending on the current default scrolling direction, as indicated by your status line. To change the direction of searches, the Change Direction key is F11 on a VT terminal and F3 on a PC.) Enter the text to search for at the `Forward Find:` prompt and press Return. EVE searches for the entered text and highlights it if it finds it. If it cannot find the text you enter, it tells you so. For example, if you tell it to search for "potrzebie" and it doesn't find it, it tells you

```
Could not find: potrzebie
```

To repeat a search, press F1 twice. The first time you press it, you will see nothing at the `Forward Find:` or `Reverse Find:` prompt; the second time, EVE searches for the next occurrence of the last search target that you entered at that prompt.

You can control whether the search is case-sensitive by pressing the Do key (F4 on a PC) to display the `Command:` prompt and entering `SET FIND CASE EXACT` to make searches case-sensitive or `SET FIND CASE NOEXACT` to tell EVE to ignore the case of the text it searches.

10.7 Saving Your Changes

To save your file, press the Do key to display the `Command:` prompt, enter the `WRITE` command with no parameters, and press Return. EVE saves your file and returns your cursor to its former position so that you can continue to edit the file. (The `SAVE FILE` command also accomplishes this, but the many options of the SAVE command besides FILE make WRITE a simpler way to save your work.) Section 10.8, "Quitting EVE," shows how to save your work and quit EVE in one command.

10.8 Quitting EVE

Enter QUIT at the Do key's Command: prompt to quit EVE and return to the DCL prompt. If you've made changes to your file without saving them, EVE displays the following:

```
Buffer modifications will not be saved, continue quitting [Yes]?
```

The square brackets show that "Yes" is the default answer. In other words, if you press Return without entering anything, EVE considers that a "Yes" and finishes the quitting process. This sends you back to the DCL prompt without saving the changes you've made since the last time you saved. Entering "N" for "No" at the Buffer modifications prompt tells EVE that you changed your mind about quitting. The prompt goes away, and EVE returns your cursor to its location before you pressed the Do key so that you can continue to edit the file.

Enter the EXIT command at the Do key's Command: prompt to save your work and quit EVE all at once.

10.9 EVE On-Line Help

EVE offers two ways to get help:

- Pressing the Help key (or on a PC emulating a terminal, F2) displays help about the use of the keyboard in EVE.

- Entering HELP at the Do key's Command: prompt displays the EVE general help menu.

Figure 10.3 shows a typical opening help screen after you press the Help key while using EVE (the actual screen you see depends on the terminal you use).

As the bottom of the screen tells you, you can display help about a specific key by pressing that key while viewing this screen. For example, press F1 (the Find key—as the diagram shows, this is the upper-left corner of the numeric keypad, which is NumLock on a PC and PF1 on an actual VT terminal) to display help about searching for text, as shown in Figure 10.4

The bottom of the screen tells you which keys scroll through this help information. On a VT terminal, these are the Prev Scrn and Next Scrn keys; when using a terminal emulation program, the Cursor Up and Cursor Down keys will probably scroll through the help information.

```
 _____ _____ _____ _____        _____ _____ _____ _____
|Move up| Move  | Move  | Move  |      | Find | HELP |Change | Do   |
|       | down  | left  | right |      |      |      |directi|      |
|_____|_____|_____|_____|      |_____|_____|_____|_____|
                                       |Select|Remove|Insert |Move  |
 To get help on commands, type a       |      |      |here   |by line|
 command or ? and press RETURN.         |_____|_____|_____|_____|
                                       |      |Move up|       |Erase |
 To list all key definitions, type     |      |       |       |word  |
 Keys and press RETURN, or press       |_____|_____|_____|_____|
 GOLD-HELP.                            | Move | Move | Move  |      |
                                       | left | down | right |Change|
 To show a key definition, use         |_____|_____|_____|mode  |
 SHOW KEY.                             | Next  screen |Previou|      |
                                       |              |screen |      |
                                       |_____|_____|_____|

                                       Synonyms for the DO key:
                                                  PF4

 Buffer: HELP
 Press the key that you want help on (RETURN to exit help):
```

Figure 10.3 Opening EVE help screen.

```
 FIND

    Searches for a string of text you specify and highlights the found text.

    Keys:  EVE Default    VT100 Keypad    EDT Keypad    WPS Keypad
           ------------------------------------------------------------------
           FIND           PF1             GOLD-PF3      GOLD-, on keyboard

    Steps:

       1.  Use FIND (see key list above).

       2.  Type the text you want to find (see examples below).

       3.  To find another occurrence of the same string,
           use FIND NEXT or press the FIND key twice.

    Examples:

       Commands                 Purposes or Effects
       ------------------------------------------------------------------
 Buffer: HELP         To see more, use:Press Up arrow or Down arrow to see more.
 Press the key that you want help on (HELP for keypad, Return to exit help):
```

Figure 10.4 Help screen for EVE's Find key.

Pressing Return without entering anything leaves the help facility and returns to the file you were editing. Pressing any other special key displays similar help about that key. Entering a question mark (?) displays the same main help screen available when you enter HELP at the Do key's Command: prompt.

```
List Of Topics (Commands)

For help on EVE topics, type the name of a topic and press RETURN.

    o  For a keypad diagram, press HELP.
    o  For help on VAXTPU builtins, type TPU and press RETURN.
    o  To exit from help and resume editing, press RETURN.

EDITING TEXT

    Change Mode            Erase Word           Restore Character
    Copy                   Insert Here          Restore Line
    Cut                    Insert Mode          Restore Selection
    Delete                 Overstrike Mode      Restore Sentence
    Erase Character        Paste                Restore Word
    Erase Line             Quote                Select
    Erase Previous Word    Remove               Select All
    Erase Start Of Line    Restore              Store Text

    BOX OPERATIONS

 Buffer: HELP        To see more, use:Press Up arrow or Down arrow to see more.
 Type the topic you want help on (press RETURN if done):
```

Figure 10.5 EVE's general help menu.

Enter HELP at the Do key's Command: prompt to display the general help menu. Figure 10.5 shows the beginning of this help.

At the Type the topic you want help on prompt, enter any of the words or phrases listed on the screen, such as Delete or Erase Character. Remember, these choices are merely the beginning; just as EDITING TEXT is a heading for a series of choices, so are BOX OPERATIONS and several other categories. Scrolling down displays the rest.

The EVE help works essentially the same as regular VMS help. If you choose a broad enough topic, its help text will end with subtopics from which to choose.

10.10 Other EVE Features

EVE has just about all the capabilities that you could ever want in a text editor or word processor. This includes:

- The ability to extend TPU by writing command files
- The ability to mark ranges and blocks of text for moving, copying, and deletion
- The ability to split the screen into multiple windows so that you can edit multiple files at once

A description of how to use these features is beyond the scope of this chapter, but you can find out more about them easily enough by exploring EVE's on-line help.

Using an OpenVMS System

11.1 Printing Text Files

Printing in VMS is simple. Enter the PRINT command followed by the name of the file to print. For example, if Joe User enters

```
PRINT ROCHESTER.TXT
```

he might see a response from the system like this:

```
Job ROCHESTER (queue SYS$PRINT,entry 203) started on SYS$PRINT
```

SYS$PRINT is the name of the default print queue; if Joe had wanted to print ROCHESTER.TXT on a different printer, he would add the /QUEUE = queuename qualifier to the end of his print command.

If other print jobs are ahead of this one in the print queue so that it must wait its turn to start printing, the started on SYSPRINT line will say pending.

11.1.1 Checking the print queue

To list the jobs waiting to print, enter the SHOW QUEUE command followed by the name of the print queue:

```
SHOW QUEUE SYS$PRINT
```

The output lists the file currently printing, as well as any waiting files:

```
Printer queue SYS$PRINT, on NEPTUNE::LCA0:, mounted form DEFAULT
Entry Jobname   Username Blocks Status
----- -------   -------- ------ ------
 588  091394JS  MJONES   2      Printing
 590  ROCHESTER JOEUSER  1      Pending
 591  TESTDCL   MJONES   1      Pending
```

The columns of information are self-explanatory, with one exception: Entry. This is how VMS identifies individual print jobs, and how you must refer to your print job if you want to cancel it.

11.1.2 Cancelling your print job

To cancel a pending print job, you use the same DELETE command that you use to delete files and subdirectories, except that you add the /ENTRY = entrynumber qualifier. The entry number is the number that showed up in the first column when you entered SHOW QUEUE SYS$PRINT. For example, Joe enters the following to delete ROCHESTER.TXT from the list of files shown above:

```
DELETE/ENTRY = 590
```

Since VMS displays no confirmation of a successful deletion from the print queue, you must enter the SHOW QUEUE command again to see if the job you deleted is gone. If you didn't get an error message when you entered the DELETE/ENTRY command, chances are that the file was successfully deleted. The following is the most common error message:

```
%DELETE-E-NOTDELETED, error deleting 590
-JBC-E-NOSUCHJOB, no such job
```

In other words, it couldn't find entry 590. Either the number was mistyped or VMS has already printed that particular job. Either way, the queue has no job with that number waiting to print.

An optional parameter for the DELETE/ENTRY command is the name of the print queue. If you omit it, VMS assumes that you mean the SYS$PRINT queue. If Joe had sent the ROCHESTER.TXT file to a queue called ACCTING, he would have checked out the queue with the following command:

```
SHOW QUEUE ACCTING
```

If ROCHESTER.TXT had an entry number of 304, he would delete it from that queue with this command:

```
DELETE/ENTRY = 304 ACCTING
```

11.2 Command Files

On most operating systems, one-line command files are the best way to make it easier to enter long but commonly used commands. Although DCL command files are useful and easy to create, VMS has an even better way to define a short string of characters to represent a much longer one: symbols.

11.2.1 Symbols

Defining a symbol assigns one string of characters to represent another. For example, if you like to use the /DATE/VER = 1/SIZE qualifiers with the DIRECTORY command, but get tired of repeatedly typing

```
DIR/DATE/VER = 1/SIZE
```

every time you want to list your file names, you can assign this command to a symbol. If the symbol is the string FILES, you would assign it like this:

```
FILES == "DIR/DATE/VER = 1/SIZE"
```

Entering FILES at the DCL command prompt would then have the same effect as entering DIR/DATE/VER = 1/SIZE.

When you create the symbol, don't forget the quotes around the string being assigned to the symbol. You don't always need both equal signs when creating a symbol at the DCL command prompt, but two are necessary when you put a symbol assignment command in a command procedure, so it's a good idea to get into the habit of using two.

A symbol assignment only lasts until you log out. If you want certain symbol assignments done every time you log in (and everyone has a few favorites), add the commands that create the symbols to your LOGIN.COM command procedure. (For more on LOGIN.COM, see Section 11.2.3, "The automatic login command file.")

11.2.2 DCL command procedures

A DCL command procedure is a file that consists of DCL commands. Each line begins with a dollar sign ($) and the last line is the following:

```
$ EXIT
```

Command files have a file type of COM, and you start them up by typing the file name preceded by an "at" sign (@).

For example, let's say Joe User has a program called SUMRPT that creates and stores a report in a text file called SUMRPT.TXT. Every time he runs this report he examines the report output with the EVE text editor, perhaps changing a few things, and then prints it. He could automate these steps by putting them in a file called SUM.COM with these lines:

```
! SUM.COM: run summary report, EVE it, print it. 2/13/94 J. User
$ SUMRPT
$ EDIT/TPU SUMRPT.TXT
$ PRINT SUMRPT.TXT
$ SHOW QUEUE SYS$PRINT
$ EXIT
```

The first line begins with an exclamation point. This tells VMS to ignore the line; it is a comment that describes the purpose of the program. Complicated command procedures need many comment lines so that someone who reads them at a later date can easily see the purpose of each part.

Except for the dollar signs, the next four lines show just what Joe would have typed at the DCL prompt to execute these steps. (The SHOW QUEUE SYS$PRINT line is an added bonus that he threw in because most people want to know immediately how long they have to wait for something that they sent to the printer.) The final line, $ EXIT, returns control to the DCL prompt.

To run this command procedure, Joe types

```
@SUM
```

at the DCL prompt. VMS looks for SUM.COM, finds it, and executes its commands one by one. (Actually, VMS first checks to make sure that there are no DCL commands with this name. This is why you should never name a COM file after an existing command, like COPY.COM or PRINT.COM.)

DCL command procedures can be much more complex than SUM.COM. It's a whole programming language, complete with branching, variables, and subroutines. Built-in functions known as *lexical functions* give DCL command procedures the ability to manipulate string expressions, convert between string and numeric data, query the operating system for information, and many other things more often associated with programming languages like C and Pascal than with an operating system command procedure language.

11.2.3 The automatic login command file

When a user first logs in to a VMS system, the system looks for a command procedure called LOGIN.COM. If it's in the user's root directory, the system executes it. This is particularly useful for defining your favorite symbols that you want to use every time you log in. Joe User's LOGIN.COM command procedure shows how you can define symbols to substitute new words for often-used commands that may be hard to remember:

```
$ SHOW QUOTA
$ FILES == "DIR/DATE/VER = 1/SIZE"
$ EVE == "EDIT/TPU"
$ SHOW == "TYPE/PAGE"
$ EXIT
```

Joe's LOGIN.COM file begins with the command SHOW QUOTA. This command, discussed in Section 8.3.2, "Querying available disk space," displays information that may be handy when you first log in.

The next three lines create symbols for Joe to use as shortcuts in his VMS session. For example, after his LOGIN.COM command file executes, Joe can type

```
eve schedule.txt
```

and VMS reacts as if he had typed this:

```
edit/tpu schedule.txt
```

It also substitutes "TYPE/PAGE" everywhere that he types SHOW at the DCL prompt and "DIR/DATE/VER = 1/SIZE" whenever he types FILES.

11.3 Communicating with Other Users

The VMS MAIL program has its own command line, commands, and on-line help to aid you in creating, sending, receiving, and managing mail messages. It's one of the best mail programs built-in to any operating system.

To start the program, enter the word MAIL at the DCL prompt. VMS tells you whether you have new messages waiting and displays the MAIL program's prompt:

```
You have 1 new message.
MAIL>
```

To send a mail message, enter the command SEND and press Return. The MAIL program prompts you for the name of the message's recipient:

```
MAIL> send
To:
```

Enter the recipient's login ID and press Return. If the system doesn't recognize the name (for example, MJOONES), it tells you this:

```
%MAIL-E-NOSUCHUSR, no such user MJOONES
```

If it does recognize the recipient's name, it prompts you for the subject of the message. Enter the subject, press Return, and the mail program displays instructions about entering your message:

```
MAIL> send
To: mjones
Subj: budget meeting
Enter your message below. Press CTRL/Z when complete, or CTRL/C to
quit:
_
```

The cursor appears under the instructions, ready for your input. You are only allowed the most primitive kind of input; each time you press Return at the end of a line, you cannot go back and edit that line. We'll see shortly how to send an existing text file, which gives you the flexibility to compose your mail message with the EVE text editor before you send it.

As the explanatory message tells you, press Ctrl + C to abort your message or Ctrl + Z when you are satisfied with it. If you abort, the MAIL program acknowledges your action with the word "Cancel" and this message:

```
%MAIL-E-SENDABORT, no message sent
```

If you press Ctrl + Z to send your message, it displays the word "Exit."

11.3.1 Sending an existing file

If you add a parameter to the SEND command described earlier, the MAIL program assumes that it names a file that you want to send. For example, if Joe enters

```
send marymemo.txt
```

at the MAIL> prompt, the MAIL program prompts him for the recipient's name and the message's subject, as usual, but it then returns him to the MAIL> prompt. If MARYMEMO.TXT doesn't exist, it displays an error message.

11.3.2 Receiving mail

If you are logged in when someone sends you a mail message, VMS displays a message similar to this on your screen:

```
New mail on node NEPTUNE from OROURKE::FDAKOVA (12:55:02)
```

If you are not logged in, your system probably displays a message that tells you how many unread messages are waiting for you the next time you log in. As we saw in Section 11.3, "Communicating with Other Users," the MAIL program also tells you how many new messages you have when you start it up.

11.3.2.1 Mail folders. The MAIL program organizes messages into groups called folders. It's easier to learn how to read, delete, save, and organize mail messages if you first understand the role of folders.

Creating folders and moving messages between them is easy. MAIL automatically creates three folders for you as you need them: NEW-

MAIL, MAIL, and WASTEBASKET. To avoid confusion, keep in mind that certain actions automatically move messages in and out of these three folders.

VMS stores new, unread messages in the NEWMAIL folder. When you leave the NEWMAIL folder, the mail program automatically moves any newly read messages from there to the MAIL folder if you didn't explicitly move them to any other folders after you read them. Deleting a message from any folder moves it to the WASTEBASKET folder.

At any given time, one folder is the current one. For example, when you start up MAIL, the NEWMAIL folder is current if you have any unread messages. If you do not have any unread messages, the MAIL folder is the current one.

To make a different folder current, enter the SELECT command at the MAIL> prompt followed by the name of the folder you want to make current. For example

```
SELECT WASTEBASKET
```

makes the WASTEBASKET folder the current one.

Use the DIR command to list the messages in a given folder. If you don't include a folder name, the MAIL program assumes that you want to list the messages in the current folder. For example, if NEW-MAIL is your current folder, entering

```
DIR
```

lists the messages in the NEWMAIL folder, and

```
DIR MAIL
```

lists the messages in the MAIL folder. A message list looks something like this:

```
MAIL
# From            Date         Subject
1 NEPTUNE::MJONES  17-AUG-1994 1995 budget
2 OROURKE::FDAKOVA 18-AUG-1994 new Windows release?
3 NEPTUNE::KBERRY  19-AUG-1994 lunch Monday
4 NEPTUNE::LSTORCH 19-AUG-1994 Giants tickets
```

To list folder names instead of information about messages, add the /FOLDER qualifier to the DIR command.

Because the MAIL program creates the NEWMAIL and WASTE-BASKET folders as you need them, they may not always exist. If you enter the MAIL program, but have no new mail, and you enter the command

```
SELECT NEWMAIL
```

you'll see an error message like this:

```
%MAIL-E-NOTEXIST, folder NEWMAIL does not exist
```

If you have no new messages, you don't have a NEWMAIL folder. A similar idea applies to WASTEBASKET: after you start up the MAIL program, you won't have a WASTEBASKET folder until you delete your first message (unless you last left the MAIL program with QUIT instead of EXIT—see Section 11.3.2.5, "Leaving the MAIL program," for more on this).

Section 11.3.2.2, "Reading mail," shows how to move messages from one folder to another.

11.3.2.2 Reading mail. Entering READ displays the first page of the oldest message in the current folder. If you have any new messages when you first start up the MAIL program, your NEWMAIL folder will be current, so MAIL will display your oldest unread message. If the message you are reading is more than one page long, press Return to advance to the next page.

As a matter of fact, since READ is the default command in the MAIL program, you only need to press Return to read the next message in the current folder. To read a different message in the current folder, enter its number, which you can learn by entering DIR to list the folder's messages.

11.3.2.3 Moving a message to another folder. The FILE command (and the MOVE command, which behaves identically) tells the MAIL program to move a message to another folder. To move the current message, enter FILE at the MAIL> prompt and the MAIL program prompts you for the name of the destination folder. If you enter the name of a nonexistent folder, MAIL asks you if you want to create a folder with that name.

For example, after he reads the following message, Joe User enters file budget95 at the MAIL> prompt. The MAIL program responds by telling him that no such folder exists, and asks if he wants to create one:

```
NEWMAIL
From: NEPTUNE::MJONES
To: JOEUSER
CC:
Subj: 1995 budget
I know it seems early, but it's already time to talk about the
budget for fiscal 1995. Get together any notes or ideas you have
and get in touch with me. I'm out of the office on Tuesday.
MAIL> file budget95
Folder BUDGET95 does not exist.
Do you want to create it (Y/N, default is N)?
```

Joe responds with a "Y" for "Yes," and the MAIL program creates the BUDGET95 folder and stores this message there.

Just as adding the first message to a folder creates that folder, moving the last message from a folder automatically deletes that folder. The MAIL program has no explicit command for deleting a folder.

Any messages that you read in the NEWMAIL folder without deleting or filing to another folder get automatically moved to the MAIL folder when you leave NEWMAIL. This happens whether you leave NEWMAIL by selecting another folder or by exiting the MAIL program. If this includes all the messages in NEWMAIL, the folder itself will be deleted until the next time you start up the MAIL program and have new mail.

11.3.2.4 Deleting messages from a folder. Entering DELETE by itself at the MAIL> prompt either deletes the message you are currently reading, if it takes up more than one screen and is pausing for you, or the message you just read, if you are between messages. You can also add one or more numbers to the DELETE command to specify which of the messages in the current folder to delete. For example, if your current folder has the messages shown in Section 11.3.2.1 earlier ("Mail folders") and you enter the following command

```
DELETE 2,4
```

and follow it with the DIR command, the MAIL program shows the following revised list:

```
MAIL
# From          Date        Subject
1 NEPTUNE::MJONES 17-AUG-1994 1995 budget
2 (Deleted)
3 NEPTUNE::KBERRY 19-AUG-1994 lunch Monday
4 (Deleted)
```

To undelete a message, select the WASTEBASKET folder and move the message in question to another folder with the FILE or MOVE command. It doesn't have to be moved to the folder where it was originally located at the time you deleted it.

11.3.2.5 Leaving the MAIL program. The MAIL program offers two ways to exit and return to the DCL command prompt:

- The QUIT command leaves anything in your WASTEBASKET folder alone when it returns to the DCL prompt. The next time you enter the MAIL program, your WASTEBASKET folder will still be there with everything that you deleted in your previous session.

- The EXIT command empties out your WASTEBASKET folder when it returns you to the DCL prompt.

11.3.2.6 Saving a message in a text file. The EXTRACT command saves the message that you read most recently (or are currently reading) into a text file in the default directory. In the following example, Joe saves the message from Mary in a file called `121794MJ.TXT`:

```
MAIL> extract 121794mj.txt
%MAIL-I-CREATED, NEPDISK:[JOEUSER]121794MJ.TXT;1 created
```

The system responds with a message that it has successfully created the file.

11.3.3 On-line help in the MAIL program

On-line help in the `MAIL` program resembles on-line help elsewhere in VMS. Enter `HELP` by itself at the `MAIL>` prompt to display an introduction to using help and a list of commands that you can learn more about. This list includes all the `MAIL` commands described in this section and several more.

As with help from the DCL prompt, if you know the command that you want to learn more about, you can enter that command name as a parameter to the `HELP` command at the `MAIL>` prompt. For example, entering

```
HELP SELECT
```

tells you about the command to make a particular folder current.

11.4 A Sample OpenVMS Session

One morning you arrive at your desk, log in to your VMS account, and see the following line along with the other login messages:

```
You have 1 new Mail message.
```

You enter `MAIL` at the DCL prompt to start the mail program, and the `MAIL>` prompt appears. Because you know that pressing Return has the same effect as entering the `MAIL` program's `READ` command and that without additional instructions it will show you the oldest unread message in your NEWMAIL folder, you press Return and this message shows up on your screen:

```
NEWMAIL
From: NEPTUNE::LNIVEN
To: JOEUSER
CC:
Subj: August 1994 numbers
I need the gross and net figures, by region, for last month.
Please run the report and send me the output by e-mail before
lunch. I need them for a 2PM meeting.
Thanks!
MAIL>
```

Since you know that the data Larry needs isn't complete, you decide to keep a disk file copy of this memo in case the unreadiness of the numbers comes back to haunt you. You enter EXTRACT NIVMEMO.TXT at the MAIL> prompt, and then EXIT to return to the DCL prompt.

Because this report must be run every month, you've already set up a command file called SUMRPT to run the report and save the data in a file named SUMRPT.TXT. You run the command file:

```
@SUMRPT
```

When the command file finishes, you take a quick look at the report output by using the TYPE command to display the SUMRPT.TXT file that was just created:

```
$ type sumrpt.txt
```

The system responds by showing you SUMRPT.TXT, as shown in Figure 11.1.

It looks like the figures aren't in yet from the Southwest and the West Coast regions, so the totals aren't that useful. However, Larry asked for them, so Larry gets them. You pull up SUMRPT.TXT in the EVE text editor to add a note:

```
EDIT/TPU SUMRPT.TXT
```

Once EVE displays the file, you add a few lines at the top, so that your screen looks like Figure 11.2.

After you add these new lines, you press F4 to display EVE's Command: prompt and type EXIT there to save your edits and return to the DCL prompt.

```
AUGUST    1994          Gross     Net
                        ------   ------
Northeast               75,732   11,890
Mid-Atlantic            69,348   11,008
Southeast               61,835    8,890
Southwest                    0        0
Midwest                 70,762   12,934
Northwest               14,242    1,634
West Coast                   0        0
                        ------   ------
AUGUST    TOTAL        291,919   26,356
```

Figure 11.1 The contents of the SUMRPT.TXT file.

```
Larry -

As you can see, we're still waiting for the figures from the southwest
and from the west coast.  I left voice mail with Ginny in Phoenix and
Jim in LA; I'll call you when I know more.


AUGUST   1994           Gross    Net
                        ------   ------
Northeast               75,732   11,890
Mid-Atlantic            69,348   11,008
Southeast               61,835    8,890
Southwest                    0        0
Midwest                 70,762   12,934
Northwest               14,242    1,634
West Coast                   0        0
                        ------   ------
AUGUST    TOTAL        291,919   26,356
[End of file]
```

Buffer: SUMRPT.TXT | Write | Insert | Forward

14 lines read from file NEPDISK:[JOEUSER]SUMRPT.TXT;4

Figure 11.2 Summary report file in EVE after editing.

Now that the file is ready, you can send it to Larry. You enter MAIL at the DCL prompt to start up the mail program and SEND SUMRPT.TXT at the MAIL program's MAIL> prompt. When the mail program asks you for the user ID of the message's recipient, you enter LNIVEN. After you enter "August numbers" in response to the MAIL program's prompt for the subject of the message, the program returns you to its MAIL> prompt. You enter EXIT to return to the DCL prompt, finally entering LOGOUT at the DCL prompt to finish your VMS session.

12

OS/400: An Introduction

OS/400 is the operating system used on IBM's line of AS/400 mini-computers. "OS" stands for "Operating System," as it does in "OS/2," and "AS" stands for "Application System." No one uses any other operating system on the AS/400, and no one installs OS/400 onto any other computers. Because they're always used together, it's common to use the terms "OS/400" and "AS/400" interchangeably when we talk about using the computer.

The combination of OS/400 and the AS/400 has an odd mix of advanced and old-fashioned approaches to computing. On the one hand, the object-oriented approach of treating system resources and their interaction as objects and messages exists in few other operating systems used on a large scale in the business world (none of the ones covered by this book) but will be seen more and more in the coming years. On the other hand, certain aspects of OS/400 and the AS/400 show their roots in aging technology, such as IBM's encouragement of developers to use RPG and COBOL and the inclusion of an 8-in. or 5¼-in. disk drive without an option for 3½-in. disk drives. Because none of these links to older IBM technology are inherent parts of an AS/400 system, I'm sure that they will be brought up to date soon if they haven't been by the time you read this. The Integrated Language Environment (ILE), available with Version 2 Release 3 of OS/400, already promises to make things easier for OS/400 developers who use the C programming language.

While features like communications, built-in database support, transaction processing, and system security were added on to other operating systems over the years, these features were all part of the design of OS/400 from the start. This may be its greatest advantage, from a design point of view—IBM included these features as intrinsic parts of the operating system from the beginning instead of patching them in over time.

From a user's perspective—or even a system administrator's—the biggest advantage of OS/400 is its ease of use. While many operating systems offer menus to make things easier for the beginner, OS/400 offers access to a greater percentage of its capabilities through menus than any other popular operating system. Its command language isn't too bad either; while the abbreviations that form the commands give them a terse, strange appearance, they're actually pretty easy to figure out once you learn the logic behind the abbreviation system.

For the system administrator, the ease of use starts as soon as the AS/400 comes out of the box. IBM went to great trouble to make the AS/400 a "plug and play" computer, doing much of the setup that a customer needs before shipping it.

All this combines to make the AS/400 a very successful computer. It has been the silver lining on some of IBM's darkest clouds; in February 1993, just when the public and stock market were taking the dimmest view of IBM's future as a major player in the computing world, IBM took out a full page ad in the *New York Times* that proclaimed in huge letters "You ain't seen nothing yet. The IBM AS/400. Success isn't complicated." The ad's copy bragged that IBM had "shipped over 200,000 AS/400s in just over four years—more than our closest competitor has in seven—to companies of all sizes...with a customer satisfaction rate just shy of 98%, we've got nothing to be shy about."

12.1 History

The 1960s saw the birth and growth of the minicomputer market. IBM got into the game fairly late; in 1969, 8 years after DEC introduced the PDP-1, IBM introduced its first minicomputer: the System/3. Although IBM had the resources to provide better support than other minicomputer makers, it didn't have a better minicomputer. IBM also managed to charge more than their competitors, so the System/3 provided no threat to DEC's market and became a historical footnote.

In 1975, IBM announced the System/32. This batch-oriented, single-tasking computer was the beginning of what people now refer to as the "System/3X" family of computers. Neither the System/32 nor its multiuser, multitasking 1977 successor, the System/34, took a firm hold in the marketplace, but the 1978 System/38 and the 1983 System/36 became very successful.

Users found the System/36 easy to use, and IBM kept this in mind when designing its replacement. The popularity of the simple interface on the System/36 and the large installed base of System/36 and System/38 minicomputers were key factors in the design of the AS/400, which IBM introduced in 1988. While the AS/400 and OS/400 had an entirely new architecture, subsystems were built in to ensure that the more than 8000 existing System/3X application packages could run on it. (You can run System/38 programs in the AS/400's System/38 mode without modification, but you must recompile System/36 programs before you can run them in the AS/400's System/36 mode.) This gave the AS/400 a big start in available applications—always an important issue with a new computer and operating system.

IBM currently offers five different series of AS/400s: the B, C, D, E, and F series. Within each series, a number attached to the letter identifies how that model relates to others in that series. The higher the number, the greater the power. For example, the F series, when first introduced, offered the F02 as the simplest model and the F95 as the most powerful.

You can upgrade many models to more advanced AS/400s. For example, models from the B and C series can be upgraded to the D series. This upgradability has always been a big selling point for the AS/400; if you get one for your small company and your company grows, your AS/400 can grow with you.

IBM had an amusing way of demonstrating this to the public. You probably remember how IBM's original television ads for the PS/2 featured all the major characters from the television show *MASH* except for Hawkeye. They saved him for the AS/400 ads. (As far as I know, these were not run on television, but run as print ads aimed at a more specialized audience.) To symbolize the ability of the AS/400 to grow with your business, he was shown watering a little plant next to a small AS/400; in the next picture, he stood proudly by a much bigger plant—ostensibly, the same as the one in the first picture, but grown larger—next to a much bigger AS/400. Warm and friendly as Alan Alda, but capable of providing all the power you need when you need it—that's the AS/400.

> BUZZWORD: "Blue shop." This is actually two buzzwords: "blue" means IBM in the computer world the same way "yellow" means "Kodak" in the world of photography. It's an adjective meaning "of or pertaining to IBM." As a noun, people often say "big blue"; for example, a trade journal might have the headline "Big Blue Announces New AS/400 Models."
>
> "Shop" refers to a given company's collection of minicomputers and mainframes. A "blue shop" means that a particular company uses only IBM's minis and mainframes.

12.1.1 Today

As more and more AS/400s are installed, and more and more applications are written for it, backwards compatibility with the System/3X computers has become less of an issue. As PCs and networked PC applications become more prevalent and more powerful, the AS/400's relationship to this growing segment of the computer world, and not its relationship to IBM's earlier minis, has come to define Big Blue's positioning of the AS/400's advantages.

Three features play a key role in this new positioning:

- *Database management.* The AS/400 was designed from the start to be a database management machine. It has a relational database manager built in as an integral part of both the operating system and the machine itself. You don't buy it as a separate piece of software; in fact, if you do install another database manager on the AS/400, it must translate everything into the AS/400 database manager's terms in order to perform any work. To learn more about the AS/400's database management capabilities, use the search index described in Section 13.4, "Available On-Line Help," to search for information about DFU (Data File Utility) and IDDU (Interactive Data Definition Utility).

- *Communications.* The AS/400 communicates with other computers—mainframes, PCs, other AS/400s, and non-IBM minis—better than any past or present IBM computer. It can communicate with other computers using protocols such as Ethernet, SNA, OSI, ISDN, TCP/IP, Novell NetWare, and others. It can support connections to three different local area networks at once.

- *Security.* Features for the implementation and maintenance of data security are also built right into the operating system and the machine itself. You can define data security in terms of objects, users, workstations, files, records, and fields.

These three features combine to make the AS/400 an ideal candidate for a database server. IBM had ideas about this from the beginning, but in the original grand plan the desktop computers attached to these servers were supposed to be PS/2s running OS/2. Over time, IBM realized that there was a greater advantage in making the AS/400 capable of being a database server for any other computer that needed it. While the database and security features mentioned above were built into the AS/400 from the beginning, many of the communications protocols were added over time (particularly with the introduction of the D series in 1991) as IBM began to reposition the AS/400 as a more general-purpose database server. Version 2 of the OS/400 operating system made it easier for developers to write applications that store and use PC files on an AS/400; this encouraged developers to write client/server applications that use the AS/400 as the server.

IBM also offers the PC Support package for the AS/400, which links PCs to an AS/400. PC Support makes it easier for PCs to act as full-featured AS/400 terminals and to use disks and printers attached to an AS/400 system.

The AS/400 doesn't always have to be a server in a client/server relationship; it can also be the client, requesting data from another system. Its extensive peer-to-peer communications abilities give it a great deal of flexibility, allowing the same AS/400 to be the server for one application and the client for another.

IBM's Minicomputer: the AS/400 or the RS/6000?

Shortly after introducing the AS/400, IBM introduced the RISC System, or RS series of computers. The RS computer is essentially an engineering workstation that runs AIX, IBM's version of UNIX. It can be run as a single- or multiple-user machine.

It sounds like a minicomputer. How does it differ from the AS/400, the successor to the System/3X line and therefore IBM's current main entry in the minicomputer market? The RS/6000's various technical differences from the AS/400 reflect one key point: it's aimed at a different audience. A scientist or engineer who must write his or her own C or C++ program to attack a complicated math problem that produces complex graphical output would not use the AS/400, a multiuser machine optimized to run common database applications such as inventories and payrolls. The technical user wants a machine that can be dedicated to the problem at hand without being slowed down by other users' programs. The RS/6000 user is familiar with UNIX and UNIX tools, knows how to combine them to solve technical problems, and wants to leverage this knowledge.

The RS machines and the AIX operating system are designed for this user. While the AS/400 competes in the marketplace with business machines like the VAX and Hewlett-Packard's minicomputers, the RS/6000 competes with other engineering workstations from companies like Sun and Silicon Graphics. And it competes very well; it has a reputation as a well-built, powerful, reasonably priced engineering workstation. This made the RS/6000, like the AS/400, a bright spot in IBM's dark days of the early 1990s.

In fact, the RS/6000 has done so well that it has ended up competing with the AS/400 after all. One of the AS/400's most promising roles is that of a PC file server, and some find the RS/6000 more suited to this than the AS/400—regardless of the applications being run on the PC.

For information on using the RS/6000 computers, see this book's chapters on UNIX (Chapters 2 to 6), particularly the sidebars in Chapter 2 titled "ULTRIX? XENIX? AIX? AUX? POSIX? DYNIX? MACH? SunOS?" and "Workstations."

12.1.1.1 Popular OS/400 software. As mentioned earlier, OS/400's built-in database manager is one of the main reasons people use the system. Another popular package available to run under OS/400 is OfficeVision. OfficeVision offers many general-purpose features needed by almost any office: calendar and scheduling software, word processing, e-mail, and integration of these facilities with the AS/400's built-in database. Although message sending and the Source Entry Utility (SEU) text editor are built into OS/400, the OfficeVision alternatives are more powerful and easier to use. (SEU has many features that still make it better for entering program source code, since OfficeVision's word processor is geared more toward correspondence and document composition.)

13

Getting Started with OS/400

13.1 Starting Up

The first thing you see when you connect to an AS/400 is its sign-on screen. Figure 13.1 provides an example.

Your screen may not look exactly like Figure 13.1. It may have additional information, and it may not tell you the release of OS/400 being used (in the example, "V2R2" means "Version 2 Release 2"). It will tell you three things about where you are signing on:

System	The name assigned by the system administrator to the particular AS/400 on which you have your account.
Subsystem	The system administrator may divide various aspects of the system into different areas known as "subsystems." Don't worry about it.
Display	The name assigned to the terminal you are using to sign on.

```
                    O'Rourke Enterprises
                       AS/400-F45
                         V2R2


System  . . . . :   NEPAS4
Subsystem . . . :   QINTER
Display . . . . :   DISP07



User  . . . . . . . . . . . . .
Password  . . . . . . . . . . .
Program/procedure . . . . . . .
Menu  . . . . . . . . . . . . .
Current library . . . . . . . .


                              (C) COPYRIGHT IBM CORP. 1980, 1992.
```

Figure 13.1 AS/400 sign-on screen.

Below this information, several fields appear for you to complete. You only need to fill out the first two. Use your Field Exit key (when emulating a terminal, this will probably be the Tab key) to move your cursor forward from field to field. If you make a typing mistake, use your Backspace key to reposition your cursor and fix the mistake.

User
: The user ID that represents your identity on the system. If you don't have one, you can't sign on, so contact your system administrator. It doesn't matter whether you type in your ID in upper- or lowercase; it displays in all capital letters.

If you enter a user ID that the system doesn't recognize, it will tell you. For example, if Joe User mistypes his JOEUSER user ID as JEOUSER, OS/400 displays a message at the bottom of the sign-on screen telling him "User JEOUSER does not exist."

Password
: The password that goes with your ID. If you enter the wrong password for the entered user ID, the system tells you "Password not correct for user profile." The user profile is the collection of information stored about a particular user—the user ID, the password, and the access rights that user has to the various parts of the system.

Program/procedure
: If you know the program that you want to run as soon as you are signed on, you can enter its name here.

Menu
: All menus in OS/400 have names. If you want to go directly to a menu other than the currently designated initial menu, enter its name here.

Current library
: A library is a collection of objects, much like a subdirectory on other operating systems is a collection of files. The current library is the first place the system looks when you request the use of a particular object. If you want a library other than the default one to be the current library for this session, enter its name here. For more information on libraries, see Section 13.3, "How Files are Organized."

After you have signed on successfully, OS/400 displays the initial menu.

This will probably be some variation of the AS/400 Main Menu (Figure 13.2), but your system administrator may set another menu as your initial one. If you prefer to designate a specific menu as the initial menu, you can easily set this up; see Section 16.2.1, "The automatic signon command file," for more information.

```
MAIN                        AS/400 Main Menu
                                                    System:    NEPAS4
Select one of the following:

     1. User tasks
     2. Office tasks
     3. General System Tasks
     4. Files, libraries, and folders
     5. Programming
     6. Communications
     7. Define or change the system
     8. Problem handling
     9. Display a menu
    10. Information Assistant options
    11. PC Support tasks

    90. Sign off

Selection or command
===>

F3=Exit   F4=Prompt   F9=Retrieve   F12=Cancel   F13=User support
F23=Set initial menu
(C) COPYRIGHT IBM CORP. 1980, 1992.
```

Figure 13.2 OS/400 main menu.

13.1.1 Finishing your OS/400 session

As you will see in Section 13.1.2, "Entering commands," there are two ways to do just about anything in OS/400: by entering a command or by picking a choice off of a menu. Menu choices are numbered, and from the OS/400 main menu (Figure 13.2) signing off is always choice number 90.

Picking a command off of a menu is actually similar to entering a command—you're just entering a number instead of typing out a word or phrase. To sign off, type 90 at the ===> prompt.

To sign off by entering a command, type SIGNOFF. Although menu choice 90 shows "sign off" as two words, remember to enter the command as one word.

The command has one particular advantage over using the number to designate the menu choice: this menu choice is only available on the main menu, while you can type SIGNOFF anywhere that you see the ===> prompt.

13.1.2 Entering commands

Along with SIGNOFF, any OS/400 command can be entered anytime you see the ===> prompt. We call these commands "CL commands" because they make up the OS/400 Command Language. (When I say "command prompt," I'm referring to the ===> prompt.) As you'll see in Section 16.2, "Command Files," OS/400 command files are known as "CL programs."

Most menus have the phrase "Selection or command" above this prompt. This means "type the number of the menu choice you want to make or a command at this command line." Some menus have no ===> prompt, but your cursor still appears at the bottom of the screen, waiting for you to type something. If the line above your cursor says "Type a menu option below," then you can't enter a command; you must enter a menu choice number. You might not even notice these clues indicating that you must enter a number and not a command, but if you start entering a command and your cursor jumps back to the first character that you typed as soon as you enter the second character, don't panic; you've found one of these menus.

Much AS/400 literature talks about how intuitive and English-like the CL commands are. When you see command names like SNDMSG, DLTF, STRSEU, and DSPMSG, you're bound to wonder: if this is English-like, then I guess UNIX commands aren't so bad after all!

Actually, CL commands aren't too bad once you learn the abbreviation system. The words of a command are usually abbreviated to three (or fewer) letters and then strung together into verb-object or verb-modifier-object order. The verb part is always three letters. (There are a few commands that deviate from this system, like GO, which you use to jump directly to a specific menu, and SIGNOFF.)

Keeping this system in mind, SNDMSG doesn't look as cryptic anymore; it means "Send Message." DLTF is "Delete File." Once you know that the Source Entry Utility (SEU) is the name of the OS/400 text editor, it's not too hard to remember that STRSEU means "Start Source Entry Utility."

Many commands use STR as an abbreviation of "start." DSP, which means "display," is also popular; DSPMSG, or "display message" is only one of many commands that begin with these three letters. Once you get used to the abbreviations for common verbs like STR and DSP and common verb objects like MSG, you can figure out many commands on your own.

The following shows some other common verb abbreviations:

CRT   Create
WRK   Work with
CHG   Change

Certain noun abbreviations also come up often:

LIB   Libraries
OBJ   Objects
CMD   Commands

13.1.2.1 Command parameters. When a command needs parameters, you enter each one in parentheses preceded by the name of the para-

```
                     Copy File (CPYF)

Type choices, press Enter.

From file  . . . . . . . . . .   _____   Name
   Library  . . . . . . . . . .    *LIBL      Name, *LIBL, *CURLIB
To file  . . . . . . . . . . .   _____   Name, *PRINT
   Library  . . . . . . . . . .    *LIBL      Name, *LIBL, *CURLIB
From member  . . . . . . . . .   *FIRST       Name, generic*, *FIRST, *ALL
To member or label . . . . . .   *FIRST       Name, *FIRST, *FROMMBR
Replace or add records . . . . .  *NONE        *NONE, *ADD, *REPLACE
Create file  . . . . . . . . .   *NO          *NO, *YES
Print format . . . . . . . . .   *CHAR        *CHAR, *HEX




                                                           Bottom
F3=Exit    F4=Prompt   F5=Refresh   F10=Additional parameters   F12=Cancel
F13=How to use this display   F24=More keys
Parameter FROMFILE required.
```

Figure 13.3 Command prompt display for the Copy File command.

meter. For example, the following command renames a file object called OLDNAME with a name of NEWNAME:

```
RNMOBJ OBJ(OLDNAME) OBJTYPE(*FILE) NEWOBJ(NEWNAME)
```

If you can't remember the name or order of the parameters, there is plenty of help.

The easiest way to deal with the parameters is the prompt key, F4. If you enter a command name and press F4 instead of Enter, OS/400 displays the *command prompt display*, which displays the parameters for that command on a form for you to fill out. To make things even easier, it highlights the required parameters that don't have default values and displays a message at the bottom telling you the next required parameter to fill out. Figure 13.3 shows the command prompt display that you get if you press F4 immediately after entering CPYF at the command prompt.

Another way to bring up the command prompt display is to precede the command with a question mark (for example, ? CPYF). This is a nice trick for making your CL programs a little more interactive—instead of filling in a command's parameters in the CL program, so that the command is executed with the same parameters every time someone runs the program, a question mark before the command brings up that command's command prompt display. This allows the CL program's user to set different parameters each time the CL program is run.

As with the signon screen, you use the Tab key to move from field to field. Press Enter when you're ready to execute the command or F3 to exit out of the command prompt display. If you press Enter before you've filled out all the required fields, your cursor jumps to the first mandatory field that you neglected to fill out and a message appears at the bottom of the screen telling you that parameter's name and the fact that it is required.

If you press F4 after filling out any of a command's parameters at the command line, those parameters will be filled in for you on the command prompt display.

Certain commands don't require any parameters, but won't do anything unless you include some. For example, the Change Profile command (CHGPRF) changes various settings that control your signon ID's working environment. If Joe User enters CHGPRF with no parameters and presses Enter, he'll see the message "User profile JOEUSER changed." Nothing about it was really changed, though, because he didn't indicate any changes to make. Although it has no mandatory parameters, the Change Profile command has so many optional ones that AS/400 users nearly always use F4 with it instead of Enter; this allows them to see the names of the various values that can be reset.

After entering a command name and any of its parameters at the command line, you can also press F1 to display the on-line help about that command. See Section 13.4, "Available On-Line Help," for more information.

13.1.2.2 Positional parameters.   When entering a command on the command line, some parameters require you to only enter their value, without the parameter name or parentheses. These are called "positional parameters" because each one's position on the command line tells OS/400 which parameter it is. The use of positional parameters is most common for required parameters, since it saves you some typing.

A common positional parameter is FILE(), which is often the first parameter for many commands. For example, to delete a file in the current library called BUDGET95, you might enter this,

```
DLTF FILE(BUDGET95)
```

but it's easier to enter this:

```
DLTF BUDGET95
```

It's not unusual to leave out the parameter names and parentheses for some of a particular command's positional parameters and to include them for other optional ones, all on the same command line.

For a more detailed case study of the use of positional parameters, see Section 14.1.4, "Copying files."

13.1.2.3 Case sensitivity. OS/400 doesn't care whether you enter commands, parameters, or parameter names in upper- or lowercase. To delete a file called DRAFT1 in the library BUDGET94 (see Section 13.3, "How Files are Organized," for more on libraries), you could type any of the following three commands:

```
DLTF FILE(DRAFT1)
dltf file(draft1)
DlTf FiLe(DrAfT1)
```

13.1.2.4 The four types of displays. OS/400 has four different kinds of screens. IBM terminology calls them four different kinds of "displays." All four display types have two things in common: a title at the top to let you know exactly which display it is and a list of available function keys across the bottom of the display. As Section 13.1.2.5 ("Important special keys") shows you, the function keys always offer you a way to back out of any screen that you displayed accidentally.

The main screen that you see after signing on (Figure 13.2) is an example of a *menu display*. Menu displays include a command prompt where you can type either CL commands or the number of the menu choice that you want to select. The upper left corner shows the name of the menu.

Knowing the names of the popular menus is useful, because entering the GO command at any command prompt lets you jump directly to any menu. For example, to jump to the MAIN menu, enter

```
GO MAIN
```

at the command prompt.

An *entry display* is a form for you to fill out. Section 13.1.2.1, "Command parameters," described how you can press F4 instead of entering a command's parameters if you are unsure of those parameters. The command prompt display that this brings up (Figure 13.3) is a good example of an entry display.

Sometimes there are hints to the right of each field on an entry display about what you can enter in that field. There are three types of clues:

Name   A name that you either make up or should already know. For example, when you copy a file, you should know its name and you will make up a name for the copy. In Figure 13.3, Name is an option for the first six fields.

generic*   A name with the asterisk wildcard that applies to multiple names. If you are issuing a command that will display a hundred object names, and entering JULYBUD will list only the JULYBUD object, then entering JULY* will list the names that begin with the letters "JULY." For more information, see Section 13.2.1, "Wildcards."

*PREDEFVAL

A *predefined value* is a name that has a specific, defined meaning to OS/400. These are usually spelled in all capital letters and begin with an asterisk. For example, when you send a message to another user with the SNDMSG command, you enter the message recipient's ID in the "To user profile" field. On the right of the blank where you enter the recipient's name, it offers the choices "Name, *SYSOPR, *ALLACT." The Name part means that you can just type in someone's user ID. *SYSOPR and *ALLACT are predefined values; *SYSOPR represents the system operator, so if you have a problem with the system and want to send a message to the system operator you don't need to know which system operator is on duty and his or her user ID. *ALLACT means "all active users." It lets you send a message to everyone who is currently signed on. (This option would be useful to the system operator to warn everyone of system problems or impending downtime.)

An entry display often displays more fields than you need to fill out. To make it easier for you to find the mandatory fields, they are highlighted for you.

Some of an entry display's fields may be filled out for you with default values. To change them, move your cursor there with your Tab or cursor keys and type a new value over the displayed one.

When you ask OS/400 to list information (for example, the files in a library), it often displays the information on a *list display*, which allows you to perform actions on items in the list. Figure 13.4 shows an example of a list that is displayed when you ask the on-line help about help topics that cover "programming."

The first column of a list display is the Option or Opt column. It shows a blank next to each list item where you enter a number to indicate what you want to do with that list item. Above the list, a key to the actions shows the numbers you can enter in the options column and what they do. For example, entering the number 6 next to a help topic title in Figure 13.4 tells OS/400 to send a copy of that help topic to the printer. Use your Tab or cursor keys to move your cursor to the appropriate place in the Opt column. (For more information on help topic lists, see Section 13.4.1, "The search index.")

List displays sometimes have a command line at the bottom. In addition to regular CL commands, you can type any additional information that OS/400 needs to perform an action indicated by a number in the option column. If this is the case, the list display will let you know just above the command line. For example, if the key to the actions above the list shows that you can enter 1, 2, 3, 4, or 5 in the options column and entering 2, 3, or 5 requires additional information, you will see the following message just above the command line:

```
                    Main Help Index for AS/400

Type options, press Enter.
  5=Display topic    6=Print topic


Option  Topic
  _     Add physical file variable-length member (ADDPFVLM) command
  _     Add program (ADDPGM) command
  _     Analyze program (ANZPGM) command
  _     APPC
  _     Application program
  _     Apply program temporary fix (APYPTF) command
  _     APPN
  _     Attention-key-handling program
  _     Automatic link and external reference
  _     BASIC
  _     Branch instruction
  _     Breakpoint program

                                                      More...
Or to search again, type new words and press Enter.
  programming


F3=Exit help   F5=All topics   F12=Cancel   F13=User support
```
Figure 13.4 Entry display of search help topics for "programming."

```
              Parameters for options 2, 3, 5, or command
```

In other words, you can enter the parameters for options 2, 3, or 5 at the command line or a regular CL command.

A list or menu display may be too long to fit on your screen. If it fits, the lower right of the screen will say "Bottom"; if it's too long, the lower right will say "More..." (as in Figure 13.4). If there is more, the Page Down and Page Up keys let you scroll through the list. (See Section 13.1.2.5, "Important special keys," for more on the use of these keys.)

13.1.2.5 Important special keys. We've already seen three special keys: F4 displays an entry screen that prompts you for a command's parameters, and Page Up and Page Down scroll through a display that doesn't fit on your screen.

When function keys are available to help you, the bottom of the display lists as many function key descriptions as will fit. Certain function keys nearly always have the same meaning:

F1   *On-line Help* displays information about the current display and your options for what to do with it. See Section 13.4, "Available On-Line Help," for more information.

F3   *Exit* ends the current program (for example, on-line help or a command prompt display) and returns to the screen that was displayed when you called that program. (Compare this with F12.)

F4   *Prompt* displays the command prompt display, an entry screen whose fields prompt you for the parameters of the command at the command line.

F9   *Retrieve* retrieves the previously entered command to the command line. This can be particularly useful to correct a typo in a long, complicated command that didn't execute because of the typo. Just press F9, correct the mistake, and press Enter.

F9 can also teach you the parameters that a command needs; if you press F4 and use the command prompt display to enter a command's parameters, pressing F9 later retrieves the command to the command line as if you had typed it out without the aid of the command prompt display.

Retrieve does not retrieve menu choice numbers typed at the command line, but only actual commands. Pressing it repeatedly retrieves earlier commands from your OS/400 session.

F12   *Cancel* leaves the current display and returns to the one before it. This is useful when you are searching through help screens and you want to return to one you just saw without leaving the help program.

If you're looking at the first screen in a particular program, this key acts like F3, returning you to the screen that was displayed when you called that program.

F13   *User Support* displays the User Support and Education menu. This offers a menu-driven way to access the various kinds of on-line help available for the AS/400. For more information, see Section 13.4, "Available On-Line Help."

F16   *Major Commands* displays the first of a series of menus that can lead you to the command you need. (The menu's title is MAJOR, so F16 is essentially a shortcut to entering GO MAJOR at the command line.)

F24   *More Keys* displays more function key descriptions if there is not enough room at the bottom of the screen to describe all of the current display's available function keys. Repeatedly pressing this key cycles through descriptions of the current display's available function keys.

When you use a terminal emulation program, certain keys may be designated as the "scroll down" and "scroll up" keys. These are analogous to the Page Up and Page Down keys, respectively. This may seem a bit backward, and can easily lead to confusion—the key that scrolls down corresponds to the Page Up key, because it scrolls the displayed text down to show you the text above it.

The AS/400 also lets you insert and delete characters at the command line the same way you would in a text editor. Pressing the Insert key turns on insert mode; everything you type is inserted at the cursor position, moving the characters to the right of the cursor further to the right.

To return to overstrike mode while using a 3270 terminal, press the key marked "Reset." The carat symbol should disappear, and newly typed text will take the place of the characters at the cursor. (When your keyboard "locks up," or refuses to accept input, the Reset key is also useful for freeing up the keyboard.) On most PCs emulating a 3270, the Insert key does the job of the 3270 keyboard's Insert key and the Escape key serves as the Reset key. Check your emulation program's documentation to make sure.

Each time you press the Delete key, it deletes the character at the cursor.

The ability to insert and delete characters is particularly useful when used in conjunction with the F9 key. To enter a series of similar commands, start by typing out the first one and pressing Enter. For each of the remaining commands, press F9 to retrieve the last one entered, make the necessary changes to turn it into the new command, and press Enter again.

13.2 Filenames

As you'll see in Section 13.3, "How Files are Organized," files and nearly everything else on an AS/400 are treated as objects. You rarely have to worry about the maximum length of the name of an object or of anything else; when you enter a name on an entry screen, you're filling out a field, and underscores show the field's maximum length. You'll see that object names can be up to 10 characters.

Names can use letters of the alphabet (case doesn't matter—lowercase is converted to uppercase) and numeric digits, and the characters $, #, @, and the period (.). Don't start a name with a numeric digit or a period.

13.2.1 Wildcards

There is only one wildcard in OS/400: the asterisk. It is used to designate "generic object names," which are essentially the same as the use of a wildcard to refer to multiple files at once on any other operating system. The string "abc*" refers to all applicable objects that begin with the letters "abc."

The asterisk must go at the end of a generic name. Remember, a name that starts with an asterisk is very different from a generic name—it is a predefined value, which is a special string that represents a specific value defined by the operating system.

A typical command that can make use of generic names is the Work with Members Using the Program Development Manager (WRKMBRPDM) command. This displays the components of a file known as "members" on a list display so that you can view and manipulate individual members. (You'll see more about this command in Section 14.1.2.1, "Listing a file's members.") If the 93 members of the QCSRC file are the C source code for 93 different programs, entering the command

```
WRKMBRPDM FILE(QCSRC) MBR(*ALL)
```

lists all 93 members on the Program Development Manager display. (Since the predefined value *ALL is the default value for the WRKMBRPDM command's MBR parameter, it doesn't need to be included in this command.) You can enter a member name as the value for the MBR() parameter; entering the command

```
WRKMBRPDM FILE(QCSRC) MBR(CTEST1)
```

tells WRKMBRPDM to only list the member named CTEST1.

A generic name is a compromise between entering *ALL amd entering a specific member name. Entering

```
WRKMBRPDM FILE(QCSRC) MBR(CTEST*)
```

tells WRKMBRPDM to list the members of the QCSRC file that begin with the letters "CTEST." With this command, the members CTEST1, CTEST2, CTEST3, and CTEST3A will all show up in the list display.

The GO command is another that accepts generic names as parameters. Because there are three different menus that begin with the letters "MA," entering the command

```
GO MA*
```

displays a list with the names and descriptions of these three menus, letting you pick the one you want.

13.3 How Files Are Organized

OS/400 treats everything as objects. This includes files, screens, commands, terminals, databases, programs, queues, and libraries.

Each *library* holds a group of related objects. For example, there is one library for each user ID, several for the operating system, one or more for each installed application, and so forth. If the concept of a library sounds similar to the concept of a directory on other operating systems, you're right, but there is one crucial difference: the QSYS library (one of the operating system libraries) is the only one that can contain other libraries. You cannot create libraries within your libraries the way you can create subdirectories on UNIX, VMS, and DOS. As a general rule, only the system administrator can create new libraries, whether they are for new users or for new application software.

Each object has an object type. This identifies what the object is and the operations that you can perform on it. When you list the objects in a library, you will see the type of each object listed with it; the following are some common object types:

*LIB   A library

`*FILE`	A file
`*CMD`	A command
`*PGM`	A program

Certain object types have an attribute (sometimes known as the "extended attribute") that describes their role more specifically than their type name does. For example, a *PGM object has an attribute describing the language in which the program was written, such as C or RPG. For *FILE objects, the attribute plays a crucial role in identifying a particular file's structure and purpose, as you'll see in Section 13.3.1, "Physical, source physical, and logical files."

When you refer to an object, you often have to identify the library where it can be found. A popular shorthand way to refer to an object's full name is `LIBNAME/OBJNAME`, where `LIBNAME` is the library name and `OBJNAME` is the object name. When the library name is included with the object name, it's known as a "qualified object name." (If an object's library is in your library list, specifying the library name is probably unnecessary. For more on library lists, see Section 13.3.2, "The library list and your current library.")

Technically, the term "file" has a more specific meaning on the AS/400 than it does on other operating systems: It is an object in a library that contains data or source code for programs. Programs and files are two different object types, so a compiled, executable program is not considered to be a file the way that it is on other operating systems.

To confuse you even further, a file can be composed of units known as *members*, which are individually comparable to a single file of source code on other operating systems. For example, a file of C source code can have multiple members, each of which might be the C source code for a different program. Members don't count as objects in the AS/400's object-oriented scheme of things, because they can't exist on their own; each member is part of a *FILE object.

Like a group of C programs on another operating system, the members of a given file generally have a similar purpose and format. In addition to storing the source code for several different programs written in the same language, a file could hold a group of data file descriptions, a group of operating system command language files, or the information necessary to display a group of menus.

If you can get used to the AS/400's fairly restricted use of the term "file," then its system of file organization—excuse me, object organization—is not really that confusing. To recap: everything is an object. Files and other objects are stored in libraries (which are also objects). A file can be subdivided into groups called members. A group of members in the same file usually have the same format and purpose, similar to a group of files with the same file extension in UNIX or DOS or files with the same file type in VM/CMS or VMS. The whole arrangement will look especially familiar to MVS users, who will recognize a strong resemblance to the concept of partitioned data sets.

13.3.1 Physical, source physical, and logical files

A *physical file* is a file that holds database data. This has broader applications on the AS/400 than a traditional database file does on other systems; while you might think of a database file as holding columns of data for a database (for example, an employee's last name, first name, Social Security Number, and hire date) on the AS/400 it might hold a simple text file. Technically, such a file is still columns of data—one for line numbers, one for the date that each record (that is, each line of the text file) was last changed, and one for the line of text itself. To see an example of a physical file that holds paragraphs of text, use the DSPPFM command described in Section 14.1.3, "Displaying a text file's contents," to look the AAAMAP member of the QATTINFO file in the QUSRTOOL library. (This IBM-supplied file describes application development and system management tools available on the system for more advanced users.)

A physical file whose members contain source code for programs, screens, or databases is known as a *source physical file*. A particular source physical file's members might be source code for several programs written in the same language. (Certain file-naming conventions make it easier to recognize the programming language by a file's name; for example, QCSRC is a common name for a source physical file of C code, and QCBLSRC is a typical name for a file of COBOL source code.) The name of the OS/400 text editor reveals its important role in creating the members of these files: the SEU is the text editor used to create and edit these files.

A *FILE object has an attribute that describes what kind of file it is. Two common values for this attribute are PF (physical file) and LF (logical file). A logical file doesn't hold database data; it holds information about an alternate format for viewing a particular physical data file or group of files. For example, if a physical file of employee data holds names, salaries, and phone numbers, a programmer might define a logical file that only shows the names and phone numbers from the physical file. A system administrator could then grant wider access to the logical file, allowing people to look up each other's phone numbers without seeing each other's salaries.

An object of *FILE can have several other possible attributes—for example, PF38 denotes a physical file moved from a System/38—but PF and LF are the most common.

13.3.2 The library list and your current library

When you want to run a program or use a data file, you don't always have to specify the library where it is located. How does OS/400 know where to find it? By searching the library list. The *library list* is a list of libraries that tell OS/400 where to look for objects and in what order.

Each user has his or her own library list. Sometimes, to use a new application program on your system, you might be told to add the library with that application's objects to your library list. (For information on doing this, see Section 14.1.7, "Editing your library list.")

The *current library* is the first library where the system looks when you request the use of an object—in other words, the first library on your library list. (Actually, it's the first library on the part of the list that you can change.) Your default current library is probably the personal library assigned for your user ID. This way, you get quick access to objects that you create.

If this book shows you an OS/400 command with FILE(filename) as a parameter, it usually takes it for granted that that file is in a library in your library list. If not, you must tell OS/400 where to find the file by either entering the library name as a separate parameter or by using the FILE(libname/filename) notation.

You can change your current library by indicating a particular library name in the "current library" field of the signon screen or by using the CHGCURLIB command. For more information, see Section 14.1.7, "Editing your library list," and Section 14.1.7.1, "Changing your current library."

13.4 Available On-Line Help

OS/400 offers many kinds of help. The most important way to get help is also the most basic: press F1. (On some keyboards, there may be an actual key labeled "Help.")

This doesn't bring up some vague help menu that forces you to search through a dozen screens to find the information that you need, as F1 does with some other systems and application programs. The OS/400 on-line help is context-sensitive, so F1 often takes you right to the information you need.

All you have to do is move your cursor to the appropriate area of the screen before pressing F1. For example:

- If you move your cursor to the lines at the bottom of the screen that list the available function keys, pressing F1 displays explanations of those function keys.

- On a menu display, pressing F1 while your cursor is positioned on one of the menu choices displays information about that menu choice.

- On an entry display, pressing F1 while your cursor is in one of the fields displays "field help," or information about that field.

```
MAIN                           AS/400 Main Menu
.........................................................................
:                        Function Keys - Help                           :
:                                                                       :
:   F1=Help                                                             :
:       Provides additional information about using the display or a    :
:       specific field on the display.                                  :
:                                                                       :
:   F3=Exit                                                             :
:       Ends the current task and returns to the display from which the task :
:       was started.                                                    :
:                                                                       :
:   F4=Prompt                                                           :
:       Provides assistance in entering or selecting a command.         :
:                                                                       :
:   F9=Retrieve                                                         :
:                                                             More...    :
:   F2=Extended help   F3=Exit help   F10=Move to top      F11=Search index :
:   F12=Cancel         F13=User support   F14=Print help   F20=Enlarge   :
:                                                                       :
:.......................................................................:
F3=Exit   F4=Prompt   F9=Retrieve   F12=Cancel   F13=User support
```
Figure 13.5 Help screen for the Main Menu's function keys.

- In a list display, pressing F1 while your cursor is in one of the columns displays help about the information in that column.

- With your cursor on an error message, F1 displays an explanation of the cause of the error message and how to fix it.

- If you enter a command or menu choice number at the command line but press F1 instead of Enter, OS/400 displays help about that command or menu choice.

Figure 13.5 shows the screen displayed after pressing F1 with your cursor on the MAIN menu's function key list.

If your cursor is on a display's command line, title, a blank line, or any part of the screen for which no specific help is available, OS/400 displays extended help. Extended help is a general description of the current display and how to use it. It's also available when you are viewing any other kind of help by pressing F2. Figure 13.6 shows the extended help for the SNDMSG (Send Message) command.

13.4.1 The search index

With many help systems, you can't find out about the use of a command unless you already know the command's name. The OS/400 Search Index makes it easy to find help on a topic when you only have a vague idea of the information you need and don't yet know the OS/400 name or terminology associated with that command.

To start the Search Index, either enter STRSCHIDX at any command line or press F11 when the bottom of a help screen tells you that F11 = Search Index. This brings up the Search Help Index

```
                        Send Message (SNDMSG)
.......................................................................
:                       Send Message - Help                          :
:                                                                     :
:    The Send Message (SNDMSG) command is used by a display station user :
:    to send an immediate message from his display station to one or more :
:    message queues.  (An immediate message is a message that is not  :
:    predefined and is not stored in a message file.)  The message can be :
:    sent to the system operator, to other display station users, to a :
:    user's message queue, all currently active users' message queues or :
:    to the system history log, QHST.  The sender can require a reply :
:    from the message receiver.  The primary users of this command are :
:    display station users and the system operator.                   :
:                                                                     :
:        Note:  Do not precede an entry with an asterisk unless that  :
:        entry is a "special value" that is shown (on the display itself :
:        or in the help information) with an asterisk.                :
:                                                                     :
:  Message text (MSG)                                                 :
:                                                             More... :
:  F3=Exit help      F10=Move to top   F11=Search index   F12=Cancel  :
:  F13=User support  F14=Print help                                   :
:                                                                     :
:.....................................................................:
```

Figure 13.6 SNDMSG extended help screen.

```
                        Search Help Index

Index Search allows you to tell the system to search for specific
information.  To use Index Search, do the following:

1.  Type the phrase or words to search for.

2.  Press Enter.

When you press Enter, the system searches for topics related to the
words you supplied and displays a list of topics found.

If you press Enter without typing anything, the system displays a list
of all available topics.




Type words to search for, press Enter.
_____


F3=Exit help    F5=All topics    F12=Cancel    F13=User support
```
Figure 13.7 Search Help Index display.

display, where you enter a word or phrase that describes the topic in question. Figure 13.7 shows the Search Help Index display.

After you enter a search phrase, press Enter. OS/400 displays a list of the relevant help topics. For a vague search phrase, there may be too many topics to fit on one screen. Figure 13.8 shows the result of entering "programming" as the search phrase; note how the message

```
                      Main Help Index for AS/400

Type options, press Enter.
  5=Display topic    6=Print topic


Option  Topic
   _       Add physical file variable-length member (ADDPFVLM) command
   _       Add program (ADDPGM) command
   _       Analyze program (ANZPGM) command
   _       APPC
   _       Application program
   _       Apply program temporary fix (APYPTF) command
   _       APPN
   _       Attention-key-handling program
   _       Automatic link and external reference
   _       BASIC
   _       Branch instruction
   _       Breakpoint program

                                                            More...
Or to search again, type new words and press Enter.
  programming


F3=Exit help    F5=All topics    F12=Cancel    F13=User support
```
Figure 13.8 Search Help Index topics for "programming."

More... in the lower right tells you that you must press Page Down (or Scroll Up) to look through the remaining topic titles. Topics are listed alphabetically, and since the list shown in Figure 13.8 doesn't even get to the topics beginning with the letter "C," it must be quite a long list.

Figure 13.9 shows the result of a search on a more specific topic, "C programming." The word "Bottom" in the lower right shows that all the topics that fit this search phrase are displayed on this one screen.

Because help topics are shown on a list display, the upper part of the screen shows the numbers that you can type in the Option column on the left to see the help topics. A 5 displays the help information for a given topic, and a 6 sends that information to the printer.

13.4.2 Navigating help screens

The important function keys in on-line help are consistent with the rest of OS/400: Page Up (or Scroll Down) and Page Down (or Scroll Up) to page through the help text, F3 to exit help, and F12 to Cancel (that is, to back up one screen). As with other situations, F1 gives you help about what you are doing—in this case, using help. Figure 13.10 shows the first "How to Use Help" screen that OS/400 displays when you press F1 while viewing any other help screen.

13.4.2.1 Expanding help windows.   Sometimes, when viewing field help after pressing F1 with your cursor on a particular entry screen field, the help information appears in a window that takes up only part of your screen. Figure 13.11 shows the help displayed by pressing F1 when the cursor is in the "Send Message" entry screen's "To user profile" recipient field.

```
                        Main Help Index for AS/400

Type options, press Enter.
  5=Display topic    6=Print topic

Option  Topic
  _       C language
  _       C language interface (Query Management)
  _       Create C locale description (CRTCLD) command
  _       Create C/400 program (CRTCPGM) command
  _       Create Structured Query Language C (CRTSQLC) command
  _       Delete C locale description (DLTCLD) command
  _       Including SQLCA in C
  _       Retrieve C locale description source (RTVCLDSRC) command



                                                         Bottom
Or to search again, type new words and press Enter.
  C programming

F3=Exit help    F5=All topics    F12=Cancel    F13=User support
```

Figure 13.9 Search Help Index topics for "C programming."

```
Help                        How to Use Help

    Help is provided for all AS/400 displays.  The type of help provided
    depends on the location of the cursor.

    o  For all displays, the following information is provided:

         -  What the display is used for
         -  How to use the display
         -  How to use the command line if there is one
         -  How to use the entry fields and parameter line if any
         -  What function keys are active and what they do

    o  The following information is also provided for specific areas,
       depending on the type of information being displayed:

         -  Menus:  Meaning of each option
         -  Entry (prompting) displays:  Meanings and use of all values
            for each entry field
         -  List displays:  Meaning and use of each column

                                                         More...
F3=Exit help    F10=Move to top    F12=Cancel    F14=Print
```

Figure 13.10 The first "How to Use Help" screen.

If a help window covers only part of your screen but has too much information to fit in the help window, the F20 (Enlarge) key expands it to take up the whole screen. Figure 13.12 shows the "To user profile" help expanded to fill up the whole screen. Much more informa-

```
                         Send Message (SNDMSG)

Type choices, press Enter.

Message text . . . . . . . . . .




To user profile  . . . . . . . .              Name, *SYSOPR, *ALLACT...
              ..................................................................
              :           To user profile (TOUSR) - Help                     :
              :                                                               :
              :  Specifies that the message is to be sent to the message     :
              :  queue specified in the user profile for the user named on    :
              :  this parameter.  This parameter cannot be used if a value    :
              :  is specified for the To message queue prompt (TOMSGQ         :
              :                                                    More...    :
              :  F2=Extended help   F10=Move to top    F11=Search index       :
F3=Exit   F4= :  F12=Cancel          F20=Enlarge        F24=More keys          :
F13=How to us :                                                               :
Parameter MSG :................................................................:
```

Figure 13.11 "To user profile" field help overlaying "Send Message" screen.

```
                         Send Message (SNDMSG)
..................................................................................
:                    To user profile (TOUSR) - Help                             :
:                                                                               :
:  Specifies that the message is to be sent to the message queue specified     :
:  in the user profile for the user named on this parameter.  This             :
:  parameter cannot be used if a value is specified for the To message         :
:  queue prompt (TOMSGQ parameter).                                            :
:                                                                               :
:  Either this parameter or the To message queue prompt (TOMSGQ parameter)     :
:  is required.                                                                 :
:                                                                               :
:  user-profile-name                                                           :
:      Specify the user profile name of the user to whom the message is        :
:      sent.                                                                    :
:                                                                               :
:  *SYSOPR                                                                      :
:      The message is sent to the system operator message queue,               :
:      QSYS/QSYSOPR.                                                            :
:                                                                    More...   :
:  F2=Extended help    F3=Exit help   F10=Move to top   F11=Search index       :
:  F12=Cancel          F13=User support  F14=Print help                        :
:                                                                               :
:..............................................................................:
```

Figure 13.12 "To user profile" field help expanded to whole screen.

tion fits in this help window, so less paging is necessary to read the whole thing.

13.4.2.2 The user support and education menu. The User Support and Education menu offers another form of access to the various kinds of

```
SUPPORT                      User Support and Education
                                                        System:    NEPAS4
Select one of the following:

     1. How to use help
     2. Search system help index
     3. How to use commands
     4. Question and answer
     5. AS/400 publications
     6. IBM product information
     7. How to handle system problems
     8. Problem handling
     9. Online education




Selection or command
===>

F3=Exit    F4=Prompt    F9=Retrieve    F12=Cancel    F16=AS/400 Main menu
(C) COPYRIGHT IBM CORP. 1980, 1992.
```
Figure 13.13 User Support and Education menu.

on-line help. You can display it by entering GO SUPPORT at any command line or by pressing F13 while viewing any screen where F13 means "User support." (This applies to nearly all OS/400 menus.)

Figure 13.13 shows an example of the User Support and Education menu. It offers the following choices:

1. *How to use help* displays the same screen that you get when you press F1 while viewing a help screen: an overview of how to use the on-line help.

2. *Search system help index* displays the Search Help Index screen, which lets you tell OS/400 to list help topics related to a word or phrase that you enter. See Section 13.4.1, "The search index," for more information.

3. *How to use commands* displays an overview of the use of the OS/400 command line and the structure of the available commands and their parameters.

4. *Question and answer* gives you access to a database of commonly asked questions about the AS/400 and their answers. Some AS/400 systems are hooked up to mainframes at IBM sites, giving them access to a wider variety of questions and answers (an excellent example of the AS/400's potential role in a large, distributed database).

5. *AS/400 publications* displays a catalog of publications that you can order from IBM that cover OS/400, the AS/400, and available IBM development and application software.

6. *IBM product information* displays information about software available for the AS/400.

7. *How to handle system problems* displays information for system administrators about ways to approach problems with their AS/400. (Although I wonder about the paragraph on the first screen that begins "If you cannot turn the system on...." If someone can't turn the system on, they'll have a tough time taking advantage of the information provided by "How to handle system problems.")

8. *Problem handling* displays information for system administrators about the use of tools such as the job log (a history of a user's activity since signing on) and various kinds of diagnostic software used to handle problems in communications, programming development, and other aspects of the AS/400.

9. *Online education* leads you to the on-line tutorials about the AS/400 and its software. A variety of tutorials may be installed; if there is only one, it will be Tutorial System Support (TSS), which gives you background in the concepts and usage of OS/400. See Section 13.4.3, "The on-line tutorial," for more information.

Choices 4 through 8 on this menu are part of something called "Electronic Customer Support," or "ECS." In much of the computer industry, "customer support" means calling up some company, being put on hold, asking your question, being put on hold again, and then being told that someone will call you back with the answer. ECS takes advantage of the computing and communications resources at your disposal to offer you a much more efficient alternative.

13.4.2.3 Hypertext links. On many help screens, you will see certain phrases highlighted or underlined, depending on the type of terminal that you are using or emulating. This highlighting tells you that the phrase is a hypertext link to more detailed information on that phrase. These phrases may be in the middle of a sentence or in a list of topics at the end of a help topic.

For example, on the help screen that you see when you press F1 while viewing the OS/400 Main Menu, one paragraph begins with the sentence "To go to another menu, use the Go to Menu (GO) command." The phrase "Go to Menu (GO) command" is highlighted, showing that if you press your Tab key to move your cursor there and then press Enter (not F1 again—remember, F1 while viewing a help screen gives you help about the use of on-line help) you'll jump directly to a screen that tells you about the GO command.

After you use a hypertext link to another screen, a new function key becomes available: F6 (Viewed Topics). This displays a window with a list of the titles of the help screens you have viewed. You can jump directly back to any of these help screens by moving your cursor

```
MAIN                            AS/400 Main Menu
............................................................
:                        Go to Menu - Help                         :
:  .......................................................         :
:  :                     Viewed Topics                    :  : nd   :
:  :                                                       :  : name. :
:  :  To return to a topic, position the cursor to that topic  :  : rom  :
:  :     and press Enter.                                  :         :
:  :                                                       :         :
:  :     AS/400 Main Menu - Help                           :  : ntry is :
:  :     Go to Menu - Help                                 :  : the  :
:  :                                                       :         :
:  :                                                       :         :
:  :                                                       :         :
:  :                                                       :         :
:  :                                          Bottom       :         :
:  :  F12=Cancel                                           :         :
:  :                                                       :         :
:  :.......................................................: Bottom  :
:  F3=Exit help    F6=Viewed topics    F10=Move to top  F11=Search index :
:  F12=Cancel      F13=User support    F14=Print help                    :
:                                                                        :
:..........................................................................:
```

Figure 13.14   Viewed Topics window listing help screens displayed with hypertext links.

to the title of your choice and pressing Enter. Figure 13.14 shows the short list of topics displayed if you press F6 after using the hypertext link described above to go from the Main Menu's help screen to the GO command's help screen.

13.4.3 The on-line tutorial

OS/400 offers various on-line tutorials to help you learn about the system. They let you work at your own pace, with exercises, reviews, and quizzes. Each course is broken down into lessons known as "modules" that can be completed in 15 to 40 minutes. Each module warns you at the beginning how long it will take. The system keeps track of which modules you have taken of which courses, which makes it easier to pick up where you left off if you haven't worked on a particular tutorial in a while. You can even leave "bookmarks" showing where you were if you have to leave a module before finishing it.

The most important course is TSS, which gives you background in the concepts and usage of OS/400. Even if many tutorials are available on your system, this is the best one to start with.

To start the on-line education, you can select Online Education from the "User Support and Education" menu described in Section 13.4.2.2 or you can enter STREDU (Start Education) from the command line.

The first time you do this, an entry display asks you for your first and last name. The system uses this information to remember which courses you have taken. Next, a list display asks you to pick from a

```
                      Select Audience Path

Course title . . . . . . . . :

Type option, press Enter.
  1=Select    5=Display modules   8=Display description

Option      Audience Path Title
  _         How to Use AS/400 Online Education
  _         All Modules in the Course
  _         Communications Implementer
  _         Database Administrator
  _         Data Processing Manager
  _         Executives
  _         Office Systems Administrator
  _         Clerical User (Secretary)
  _         Office Implementer
  _         Experienced S/36 System Operator
  _         Experienced S/38 System Operator
  _         Programmer/Implementer
  _         Professional User
                                            More...
F3=Exit    F9=Print list   F12=Cancel   F17=Top   F18=Bottom
```

Figure 13.15 List display asking you to pick an audience path for an on-line course.

list of available courses. After you pick one, another list asks you to pick an audience path, as shown in Figure 13.15.

The "audience path" concept is a nice design touch. Of the many modules available for each course, certain combinations have been grouped into "paths" for different audiences. For example, Figure 13.15 shows different paths for database administrators, secretaries, executives, and programmers. While all four of these paths have the modules "Getting Started with Online Education" and "Working with System Displays," only the database administrator and programmer paths have the modules "Object Management Concepts." Note also the path "All Modules in the Course"—while time-consuming, this would obviously give you the most detailed background on the use of the AS/400.

Once you've selected a path, the "Select Course Option" menu offers you the following choices:

- Start the next module in your path.

- Select a different module.

- Return to the displays where you picked your course or your path.

Once you start a module, the on-line education leads you through the step-by-step tutorial.

13.4.4 Other helpful features

OS/400 includes several other features that, while not actually part of on-line help, make it much easier to navigate and use the system.

The Display Keyboard Map command (DSPKBDMAP) displays a series of help screens that describe the use of the keys on the terminal that you are using or emulating. If an OS/400 screen refers to a key that isn't on your keyboard, use DSPKBDMAP to find out which of your keyboards's keys are doing the unfamiliar key's job.

OS/400 enables you to do so much by using menus that some menus can overwhelm many users. A useful feature called the Operational Assistant can ease this problem. The Operational Assistant is a set of simple menus with a minimum of fancy terminology that let you find the most important tasks quickly and easily. In addition to allowing the basic tasks required by all users, it enables a system administrator to add new users, to backup the hard disk to tape, and to do other tasks that are crucial to running the system. This kind of feature makes the AS/400 one of the most "plug and play" large computers ever available, because it allows novice AS/400 users to set up the computer and become productive very quickly with a minimum of technical assistance.

To see the first Operational Assistant menu, enter GO ASSIST. Figure 13.16 shows this menu.

```
ASSIST              AS/400 Operational Assistant (TM) Menu
                                              System:   NEPAS4
To select one of the following, type its number below and press Enter:

     1. Work with printer output
     2. Work with jobs
     3. Work with messages
     4. Send messages
     5. Change your password

    75. Information and problem handling

    80. Temporary sign-off




Type a menu option below


F1=Help   F3=Exit   F9=Command line   F12=Cancel
```
Figure 13.16 Operational Assistant main menu.

14

Using Files in OS/400

14.1 The 12 Most Important Commands

OS/400 seems to have a larger number of crucial commands than other operating systems because of the file/member system. You want the ability to perform the basic operations on files and on members within files. This doesn't really require memorizing more commands, because the OS/400 menus and on-line help make it easy to find the commands whose names you can't remember.

The 12 most important commands in OS/400 are:

DSPLIB	Lists the files (and other objects) in a library
DSPFD	Lists the members in a file
DSPPFM	Displays a file or file member's contents
CRTDUPOBJ	Copies files and other objects
CPYSRCF	Copies file members
RNMOBJ	Renames files and other objects
RNMM	Renames file members
DLTF	Deletes files
RMVM	Deletes file members
EDTLIBL	Edits your library list
CRTLIB	Creates libraries
DLTLIB	Deletes libraries.

14.1.1 Common error messages

Remember, the greatest thing about OS/400 error messages is that you can always move your cursor to them and press F1 to display an explanation of what they mean if a message is too cryptic. For example, let's look at the error message that you get when you pick a

```
MAIN                           AS/400 Main Menu
                                                        System:    NEPAS4
Select one of the following:

     1. User tasks
     2. Office tasks
     3. General System Tasks
     4. Files, libraries, and folders
     5. Programming
     6. Communications
     7. Define or change the system
     8. Problem handling
     9. Display a menu
    10. Information Assistant options
    11. PC Support tasks

    90. Sign off

Selection or command
===> 75

F3=Exit    F4=Prompt    F9=Retrieve    F12=Cancel    F13=User support
F23=Set initial menu
Specified menu selection is not correct.
```

Figure 14.1 Main menu with error message for incorrect menu choice.

nonexistent menu choice. After you enter 75 at the command line while viewing the main menu, OS/400 responds with the error message shown at the bottom of Figure 14.1.

If you move your cursor to the line "Specified menu selection is not correct" and press F1, OS/400 displays the more detailed "Additional Message Information" about the error message, as shown in Figure 14.2.

Another common error message tells you that OS/400 can't find an object that you asked to use. If you enter a command that uses a nonexistent object named "POTRZEBIE" (for example, try entering GO POTRZEBIE) you get an error message similar to this:

```
Object POTRZEBIE in library *LIBL not found
```

*LIBL is the OS/400 predefined value that refers to the library list. The error message means that the object POTRZEBIE cannot be found in any of the libraries in the library list.

*LIBL, as a representative of all the libraries in the library list, sometimes takes the place in error messages of a specific library name. If you had indicated a specific nonexistent library when you identified the object to use (for example, LOOBRARY/POTRZEBIE), you might have seen that library's name instead of *LIBL in the error message.

```
                       Additional Message Information
Message ID . . . . . . :   CPD6A64
Date sent  . . . . . . :   07/10/93     Time sent . . . . . . :    19:33:53

Message . . . . :   Specified menu selection is not correct.

Cause . . . . . :    The selection that you have specified is not correct for
  one of the following reasons:
    -- The number selected was not valid.
    -- Something other than a menu option was entered on the option line.
Recovery  . . . :    Select a valid option and press the Enter or Help key
  again.



                                                                   Bottom
Press Enter to continue.
```

Figure 14.2 Additional information about the "Specified menu selection is not correct" error message.

The "not found" error message can be more specific about what it's looking for than just calling it an "object." For example, if you were copying a file and specified a nonexistent "from file" (that is, the file that you are making a copy of, or copying "from") called HELLFILE, the error message would tell you the following:

```
From-file HELLFILE in *LIBL not found.
```

Entering the nonexistent command CLEANRUG at the command prompt gives you this error message:

```
Command CLEANRUG in library *LIBL not found.
```

Let's say that the POTRZEBIE program does exist in the library SUPERLIB, but you're not authorized to use it. You'll get a fairly straightforward error message:

```
Not authorized to object POTRZEBIE in SUPERLIB type *PGM.
```

One more hint about dealing with errors: if you make a mistake when filling out a command prompt display (the screen you get when you press F4 after entering a command at the command line) OS/400 returns you to the previous screen and displays the command line version of the command on the command line with the appropriate error message underneath it. Of course, you can move your cursor to the error message and press F1, but if you want some background on using that command, you can also move your cursor to the command line and press F1.

14.1.2 Listing filenames

On the AS/400, you'll want to list more than just filenames. In addition to listing the names of a given library's files and other objects, it's also handy to be able to see the members of a given file. This is covered in Section 14.1.2.1, "Listing a file's members."

Use the Display Library command (DSPLIB) to list the objects in a library. (Don't confuse it with the similarly spelled Display Library List command, DSPLIBL—see Section 14.1.7, "Editing your library list," for more information on this.)

From the command line, you tell OS/400 to list the contents of a particular library by entering DSPLIB with the library name as the LIB parameter. For example, to look at the JOEUSER library, Joe would enter the following:

```
DSPLIB LIB(JOEUSER)
```

If you leave out the LIB() part, the system assumes that the DSPLIB command's single parameter is a library name, so the following works just as well:

```
DSPLIB JOEUSER
```

If you type DSPLIB with no parameters and press Enter, the system assumes a default parameter of LIB(*LIBL), which tells it "I want to look at a list of objects from one of the libraries in my library list. List them out and then I'll pick one." This brings up a screen like the one shown in Figure 14.3.

As the display tells you, all you need to do to list the objects in one of these libraries is to enter a 5 in the Opt column next to a library name and press Enter. For example, entering a 5 next to QGPL and pressing Enter displays a screen similar to the one shown in Figure 14.4. Note the "More..." message at the bottom; QGPL has more objects than will fit on one Display Library screen, and you will need your Page Down and Page Up (or Scroll Up and Scroll Down, respectively) keys to see the other objects in the list.

As described earlier, the commands

```
DSPLIB LIB(QGPL)
```

or

```
DSPLIB QGPL
```

would have taken you right from the command line to the list of objects in the QGPL library.

To the right of the Opt column, the other columns in the library object list tell you the following information:

```
                         Display Libraries
                                              System:     NEPAS4
 Libraries:    *LIBL

 Type options, press Enter.
  5=Display objects in library

 Opt   Library    Type        Text
       QSYS       SYS         System Library
       QSYS2      SYS         System Library for CPI's
       QUSRSYS    SYS         *IN USE
       QHLPSYS    SYS
       JOEUSER    CUR         Joe User's Library
       QTEMP      USR
       QGPL       USR         GENERAL PURPOSE LIBRARY
       QUSRTOOL   USR
       QTEMP      USR
       QGDDM      USR


                                                         Bottom
 F3=Exit    F12=Cancel    F17=Top    F18=Bottom
```

Figure 14.3 Sample list of libraries displayed when you press Enter after entering DSPLIB with no parameters.

Object	The object's name.
Type	The object's type, as described in Section 13.3, "How Files are Organized."
Attribute	If applicable, the object's attribute, as described in Section 13.3.1, "Physical, source physical, and logical files."
Freed	Whether the object's storage space has been freed up. This only concerns advanced users.
Size	The object's size in bytes. If you are not authorized to use the object, a zero appears here.
Text	Descriptive text that can be added when the object is created. If the whole description does not appear on the library object list screen, entering either 5 or 8 in the Opt column displays the complete description along with other technical information about the object.

According to the Type column in Figure 14.4, most of the objects in the QGPL library look like programs. A personal library would have more objects of type *FILE. For example, entering the command

```
DSPLIB LIB(JOEUSER)
```

shows the object's in Joe User's library, as shown in Figure 14.5.

14.1.2.1 Listing a file's members. The Display File Description command (DSPFD) will tell you more than you ever want to know about a given file. Fortunately, there is a way to tell this command, "Don't tell me every little technical detail about this file; just tell me the

```
                        Display Library

Library  . . . . . . :   QGPL          Number of objects  . :   208
Type . . . . . . . . :   PROD          ASP of library . . . :   1
Create authority . . :   *SYSVAL

Type options, press Enter.
  5=Display full attributes   8=Display service attributes

Opt   Object      Type     Attribute    Freed        Size  Text
      ALRC        *PGM     CLP          NO           7680  Does ADDLIBLE NEW (
      CC          *PGM     C            NO          54784  compile with as400
      CC_CMD      *PGM     C            NO          55808  compile with as400
      CCSYSTEM_   *PGM     C            NO          12288
      DKJFOCCLP   *PGM     CLP          NO          22528
      DKJSINKC    *PGM     CLP          NO          19968
      FUNCLP      *PGM     CLP          NO          22016
      FUNCLP2     *PGM     CLP          NO          20992  FUN System Developm
      INZQBATCH   *PGM     CLP          NO          11776  Pgm called when QBA
      QDCUPF      *PGM     PAS          NO          44544
      QRZHWUG1    *PGM                                 0   *NOT AUTHORIZED
                                                             More...

F3=Exit   F12=Cancel   F17=Top   F18=Bottom
(C) COPYRIGHT IBM CORP. 1980, 1992.
```

Figure 14.4 List of objects in the QGPL library.

```
                        Display Library

Library  . . . . . . :   JOEUSER       Number of objects  . :   31
Type . . . . . . . . :   PROD          ASP of library . . . :   1
Create authority . . :   *SYSVAL

Type options, press Enter.
  5=Display full attributes   8=Display service attributes

Opt   Object      Type     Attribute    Freed        Size  Text
      SETUP       *PGM     CLP          NO           1022
      STRIPPRN    *PGM     C            NO           3234  Strip codes from pr
      RPGTEST     *PGM     RPG          NO            894  My first RPG progra
      JOEUSER     *OUTQ                 NO           4608
      OUTPUT      *OUTQ                 NO           8704
      BUDGET93    *FILE    PF           NO          11822
      BUDGET94    *FILE    PF           NO          10432
      D2235324    *FILE    PF           NO          18944
      DEF         *FILE    PF           NO          15360
      JOETEST     *FILE    PF           NO           9216  Sample data to play
      SALES93     *FILE    PF           NO           7320
                                                             More...

F3=Exit   F12=Cancel   F17=Top   F18=Bottom
(C) COPYRIGHT IBM CORP. 1980, 1992.
```

Figure 14.5 Objects in Joe User's personal library.

file's members." As its command prompt display tells you, it has an optional field called "Type of information." The default value is *ALL, but if you don't want to scroll through all the technical details to find the member list, you can enter a TYPE of *MBRLIST. If Joe User

```
                         Display Spooled File
File  . . . . . :   QPDSPFD                    Page/Line   1/36
Control . . . . .                              Columns     1 - 78
Find  . . . . . .
*...+....1....+....2....+....3....+....4....+....5....+....6....+....7....+...
   CONVERT          25322 C     07/18/93 07/18/93 16:07:37        4
     Text:  Conversion routines
   CTEST1            4096 C     07/09/93 05/16/93 09:26:36         4
     Text:  my first C/400 program
   CTEST2            6144 C     07/16/93 05/16/93 09:35:45        30
     Text:  Another C programming test
   GETDATA           4096 C     07/18/93 07/18/93 16:02:48        20
     Text:  Get data from main file
   LKNGLASS          8198 C     07/16/93 07/16/93 09:44:17         4
     Text:  Alice's Adventures Through the Looking Glass
   MAIN344           4096 C     07/18/93 07/18/93 16:04:11        20
     Text:  Module 344 of main procedure
   MAIN346           9416 C     07/18/93 07/30/93 09:23:45        20
     Text:  Module 346 of main procedure
   MAIN347          12844 C     07/18/93 07/23/93 13:36:11        20
     Text:  Module 347 of main procedure
                                                       More...

F3=Exit    F12=Cancel   F19=Left    F20=Right    F24=More keys
```

Figure 14.6 The members of Joe User's QCSRC file as listed by the DSPFD command.

wants to enter a command at the command line that displays a list of his CL program source code members, which are in the file QCLSRC, he enters

```
DSPFD FILE(JOEUSER/QCSRC) TYPE(*MBRLIST)
```

or even just this:

```
DSPFD QCSRC TYPE(*MBRLIST)
```

The first screen displayed by this command shows some summary information about the file. To see the beginning of the list of member names, press Page Down (or Scroll Up) once.

Figure 14.6 shows the results of paging down once after executing this command with the JOEUSER/QCSRC file. As you can see, DSPFD shows more than just the members' names—it also shows the size, creation date, and the date and time that each member was last modified.

14.1.2.2 Listing a file's members with the program development manager.
Another quick way to list a file's members is to use the Work with Members using the Program Development Manager WRKMBRPDM command. (Like OfficeVision, the Program Development Manager is an IBM "Licensed Program Product" or "LPP" and therefore not included as part of OS/400, so you may not have it installed on your system.) Entering the command

```
                        Work with Members Using PDM

File  . . . . . .     QCSRC
  Library . . . .       JOEUSER              Position to  . . . . .

Type options, press Enter.
  2=Edit          3=Copy       4=Delete      5=Display      6=Print
  7=Rename        8=Display description      9=Save         13=Change text ...

Opt  Member      Type         Text
     CONVERT     C            Conversion routines
     CTEST1      C            my first C/400 program
     CTEST2      C            Another C programming test
     GETDATA     C            Get data from main file
     LKNGLASS    C            Alice's Adventures Through the Looking Glass
     MAIN344     C            Module 344 of main procedure
     MAIN346     C            Module 346 of main procedure
     MAIN347     C            Module 347 of main procedure
                                                                  More...
Parameters or command
===>
F3=Exit          F4=Prompt            F5=Refresh            F6=Create
F9=Retrieve      F10=Command entry    F23=More options      F24=More keys
```

Figure 14.7 The members of Joe User's QCSRC file as listed by the WRKMBRPDM command.

```
        WRKMBRPDM FILE(libname/filename)
```

displays a file's members on a list display. Because the program lets you "work with" the members, you can use this list to edit, copy, delete, display, print, and rename a file's members, as we'll see later in this chapter. Figure 14.7 shows how WRKMBRPDM lists the members of Joe User's QCSRC file.

Many people find WRKMBRPDM easier to use than DSPFD, but keep in mind that it is not available on all AS/400 installations.

14.1.3 Displaying a text file's contents

When you want to see text stored in a file on an AS/400, you want to see a particular member of a file. Do this with the Display Physical File Member (DSPPFM) command. This command needs to know the name of the file and the name of the member that you want to see within that file. (It doesn't really need to know a member name; if you fail to supply one, it displays the first member of that file.)

In Joe User's QCSRC file, he has a C source code member called WNDRLAND that displays a passage from *Alice in Wonderland*. To view it, he enters the following:

```
        DSPPFM FILE(JOEUSER/QCSRC) MBR(WNDRLAND)
```

(If the JOEUSER library is in Joe's library list he doesn't really need to include the qualified object name for QCSRC. He could have just written FILE(QCSRC) as the DSPPFM command's first parameter.)

```
                     Display Physical File Member
File . . . . . . :    QCSRC            Library . . . . :    JOEUSER
Member . . . . . :    WNDRLAND         Record . . . . . :    1
Control . . . .                        Column . . . . . :    1
Find . . . . . . .
*...+....1....+....2....+....3....+....4....+....5....+....6....+....7....+...
000100930709#include <stdio.h>
000200930709main() {
000300930716    printf("Soon her eye fell on a little glass box that was lying\
000400930716    printf("under the table: she opened it, and found in it a very\
000500930716    printf("small cake, on which the words \"EAT ME\" were \n");
000600930716    printf("beautifully marked in currants.  \"Well, I'll eat it,\"
000700930716    printf("said Alice, \"and if it makes me grow larger, I can\n")
000800930716    printf("reach the key; and if it makes me grow smaller, I can\n
000900930716    printf("creep under the door: so either way I'll get into the \
001000930716    printf("garden, and I don't care which happens!\"\n\n");
001100930716    printf("She ate a little bit, and said anxiously to herself\n")
001200930716    printf("\"Which way?  Which way?\", holding her hand on the top
001300930716    printf("of her head to feel which way it was growing; and she\n
001400930716    printf("was quite surprised to find that she remained the same
001500930716    printf("size.  To be sure, this is what generally happens when\
                                                                   More...
F3=Exit   F12=Cancel   F19=Left   F20=Right   F24=More keys
```

Figure 14.8 The first fifteen lines of the WNDRLAND program as displayed by DSPPFM.

Figure 14.8 shows the result of this command: the Display Physical File Member screen with the first 15 lines of the WNDRLAND program.

This file has three columns, although the first two appear as one big column. These two show the number and the date of the last change for each line. In Figure 14.8, the first two lines were created on July 9, 1993, and the rest were added a week later on the 16th.

The third column, which takes up most of the screen, is the text file itself. Lines that are too long to fit on the screen end with the slash (\) character; we'll see a way to scroll to the right to see what we're missing. (The other slashes are part of the C program. A slash before a quotation mark tells the computer that that quotation mark is part of the text that the program should output onto the screen, and a slash before the letter "n" causes a carriage return in the program's output.)

To move around in the file, the description of the function keys at the bottom of the screen shows that F19 and F20 will scroll a screenful to the left and right. Your Page Down (or Scroll Up) and Page Up (or Scroll Down) keys have the same effect here that they have when you view anything else too long to fit on the screen.

The following commands, which you enter in the Control field at the top of the screen, give you additional options for scrolling text that doesn't fit on the screen:

n	Make line n the top line on the screen
+n	Move forward n lines
-n	Move back n lines
W + n	Shift the text n characters to the left

```
                     Display Physical File Member
File . . . . . . :   QCSRC              Library  . . . . :   JOEUSER
Member . . . . . :   WNDRLAND           Record . . . . . :   17
Control  . . . . .                      Column . . . . . :   5
Find . . . . . . .   dull and stupid
+....1....+....2....+....3....+....4....+....5....+....6....+....7....+....8..
00930716    printf("of expecting nothing but out-of-the-way things to\n");
00930716    printf("happen, that it seemed quite dull and stupid for life\n");
00930716    printf("to go on the common way.\n");
00930709}
                    ****** END OF DATA ******




                                                                    Bottom
F3=Exit    F12=Cancel    F19=Left    F20=Right    F24=More keys
String found in column 53 in record 18.
```

Figure 14.9   Result of searching the WNDRLAND file for the string "dull and stupid."

      W-n   Shift the text n characters to the right

The Find field at the top of the screen makes it easy to search for a string of text. Enter a string there, press F16, and the system puts the first line with that string near the top of the screen with the target string highlighted. (Although there was nothing at the bottom of Figure 14.8 about F16, pressing F24 for "More keys" once or twice would have shown you that F16 meant "Find.") Figure 14.9 shows the result of a search for the string "dull and stupid." Note the message at the bottom of the screen that tells the column and record (that is, line of the file) where the string was found.

When you are finished looking at the file member, press F3 to exit DSPPFM.

14.1.3.1 Displaying a file's members with the program development manager. If you use the Program Development Manager to list the names of a file's members, as shown in Section 14.1.2.2, "Listing a file's members with the program development manager," you can display one of the listed members by simply entering the number 5 next to that member's name in the Opt column.

14.1.4 Copying files

OS/400 does have a command called CPYF to copy files, but its most popular uses can be a bit specialized. An easier, more versatile command is "Create Duplicate Object," or CRTDUPOBJ.

The CRTDUPOBJ needs to know four things:

OBJ()   The name of the object being duplicated.

FROMLIB()   The library where this object is stored.

OBJTYPE()   The type of the object being duplicated. Because you can have
                two objects with the same name in the same library (as long as
                they have different types) specifying the object type tells
                OS/400 more specifically which one you want to duplicate. If
                you want to copy everything in the FROMLIB() library with the
                name given by OBJ(), enter the predefined value *ALL as the
                OBJTYPE. To copy a file object, enter an OBJTYPE() of *FILE.

NEWOBJ()   The new object's name. If an object with this name already
                exists, OS/400 displays an error message and does not make
                the copy.

When used to copy a file, CRTDUPOBJ copies the file and all of its
members. But it doesn't necessarily copy the contents of these members—you have to tell it to do that with an additional parameter:
DATA(). A value of *NO is the default; this tells CRTDUPOBJ not to
copy the records in the file's members. A parameter of DATA(*YES)
tells CRTDUPOBJ to copy the members' text when the file is copied.

To copy his QCSRC file and all the C source code in it to a file called
CCODE, Joe User could enter the following:

```
CRTDUPOBJ OBJ(QCSRC) FROMLIB(JOEUSER) OBJTYPE(*ALL) NEWOBJ(CCODE)
DATA(*YES)
```

What if Joe tries this command without the parameter names? He enters this:

```
CRTDUPOBJ QCSRC JOEUSER *ALL CCODE
```

and sees this:

```
Library CCODE not found.
```

If the fourth parameter doesn't have a parameter name, CRTDUPOBJ
assumes that it's the name of the library to which you are copying the
object—the TOLIB(). If you leave out the TOLIB(), CRTDUPOBJ assumes that you want to put the copy in the same library as the original. If you leave out the TOLIB() but want to include more than
three parameters, everything after the third must therefore have a
parameter name. Otherwise, the program thinks that your fourth parameter is the TOLIB(). In Joe's last attempt at copying QCSRC,
CRTDUPOBJ saw CCODE in the fourth position, looked for a library by
that name, and didn't find it.

Positional parameters are not an all-or-nothing proposition. You
can include positional parameters without the parameter names and

parameters that include the parameter names in the same command, as long as all positional parameters come before all named parameters. Joe will have no trouble if he enters the command like this:

```
CRTDUPOBJ QCSRC JOEUSER *ALL NEWOBJ(QCSRC1) DATA(*YES)
```

14.1.4.1 Copying members.   The Copy Source File (CPYSRCF) command lets you copy individual source file members. The copy can go in the same source file or to a different one.

CPYSRCF needs to know at least three things:

FROMFILE()   The file with the member you are copying.

TOFILE()   The file where the copy should go. Even if the copy will go in the same file as the original, this must be included.

FROMMBR()   The name of the member being copied.

When you copy a member from one file to another, the new member can have the same name as the old one. If your copy is going to be in the same file as the original (that is, the TOFILE() is the same as the FROMFILE()), the command will need to know something else: the name that you want to give the copy. Use the TOMBR() parameter for this.

If you specify an existing file member as the TOMBR(), CPYSRCF copies the FROMMBR() right over it with no warning.

Joe User's first C source code program on the AS/400 was the member CTEST1 in his QCSRC file. He wants to try a variation on this program, but he wants to keep the original intact, so he makes a copy in the same file called CTEST1A with the following command:

```
CPYSRCF FROMFILE(JOEUSER/QCSRC) TOFILE(JOEUSER/QCSRC) FROMMBR(CTEST1)
TOMBR(CTEST1A)
```

He can then edit CTEST1A to try out his new ideas.

Next, Joe's QCSRC file has a member called CONVERT which has the code for several data conversion routines. He needs this in another file called BIOINPUT and copies it with the following command:

```
CPYSRCF QCSRC BIOINPUT CONVERT
```

Because all the parameters that he needed to enter were required, he entered them as positional parameters without their parameter names and saved himself some typing.

14.1.4.2 Copying members with the program development manager.   Once you've listed a file's members with the Program Development Manager, you can copy one of these members by entering the number 3 next to that member's name in the Opt column. The Program Development Manager then displays the screen shown in Figure

```
                            Copy Members

From file . . . . . . . :    QCSRC
  From library . . . . :       JOEUSER

Type the file name and library name to receive the copied members.

  To file . . . . . . .      QCSRC          Name, F4 for list
    To library . . . . .       JOEUSER

To rename copied member, type New Name, press Enter.

Member          New Name
CTEST1          _____




                                                          Bottom
F3=Exit              F4=Prompt     F5=Refresh     F12=Cancel
F19=Submit to batch
```

Figure 14.10 The Program Development Manager's "Copy Members" display.

14.10 to find out the name that you want to give the new member. If you want to put the copy in a different file or library, enter their names here as well. (If you don't want to put it in a new file or library, note that the FROMFILE's file and library names are already entered as the default values.)

14.1.5 Renaming files

Instead of a command for renaming files, OS/400 has a command for naming objects: RNMOBJ. This makes things easier, because you use the same command to rename files, programs, and libraries.

If you enter RNMOBJ by itself and press F4, you get the command prompt display shown in Figure 14.11. Enter the object's name in the Object field, its library in the Library field (if you leave the default value of *LIBL, OS/400 searches the library list for the appropriate one) and the object's type in the field with that name. (As with copying, you need to specify this because you can have two objects with the same name in the same library, as long as they have two different object types.) In the New object field, enter the new name for the object.

To rename a file called SALES93 to SALES93A, enter SALES93 in the Object field, *FILE in the Object type field, and SALES93A in the New object field. Assuming that SALES93 was in a library in your library list, you could leave the Library field at its default value of *LIBL.

To do the same thing from the command line, enter this command:

```
RNMOBJ OBJ(SALES93) OBJTYPE(*FILE) NEWOBJ(SALES93A)
```

```
                      Rename Object (RNMOBJ)

Type choices, press Enter.

Object . . . . . . . . . . . . .    _____     Name
  Library  . . . . . . . . . .      *LIBL___     Name, *LIBL, *CURLIB
Object type  . . . . . . . . .      _____     *ALRTBL, *AUTL, *CFGL...
New object . . . . . . . . . .      _____     Name




                                                              Bottom
F3=Exit    F4=Prompt    F5=Refresh    F12=Cancel    F13=How to use this display
F24=More keys
```

Figure 14.11 **Rename Object command prompt display.**

After you rename a file with either the command prompt display or
the command line, OS/400 displays a message confirming the rename:

```
Object SALES93 in JOEUSER type *FILE renamed SALES93A.
```

To rename a program, use the same syntax—just be sure to put *PGM
as the object type:

```
RNMOBJ OBJ(RPGTEST) OBJTYPE(*PGM) NEWOBJ(EMPRPT)
```

Renaming a library would be similar, except that you enter an object
type of *LIB.

14.1.5.1 Renaming members.   Use the RNMM command to rename a
member within a file. It needs to know three things:

FILE()	The file where the member can be found
MBR()	The name of the file to rename
NEWMBR()	The member's new name

In the following example, Joe User renames the CTEST1 member of
his QCSRC file with a new name of CTEST1A:

```
RNMM FILE(QCSRC) MBR(CTEST1) NEWMBR(CTEST1A)
```

Because the command needs such simple, obvious information, it's
easy to enter it with positional parameters instead. The following
command works just as well:

```
RNMM QCSRC CTEST1 CTEST1A
```

14.1.5.2 Renaming members with the program development manager.
Once you've listed a file's members with the Program Development
Manager, you can rename one by entering the number 7 next to that
member's name in the `Opt` column. The Program Development
Manager will display the "Rename Members" screen, which has only
one field for you to fill out: the new name of the member.

14.1.6 Deleting files

Delete files with the `DLTF` command. Delete the file `CTEST1A` by entering

```
DLTF FILE(SALES93A)
```

or by entering the positional version:

```
DLTF SALES93A
```

Because programs are a different object type from files, there is a different command to delete them: `DLTPGM`. It uses the same syntax as
`DLTF`. To delete a program called `CTEST1`, enter this:

```
DLTPGM CTEST1
```

14.1.6.1 Deleting members.   Use the `RMVM` command to delete a member from a file. The `RMVM` command needs to know the name of the file
and the name of the member within that file to delete. To delete the
`CTEST1A` member from the `QCSRC` file, enter

```
RMVM FILE(QCSRC) MBR(CTEST1A)
```

or the positional version:

```
RMVM QCSRC CTEST1A
```

14.1.6.2 Deleting members with the program development manager.   Once
you've listed a file's members with the Program Development
Manager, you can delete one of these members by entering the number 4 next to that member's name in the `Opt` column.

The Program Development Manager will display the "Delete
Members" screen. This has no fields to fill out; it shows the name of
the member that you want to delete and a message at the top that
tells you to "Press Enter to confirm your choices for Delete." (The
plural "choices" is used because you could have entered the number 4
next to more than one member.) To abort the deletion, press F12 to
return to the "Work with Members Using PDM" list of the file's
members.

14.1.7 Editing your library list

Use the Edit Library List (EDTLIBL) command to do just what it says. (The Change Library List command—CHGLIBL—completely replaces the library list with a new one, as opposed to merely making edits. That's for advanced users, and is particularly useful in CL programs where altering the library list needs to be automated.)

The Display Library List command (DSPLIBL) displays a list of the libraries in your member list, if you just want to see what your library list looks like. (Don't confuse this with DSPLIB, the "Display Library" command, which lists the objects in a library.) Although DSPLIBL is not really an essential command, taking a look at its output makes it easier to understand some important things about library lists. Figure 14.12 shows the result when Joe User enters the DSPLIB command, which takes no parameters.

When Joe enters EDTLIBL, he will see a list of libraries, but he won't see as many as he sees when he enters DSPLIBL. That's because a complete library list has several parts, and EDTLIBL only lets him edit one part: the user part. Figure 14.13 shows what happens when he enters EDTLIBL.

The user part of the library list, which comes at the end of the complete library list, is the part that you can control. You can reorder, delete, and add to its list of libraries.

As it shows in Figure 14.13, you manipulate the libraries and their order in the list by entering their names in the Library column and entering new numbers in the Sequence Number column. Each time

```
                        Display Library List
                                                     System:    NEPAS4


Type options, press Enter.
  5=Display objects in library

Opt   Library     Type        Text
      QSYS        SYS         System Library
      QSYS2       SYS         System Library for CPI's
      QUSRSYS     SYS         *IN USE
      QHLPSYS     SYS
      JOEUSER     CUR         Joe User's library
      URBASE      USR         UpRiteBase system library
      QTEMP       USR
      QGPL        USR         GENERAL PURPOSE LIBRARY
      USERTOOLS   USR
      QUSRTOOL    USR




                                                            Bottom
F3=Exit    F12=Cancel    F17=Top    F18=Bottom
(C) COPYRIGHT IBM CORP. 1980, 1992.
```

Figure 14.12 DSPLIBL output for Joe User.

```
                      Edit Library List

Type new/changed information, press Enter.
  To add a library, type name and desired sequence number.
  To remove a library, space over library name.
  To change position of a library, type new sequence number.


Sequence                    Sequence                    Sequence
Number      Library         Number      Library         Number      Library
  010                         120                         230
  020       URBASE            130                         240
  030       QTEMP             140                         250
  040       QGPL              150
  050       USERTOOLS         160
  060       QUSRTOOL          170
  070                         180
  080                         190
  090                         200
  100                         210
  110                         220


F3=Exit              F5=Refresh              F12=Cancel
```

Figure 14.13 Edit Library List (EDTLIBL) screen.

you press Enter, the Edit Library List program makes (or tries to make) the changes that you indicated and reorders the numbers. The first library name on the list is always next to the number 20; you use the number 10 to indicate a library name that you want to move to the beginning of the list. For example, Figure 14.14 shows that Joe entered a "10" over the "40" next to the QGPL library's name.

Figure 14.15 shows that after he presses Enter, EDTLBL moves QGPL to the beginning of the list, ahead of the URBASE library. The list has been renumbered, and QGPL becomes the new line 20, now that it's first on the list.

To move a library name between two others, enter a number in the sequence column next to it that falls between the two numbers at its destination. For example, to move the URBASE library name between the USERTOOLS and QUSRTOOL libraries, you could enter the number 55 (or any other number between 50 and 60) next to it and press Enter.

To delete a library from the library list, type over its name with the space bar and press Enter.

To insert a new library:

1. Enter its name in any blank space in the Library column.

2. Give it a number showing where you want it to be placed in the list.

3. Press Enter.

```
                        Edit Library List

Type new/changed information, press Enter.
  To add a library, type name and desired sequence number.
  To remove a library, space over library name.
  To change position of a library, type new sequence number.


Sequence                   Sequence                   Sequence
 Number    Library          Number    Library          Number    Library
  010                        120                        230
  020     URBASE             130                        240
  030     QTEMP              140                        250
  010     QGPL               150
  050     USERTOOLS          160
  060     QUSRTOOL           170
  070                        180
  080                        190
  090                        200
  100                        210
  110                        220


F3=Exit           F5=Refresh              F12=Cancel
```

Figure 14.14 Entering the new sequence number to move QGPL to the top of the library list.

```
                        Edit Library List

Type new/changed information, press Enter.
  To add a library, type name and desired sequence number.
  To remove a library, space over library name.
  To change position of a library, type new sequence number.


Sequence                   Sequence                   Sequence
 Number    Library          Number    Library          Number    Library
  010                        120                        230
  020     QGPL               130                        240
  030     URBASE             140                        250
  040     QTEMP              150
  050     USERTOOLS          160
  060     QUSRTOOL           170
  070                        180
  080                        190
  090                        200
  100                        210
  110                        220


F3=Exit           F5=Refresh              F12=Cancel
```

Figure 14.15 The effect of pressing Enter after entering a 10 next to the QGPL library to move it to the front of the list.

After you make any successful change to your library list, you'll see the message "Library list changed" at the bottom of your screen.

A typical unsuccessful change would be the attempted addition of a nonexistent library. If you tried to add the nonexistent library POTRZEBIE to your list, you get the message "Library POTRZEBIE not found."

Any changes you make to your library list will only remain in effect for the current OS/400 session. For help in making permanent changes to your library list, see your system administrator.

14.1.7.1 Changing your current library.   There are two ways to reset your current library:

- As we saw in Section 13.1, "Starting Up," you can enter a specific library in the "Current library" field of the signon screen when you enter you user ID and password.

- You can use the CHGCURLIB command. This command's command prompt display shows that it only needs one parameter: the name of the library to make current. To change your current library to one called URBASE from the command line, enter

```
CHGCURLIB CURLIB(URBASE)
```

or even just this:

```
CHGCURLIB URBASE
```

14.1.8 Creating and deleting libraries

There's a good chance that the first time you sign on, you will find that the system administrator has created a personal library named after your user ID and that you do not have the privileges to create or delete other libraries. In this situation, you keep your files in your own library and leave the creation and deletion of libraries to the system administrator.

On the other hand, you may be told "Here's your user ID name. The first thing you have to do when you sign on is to create a library for yourself." The Create Library (CRTLIB) command makes it easy. To create a library called MYLIB, enter the following:

```
CRTLIB LIB(MYLIB)
```

Because libraries are objects, just as files are, you follow the same rules for making up library names that you do for filenames. (For more information, see Section 13.2, "Filenames.") The one extra rule—a guideline, really, because the system won't prevent you from doing this—is to avoid beginning a library name with the letter "Q," because this indicates a system library, and could give other users the wrong idea.

If the command worked, you will see the message "Library MYLIB created" at the bottom of your screen.

To delete a library, use the Delete Library (DLTLIB) command:

```
DLTLIB LIB(MYLIB)
```

If successful, you will see the message "Library MYLIB deleted" at the bottom of your screen.

Because both of these commands have only one required parameter, there is no problem with entering that parameter without its parameter name. Entering

```
CRTLIB MYLIB
```

or

```
DLTLIB MYLIB
```

will both work.

15

The OS/400 SEU Text Editor

As we saw in Section 13.3.1, "Physical, source physical, and logical files," the most popular use of the OS/400 Source Entry Utility (SEU) text editor—in fact, the reason for its name—is for creating and editing source code. However, you don't have to limit your use of SEU to this; you can use it to create any text file you like.

15.1 Entering SEU

To enter SEU, use the Start SEU command (STRSEU). If you enter it with no parameters and press F4, you'll see its command prompt display screen, as shown in Figure 15.1.

You need to tell STRSEU the file with the member that you want to edit and the name of the member. Note how the default values for both of these are *PRV; these mean "previous value." In other words, if you had entered STRSEU with no parameters and pressed Enter, it would have brought up the file member that you had most recently edited.

STRSEU will not create a new file for you, but it will create a new member in an existing file. In addition to entering the member's name in the "Source Member" field, enter its type in the "Source Type" field. The default source type is TXT. (Even if the member exists, nothing prevents you from entering a new value in the "Source Type" field. In fact, this is the easiest way to change a file member's type.)

Of course, you could skip the command prompt display screen by entering the file and member name at the command line. For example, let's say you have a file called YEATS and you want to edit a member called BYZANTIUM. If you include the parameter names, you would enter the following:

```
                    Start Source Entry Utility (STRSEU)

Type choices, press Enter.

Source file . . . . . . . . . .    *PRV         Name, *PRV
  Library . . . . . . . . . . .                 Name, *LIBL, *CURLIB, *PRV
Source member . . . . . . . . .    *PRV         Name, *PRV, *SELECT
Source type . . . . . . . . . .    *SAME        Name, *SAME, BAS, BASP, C...
Option . . . . . . . . . . . .     *BLANK       *BLANK, ' ', 2, 5, 6
Text 'description' . . . . . . .    *BLANK






                                                                       Bottom
F3=Exit    F4=Prompt    F5=Refresh    F12=Cancel    F13=How to use this display
F24=More keys
```

Figure 15.1 The STRSEU text editor's command prompt display screen.

```
STRSEU SRCFILE(YEATS) SRCMBR(BYZANTIUM)
```

If you wanted to leave out the parameter names and enter the file and member names as positional parameters, you would enter this:

```
STRSEU YEATS BYZANTIUM
```

SEU starts up, and if the member exists, it shows the beginning of the member. Otherwise, it shows a blank editing area and a message at the bottom informing you that the member has been added to the file. Figure 15.2 shows an example of this.

The SEU==> prompt points to the SEU command line, where you can enter certain SEU commands. The F10 key moves the cursor back and forth between the SEU command line and the data area.

The column of apostrophes (' ' ' ' ' ' ') down the left shows the location of the sequence number field for each line. This will show numbers next to a file member's lines once they exist; before then, the apostrophes show places where you can enter new lines of text. This is where you enter the commands known as *line commands*, which you use to delete, copy, and move lines of your file member.

The Columns: 1 71 message in the upper left show that you are looking at columns 1 through 71 of the file member named in the upper-right. SEU can edit file members that are too wide for the display and has commands to scroll to the left or right to look at different parts of it. In these situations, the Columns part of the screen is pretty handy.

```
Columns . . . :   1  71           Edit                  JOEUSER/YEATS
SEU==>                                                   BYZANTIUM
FMT **   ...+... 1 ...+... 2 ...+... 3 ...+... 4 ...+... 5 ...+... 6 ...+... 7
         *************** Beginning of data ********************************
''''''''
''''''''
''''''''
''''''''
''''''''
''''''''
''''''''
''''''''
''''''''
''''''''
''''''''
''''''''
''''''''
''''''''
''''''''
         ***************** End of data ****************************************

F3=Exit    F4=Prompt    F5=Refresh    F9=Retrieve   F10=Cursor
F16=Repeat find        F17=Repeat change            F24=More keys
Member BYZANTIUM added to file JOEUSER/YEATS.
```

Figure 15.2 Opening SEU screen for a new member.

15.1.1 Entering SEU from the program development manager

When you've listed a file's members with the Program Development Manager, you can edit one of these members by entering the number 2 next to that member's name in the Opt column. The Program Development Manager will start up SEU with that member for you to edit.

15.2 Line Commands

In addition to command-line commands entered at the SEU==> prompt, many SEU operations are performed with line commands entered in the sequence number column. You can add, delete, copy, and move lines by entering one- or two-character commands in this column and pressing the Enter key. (This will be familiar to users of the MVS ISPF editor, and CMS users who detect a similarity to the XEDIT text editor will find that line commands are SEU's counterpart to XEDIT line commands.)

Line commands are not limited to the sequence number column of the contents of your file; you can also enter them in the sequence number column of the *** Beginning of data *** and *** End of data *** lines.

You can enter a line command anywhere on the sequence number. For example, you can enter the command to delete two lines (D2) on the line numbered "0001.00" like this

D201.00

or

```
00D2.00
```

This can obviously lead to confusion if you enter line commands that use numbers (like D2) on a sequence number column that is displayed as numbers instead of as apostrophes (like "0001.00") so be careful.

If you ever enter a line command and then realize, before you press Enter, that you didn't mean to enter it, just type spaces over it. The next time you press Enter, SEU restores the numbers that were there before you entered the line command.

15.2.1 Adding new lines

We saw that apostrophes next to a line on the display mean that you can enter new lines of text there. Since new lines are automatically numbered when you press Enter, all existing lines will have numbers to the left of them. You can type over the text of existing lines as easily as you can enter new text on blank lines.

When you press Enter, SEU removes any blank lines that still have apostrophes in the sequence number field and that are below the last newly entered line, and the End of data message jumps up to just below the last real line of the file member.

Figure 15.3 shows the same screen as Figure 15.2 with several lines of text that Joe User has added. He has not pressed Enter yet.

Figure 15.4 shows the same screen after Enter is pressed. Notice how the entered lines have been numbered, and the blank lines are gone.

```
Columns . . . :    1  71              Edit                    JOEUSER/YEATS
SEU==>                                                          BYZANTIUM
FMT **   ...+... 1 ...+... 2 ...+... 3 ...+... 4 ...+... 5 ...+... 6 ...+... 7
         *************** Beginning of data ********************************
''''''' Marbles of the dancing floor
''''''' Break bitter furies of complexity
''''''' Those images that yet
''''''' Fresh images beget
''''''' That dolphin-torn, that gong-tormented sea.
'''''''
'''''''
'''''''
'''''''
'''''''
'''''''
'''''''
'''''''
'''''''
'''''''
         ***************** End of data *****************************************


F3=Exit    F4=Prompt    F5=Refresh    F9=Retrieve    F10=Cursor
F16=Repeat find         F17=Repeat change           F24=More keys
Member BYZANTIUM added to file JOEUSER/YEATS.
```

Figure 15.3 Empty SEU screen with some text entered, before Enter is pressed.

```
Columns . . . :    1  71              Edit                    JOEUSER/YEATS
SEU==>                                                        BYZANTIUM
FMT **    ...+... 1 ...+... 2 ...+... 3 ...+... 4 ...+... 5 ...+... 6 ...+... 7
*************** Beginning of data ***********************************
0001.00 Marbles of the dancing floor
0002.00 Break bitter furies of complexity
0003.00 Those images that yet
0004.00 Fresh images beget
0005.00 That dolphin-torn, that gong-tormented sea.
***************** End of data ***************************************




F3=Exit    F4=Prompt    F5=Refresh    F9=Retrieve    F10=Cursor
F16=Repeat find         F17=Repeat change            F24=More keys
```

Figure 15.4 Effect of pressing Enter when viewing the screen shown in Figure 15.3.

```
FMT **    ...+... 1 ...+... 2 ...+... 3 ...+... 4 ...+... 5 ...+... 6 ...+... 7
*************** Beginning of data ***********************************
0001.00 Marbles of the dancing floor
I302.00 Break bitter furies of complexity
0003.00 Those images that yet
0004.00 Fresh images beget
0005.00 That dolphin-torn, that gong-tormented sea.
***************** End of data ***************************************
```

Figure 15.5 Entering the line command to insert blank lines after line 2.

You can easily insert blank lines for new lines of text with the I line command. If you type an I over the number in a line's sequence number field, the next time you press Enter, a new blank line is inserted after that line. (To insert new lines before the current first line, enter the I command in the same position on the Beginning of data line.)

If you enter a number after the I, that many new lines are inserted. For example, in Figure 15.5, Joe User has entered I3 to the left of line 2, but he has not pressed Enter yet. Figure 15.6 shows the effect of pressing Enter to insert those three lines.

In Figure 15.6, new lines have not really been added yet; note that line 2 is still line 2 and line 3 is still line 3. You have three potential new lines that serve the same purpose as the blank lines that you saw when you first started up SEU with a new file member.

If you enter text on only one of these new lines, as shown in Figure 15.7, and then press Enter, you'll get the result shown in Figure 15.8: the line with new text and the blank line before it are assigned line numbers and the blank line after it is removed.

```
FMT **    ...+... 1 ...+... 2 ...+... 3 ...+... 4 ...+... 5 ...+... 6 ...+... 7
          *************** Beginning of data ***********************************
0001.00 Marbles of the dancing floor
0002.00 Break bitter furies of complexity
'''''''
'''''''
'''''''
0003.00 Those images that yet
0004.00 Fresh images beget
0005.00 That dolphin-torn, that gong-tormented sea.
          ***************** End of data ***************************************
```
Figure 15.6 The effect of pressing Enter after entering the command shown in Figure 15.5.

```
FMT **    ...+... 1 ...+... 2 ...+... 3 ...+... 4 ...+... 5 ...+... 6 ...+... 7
          *************** Beginning of data ***********************************
0001.00 Marbles of the dancing floor
0002.00 Break bitter furies of complexity
'''''''
''''''' Bitter furies of complexity!  I'll say!  That crazy Yeats!
'''''''
0003.00 Those images that yet
0004.00 Fresh images beget
0005.00 That dolphin-torn, that gong-tormented sea.
          ***************** End of data ***************************************
```
Figure 15.7 Entering text on only one of the new lines inserted in Figure 15.6.

```
FMT **    ...+... 1 ...+... 2 ...+... 3 ...+... 4 ...+... 5 ...+... 6 ...+... 7
          *************** Beginning of data ***********************************
0001.00 Marbles of the dancing floor
0002.00 Break bitter furies of complexity
0002.01
0002.02 Bitter furies of complexity!  I'll say!  That crazy Yeats!
0003.00 Those images that yet
0004.00 Fresh images beget
0005.00 That dolphin-torn, that gong-tormented sea.
          ***************** End of data ***************************************
```
Figure 15.8 The effect of pressing Enter after entering the new line shown in Figure 15.7.

Note how the new line numbers are decimal numbers between 2.00 and 3.00. When you save the file member, SEU offers you the choice of renumbering the lines with whole numbers or leaving them as they are. Renumbering them with whole numbers is the default.

If you press Enter after adding text to the last of the new lines that are waiting for text, SEU inserts a new blank line under it and positions your cursor at its beginning. This is handy for entering many lines of text, because you can just type a line, press Enter, type another line, press Enter, and repeat this until you have entered all of your text.

15.2.2 Moving your cursor around

Your up, down, left, and right cursor keys move the cursor in the direction in which they point.

The Tab key helps you move around more quickly. To move your cursor to the beginning of the previous line, use the Backtab key (with a PC that is emulating a 3270 terminal, press the Shift key and the Tab key simultaneously). If your cursor is on a line of text, Tab or Backtab move your cursor to the sequence number column. If your cursor is on the sequence number column, pressing either key jumps your cursor to the beginning of the appropriate line.

15.3 Inserting, Deleting, and Typing over Words and Characters

To add text to blank lines, just move your cursor to the line and type. When you need to move your cursor back to the command line, press F10.

To delete an individual character, move your cursor there and press your Delete key. On a 3270 terminal, the delete key has a lowercase "a" with a proofreader's symbol for deletion: a line through it that forms a loop. When emulating a 3270 terminal, your emulation software probably has your PC's Delete key doing this job.

To type over existing text, just move your cursor where you want the new text and type.

To insert text, move your cursor to the place where you want to insert it and press the Insert key. On a 3270 terminal, this key has the letter "a" with a carat symbol (^) over it. When you press it, a carat symbol should appear at the bottom of your screen to indicate that you are in insert mode. (When emulating a 3270, your cursor may change shape.) Text that you type in moves any text currently to the right of the cursor further to the right.

To return to overstrike mode while using a 3270 terminal, press the key marked "Reset." The carat symbol should disappear, and newly typed text takes the place of the characters at the cursor. (When your keyboard "locks up," or refuses to accept input, the Reset key is also useful for freeing up the keyboard.) On most PCs emulating a 3270, the Insert key puts you in insert mode and the Escape key stands in for the Reset key.

15.3.1 Duplicating lines

Think of it as "repeating" lines, and it will be easier to remember the line command: RP. Enter RP by itself and press Enter to make a single copy of a line. For example, if you enter RP on the third line in the text shown in Figure 15.9, and then press Enter, you get the result shown in Figure 15.10.

Entering a number after the RP command tells SEU to repeat the line that many times. For example, if RP3 had been entered on line 2 of Figure 15.9 instead of RP, the result would have looked like Figure 15.11.

```
*************** Beginning of data ***********************************
0001.00 Marbles of the dancing floor
00RP.00 Break bitter furies of complexity
0003.00 Those images that yet
0004.00 Fresh images beget
0005.00 That dolphin-torn, that gong-tormented sea.
***************** End of data **************************************
```

Figure 15.9 Entering the command to repeat a line.

```
*************** Beginning of data ***********************************
0001.00 Marbles of the dancing floor
0002.00 Break bitter furies of complexity
0002.01 Break bitter furies of complexity
0003.00 Those images that yet
0004.00 Fresh images beget
0005.00 That dolphin-torn, that gong-tormented sea.
***************** End of data **************************************
```

Figure 15.10 Effect of pressing Enter after entering RP command in Figure 15.9.

```
*************** Beginning of data ***********************************
0001.00 Marbles of the dancing floor
0002.00 Break bitter furies of complexity
0002.01 Break bitter furies of complexity
0002.02 Break bitter furies of complexity
0002.03 Break bitter furies of complexity
0003.00 Those images that yet
0004.00 Fresh images beget
0005.00 That dolphin-torn, that gong-tormented sea.
***************** End of data **************************************
```

Figure 15.11 Effect of pressing Enter if RP3 had been entered at line 2 in Figure 15.9.

```
*************** Beginning of data ***********************************
0001.00 Marbles of the dancing floor
000D200 Break bitter furies of complexity
0003.00 Those images that yet
0004.00 Fresh images beget
0005.00 That dolphin-torn, that gong-tormented sea.
***************** End of data **************************************
```

Figure 15.12 Entering the D2 line command to delete two lines in SEU.

15.3.2 Deleting lines

The letter D in a line's sequence number field deletes that line the next time you press Enter. A number immediately following it tells SEU to delete that many lines, starting with the line where the command is entered. In Figure 15.12, two lines are about to be deleted.

After you press Enter, they're gone. Figure 15.13 shows the result; note how the lines have not been renumbered.

Put the letter D twice in a sequence number field without any number to indicate that the line begins or ends a block that you want to delete. If you press Enter while only one line has the DD, SEU leaves it there until it has a partner, and displays the message "Block com-

```
*************** Beginning of data ************************************
0001.00 Marbles of the dancing floor
0004.00 Fresh images beget
0005.00 That dolphin-torn, that gong-tormented sea.
***************** End of data ***************************************
```

Figure 15.13   Result of the D2 line command entered in Figure 15.12.

```
*************** Beginning of data ************************************
0001.00 Marbles of the dancing floor
DD02.00 Break bitter furies of complexity
0003.00 Those images that yet
00DD.00 Fresh images beget
0005.00 That dolphin-torn, that gong-tormented sea.
***************** End of data ***************************************
```

Figure 15.14   Entering the DD line command to delete a block of lines in SEU.

mand not complete" as a reminder. In Figure 15.14, SEU is ready to delete all but the first and last lines of text the next time you press Enter.

After you press Enter, the lines with the DD commands and all the lines between them are removed.

This command is particularly useful when the beginning and end of the block that you want to delete are not on the same screen, because the alternative (counting the number of lines so that you can put a number after a single D) is a lot of trouble.

15.3.3 Copying lines

Copying is similar to deletion except that you use the letter C to indicate the line or lines to copy and you must indicate a destination for the copied text. SEU gives you three options for indicating the text to copy:

- Enter a single C in a line's sequence number field if you only want to copy that one line.

- Enter a single C followed by a number to indicate how many lines to copy.

- Enter CC at the first and last lines of the block to copy.

In addition to indicating the line or lines to copy, you must indicate where to copy them. Two line commands make this possible:

B   When Enter is pressed, copy the block to the line before the line with this command.

A   When Enter is pressed, copy the block to the line after the line with this command.

In Figure 15.15, the third, fourth, and fifth lines are about to get copied above the first line, to the beginning of the file member.

Figure 15.16 shows how it looks after you press Enter.

```
*************** Beginning of data *************************************
000B.00 Marbles of the dancing floor
0002.00 Break bitter furies of complexity
CC03.00 Those images that yet
0004.00 Fresh images beget
0CC5.00 That dolphin-torn, that gong-tormented sea.
***************** End of data **************************************
```

Figure 15.15 Using the CC and B line commands to copy a block in SEU.

```
*************** Beginning of data *************************************
0000.01 Those images that yet
0000.02 Fresh images beget
0000.03 That dolphin-torn, that gong-tormented sea.
0001.00 Marbles of the dancing floor
0002.00 Break bitter furies of complexity
0003.00 Those images that yet
0004.00 Fresh images beget
0005.00 That dolphin-torn, that gong-tormented sea.
***************** End of data **************************************
```

Figure 15.16 Result of the CC and B line commands entered in Figure 15.15.

15.3.4 Moving lines

Moving is similar to copying, except that after you press Enter, the original lines are no longer there—they're moved to their new location. As with copying, there are three ways to specify the block to move, but these use the letter M:

- Enter a single M in a line's sequence number field if you only want to move that one line.

- Enter a single M followed by a number to indicate how many lines to move.

- Enter MM at the first and last lines of the block to move.

To specify the destination of the block to move, use the letters B or A the same way you do to specify the destination of a block to copy.

15.4 Searching for Text

To search for text, use the FIND command from the SEU command line. (Use the F10 key to move your cursor to the command line.) If you like, you can abbreviate FIND to just F. If your search target has spaces in it, enclose it in apostrophes or quotation marks.

Figure 15.17 shows the command to search for the string "images" just before Enter is pressed.

After you press Enter, if the search was successful, the cursor jumps to the beginning of the found string and a message at the bot-

```
Columns . . . :   1  71            Edit                    JOEUSER/YEATS
SEU==> find images                                         BYZANTIUM
FMT **   ...+... 1 ...+... 2 ...+... 3 ...+... 4 ...+... 5 ...+... 6 ...+... 7
         *************** Beginning of data *********************************
0001.00 Marbles of the dancing floor
0002.00 Break bitter furies of complexity
0003.00 Those images that yet
0004.00 Fresh images beget
0005.00 That dolphin-torn, that gong-tormented sea.
         ****************** End of data ***************************************
```

Figure 15.17 Entering the command to search for the string "images" on the SEU command line.

```
Columns . . . :   1  71            Edit                    JOEUSER/YEATS
SEU==>                                                     BYZANTIUM
FMT **   ...+... 1 ...+... 2 ...+... 3 ...+... 4 ...+... 5 ...+... 6 ..+... 7
         *************** Beginning of data *********************************
0001.00 Marbles of the dancing floor
0002.00 Break bitter furies of complexity
0003.00 Those images that yet
0004.00 Fresh images beget
0005.00 That dolphin-torn, that gong-tormented sea.
         ****************** End of data ***************************************













 F3=Exit   F4=Prompt   F5=Refresh   F9=Retrieve   F10=Cursor
 F16=Repeat find       F17=Repeat change          F24=More keys
 String images found.
```

Figure 15.18 Result of a successful search in SEU.

tom of the screen informs you that the string was found. Figure 15.18 shows an example.

If this search had been unsuccessful, the cursor would have remained on the command line and the status line at the bottom of the screen would have told you "String images not found."

As the bottom of the screen shows, pressing F16 searches for the next occurrence of the same string.

15.4.1 Case sensitivity

The FIND command can do case-sensitive and case-insensitive searches. You control this with the SET MATCH command. To make the searches case-sensitive, enter

```
SET MATCH ON
```

at the SEU command line. All uses of the FIND command will then look for exact case matches. To set it to ignore case when searching, you can guess what the command is:

```
SET MATCH OFF
```

15.5 Saving Your Changes

To save your file member and then continue working, simply enter SAVE at the SEU command line. To save the edited file under a new name, enter SAVE followed by that name. For example, entering

```
SAVE OHYEAH
```

saves the file member with the name OHYEAH. If there is no such member in the file, SEU creates it and displays a message similar to the following at the bottom of the screen:

```
Member OHYEAH added to file JOEUSER/YEATS.
```

If a member by this name had already existed, SEU would have warned you with the following message:

```
Member OHYEAH already exists. Press Enter to confirm.
```

If you want to abort this save, space over the SAVE command at the SEU command line before the next time you press Enter.

15.6 Quitting SEU

To quit SEU, press F3. SEU displays a screen similar to the one shown in Figure 15.19.

If you had any unsaved changes, the default value for "Change/create member" will be "Y" for "Yes."

The other fields in Figure 15.19 are self-explanatory. As with any entry display, you can use your Tab or cursor keys to move your cursor to any field and then type in a new value or press F1 to find out more about that field.

15.7 Other SEU Features

15.7.1 SEU on-line help

On-line help in SEU follows the same conventions that it does elsewhere in OS/400:

- To learn more about function keys, move your cursor to the their descriptions at the bottom of the screen and press F1.

```
                              Exit

Type choices, press Enter.

   Change/create member  . . . . . . .    N            Y=Yes, N=No
      Member  . . . . . . . . . . . . .    BYZANTIUM    Name, F4 for list
      File  . . . . . . . . . . . . .      YEATS        Name, F4 for list
         Library . . . . . . . . . . .       JOEUSER    Name
   Text  . . . . . . . . . . . . .

   Resequence member . . . . . . . .      Y            Y=Yes, N=No
      Start . . . . . . . . . . . . .      0001.00      0000.01-9999.99
      Increment . . . . . . . . . .        01.00        00.01-99.99

   Print member  . . . . . . . . . .      N            Y=Yes, N=No

   Return to editing . . . . . . . .      N            Y=Yes, N=No

   Go to member list . . . . . . . .      Y            Y=Yes, N=No




F3=Exit   F4=Prompt   F5=Refresh   F12=Cancel
```

Figure 15.19 The "Exit SEU" screen.

- To learn more about SEU commands, move your cursor to the sequence number field or the SEU command line and press F1.

- To learn more about a specific command, enter that command at the SEU command line and press F1 instead of Enter.

15.7.2 Syntax prompting

SEU has built-in intelligence that can be a great help in writing programs in any language. Because it knows the extended attribute of the file member you are editing, it knows the programming language you are using to write your source code. This means that it can help you with that particular language and point out syntax errors as you write so that you don't have to wait for your compilation to bomb to see what's wrong with your source code.

This is particularly useful when writing CL programs. For more information, see Section 16.2, "Command Files."

16

Using an OS/400 System

16.1 Printing Text Files

Many OS/400 programs offer printing as one of their features; Section 16.1.1, "Printing a file member from the program development manager or SEU," describes two handy ways to print file members.

To print something from the OS/400 command line, we can use a command that we've already seen: CPYSRCF (Copy Source File). The following command uses the predefined value *PRINT to tell OS/400: "copy the BYZANTIUM member of the YEATS file, but not to another file member—instead, send it to the printer."

```
CPYSRCF FROMFILE(JOEUSER/YEATS) TOFILE(*PRINT) FROMMBR(BYZANTIUM)
```

Using positional parameters, the command would look like this:

```
CPYSRCF YEATS *PRINT BYZANTIUM
```

When you tell the system to print something, it doesn't really send it directly to the printer. Instead, it goes to a program called a print spooler, which acts as a traffic cop for the various print jobs as they come up.

Once you've sent something to a print spooler, that doesn't mean that it's going to be printed. A program known as a printer writer must take the print job from the spooler and pass it along to the printer.

This and several other useful tasks (like checking the print queue and cancelling print jobs, as you'll see in the following sections) can be done with the Work with Spooled Files (WRKSPLF) command, which displays the "Work with Printer Output" display. WRKSPLF doesn't need any parameters, although there are several optional ones that you can learn about by entering the command and pressing

```
                    Work with Printer Output
                                              System:   NEPAS4
User . . . . . :    JOEUSER

Type options below, then press Enter.  To work with printers, press F22.
  2=Change    3=Hold    4=Delete    5=Display         6=Release    7=Message
  9=Work with printing status      10=Start printing  11=Restart printing


`    Printer/
Opt    Output      Status
     Not Assigned
       QSYSPRT      Not assigned to printer (use Opt 10)






                                                            Bottom
F1=Help       F3=Exit    F5=Refresh    F9=Command line   F11=Dates/pages/forms
F12=Cancel    F21=Select assistance level    F22=Work with printers
```

Figure 16.1 WRKSPLF display for controlling printer output.

F4 instead of Enter. (Another way to display the "Work with Printer Output" screen is by selecting choice 1 from the Operational Assistant. Type GO ASSIST to start up the Operational Assistant.)

Figure 16.1 shows a sample "Work with Printer Output" display after Joe User entered the command above to print the BYZANTIUM member of the YEATS file.

Notice that it doesn't mention "YEATS" or "BYZANTIUM" anywhere. Instead, it shows the name assigned by the program that put it in the print spooler (in this case, CPYSRCF): QSYSPRT. To make sure that QSYSPRT is the print job that you think it is, you can display it by moving your cursor into the Opt column next to it and entering the number 5. This displays the text that is waiting to go to the printer on a screen similar to the one used by the Display Physical File Member (DSPPFM) command.

The column showing QSYSPRT is labeled "Printer/Output." It shows the names of the various printers available, and indented under each printer name, the jobs waiting to go there. Jobs that are not bound for any particular printer are indented under the name "Not Assigned."

Figure 16.1 shows that QSYSPRT is not headed for any printer. The top of the display shows that entering the number 10 next to QSYSPRT will "start printing" it. Figure 16.2 shows what happens when we do this to a printer output file that has not been assigned to a printer.

As the "Assign Output to a Printer" screen shows, pressing F4 displays a list of the valid printers that are connected to your AS/400, allowing you to pick one as the destination for your print job. If you

```
                    Assign Output to a Printer

  Printer output . . :   QSYSPRT

This printer output is not assigned to a printer.
To print the output, type the printer name below and then press Enter.

  Printer  . . . . .  _____      Name, F4 for list


















F1=Help    F3=Exit    F12=Cancel
```

Figure 16.2 Assigning printer output to a particular printer.

```
                    Work with Printer Output
                                            System:    NEPAS4
User . . . . . :   JOEUSER

Type options below, then press Enter.  To work with printers, press F22.
  2=Change    3=Hold    4=Delete    5=Display      6=Release    7=Message
  9=Work with printing status     10=Start printing    11=Restart printing


     Printer/
Opt    Output     Status
     NEPPRT1
      QPSUPRTF    Printing starting or ending (use F5)








                                                            Bottom
F1=Help      F3=Exit    F5=Refresh    F9=Command line    F11=Dates/pages/forms
F12=Cancel   F21=Select assistance level    F22=Work with printers
```

Figure 16.3 The print job on its way to the printer.

don't know the name assigned to the printer where you want to send
your output, ask your system administrator.

Figure 16.3 shows how the "Work with Printer Output" screen
looks once the print job is in progress. The printer assigned in Figure
16.2 was called NEPPRT1.

The Status column shows the status of the print job at the instant the screen is displayed. To update the display press F5, the "Refresh" key. Other typical status messages are "Waiting to print" for a job that has been assigned to a printer but hasn't reached its turn yet and "Printing page 1 of 1" (with whatever appropriate numbers) for a job currently being printed.

If your printer output doesn't automatically get sent to a printer, it would be pretty annoying to have to go through all of these steps every time you print something. Your user profile stores the name of your default printer destination, and you can change your profile with the CHGPRF command with the following steps:

1. Enter CHGPRF and press F4 to see the CHGPRF parameters. It will only show you a few of the parameters, and "Print Device" won't be one of them.

2. The bottom of this screen will tell you that pressing F10 shows you "Additional Parameters." Press F10, and you will see additional parameters, but you still won't see "Print Device."

3. You will see the More... message in the lower right, and after pressing Page Down (or Scroll Up) you will see the "Print Device" field. Enter the name of the printer you learned about from the "Assign Output to a Printer" screen (or from your system administrator) here and all of your printed output will then be sent to that printer.

4. Press Enter to show that you are done editing the CHGPRF parameters.

16.1.1 Printing a file member from the program development manager or SEU

When you've listed a file's members with the Program Development Manager, you can print one of these members by entering the number 6 next to that member's name in the Opt column. The Program Development Manager will send that member to a print queue, if one has been assigned.

When you finish editing a file member in SEU, the "Exit SEU" screen offers "Print member" among its various options. The default value is "N" for "No," but you can easily Tab your cursor to that field and change it to "Y" if you want to print that member.

16.1.2 Checking the print queue

As we saw in Section 16.1, "Printing Text Files," the Work with Spooled Files (WRKSPLF) command lists jobs that are waiting to print. Figure 16.4 shows an example.

Across the top of the screen is the key to the various actions you can take on a waiting print job. We already saw that option 5 shows you what the waiting print job looks like.

```
                    Work with Printer Output
                                              System:    NEPAS4
User . . . . . :    JOEUSER

Type options below, then press Enter.  To work with printers, press F22.
  2=Change    3=Hold    4=Delete    5=Display        6=Release    7=Message
  9=Work with printing status    10=Start printing   11=Restart printing


     Printer/
Opt    Output       Status
     NEPPRT1
       QSYSPRT      Printing page 1 of 1
       QSYS2        Waiting to print
     NEPPRT2
       QSYS3        Held (use Opt 6)




                                                            Bottom
F1=Help      F3=Exit    F5=Refresh    F9=Command line    F11=Dates/pages/forms
F12=Cancel   F21=Select assistance level    F22=Work with printers
```

Figure 16.4 The Work with Printer Output screen.

Option 2 is a handy one. It displays the "Change Printer Output" screen, which lets you change certain aspects of the print job. One of the most useful fields on the "Change Printer Output" screen is "Printer to Use." This lets you redirect your print job to a different printer.

Options 3 and 6 are also useful. In Figure 16.4, whoever sent job QSYS3 to the printer has selected 3 to hold the job. It will remain held until that user selects 6 to release the job, allowing it to print. Note how the status message of a held job reminds you that option 6 releases it. Holding a job is useful if you want to select option 2 to change some aspect of how the job is printed. It's also a way to be a nice guy when you have a huge job in front of someone else's smaller job, because holding your job lets the smaller job print first.

16.1.3 Canceling your print job

Option 4 of the "Work with Printer Output" screen described in Section 16.1.2, "Checking the print queue," deletes a print job. If you enter 4 next to one of your jobs and press Enter, it won't be deleted right away; another screen will first prompt you to confirm that you really want to delete that printer job.

16.2 Command Files

A stored collection of CL commands that you can execute as a program is called a "CL program." After you use the SEU editor to create a source member of CL commands, it's easy to create a program from that source member and to then use that program from the OS/400 command line.

On most operating systems, the text file that you create as a command file is the same file that you tell the system to run as a program. With OS/400, the file that you create is just the source code for the program that you will run. The source code must be compiled into a program, just like the source code for a program written in C or Pascal. (Don't worry—as we'll see, it's one quick, simple extra step.) This is a great advantage, because a compiled program runs much faster than its text file equivalent.

As we examine the steps in the creation of a CL program and the built-in features of SEU that help us write a CL program, we'll create a sample program that does four things:

1. Run the UpRiteBase database program, telling it to run the report called SUMRPT.

2. Display the report output with the SEU editor, allowing us to make any necessary changes.

3. Print the edited report.

4. Check the print queue to see how long we'll have to wait for the printout.

If this is your first CL program, you'll need to create a file to hold CL programs as members. You can call the file anything you want, but the AS/400 convention for naming a CL program file is QCLSRC. Instead of copying another file to create it, you can create it with the Create Source Physical File command:

```
CRTSRCPF FILE(QCSLRC)
```

Start SEU, telling it you want to edit a member in QCSLRC called SUMMARY.

```
STRSEU QCSLRC SUMMARY
```

Since this member doesn't exist, SEU creates it for you.

All CL programs must begin with the line PGM and end with the line ENDPGM, so you start the SUMMARY program with these three lines:

1. PGM

2. The line that tells the URBASE (UpRiteBase) program to run the SUMRPT report.

3. The line that starts the SEU editor up to edit the SUMRPT member of the RPTS file.

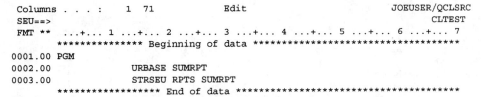

```
Columns . . . :   1  71          Edit              JOEUSER/QCLSRC
SEU==>                                                       CLTEST
FMT **  ...+... 1 ...+... 2 ...+... 3 ...+... 4 ...+... 5 ...+... 6 ...+... 7
       *************** Beginning of data **********************************
0001.00 PGM
0002.00             URBASE SUMRPT
0003.00             STRSEU RPTS SUMRPT
       ***************** End of data ***********************************
```

Figure 16.5 SEU editor with the first three lines of CL program SUMMARY entered.

It's good programming practice to indent blocks of code, and everything between PGM and ENDPGM is considered a block. Figure 16.5 shows the SEU editor with these three lines added.

Because you are adding a member to a file called QCLSRC, SEU knows that you are entering a CL program, and has two ways to help you:

- SEU points out errors in syntax while you are still composing the CL source program.

- Pressing the F4 key brings up the command prompt display to help you with command syntax the same way that it does when you're entering commands at the command line.

The next line to add to the SUMMARY program shown in Figure 16.5 will print the SUMRPT member with the CPYSRCF command, but what if you can't remember the complete CPYSRCF syntax? If you are entering any command in a CL program and forget the syntax for its parameters, just press F4.

If (after inserting a new blank line with the I line command) you entered CPYSRCF and nothing else on the fourth line of the SUMMARY program and then pressed F4, you would see the screen shown in Figure 16.6—the same screen that you see when you press F4 after entering CPYSRCF at the OS/400 command line.

Actually, there is one difference: the optional "Label" field at the top, where you can enter a label to identify that line of the program.

```
                    Copy Source File (CPYSRCF)

Type choices, press Enter.

Label  . . . . . .  1  . . .+. . .
Data base source file . . . . .          Name
  Library . . . . . . . . . .   *LIBL    Name, *LIBL, *CURLIB
To file . . . . . . . . . . .            Name, *PRINT
  Library . . . . . . . . . .   *LIBL    Name, *LIBL, *CURLIB
From member  . . . . . . . . .           Name, generic*, *FIRST, *ALL
To member or label . . . . . . *FROMMBR  Name, *FROMMBR, *FIRST
Replace or add records . . . . *REPLACE  *REPLACE, *ADD
Source update options  . . . . *SAME     *SAME, *SEQNBR, *DATE
```

Figure 16.6 Copy Source File command prompt display from within SEU.

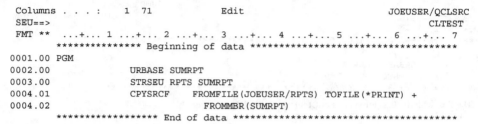

```
Columns . . . :   1  71          Edit                    JOEUSER/QCLSRC
SEU==>                                                            CLTEST
FMT **   ...+... 1 ...+... 2 ...+... 3 ...+... 4 ...+... 5 ...+... 6 ...+... 7
         *************** Beginning of data *********************************
0001.00 PGM
0002.00           URBASE SUMRPT
0003.00           STRSEU RPTS SUMRPT
0004.01           CPYSRCF    FROMFILE(JOEUSER/RPTS) TOFILE(*PRINT) +
0004.02                      FROMMBR(SUMRPT)
         ***************** End of data *************************************
```

Figure 16.7 CPYSRCF syntax, automatically filled in by SEU.

In more advanced programming, an instruction of the program could tell the program to jump to that line, and it would use this label to identify the destination of the jump.

After you fill out the screen by entering RPTS as the "Data base source file," *PRINT as "To file," and SUMRPT as the "From member," pressing Enter returns you to the SEU screen. The parameters of the CPYSRCF command have been added for you, as shown in Figure 16.7.

Note how, even if you had entered CPYSRCF on the left side of the screen before pressing F4, it gets indented for you after you fill out the command prompt display.

It also added the parameter names, which makes the line easier to read. However, the indenting plus the parameter names meant that the whole command wouldn't fit on the line. No problem; a plus sign (+) at the end of a line means that the next line is a continuation of that line.

SEU can help you with the syntax of more than just CL programs. It can provide intelligent assistance with the creation of programs written in other languages, like RPG, and even with objects that are not program source code, like the Data Definition Specification (DDS) source code sometimes used as an alternative to IDDU to create databases.

If you make a mistake while entering a CL program, SEU is glad to let you know about it so that you don't have to wait until you attempt to compile the program to find out whether you made a syntax mistake. For example, let's say you forgot the "E" in "STRSEU" and entered "STRSU RPTS SUMRPT" as the third line of the SUMMARY program. After you press Enter, SEU highlights the offending line and displays the same error message at the bottom of the screen that it would have displayed if you had entered STRSU at the OS/400 command line, as shown in Figure 16.8.

Once you've properly entered the STRSEU and CPYSRCF commands and then added the final two lines of the CL program, the complete SUMMARY program looks like this:

PGM

```
 Columns . . . :   1  71              Edit                    JOEUSER/QCLSRC
 SEU==>                                                                 CLTEST
 FMT **  ...+... 1 ...+... 2 ...+... 3 ...+... 4 ...+... 5 ...+... 6 ...+... 7
         *************** Beginning of data ********************************
0001.00 PGM
0002.00 STRSU RPTS
         ***************** End of data **********************************










 F3=Exit   F4=Prompt   F5=Refresh   F9=Retrieve   F10=Cursor
 F16=Repeat find        F17=Repeat change        F24=More keys
Command STRSU in library *LIBL not found.
```

Figure 16.8 SEU's reaction to a mistyped "STRSEU" command entered as part of a CL program.

```
URBASE SUMRPT
STRSEU RPTS SUMRPT
CPYSRCF     FROMFILE(JOEUSER/RPTS) TOFILE(*PRINT) +
     FROMMBR(SUMRPT)
  WRKSPLF
ENDPGM
```

After saving this file member, you can't run it, because you've only created a member of a source physical file. In other words, you've created the source code for your CL program, not the program itself. Remember, a program is a different kind of object.

To turn your source code into a program, use the Create CL Program command (CRTCLPGM). You only need one parameter for this command: the name that you want to assign to your working CL program. If you omit the name of the file where the source code is stored, CRTCLPGM assumes that it's stored in a file called QCLSRC. If you omit the name of the library where QCLSRC is stored, CRTCLPGM assumes that it will find it in your library list. If you omit the name of the member of QCLSRC holding the source code, CRTCLPGM assumes that it has the same name as the program that you are creating. So, if the SUMMARY source member is in the QCLSRC file in a library in your library list, you can compile it into a program by merely typing

```
CRTCLPGM PGM(SUMMARY)
```

or even just this:

```
CRTCLPGM SUMMARY
```

Once it's been created, the Display Library (DSPLIB) command shows SUMMARY as a new object in your library with an object type of *PGM.

To run the program, enter the CALL command followed by the program name. (On some operating systems, every command starts up a corresponding program, but OS/400 makes a distinction between commands and programs. The CALL command is used to run programs.) For the SUMMARY program, this would mean entering this:

```
CALL SUMMARY
```

All the commands entered in the SUMMARY program will be executed one after the other. Each program also pauses for input in the same places that it normally does—for example, when you press F3 to show that you're finished editing the summary report with SEU, the editor displays the "Exit SEU" screen, allowing you to change the parameter values that control whether the file member is printed, whether its lines are renumbered, and so forth.

You can make your CL programs pause for user input. As we saw in Section 13.1.2.1, "Command parameters," entering a question mark (?) before a command and then pressing Enter has the same effect as typing in that command and pressing F4 instead of Enter: it brings up the command prompt display and waits for the user to enter the parameters. This same trick works in CL programs.

For example, if the third line of the SUMMARY program had been

```
? STRSEU
```

instead of

```
STRSEU RPTS SUMRPT
```

the SUMMARY program would have displayed SEU's command prompt display and waited for the user to enter in the file and member names. After the user was done with SEU, SUMMARY would continue with the remaining CL program lines normally.

This adds flexibility to a CL program, because the program's user can fill in different parameters each time while still getting the benefits of an automated series of commands.

16.2.1 The automatic signon command file

The Change Profile (CHGPRF) command mentioned in Section 16.1, "Printing Text Files," has a field on its first display prompt screen called "Initial program to call." Enter the name of a CL program here, and OS/400 will execute that program for you as soon as you sign on, just as if you had entered the CALL command to run it as soon as the OS/400 prompt appeared.

Another field on the Change Profile display is called "Initial menu." If you enter a menu name here (remember, each menu has its menu name in the upper left corner) it will be the first menu to display when you sign on. The ASSIST menu (the main menu of the Operational Assistant) is a popular choice for beginners as the initial menu. If you specify both an "Initial program to call" and an "Initial menu" on the Change Profile command prompt display, the specified program runs first and then the system displays the menu when the program is finished.

A popular shortcut for specifying the initial menu is the F23 key. While viewing any OS/400 menu, pressing F23 indicates that you want that menu to be the first menu to appear after signing on. If you look at the Change Profile command prompt display after doing this, you will see that pressing F23 just fills out the "Initial menu" field with the menu's name.

16.3 Communicating with Other Users

Part of the AS/400's object-oriented approach is its use of messages for communication between the operating system, users, and programs. The operating system communicates to the user via messages—for example, error messages. It communicates to programs via messages—for example, it might tell a program that a given file that it wants to use is not available. The person using this program is unaware of this communication between the operating system and the program, but the program might be designed to pass along its own version of the same message to the user, because programs can also send messages to users.

And users can send messages to other users just as easily. You can send a message to a mailboxlike storage area called a message queue to wait until the recipient wants to read their waiting messages. In fact, because programs and the operating system can send messages just as users can, you will find messages in your message queue from all three sources.

There are two kinds of messages that you can send:

- *Informational messages*, which simply show up in someone's message queue

- *Inquiry messages*, which request a reply from the message's recipient

Send messages with the Send Message (SNDMSG) command. After you enter it at the OS/400 command line, pressing F4 or Enter displays the screen shown in Figure 16.9. There are two fields: the long, multiline one where you enter the message and the one for the name (the signon ID) of the message's recipient.

```
                    Send Message (SNDMSG)

Type choices, press Enter.

Message text . . . . . . . . .    _____
_____
_____
_____
_____
_____

To user profile . . . . . . . .    _____    Name, *SYSOPR, *ALLACT...




                                                                   Bottom
F3=Exit    F4=Prompt   F5=Refresh    F10=Additional parameters   F12=Cancel
F13=How to use this display        F24=More keys
Parameter MSG required.
```

Figure 16.9 Entry screen for Send Message command.

When you enter the message, keep in mind that it will be reformatted. The end of a line on the Send Message command prompt display won't necessarily be the end of the line when the message's recipient reads the message. This means that if a word gets split at the end of the line it won't appear that way to the message's recipient. If you do enter the last character of a word on the end of a line and the first letter of the next word on the beginning of the following line, with no space between the two, they will probably be displayed as one word to the message's recipient.

Figure 16.10 shows a sample message that Joe User has entered. There are three things of interest in this particular message:

- Before sending a real message to another user, he wants to get familiar with OS/400's message sending capabilities, so he's entering his own ID as the message recipient.

- The words "pretty," "sending," and "queue" are each split up over two lines. We'll see how they look when Joe "receives" the message. According to what I said above, they shouldn't cause any problem.

- The words "to" at the end of the first line and "get" at the beginning of the second line seem separate enough, but there is no space between them. I warned against this, and we'll see how it looks when the message reaches Joe's message queue.

When you have finished filling out the Send Messages screen, press Enter to show that you are done.

```
                        Send Message (SNDMSG)

Type choices, press Enter.

 Message text  . . . . . . . . . .     This is a test message that I am entering to
get familiar with the sending and receiving of messages with OS/400.  It seems p
retty simple.  I just enter SNDMSG, press Enter, enter the message and the ID of
 the person I want to send it to, press Enter again, and I'm all done.  I'm send
ing this to myself, and soon I'll see how it looks when it's in the message queu
e.

 To user profile  . . . . . . . .     JOEUSER        Name, *SYSOPR, *ALLACT...








                                                                     Bottom
 F3=Exit    F4=Prompt    F5=Refresh    F10=Additional parameters    F12=Cancel
 F13=How to use this display        F24=More keys
 Parameter MSG required.
```

Figure 16.10 Sample message entered by Joe User to send to himself.

```
                        Work with Messages
                                                  System:   NEPAS4
 Messages for:   JOEUSER

 Type options below, then press Enter.
   4=Remove    5=Display details and reply

 Opt    Message
                          Messages needing a reply
      (No messages available)

                        Messages not needing a reply
      This is a test message that I am entering toget familiar with the
      sending and receiving of messages with OS/400.  It seems pretty
      simple.  I just enter SNDMSG, press Enter, enter the message and the
      ID of the person I want to send it to, press Enter again, and I'm all
      done.  I'm sending this to myself, and soon I'll see how it looks when
      it's in the message queue.
      From  . . :   JOEUSER        08/15/93    20:17:16
                                                                  Bottom
 F1=Help    F3=Exit    F5=Refresh    F6=Display system operator messages
 F16=Remove messages not needing a reply    F17=Top    F24=More keys
```

Figure 16.11 Message composed in Figure 16.10 as shown by the Display Message command.

16.3.1 Receiving mail

Use the Display Message (DSPMSG) command to display the Work with Messages screen, which shows the messages waiting in your message queue. If Joe User enters DSPMSG after he sends the message shown in Figure 16.10, he will see a Work with Messages screen similar to the one shown in Figure 16.11.

(Another way to display the "Work with Messages" screen is by selecting choice 3 from the Operational Assistant. Type GO ASSIST to start up the Operational Assistant.) The upper part of the Work with Messages screen shows any inquiry messages in the queue. In Figure 16.11, the line "(No messages available)" shows that there are none.

In the informational messages ("Messages not needing a reply") part of the screen, note how the words "pretty," "sending," and "queue" are not split up, as they appeared to be when Joe entered the message. The word "to" on the first line is no longer at the end of a line, and since there was no space entered between it and the word "get," they show up in the message as one word: "toget." Clearly, you need to enter a space after every word, even if a word appears to be separated from the following word by a line break.

Of the actions possible in the Opt column, "Display details and reply" only applies to inquiry messages. The only action that Joe can take with this informational message is to enter the number 4 in the Opt column, removing the message. If he has several messages and reads them all, F16 provides a shortcut to removing all the messages in the bottom half of the screen at once.

16.3.2 Inquiry messages

Inquiry messages request a response from the recipient. To send one, you enter SNDMSG, just like you to do send an informational message. On the "Send Message" screen shown in Figure 16.10, note how the F10 key displays "Additional Parameters." Pressing it when viewing a blank "Send Message" screen adds several fields to the screen, as shown in like Figure 16.12.

The "More..." message at the bottom of the screen shows that there are more parameters than will fit, but the one we want is there on the screen: "Message type." The default value is *INFO, for "informational message." For an inquiry message, enter *INQ. If you set "Message type" to *INQ, the message that you enter will appear on the recipient's "Work with Messages" screen under "Messages needing a reply." (If you know that you want to send an inquiry before you enter SNDMSG at the OS/400 command line, you can add the parameter MSGTYPE(*INQ) to the SNDMSG command. Except for short messages, AS/400 users generally don't enter all SNDMSG parameters at the OS/400 command line because it's easier to edit the actual message on the SNDMSG command prompt display than to include it on the OS/400 command line.)

To see how this works, Joe sets "Message type" to *INQ, enters his own ID in the "To user profile" field, enters a message of "How will this look?", and presses Enter. When the OS/400 command line reappears, he enters DSPMSG and sees the screen shown in Figure 16.13.

He replies to the message by entering a 5 in the Opt column next to the message and pressing Enter. The Display Message program dis-

```
                         Send Message (SNDMSG)

 Type choices, press Enter.

 Message text . . . . . . . . . .    _____
 _____
 _____
 _____
 _____
 _____
 _____

 To user profile  . . . . . . . .       Name, *SYSOPR, *ALLACT...

                         Additional Parameters

 To message queue . . . . . . . .        Name, *SYSOPR
   Library  . . . . . . . . . . .   *LIBL      Name, *LIBL, *CURLIB
                + for more values
                                    *LIBL
 Message type . . . . . . . . . .   *INFO      *INFO, *INQ
                                                           More...
 F3=Exit   F4=Prompt   F5=Refresh   F12=Cancel   F13=How to use this display
 F24=More keys
 Parameter MSG required.
```

Figure 16.12 "Send Message" screen with additional parameters displayed.

```
                       Work with Messages
                                             System:    NEPAS4
 Messages for:   JOEUSER

 Type options below, then press Enter.
   4=Remove    5=Display details and reply

 Opt    Message
                         Messages needing a reply
        How does this look?
          From  . . :   JOEUSER       08/17/93   10:04:57

                       Messages not needing a reply
        (No messages available)




                                                              Bottom
 F1=Help    F3=Exit    F5=Refresh    F6=Display system operator messages
 F16=Remove messages not needing a reply    F17=Top    F24=More keys
```

Figure 16.13 Work with Messages display of a message needing a reply.

plays the "Additional Message Information" screen for an inquiry message, which tells him to "Type reply below" at the bottom of the screen. Joe enters the response shown in Figure 16.14 and presses Enter.

After he responds to the inquiry, he sees the "Work with Messages" screen again, and it has changed: because he has responded to the "How does this look?" message, it no longer needs a reply. It is now

```
                    Additional Message Information
From . . . . . . . . . :    JOEUSER
Date sent  . . . . . . :    08/17/93      Time sent  . . . . . . :    10:04:57

Message . . . . :    How does this look?




                                                                    Bottom
Type reply below, then press Enter.
Reply  . . . .    It looks pretty reasonable.
```

Figure 16.14 Responding to an inquiry message.

```
                        Work with Messages
                                                   System:    NEPAS4
Messages for:   JOEUSER

Type options below, then press Enter.
  4=Remove    5=Display details and reply

Opt   Message
                      Messages needing a reply
     (No messages available)

                      Messages not needing a reply
      How does this look?
        From  . . :   JOEUSER        08/17/93   10:04:57
        Reply . . :    It looks pretty reasonable.




                                                                    Bottom
F1=Help   F3=Exit   F5=Refresh   F6=Display system operator messages
F16=Remove messages not needing a reply   F17=Top   F24=More keys
```

Figure 16.15 Work with Messages screen after response to inquiry message.

displayed, with its answer, under "Messages not needing a reply," as shown in Figure 16.15.

Do the inquiry message ("How does this look") and the response now appear under "Messages not needing a reply" because Joe was the originator of the inquiry or because he was the recipient? The answer is both. After an inquiry recipient responds to the inquiry, the inquiry and its response appear under "Messages not needing a reply" for both the sender and the recipient to give them a record of their exchange. The exchange remains there until they delete it by entering 4 in the `Opt` column next to it or by pressing F16.

16.3.3 Sending an existing file

The Send Network File (`SNDNETF`) command can send file members to other users on your AS/400 or, as its name implies, to other users on systems attached to your AS/400 over a network—even if the system they are using is not an AS/400.

To send the `SUMRPT` member of the `RPTS` file to Mary Jones' MJONES user ID on the JUPITER system, Joe User enters the following:

```
SNDNETF FILE(RPTS) TOUSRID((MJONES JUPITER)) MBR(SUMRPT)
```

If he omitted the parameter names and entered the positional parameter version, he would enter this:

```
SNDNETF RPTS ((MJONES JUPITER)) SUMRPT
```

There are several interesting things to note about this command:

- If RPTS wasn't in a library in Joe's library list, he would have to specify which library it was in with the (`libname/filename`) syntax.

- The destination user ID and system name are enclosed together in two pairs of parentheses, even in the positional parameter version of the command.

- The system name `JUPITER` might represent an AS/400, but it might not. The system name of your particular AS/400 will be displayed on the signon screen; in Figure 13.1, it's `NEPAS4`. This means that someone sending a file to Joe from their AS/400 ID would send it to (`(JOEUSER NEPAS4)`). (From a UNIX system connected over the same network, they would send it to `JOEUSER@NEPAS4`, and from a VM ID it would be addressed to `JOEUSER AT NEPAS4`.)

- Unlike similar commands on other computers, you must specify the destination system name even if you send it to an ID on the same system that you are using. (Other operating systems usually assume "same system" as a default if you omit the system name when identifying a recipient.)

- Don't take it for granted that you have permission to use `SNDNETF`. If you try it and get the message "User not enrolled in system distribution directory," speak to your system administrator about being enrolled to use the command.

```
                    Work with Network Files                  NEPAS4
                                              02/19/94  19:38:51
User . . . . . . . . . . . . . :    JOEUSER
User ID/Address . . . . . . . :    JOEUSER    NEPAS4

Type options, press Enter.
   1=Receive network file    3=Submit job   4=Delete network file
   5=Display physical file member


                         File  -------From-------  ----Arrival----
Opt   File      Member    Number  User ID  Address  Date      Time
      RPTS      JULYRPT       1    MJONES   JUPITER  02/19/94  10:16
      QCSRC     IOTEST        6    JCASEY   NEPTUNE  02/19/94  11:38




                                                              Bottom
Parameters or command
===>
F3=Exit    F4=Prompt    F5=Refresh    F9=Retrieve    F11=Display type/records
F12=Cancel
```

Figure 16.16 The Work with Network Files screen displayed by the WRKNETF command.

16.3.3.1 Receiving a file.   The Work with Network Files command (WRKNETF) displays the screen shown in Figure 16.16. This lets you look at and receive the files that have been sent to you with SNDNETF or with the equivalent command on other computers connected to your system over a network. (Like SNDNETF, you must be enrolled by the system administrator to use WRKNETF.)

The F11 key changes the display so that the type and number of records of the waiting files are shown instead of the User ID and Address columns. Figure 16.17 shows an example.

In Figure 16.17, we see that the JULYRPT member of the RPTS file is a simple data file with 62 lines of text. The other file is source code for a program (judging from the file name, it's written in C) and it's about three times longer than JULYRPT.

The command key at the top shows that entering a 1 in the Opt column will store the waiting member in a file. When you do this, the system assumes that you already have a file with the name shown in the File column for that member, and it stores the member there. If you don't have a file by that name, press F4 instead of Enter after entering the 1 in the Opt column. This displays the Receive Network File command prompt display, where you can enter any file name you like.

16.4 A Sample OS/400 Session

One morning you sign on to your OS/400 ID and check your messages with the DSPMSG command, and you see the screen shown in Figure 16.18.

```
                    Work with Network Files              NEPAS4
                                              02/19/94  19:38:51
User . . . . . . . . . . . . :     JOEUSER
User ID/Address  . . . . . . :     JOEUSER    NEPAS4

Type options, press Enter.
  1=Receive network file    3=Submit job    4=Delete network file
  5=Display physical file member


                                     Record  -----Send------
Opt  File       Member      Type     Records Length  Date      Time
     RPTS       JULYRPT     *DTA         62      29  02/19/94  18:15
     QCSRC      IOTEST      *SRC        182      92  02/19/94  19:38




                                                          Bottom
Parameters or command
===>
F3=Exit   F4=Prompt   F5=Refresh   F9=Retrieve   F11=Display user ID/address
F12=Cancel
```

Figure 16.17 The Work with Network Files screen with object type, number of records, and record length of the waiting files displayed.

```
                    Work with Messages
                                           System:   NEPAS4
Messages for:   JOEUSER

Type options below, then press Enter.
  4=Remove    5=Display details and reply


Opt    Message
                    Messages needing a reply
      You said that you know how to write CL programs, right?  I need one
        for the guys in the warehouse.  We're going to send them a file
        with a list of orders over the network each day, and I don't want
        to have to teach them about WRKNETF and printing.  The member
        will be called ORDERS and go into a file called INVEN (they
        already have this file, so don't worry about creating it).  When
        they type CALL GETORDERS, I want this program to get ORDERS out
        of the queue of network files and send it to their printer,
        which is called WRHOUSE.  Can you handle this?
        From  . . :   MARYJONES    04/27/94   10:03:22

                    Messages not needing a reply
      (No messages available)
                                                          Bottom
F1=Help   F3=Exit   F5=Refresh   F6=Display system operator messages
F16=Remove messages not needing a reply    F17=Top    F24=More keys
```

Figure 16.18 Message from Mary about CL program to write.

```
                    Receive Network File (RCVNETF)

Type choices, press Enter.

From file  . . . . . . . . . . . >  QCSRC          Character value
To data base file  . . . . . . . >  *FROMFILE      Name, *FROMFILE
  Library  . . . . . . . . . . .     *LIBL          Name, *LIBL, *CURLIB
Member to be received  . . . . . >  CTEST1         Character value, *ONLY
To member  . . . . . . . . . . .     *FROMMBR       Name, *FROMMBR, *FIRST






                                                              Bottom
F3=Exit    F4=Prompt    F5=Refresh    F10=Additional parameters    F12=Cancel
F13=How to use this display          F24=More keys
```

Figure 16.19 Receive Network File command prompt display, as displayed by WRKNETF program.

You type in a 4 next to the first line of Mary's message, press
Enter, and enter "No problem, Mary, you'll have it by this afternoon"
as your reply.

But there is a slight problem: you know how to receive a network
file with WRKNETF, but how would you automate this? You use
WRKNETF by making choices on a list display; you can't tell it what to
do by entering WRKNETF on the OS/400 command line with a couple of
parameters after it. It would be a good idea to review the process of
receiving a file, so you send yourself a short little file—the source
code to the first C program that you wrote on the AS/400—over the
network with the following command:

```
SNDNETF FILE(QCSRC) TOUSRID((JOEUSER NEPAS4)) MBR(CTEST1)
```

You then enter WRKNETF to bring up the Work with Network Files
screen and enter a 1 next to the CTEST1 member of the QCSRC file.
Instead of pressing Enter, you press F4 to see how much control you
can have over the receiving of a file. This displays the Receive
Network File screen, as shown in Figure 16.19.

The RCVNETF after the screen's title makes you realize something:
when you entered the 1 at the Work with Network Files screen, it just
called a program called RCVNETF. You could have your CL program call
RCVNETF directly, and skip over the Work with Network Files screen.

First, you should test this idea. You press F3 a couple of times to go
back to the command line, enter RCVNETF by itself, and press F4.
When you see the screen shown in Figure 16.20, you recognize it as

```
                    Receive Network File (RCVNETF)

Type choices, press Enter.

From file  . . . . . . . . . . .                Character value
To data base file  . . . . . . .    *FROMFILE   Name, *FROMFILE
  Library  . . . . . . . . . . .      *LIBL     Name, *LIBL, *CURLIB
Member to be received  . . . . .    *ONLY       Character value, *ONLY
To member  . . . . . . . . . . .    *FROMMBR    Name, *FROMMBR, *FIRST




                                                                   Bottom
F3=Exit    F4=Prompt    F5=Refresh    F10=Additional parameters    F12=Cancel
F13=How to use this display    F24=More keys
```

Figure 16.20   Receive Network File command prompt display, as displayed by entering RCVNETF command.

the same screen that WRKNETF displayed when you entered a 1 in the Opt column. So WRKNETF really was just calling RCVNETF!

To receive the file that you sent yourself as a test, you enter "QCSRC" in the "From file field," "CTEST1" in the "Member to be received" field, and press Enter. The system returns to the main menu, and displays the message

```
File QCSRC member CTEST1 number 14 received.
```

at the bottom. It worked! You press F9 to retrieve the command that you would have typed at the command line, and you see this:

```
RCVNETF FROMFILE(QCSRC) FROMMBR(CTEST1)
```

So that's the command that you'll need for your GETORDERS CL program, only with a file name of INVEN and a member name of ORDERS. So, you start up SEU and tell it to create the GETORDERS member of your QCSLSRC file with the following command:

```
STRSEU QCLSRC GETORDERS
```

You enter PGM as the program's first line, because that's the first line of the source code in all CL programs, and the RCVNETF command as the second line, with INVEN and ORDERS as its parameters.

The GETORDERS program's next task is to print the newly received member. You remember that this is done with some trick using the CPYSRCF command, but you don't remember the exact syntax. You

```
                          Copy Source File (CPYSRCF)

Type choices, press Enter.

Label  . . . . . . . . . . . .
Data base source file  . . . . .            Name
  Library  . . . . . . . . . .    *LIBL     Name, *LIBL, *CURLIB
To file  . . . . . . . . . . .              Name, *PRINT
  Library  . . . . . . . . . .    *LIBL     Name, *LIBL, *CURLIB
From member  . . . . . . . . .              Name, generic*, *FIRST, *ALL
To member or label . . . . . . .  *FROMMBR  Name, *FROMMBR, *FIRST
Replace or add records . . . . .  *REPLACE  *REPLACE, *ADD
Source update options  . . . . .  *SAME     *SAME, *SEQNBR, *DATE




                                                               Bottom
F3=Exit    F4=Prompt    F5=Refresh   F12=Cancel   F13=How to use this display
F24=More keys
```

Figure 16.21 Copy Source File command prompt display from within SEU.

```
FMT **   ...+... 1 ...+... 2 ...+... 3 ...+... 4 ...+... 5 ...+... 6 ...+... 7
         *************** Beginning of data ********************************
0001.00 PGM
0002.00            RCVNETF    FROMFILE(INVEN) FROMMBR(ORDERS)
0003.00            CPYSRCF    FROMFILE(INVEN) TOFILE(*PRINT) FROMMBR(ORDERS)
         ***************** End of data ********************************
```

Figure 16.22 First three lines of the GETORDERS CL program's source code.

enter CPYSRCF as the third line of the CL program's source code and press F4 to find out more about its potential parameters. SEU displays the screen shown in Figure 16.21.

Once you see the displayed screen, you know that you enter INVEN as the "Data base source file" and ORDERS as the "From member." Looking to the right of "To file," you see that *PRINT is a possible option, instead of "Name." So that was the trick. Entering a name would have copied the member to another member with the specified name, but entering *PRINT sends it to the printer. You enter "*PRINT," press Enter, and the system returns you to the SEU screen where it has filled out the CPYSRCF line for you, as shown in Figure 16.22.

Most people want to see the print queue after they send something to the printer, to determine whether they should walk to the printer right away to get their print job or if they should wait because of some other print jobs in front of theirs. You add WRKSPLF as the fourth line of GETORDERS so that the print queue gets automatically displayed, and then ENDPGM to finish the source code. At this point, your program looks like Figure 16.23.

```
FMT **   ...+... 1 ...+... 2 ...+... 3 ...+... 4 ...+... 5 ...+... 6 ...+... 7
*************** Beginning of data **********************************
0001.00 PGM
0002.00          RCVNETF     FROMFILE(INVEN)
0003.00          CPYSRCF     FROMFILE(INVEN) TOFILE(*PRINT) FROMMBR(ORDERS)
0004.00          WRKSPLF
0005.00 ENDPGM
***************** End of data **************************************
```

Figure 16.23 Finished source code for GETORDERS.

You quit out of SEU, saving the file, and enter the command to compile this source code into a working program:

```
CRTCLPGM GETORDERS
```

When you see the message "Program GETORDERS created in library JOEUSER," you know that it successfully compiled. But you still have to test it; you create a file called INVEN with a dummy member named ORDERS. You send a copy of ORDERS to your message queue with the command

```
SNDNETF FILE(INVEN) TOUSRID((JOEUSER NEPAS4)) MBR(ORDERS)
```

and then delete ORDERS from the INVEN file with the RMVM command. This way, if your program works correctly and pulls ORDERS out of the message queue and puts it in INVEN, you'll know that it was put there by GETORDERS and not left over from the original one that you created.

Time for the big test. You enter

```
CALL GETORDERS
```

and press Enter. Shortly after that, you're looking at the Work with Network Files screen, and there's the print job sent by your GETORDERS program. You press F3 to return to the command line and list the members in INVEN by entering

```
DSPFD INVEN TYPE(*MBRLIST)
```

and there is ORDERS, even though you deleted it a minute ago. Now you know that GETORDERS put it there like it was supposed to.

It looks like the GETORDERS program works, so you send it to Mary with the command

```
SNDNETF FILE(QCLSRC) TOUSRID((MJONES NEPAS4)) MBR(GETORDERS)
```

and then use SNDMSG to send the message shown in Figure 16.24 to her as well.

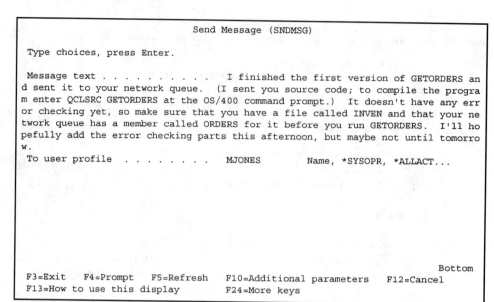

```
                          Send Message (SNDMSG)

 Type choices, press Enter.

  Message text . . . . . . . . .   I finished the first version of GETORDERS an
d sent it to your network queue.  (I sent you source code; to compile the progra
m enter QCLSRC GETORDERS at the OS/400 command prompt.)  It doesn't have any err
or checking yet, so make sure that you have a file called INVEN and that your ne
twork queue has a member called ORDERS for it before you run GETORDERS.  I'll ho
pefully add the error checking parts this afternoon, but maybe not until tomorro
w.
  To user profile . . . . . . .   MJONES          Name, *SYSOPR, *ALLACT...
```

```
                                                                       Bottom
 F3=Exit   F4=Prompt   F5=Refresh   F10=Additional parameters   F12=Cancel
 F13=How to use this display      F24=More keys
```

Figure 16.24 Message to Mary about GETORDERS.

Now all that's left is the error checking. You enter STRSCHIDX to start up the search index and then enter "CL program" as the search string, confident that you will find what you need in the OS/400's extensive help system.

17

VM/CMS: An Introduction

Before we begin with VM/CMS, you must understand one crucial concept: the operating system you are using. This may seem obvious; after all, the name of this part of the book is "VM/CMS." But, as you often hear people refer to the operating system as VM and as CMS, learning the relationship between the two is the first step in understanding it.

17.1 History

IBM developed VM ("Virtual Machine") in 1964. Like any operating system, VM controlled the computer's resources. It also added a feature that had never existed before: the illusion, for each of its users, that they had a whole computer to themselves. (Because IBM developed VM well before the invention of the PC, having even a simulation of your own computer was a Big Deal.) If 20 people use a VM system at once, it gives them the illusion that they are using 20 different computers.

The most interesting part is that each of these simulated "computers" can run its own operating system. IBM has developed versions of MVS, UNIX, DOS/VSE, and even PC/DOS to run under VM (we call an operating system that runs one of VM's simulated computers a "guest" operating system running "under" VM), but the most popular is the one that was designed from the ground up to take the fullest possible advantage of the VM environment: CMS. (VM actually evolved from an earlier version of CMS called CTSS, but this all happened at IBM's Cambridge Scientific Center in Massachusetts, before either was released as a commercial product. The MIT engineers who designed CTSS went on to design MULTICS, an ancestor of UNIX, which makes CMS a cousin of UNIX!)

Because the vast majority of people who use VM run CMS as the guest operating system, most VM user IDs are set up to automatically run CMS when someone logs on to their VM ID. Many users doesn't realize that this extra step is taking place and assume that it's all part of the normal process of logging on to the "VM/CMS" operating system. Think of it this way: once this logon process is complete, you interact with the CMS operating system, but behind the scenes, the VM operating system runs the show.

CMS originally stood for "Cambridge Monitor System," but IBM decided that its hundreds of TLAs (three-letter acronyms) weren't quite confusing enough and changed the official meaning of this one to "Conversational Monitor System." The idea of a "conversation" with the computer, where you type something, it immediately responds, and you continue this interchange, was also a Big Deal in the days when "input" often meant dropping off a pile of punch cards with the guy who fed them into the card reader and "output" meant picking up a printout and maybe another pile of cards from the same guy—not necessarily on the same day. In the days before Apple convinced everyone that moving a mouse pointer to a little picture of a garbage can was a more intuitive way to erase a file than typing the word "erase" followed by a file's name, CMS was actually considered down-right user-friendly.

> BUZZWORD: "Virtual." Unlike most computer buzzwords, this one usually holds true to its dictionary definition when it refers to hardware or software. *The Random House College Dictionary* defines "virtual" as "being such in force or effect, though not actually or expressly such." On a computer, it usually applies to software or hardware that pretends to be something it isn't. You can designate a portion of RAM on a PC to be treated as a fast, efficient hard disk; we often call this a "virtual disk," because you use it as a disk, when it's not really a disk. Sometimes you can do the opposite—on some systems, software utilities exist that let you designate a portion of your hard disk to act like RAM, giving your computer the effect of having more memory than it really has. We call this "virtual memory," because you use it as memory, without it actually being memory in the modern sense.
>
> The virtual machines created by a VM system aren't real machines, but rather simulations of separate machines created by the VM operating system. VM also gives its users virtual card punchers and virtual card readers, when actual computer punch cards and the machinery to deal with them are virtually (that word again!) obsolete. (For more on these, see the sidebar in Chapter 18: "This Is the Nineties. Why Do I Need a Card Puncher or a Card Reader?")

Because it does not manage multiple users, CMS is not a multi-user operating system. If 20 people want to use CMS simultaneously, 20 copies of CMS get started up. VM handles the multiuser part. If 10 people try to print a file at once, their individual copies of CMS pass these requests through CP to VM, which deals with print job scheduling.

17.1.1 CP: The control program

But what is CP? More IBM initials to worry about? It stands for "Control Program." Different parts of VM deal with the various aspects of the computer's activities in the computer—the disk drives, memory, and so on. CP is the part that deals with CMS. It starts a CMS session and functions as a mediator between the CMS sessions and the hardware.

CP has its own set of commands, but you only need to worry about the one that instructs it to start up a CMS session. (Section 18.1, "Starting Up," covers this in greater detail.) You may hear that some of the commands you use in CMS are actually CP commands, but don't worry; you don't need to treat these commands differently. You don't even need to remember which are CMS commands and which are CP commands. When you type a CP command at the CMS prompt, CMS automatically passes it along to CP.

VM/370? VM/IS? VM/SP? VM/XA? VM/ESA?

You might see other initials besides "CMS" after "VM." Usually, these show the version of VM being used. Various versions developed over the years take advantage of the hardware in different ways; these differences aren't anything for you to worry about. They all run CMS, and the commands that you type are the same for all of them. You might get a memo saying "On Friday the 12th from midnight to 6 AM the VM system will be shut down so that we can upgrade from VM/SP to VM/XA. The increased functionality of VM/XA will allow us to utilize the blah blah blah... ." Don't worry. The logon screen might look a little different, but you shouldn't need to do anything differently.

18

Getting Started with VM/CMS

18.1 Starting Up

Logging on to a VM/CMS system consists of two or three basic steps:

- Entering your user ID.
- Entering your password.
- Telling the CP part of VM to start up CMS. This may be unnecessary.

If CP does not automatically start up CMS, ask your VM administrator (the VM term for a system administrator) to set up your CP directory to take care of this. The CP directory keeps track of who can do what on the system. Only the system administrator has access to the CP directory.

After you turn on your terminal or hook up to a VM system from a PC running terminal emulation software, and before you log on, you will probably see the logon screen with the logo of either the company that owns the system or the version of VM being used.

18.1.1 The logon screen

The logon screen will look similar to Figure 18.1.

Your cursor should be on the USERID line, waiting for you to type your ID. Type it in, and press your Tab key to move your cursor to the PASSWORD line. Type in your password. As the screen tells you, the characters of your password will not appear as you type them, but the cursor moves along to show how many characters you have typed.

After you type your password, you could press Tab again to move your cursor to the COMMAND prompt and enter a command for the system to execute as soon as your logon is complete, or you could press Enter immediately to show that you are done with the logon screen. If

```
VM/XA SP ONLINE


                VV          VV
                 VV        VV
                  VV      VV
                   VVVVV  MMM    MMM
                     V    MMM    MMM
                          MM M M MM
                          MM  M  MM
                          MM     MM




Fill in your USERID and PASSWORD and press ENTER
(Your password will not appear when you type it)
USERID   ===>  _
PASSWORD ===>

COMMAND  ===>
```

Figure 18.1 Sample VM logon screen.

you press Enter at any time before you enter your user ID and password, the system prompts you to enter the next piece of information it needs.

If you press Enter as soon as you see the logon screen, before you even enter your user ID, the screen clears and you see a prompt like this:

```
Enter one of the following commands:
LOGON userid (Example: LOGON VMUSER1)
LOGOFF
```

(You may see additional commands suggested, but these two are the important ones.) Enter LOGOFF if you want to give up on logging on. To continue the logon procedure, enter LOGON followed by your user ID.

If you've entered your user ID but the system still needs your password, it prompts you for it:

```
VMXACI104R Enter logon password:
```

If you entered your user ID and password correctly, the system starts up a session for you. If you enter a user ID that the system doesn't recognize—in this example, JEOUSER—it displays something similar to this:

```
HCPLGO053E JEOUSER not in CP directory
Enter one of the following commands:
LOGON userid (Example: LOGON VMUSER1)
LOGOFF
```

If you entered the password incorrectly, the system tells you

```
HCPLGO050E LOGON unsuccessful—incorrect password
```

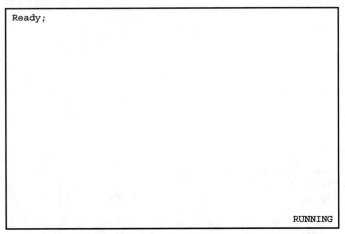

```
Ready;




                                                      RUNNING
```

Figure 18.2 Blank CMS screen with Ready; prompt waiting for a command.

followed by the prompt that tells you the syntax for logging on or off. Don't panic right away if your first attempt at logging on doesn't work; the VM system will let you make several more attempts. However, you don't get an unlimited number of chances, because a security feature of the system closes the connection if someone makes too many successive attempts to log on to a particular ID without succeeding. It could be an unauthorized person trying to guess a password, and you don't want to give anyone an unlimited number of guesses.

Once the logon procedure finishes, if you automatically enter CMS, you see the CMS Ready; prompt (as shown in Figure 18.2) which tells you that the system is ready to accept your commands.

Instead of the word Ready; you might just see R; as the prompt. The prompt may also include the amount of time that the computer's processor spent on the last task you requested and the current time of day. For example, at 6:43 PM it might look like this:

```
Ready; T = 0.01/0.01 18:43:47
```

18.1.2 Entering CMS

If you don't see a CMS prompt, you will see a screen waiting for a CP command like the one in Figure 18.3.

The only CP command you need to worry about is the one that starts up CMS. Enter

```
IPL CMS
```

IPL stands for "Initial Program Load." After you type in this command and press Enter you will see some variation of the CMS Ready; prompt as described above. (You may need to press Enter one or two more times.)

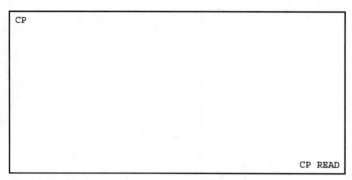

Figure 18.3 Blank CP screen waiting for a CP command.

The IPL CMS command may come in handy later in your session. If something goes drastically wrong with your CMS session, you may find yourself back in CP, with a prompt screen just like Figure 18.3. If this happens, type

    BEGIN

which will, with luck, resume the CMS session that you just lost. If this doesn't work, type

    IPL CMS

as if you were starting up a brand new session. You really are starting up a brand new session, because you have permanently lost your original session.

18.1.3 Entering commands

If you press Enter without typing a command, the system displays a message that tells you which environment you are currently in (either CMS or CP.) This is a handy trick if you are unsure of your present situation.

When you type a command it appears, as you type it, at the bottom of your screen, like the list all * being entered in Figure 18.4.

Although you might be entering your command 22 lines below the line where Ready; is displayed, we still speak of entering a command "at" the Ready; prompt. When you press Enter, the typed command jumps to the line below the most recently displayed line on your screen and the system's response appears under it, as shown in Figure 18.5.

If you enter a command like COPY or RENAME and no problems occur when you execute it, CMS won't display any message telling you that the command executed successfully. If you don't get an error message, you can assume that the command worked as you had hoped.

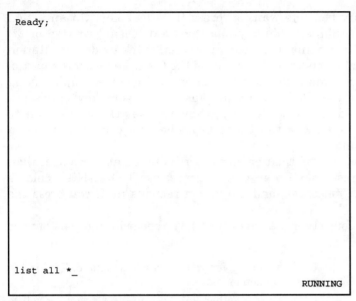

```
Ready;




















list all *_
                                              RUNNING
```

Figure 18.4 Command being entered on CMS screen.

```
Ready; T=0.01/0.01 18:48:56
list all *
ALL        BACKUP   A1
ALL        NOTEBOOK A0
ALL        NOTEINDX A0

















                                              RUNNING
```

Figure 18.5 CMS response to command entered in Figure 18.4.

18.1.3.1 MORE... .   Unlike other command-driven operating systems you may have used, CMS doesn't scroll your typed commands and the system's responses off the top of the screen when the screen fills up. Instead, the message "MORE..." appears in the screen's lower right-hand corner, to indicate that there is more to see in addition to the currently displayed text. If you wait 60 seconds CMS automatically clears the current screen and displays the next screen.

If you don't feel like waiting, press the Clear key. On an actual mainframe terminal, this key has the word "Clear" written on it. When using a terminal emulation program, check its documentation to see which key on your PC serves as the Clear key with the particular terminal emulation setting being used. (For example, using Procomm on a DOS PC, the gray plus key on your keyboard's numeric keypad is the Clear key when you set the emulation to "3270/950," but F2 is the Clear key when Procomm emulates a VT220 terminal.)

If you want the information on the screen to remain for longer than a minute, press your Enter key. The message "HOLDING" replaces the "MORE..." message, and the screen remains until you press the Clear key.

There are four other messages that may appear in that part of your screen:

RUNNING	CMS is waiting for you to type a command. This is the most common message.
VM READ	CMS (or some other VM program) is waiting for you to enter something. Unlike RUNNING, this appears when the system has asked you for something and is waiting for your answer.
READ	CP is waiting for a CP command (as when you first log on, if you need to start up CMS).
NOT ACCEPTED	You entered a command and pressed Enter before the system was ready for a command, so it couldn't accept it. Press the Reset key (on a PC emulating a 3270 terminal, this is usually the Escape key) and try again.

18.1.3.2 Aborting screen output. If a program has so much output that you press the Clear key over and over and still see the MORE... message, you may get tired of pressing the Clear key. For example, if you list filenames alphabetically and only start to see filenames that begin with the letter "B" after you press Clear eight times, you may regret issuing the command to list filenames. (Actually, CMS refers to the names of files as "file IDs," not "filenames." See Section 18.2, "Filenames," for more on this.)

There is help: the Halt Type command, abbreviated as HT. In Figure 18.6, Joe User saw the MORE... message in the lower right and decided that he didn't want to see any more file IDs, so he entered HT to Halt the Typing.

After he presses Enter, CMS displays only one more line of output and goes back to the Ready; prompt, as shown in Figure 18.7.

Remember, this not only works for the command that lists file IDs, but for any command that requires you to press the Clear key too often when you look at command output.

```
BSHFFUTL EXEC     F1 F         80        119         3  9/11/93  1:33:42 65Y370
BSHFINST EXEC     F1 F         80         68         2  9/11/93  1:33:52 65Y370
BSHFPNTR EXEC     F1 F         80        167         4  9/11/93  1:34:02 65Y370
BSHFPROF DATA     F1 F         80         20         1  2/04/94 14:13:15 65Y370
BSHFQCKG EXEC     F1 F         80         39         1  9/11/93  1:34:12 65Y370
BSHFSHLL EXEC     F1 F         80        526        11  2/04/94 14:17:01 65Y370
BSHFSHOW EXEC     F1 F         80         30         1  9/11/93  1:34:34 65Y370
BSHFSMNU EXEC     F1 F         80        184         4  9/11/93  1:34:44 65Y370
BSHFSXST EXEC     F1 F         80        376         8  9/11/93  1:34:56 65Y370
BSHFTOOL EXEC     F1 F         80        119         3  9/11/93  1:35:06 65Y370
BSHFTUTL EXEC     F1 F         80        159         4  9/11/93  1:35:17 65Y370
BSHFVIEW EXEC     F1 F         80        314         7  9/11/93  1:35:28 65Y370
BSHFXFER EXEC     F1 F         80        455         9  9/11/93  1:35:39 65Y370
BSHHFUT1 ERRORS   F1 F         80        149         3  9/11/93  1:36:02 65Y370
BSHHFUT2 ERRORS   F1 F         80        119         3  9/11/93  1:36:12 65Y370
BSHHMFD  ERRORS   F1 F         80        167         4  9/11/93  1:36:22 65Y370
BSHHSHLL ERRORS   F1 F         80        151         3  9/11/93  1:36:32 65Y370
BSHHSHL2 ERRORS   F1 F         80        134         3  9/11/93  1:36:43 65Y370
BSHHTOL2 ERRORS   F1 F         80         76         2  9/11/93  1:36:53 65Y370
BSHHTOOL ERRORS   F1 F         80        166         4  9/11/93  1:37:03 65Y370
BSHHTUTL ERRORS   F1 F         80        115         3  9/11/93  1:37:13 65Y370
BSHMSACC EXEC     F1 F         80          1         1  9/11/93  1:39:29 65Y37
ht
                                                        MORE...
```

Figure 18.6 Halt Typing (ht) command entered to stop CMS output.

```
BSHMSACC HLP      F1 F         80         11         1  9/11/93  1:38:23 65Y370
ht
Ready; T=0.07/0.36 18:09:37




                                                        RUNNING
```

Figure 18.7 Result of Halt Typing command.

This is the Nineties. Why Do I Need a Card Puncher or a Punch Card Reader?

The "virtual computer" created for you as a part of the VM system includes a virtual card reader and a virtual card puncher. Why would anyone want even a software simulation of such archaic pieces of hardware? Before sending files from one user (or computer) to another was as simple as it is today, you sent someone a file by issuing a command to the computer to create a punch card version of the file in the recipient's card reader. In other words, you "punched" it to him. He then "read" the stack of cards by entering the command that told the card reader to read each card in that stack and turn it into a line of a disk file.

One of VM's original advantages was its ability to let people emulate these processes in software, so that physical card punchers and readers became much less necessary. Now that these machines are virtually obsolete, the terminology is still with us. In fact, you may still see references to "cards" now and then on your screen. Instead of referring to those rectangular pieces of paper, your computer is referring to an 80-character unit of information—the amount that a single card used to store.

18.1.3.3 Case sensitivity. CMS is not case-sensitive. Your commands have the same effect whether you enter them in upper- or lowercase. The same applies to file IDs: when you create or refer to a file, whether you write out its name in upper- or lowercase, CMS translates it to uppercase.

18.1.4 Finishing your CMS session

Logging off is simple. Just type

```
LOGOFF
```

at the Ready prompt. This one command ends both your CMS session and the CP session underlying it. You also get a short report on the statistics of your finished session:

```
CONNECT =  00:02:30 VIRTCPU =  000:01.22 TOTCPU =  000:01.52
LOGOFF AT 09:20:42 EST MONDAY 011/06/94
```

CONNECT shows how long you were connected to the system, and the other figures show various aspects of the Central Processing Unit time that you used.

18.2 Filenames

In CMS, we don't refer to a file's name as a "filename." It has three parts, and the first by itself is known as a "filename." Some IBM literature refers to the combination of the three parts as a "file label"; other IBM literature refers to a file's full name as the "fileid," with the last two letters pronounced out loud, as if it had been written "file ID." The three parts have the following purposes:

filename If you compare the filename and filetype to a person's first and last name, then the filename is the first name. While a series of files with the same filetype are all in the same family, different filenames distinguish each from the other. The filename can have from one to eight characters and can include letters of the alphabet, numeric digits, and the characters @, #, $, +, -, ;, and _. As suggested in Section 1.5, "General Advice," stick with letters, numbers, and the underscore character (_) to stay out of trouble.

filetype This shows what family the file belongs to. For example, a filetype of EXEC shows that the file is a CMS command file (in Section 21.2, "Command Files," we'll see how to write these); a filetype of XEDIT shows that the file is a series of commands used by the CMS text editor XEDIT as a macro; a filetype of COBOL shows that the file contains source code written in the COBOL programming language. The filetype can have from one to eight characters, and can contain the same characters that a filename can.

filemode This identifies the minidisk where the file is stored. As you'll see in Section 18.3, "How Files Are Organized," CMS stores files on disks named after letters of the alphabet, with your own personal disk named A. (Disks A, B, and C may actually be on the same physical disk. To make things easier to organize, disks are divided into sections with each named as if it were a separate disk.) If you omit the filemode when you refer to a file, CMS usually assumes that you're talking about a file with a filemode of A.

When you list file labels, you may see a numeric digit from 0 to 6 after the filemode letter. Different numbers represent different purposes and access rights that users have over the file. The most common digit is 1, the default for files that you create. Files created on your minidisk by the system usually have a 0, which prevents other users from looking at the file, even when they have access to your minidisk. Files that several users may want to share often have a 2 as their filemode digit. (Section 19.2, "Sharing Files Between Users," explains how one user can gain access to another's minidisk.)

Here are some typical file labels:

```
MAY_BUDG SCRIPT    A1
NOTEBOOK ALL       A0
MAINMENU EXEC      B2
120794CR MEMO      A1
```

18.2.1 Wildcards

The use of wildcards gives you a fair amount of flexibility with `listfile`, the command used to list file IDs, but very little with other commands. The two wildcard characters are the asterisk, which represents multiple characters, and the percent sign, which represents individual characters.

In the examples used to explain these characters, assume that your A minidisk has the these files on it:

```
111494JJ MEMO       A1
112894BD MEMO       A1
120794CR MEMO       A1
121794BD MEMO       A1
121794CR MEMO       A1
122094JJ MEMO       A1
LINKUTIL EXEC       A1
MAY_BUD  SCRIPT     A1
JUN_BUD  SCRIPT     A1
NOTEBOOK ALL        A0
PHONLIST TXT        A1
SUM_RPT  EXEC       A1
SUM_RPT  HLP        A1
```

18.2.1.1 The asterisk. In many commands that operate on files, you can use the asterisk to substitute for the filename, filetype, or file-mode. To use the LISTFILE command to list all files with a filename of SUM_RPT, the command

```
LISTFILE SUM_RPT *
```

produces this output:

```
SUM_RPT EXEC        A1
SUM_RPT HLP         A1
```

To list files with a filetype of EXEC, the command

```
LISTFILE * EXEC
```

produces this output:

```
LINKUTIL EXEC       A1
SUM_RPT  EXEC       A1
```

To list all the EXEC files on your minidisk and all the ones that you have access to, you could enter

```
LISTFILE * EXEC *
```

but be prepared to use the ht command described in Section 18.1.3.2, "Aborting screen output." An EXEC is a CMS command file, and you will probably find a large number of them on other disks.

The ERASE command, which erases files, can also use the asterisk. Typing

```
ERASE * EXEC
```

would erase all of your EXEC files. Typing

```
ERASE * EXEC *
```

wouldn't erase all the EXEC files on all of the disks to which you have access; you shouldn't have privileges to alter or erase files on any minidisk besides your own A disk.

Used with the LISTFILE or COPY commands, you can use the asterisk in combination with other letters. Typing

```
LISTFILE 11* MEMO
```

produces the following output:

```
111494JJ MEMO A1
112894BD MEMO A1
```

The asterisk doesn't need to go at the end of the filename or filetype in the command. For example, you could type

```
LISTFILE *BD MEMO
```

and get this output:

```
112894BD MEMO A1
121794BD MEMO A1
```

18.2.1.2 The percent sign.   You can use the percent sign with some commands to represent a single character. Use multiple percent signs to represent several letters. For example, using three percent signs to represent three letters in this command

```
LISTFILE SUM_RPT %%%
```

produces this output:

```
SUM_RPT HLP A1
```

while doing this with four percent signs,

```
LISTFILE SUM_RPT %%%%
```

produces the following output:

```
SUM_RPT EXEC A1
```

18.3 How Files Are Organized

In keeping with the VM philosophy of giving you a simulation of your own computer all to yourself, VM also gives you a simulation of your own disk on which to store your files. Wow! Big stuff, right? Well, it was in 1964.

The mainframe you use may have many hard disks, but in practice it's easier to think of them as one big one divided into multiple minidisks. The minidisk is the basic division of hard disk space; it is analogous to the concept of a volume, directory, or folder on other systems. (Unlike directories or folders, however, you cannot divide up a minidisk into smaller minidisks.)

CMS assigns a letter to each minidisk to make it possible to distinguish a file on one minidisk from a file with the same filename and filetype on another minidisk. The filemode letter represents the minidisk on which a file is stored. (See Section 18.2, "Filenames," for more on naming files.) Everyone knows their personal minidisk as disk A. The files that comprise the CMS system programs are stored on the S and Y disks.

In Section 19.2, "Sharing Files Between Users," you'll see that commands are available to make your minidisk accessible to other users and to gain access to other users' minidisks. When you execute AC-CESS, the second of the two commands necessary to use someone else's minidisk, part of the command's syntax specifies the letter that you plan to use as a filemode for files on that minidisk. If the system lets you pick the letter yourself, the letters used to designate minidisks are clearly not hard and fast names. If you gain access to Mary Jones' personal disk and call it disk M, she still treats it as her A disk. The next day, you might use the same commands to access her minidisk but choose the letter G to represent it; you'll still be using the same files.

18.3.1 Free space on your disk

When you execute the command QUERY DISK, CMS tells you information about the various minidisks to which you currently have access. In addition to your own A disk and the S and Y disks, your system may have other letters assigned to the minidisks that store application software. The output from the QUERY DISK might look like this:

LABEL	VDEV	M	STAT	CYL	TYPE	BLKSIZE	FILES	BLKS USED-(%)	BLKS LEFT	BLK TOTAL
DSK191	191	A	R/W	2	3390	4096	110	202-56	158	360
65Y-XA	19F	F	R/O	32	3380	4096	727	3915-82	885	4800
MNT190	190	S	R/O	70	3380	4096	279	6547-62	3953	10500
CMSLIB	19E	Y/S	R/O	45	3380	4096	670	6163-91	587	6750

The most important columns of information right now are the M column, which shows the letters assigned to the available minidisks, and the BLKS USED-(%) column. Actually, only the first line of the BLKS USED-(%) column is important, because it applies to your own A minidisk. The second number tells how full it is. In the above illustration, A is 56 percent full. If this figure exceeds 90 percent, it's time to either make room on your A disk by erasing some files or to lobby with your system administrator for more space—that is, for a bigger chunk of hard disk space to be allocated as your A disk. (To help your bargaining position, sometimes they're willing to grant you extra space for only a limited time—for example if a big project means that you'll only need more space until you can get rid of the files needed for the project.)

18.4 Available On-Line Help

CMS has extensive on-line help, accessible from either menus or the command line. With either, you will find two types of help: brief and detailed.

Brief help rarely exceeds half a screen in length. It shows the syntax of a command and one or two examples. For example, Figure 18.8 shows the brief help for the LISTFILE command. It's quite brief—the upper right, where it says "line 1 of 10," shows that the 10 lines that you see (counting the four blank lines) are all that it has. It shows the format, or syntax of the command, and one example of its use. Although the format shows where to put the options to the command (after a left parenthesis following the command name), it doesn't tell you what the options are.

Note the use of upper- and lowercase to show the essential part of the command. All you really need to type is the uppercase part. For the LISTFILE command, only the "L" is really necessary (making some CMS commands even terser than UNIX commands!). If you just type the letter "L" at the command line,

```
 COMMANDS LISTFILE        Brief Help Information      line 1 of 10

The LISTFILE command lists the names of files on any disk or SFS
directory you access.

FORMAT:  Listfile (options

EXAMPLE: If you need to see a listing, then enter:

                 listf







 PF1= All      2= Top     3= Quit    4= Return    5= Clocate   6= ?
 PF7= Backward 8= Forward 9= PFkeys  10=          11= Related  12= Cursor
DMSHEL241I Press PF11 to get related information.
====>
                                            Macro-read 1 File
```

Figure 18.8 Brief help for LISTFILE command.

```
1
```

this has the same effect has typing

```
listfile
```

by itself. Of course, you can put any options after the 1 that you can put after the fully spelled-out LISTFILE command.

Some commands require more than the first letter; for example, the format part of the help screen for the COPYFILE command shows it as COPYfile; this means that you must use at least the first four letters of the word.

While viewing a brief help screen, press PF1 for "All" to display the complete, detailed help about this command. Figure 18.9 shows how the beginning of this help might look for the LISTFILE command.

The "line 1 of 610" shows that this is only the tip of the iceberg. If you wish, you can page down and page down and read more help about the LISTFILE command than you'll ever need.

18.4.1 Help function keys

On either the brief or detailed help screens, the following are the important function keys:

PF1   *Help* or *All* or *Brief*: On a help menu screen, PF1 is the Help key, which has the same effect as the Enter key: when you move your cursor to a choice on the menu and press it, CMS displays help information about the chosen menu item.

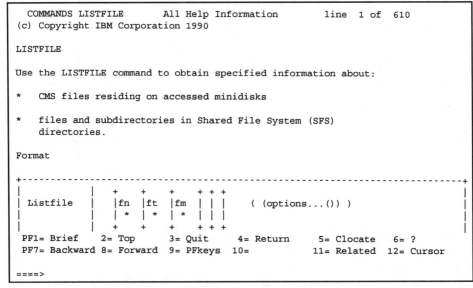

Figure 18.9 Beginning of detailed help for the LISTFILE command.

On a screen that displays help about a particular command, PF1 gives you the All (that is, detailed) help screen instead of the Brief help screen. When viewing a Detailed help screen, PF1 gives you the Brief help.

PF2   *Top*: If you used PF8 to page through a few screens of help information, PF2 returns you to the top.

PF3   *Quit*: Quit the current help screen. When using help menus, you may go from one screen to another as you narrow your search for the information that you need. The Quit key returns you to the previous screen that you were viewing. Repeatedly pressing it brings you back to the CMS Ready; prompt.

PF4   *Return*: Return directly back to the Ready; prompt, no matter how many levels of help you went through to get to the current screen.

PF7   *Backward*: Page up, or view help text above the currently displayed text.

PF8   *Forward*: Page down, or view help text below the currently displayed text.

PF11   *Related*: Display a menu of related help topics to choose from.

PF12   *Cursor*: If the cursor is on the menu part of a help menu, put it at the command line; if it's at the command line, put it at its previous position on the screen.

18.4.2 Help menus

Type the word HELP by itself at the CMS Ready; prompt to start up the Help program. The first screen you see, shown in Figure 18.10, is its main menu.

STATEMTS is not the last choice on this menu; press PF8 to page forward, and you see more of the menu, as shown in Figure 18.11.

That's everything for this particular menu. The first clue about its total number of choices was the first screen's upper right-hand corner, which said line 1 of 25. This meant that the top of your screen had the first of a total of 25 lines in this help file. (The second clue is the line at the bottom of the second screen that says * * * End of File * * *.) Other help files are longer; the PF8 key lets you go through them a page at a time.

Press PF7 to go back to the first screen. Note that part of the description for the TASKS menu choice says "Good choice for beginners." That sounds good; move your cursor to any position on that line and press either Enter or PF1. CMS displays the TASK HELP menu, shown in Figure 18.12.

This is great, because on most computers, if you want help with a command, you must remember the command's name to ask for help with it. In CMS, this help screen helps you find the information you need even when you don't know the command's name. (Forgetting the command names is difficult—one of the nice things about CMS is the

```
 ┌──────────────────────────────────────────────────────────────────────┐
 │  HELP TASKS         Task Help Information          line  1 of  25      │
 │  (c) Copyright IBM Corporation 1990                                    │
 │                                                                        │
 │  Move the cursor to the task that you want, then press the ENTER key   │
 │  or the PF1 key.                                                       │
 │                                                                        │
 │                                                                        │
 │  TASKS        - Help if you don't know VM/ESA commands.                │
 │                 Good choice for beginners                              │
 │  MENUS        - List the HELP component MENUs                          │
 │  HELP         - Explain some ways for using HELP                       │
 │  COMMANDS     - List VM/ESA commands that you can use                  │
 │  CMS          - Show only CMS commands                                 │
 │  CP           - Show only CP commands                                  │
 │  OPTIONS      - Show options for the QUERY and SET                     │
 │                 commands of both CMS and CP                            │
 │  SUBCMDS      - List VM/ESA subcommands that you can                   │
 │                 use, such as XEDIT                                     │
 │  STATEMTS     - Show statements for REXX, EXEC2, and EXEC              │
 │  PF1= Help      2= Top      3= Quit     4= Return    5= Clocate  6= ?  │
 │  PF7= Backward 8= Forward  9= PFkeys 10=           11=         12= Cursor│
 │                                                                        │
 │  ====>                                                                 │
 │                                                   Macro-read 1 File    │
 └──────────────────────────────────────────────────────────────────────┘
```

Figure 18.10 First page of main CMS help menu.

```
 ┌──────────────────────────────────────────────────────────────────────┐
 │   HELP TASKS         Task Help Information         line  9 of  25      │
 │   MENUS        - List the HELP component MENUs                         │
 │   HELP         - Explain some ways for using HELP                      │
 │   COMMANDS     - List VM/ESA commands that you can use                 │
 │   CMS          - Show only CMS commands                                │
 │   CP           - Show only CP commands                                 │
 │   OPTIONS      - Show options for the QUERY and SET                    │
 │                  commands of both CMS and CP                           │
 │   SUBCMDS      - List VM/ESA subcommands that you can                  │
 │                  use, such as XEDIT                                    │
 │   STATEMTS     - Show statements for REXX, EXEC2, and EXEC             │
 │   ROUTINES     - Show callable routines                               │
 │   MACROS       - Show Assembler Language Macros for                    │
 │                  CMS, APPC/VM, and IUCV                                │
 │   MESSAGES     - Explain how to get help for messages                 │
 │   OTHER        - Show commands for other products,                     │
 │    PRODUCTS      such as RSCS and SQLDS                                │
 │   LIBRARY      - Describe the VM/ESA library                           │
 │  * * * End of File * * *                                               │
 │   PF1= Help      2= Top      3= Quit     4= Return    5= Clocate  6= ? │
 │   PF7= Backward 8= Forward  9= PFkeys 10=           11=         12= Cursor│
 │                                                                        │
 │   ====>                                                                │
 │                                                   Macro-read 1 File    │
 └──────────────────────────────────────────────────────────────────────┘
```

Figure 18.11 Second page of main CMS help menu.

sensible choice of command names: ERASE to erase a file, COPY to copy a file, RENAME to rename a file, LIST to list their names, and so forth.)

Of the choices on this screen, Manage files covers the most basic ways to manipulate files; if you move your cursor there and press Enter or PF1, CMS displays the screen shown in Figure 18.13.

```
TASK TASK         Task Help Information        line  1 of  23
(c) Copyright IBM Corporation 1990


Each VM/ESA task below leads to a more detailed
list of tasks for you to choose from.


Move the cursor to the task that you want, then press the ENTER key
or the PF1 key.


Create or change (edit) files
Manage files (copy, rename, erase, etc.)
Work with windows in fullscreen CMS
Work with virtual screens in CMS
Scroll data in a window
Communicate with other users
Use the CMS Shared File System (SFS)
Debug programs and EXECs
Develop programs and EXECs
PF1= Help      2= Top      3= Quit     4= Return     5= Clocate   6= ?
PF7= Backward 8= Forward  9= PFkeys  10=            11=           12= Cursor

====>
                                              Macro-read 2 Files
```

Figure 18.12 First screen of "Task Help" menu.

```
MANAGE TASK        Task Help Information        line  1 of  18
(c) Copyright IBM Corporation 1990

PURPOSE: To help you manage your files.

Move the cursor to the task that you want, then press the ENTER key
or the PF1 key.


List files and associated information
List the files on a minidisk (names only)
Print files
Make copies of files
Rename files
Compare files
Discard or Erase files
Send files to other users
Work with files sent by other users
Specify patterns in file identifiers
PF1= Help      2= Top      3= Quit     4= Return     5= Clocate   6= ?
PF7= Backward 8= Forward  9= PFkeys  10=            11=           12= Cursor

====>
                                              Macro-read 3 Files
```

Figure 18.13 Beginning of "Manage Files" help menu.

If you pick List files on a minidisk, the help system displays Brief help explaining the command that lists file IDs, as shown in Figure 18.14.

Section 18.4.3, "Command-line help," shows a quicker way to find help about a particular command.

```
 CMS LISTFILE        Brief Help Information        line  1 of  10

The LISTFILE command lists the names of files on any disk or SFS
directory you access.

FORMAT:  Listfile (options

EXAMPLE: If you need to see a listing, then enter:

                        listf




 PF1= All       2= Top      3= Quit     4= Return    5= Clocate    6= ?
 PF7= Backward 8= Forward  9= PFkeys  10=            11= Related  12= Cursor
DMSHEL241I Press PF11 to get related information.
====>
                                                    Macro-read 4 Files
```

Figure 18.14 Brief help for "List files on a minidisk."

18.4.3 Command-line help

We saw earlier that typing HELP by itself at the command line brings up the help program's main menu. If you add the name of a command to the HELP command, it skips the menus and displays help information about that command. For example, if you type

```
HELP COPY
```

at the Ready; prompt, the help program jumps right to the screen shown in Figure 18.15.

This shows the brief version of help for the COPYFILE command. If you want to go directly from the Ready; prompt to the detailed help about a command, enter

```
HELP command (DETAIL
```

where command is the name of the command with which you need help.

If we can abbreviate LISTFILE to one letter and COPYFILE to four, maybe we don't need to completely spell out DETAIL. Let's use the HELP program to find out. Since we want to know about the syntax of the HELP command, enter HELP followed by the name of the command you're inquiring about:

```
HELP HELP
```

```
  COMMANDS COPY        Brief Help Information        line  1 of  9
The COPYFILE command lets you copy and/or modify files located on
CMS minidisks or in an SFS directory.

FORMAT:   COPYfile fname1 ftype1 fmode1 fname2 ftype2 fmode2
(options

EXAMPLE: To copy HISTORY SCRIPT H to HISTORY SCRIPT A, enter:
             copy history script h history script a




  PF1= All       2= Top      3= Quit      4= Return     5= Clocate   6= ?
  PF7= Backward 8= Forward  9= PFkeys  10=            11= Related  12= Cursor
DMSHEL241I Press PF11 to get related information.
====>
                                            Macro-read 1 File
```

Figure 18.15 Brief help for COPYFILE command.

The HELP program displays the screen shown in Figure 18.16.

It looks like the brief help is a little too brief to answer our question. Press PF1 to display the detailed help shown in Figure 18.17.

There's nothing about the word DETAIL here, but the detailed help information about the HELP command is 678 lines long. You could press PF8 over and over to look for the information you need, but there's a better way: PF5, the Clocate key.

"Clocate" stands for "Column Locate." As you'll see in the section on XEDIT (the CMS text editor) the LOCATE command finds the line with a specified search target; the CLOCATE command finds the line and the column. In other words, it finds the line and puts the cursor right on the first letter of the word you're searching for.

The PF5 key makes it unnecessary to type out the actual command. Just type the word you're looking for on the help screen's command line

```
detail
```

and press PF5. It doesn't matter whether you type your search target in upper- or lowercase; PF5 finds the next occurrence even if it's spelled "dEtAiL." Figure 18.18 shows what happens when the on-line help finds the target string: it moves that line to the top of your screen.

It looks like it found the word "DETAIL," but not the information we want. The detailed help on the syntax of the HELP command

```
   COMMANDS HELP          Brief Help Information          line  1 of  10

The HELP command tells you how to use VM/ESA HELP.  For
introductory information on the VM/ESA HELP Facility itself, enter
HELP SELF.

FORMAT:  Help component-name command-name (options

EXAMPLE: You forgot how to use the ACCESS command.  If you want to
         get help for that command, then enter:
                          help cms access




   PF1= All       2= Top      3= Quit      4= Return     5= Clocate    6= ?
   PF7= Backward 8= Forward  9= PFkeys  10=             11=          12= Cursor

====>
                                                  Macro-read 1 File
```

Figure 18.16 Brief help for HELP command.

```
   COMMANDS HELP        All Help Information        line  1 of  678
   (c) Copyright IBM Corporation 1990

HELP

Use the HELP command to display online information from the VM/ESA
HELP Facility.  Online HELP provides information for both new and
experienced users.

*   Tasks

    -   End-user, application programmer, and administrator

*   Commands

    -   For VM/ESA (ESA Feature): CMS, CP, AVS, TSAF, VMSES and
        dump viewing facility

    -   For VM/ESA (370 Feature): CMS, CP370, AVS, TSAF, VMSES and
   PF1= Brief     2= Top      3= Quit      4= Return     5= Clocate    6= ?
   PF7= Backward 8= Forward  9= PFkeys  10=             11=          12= Cursor

====>
                                                  Macro-read 1 File
```

Figure 18.17 Beginning of detailed help for the HELP command.

```
  COMMANDS HELP        All Help Information        line  60 of  678
2.  DETAIL - complete information (including messages)

3.  RELATED - information about similar commands.

Format

+-------------------------------------------------------------------+
|       | +                       +                                 |
| Help  | |TASKs                  |                                 |
|       | |Help                   |                                 |
|       | |taskname TASKs         |    +                       + |  |
|       | |menuname MENU          |    | ( (optionA) (optionB) (optionC)()) | |
|       | |component-name cmd-name|    +                       + |  |
|       | +                       +                                 |
|       | +       +                                                 |
|       | |MESSAGE| message-id                                      |
|       | |MSG    |                                                  |
|       | +       +                                                 |
PF1= Brief     2= Top      3= Quit      4= Return    5= Clocate   6= ?
PF7= Backward 8= Forward 9= PFkeys  10=             11=         12= Cursor


====>
                                         Macro-read 1 File
```

Figure 18.18 Result of first search for the string "detail."

seems to begin just below this screen, so the information about the use of the word "detail" can't be far off.

If you continue to press PF5 after finding a search target, it continues to search for more occurrences of the target. Press it a second time after you get the screen in Figure 18.18 and you'll see a screen similar to the one shown in Figure 18.19.

There it is: the word "DETail" as part of the detailed help on the HELP command's format. It looks like you only need the first three letters. In the future, to go directly to the detailed help about any command, you only need to type

```
HELP cmdname (DET
```

where cmdname is the name of the command you want to learn about. You'll find that many CMS programs, like the XEDIT text editor, have their own built-in help. While using a program, there are two easy ways to check whether it has its own help facility:

- If the program has its own command line, type HELP there and press Enter.
- Press the PF1 key. CMS programs are pretty consistent about always using this as the Help key.

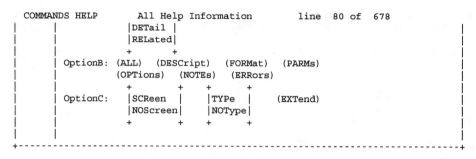

```
COMMANDS HELP        All Help Information        line  80 of  678
|       |      |DETail |
|       |      |RELated|
|       |      +         +
|       | OptionB: (ALL) (DESCript)  (FORMat)   (PARMs)
|       |         (OPTions)  (NOTEs)   (ERRors)
|       |      +       +      +        +
|       | OptionC:  |SCReen  |   |TYPe  |      (EXTend)
|       |           |NOScreen|   |NOType|
|       |      +       +      +        +
|       |
+---------------------------------------------------------------------+
```

Operands

    Help, specified without any parameters, displays a task menu if
    you are using the VM/ESA HELP files. If you are using files
    other than the VM/ESA HELP files and if the HELP HELPMENU file
    has been created, then you will get the HELP HELPMENU file.
PF1= Brief   2= Top   3= Quit   4= Return   5= Clocate   6= ?
PF7= Backward 8= Forward 9= PFkeys 10=   11=   12= Cursor

====>

                                            Macro-read 1 File

Figure 18.19 Result of second search for the word "detail."

18.4.3.1 Command-line help and error messages.   When you get an error
message in CMS, you usually get a cryptic code along with the brief
description of what went wrong. Command-line help can use this code
to get much more detailed help about the error. See Section 19.1.2,
"Common error messages," for more information.

Using Files in VM/CMS

19.1 The Five Most Important Commands

The five most important commands in VM/CMS are:

LISTFILE	Lists file IDs
TYPE	Displays the contents of files
COPY	Copies files
RENAME	Renames files
ERASE	Deletes files

In addition to these commands, CMS has a program that many people use to perform all these functions and more. Section 21.4, "The FILELIST Program," introduces this program.

19.1.1 Command options

CMS uses a left parenthesis to indicate the beginning of special instructions about how a command should operate. A right parenthesis is optional, and has no effect. For example, the LISTFILE command lists file IDs by themselves with no other options, but adding the LABEL option indicates that the system should also list other information about the files:

```
LISTFILE (LABEL
```

When you use the on-line help in CMS, the brief version of help shows you where to put the options, but you need to view the detailed help about a command to learn the available options and the syntax for using them. See Section 18.4, "Available On-Line Help," for more about brief versus detailed help.

19.1.2 Common error messages

When you type anything at the `Ready;` prompt, CMS looks for a program with that name and executes it. If you make a typing mistake, for example

```
HLEP COPY
```

when you meant to type `HELP COPY`, CMS tells you:

```
Unknown CP/CMS command
```

In other words, there is no CMS or CP command called `HLEP`.

Many commands expect some information after the command. For example, when you copy a file, you must indicate the file to copy and the name you want to give to the new copy. If you type the `COPY` command by itself without any filenames, the system responds with the message

```
DMSCPY042E No fileid(s) specified
```

The second part of this tells you the problem: you didn't specify any file ID with the command, which needed at least one. And remember: a complete file ID has three parts, and forgetting the third part is another common cause of error messages. For example, the command

```
copy profile exec
```

causes the system to respond with this message:

```
DMSCPY054E Incomplete fileid specified
```

The letters and numbers at the beginning of these error messages look pretty ugly, but they actually provide the key to some of the best error messages you will find in any operating system. Using the HELP program with one of these codes as a parameter tells you much more about your error. For example, entering

```
HELP DMSCPY054E
```

at the `Ready;` prompt displays the screen shown in Figure 19.1.

The crucial parts of this are the Explanation, which explains the problem in complete sentences, and the User Response, which tells how to correct the problem.

This is a normal help screen. All of its function keys perform identically to their descriptions in Section 18.4.1, "Help function keys."

Another popular cause of error messages is instructions that tell the system to perform an action on a nonexistent file. For example, let's

```
   MSG DMSCPY054E        All Help Information        line  1 of  14
 (c) Copyright IBM Corporation 1990

 054E      Incomplete <fileid|execid> specified

 Explanation:  You must specify the file name and file type or execname
 and exectype in order for the command to be executed.  In addition,
 for some commands you must specify the file mode.

 System Action:  RC=24.
 Execution of the command is terminated.  The system status remains the
 same.

 User Response:  Check the description of the command, correct the
 command line, and reissue the command.
 * * * End of File * * *




 PF1=          2= Top      3= Quit    4= Return    5= Clocate   6= ?
 PF7= Backward 8= Forward  9= PFkeys 10=          11=          12= Cursor

 ====>
```

Figure 19.1 Help description of the DMSCPY054E error code.

say you want to copy a file called TEMPLATE TXT and call the copy
MAY_BUD TXT, but you make a typo and enter the following command:

```
COPY TEMPALTE TXT A MAY_BUD TXT A
```

The CMS system responds with

```
DMSCPY002E INPUT file TEMPALTE TXT A not found
```

which means "The COPY program can't find the input file that you
named." Again, you can use its error code to learn more if you wish.

Remember, the COPY command is just used as an example here.
Similar mistakes with many different commands elicit similar error
messages. For a more detailed explanation of the use of the COPY
command, see Section 19.1.5, "Copying files."

19.1.3 Listing filenames

The full name of the command to list file IDs is LISTFILE. Used by
itself without any parameters, it gives you the names of all the files
on your own minidisk (the A disk).

Many users abbreviate the LISTFILE command as LISTF or LIST.
Its help screen shows that you can abbreviate it down to one character: the "L."

In Figure 19.2, the user types LISTFILE and presses Enter; CMS
then responds with the first screenful of names.

As you can see, there could be more file IDs than will fit on your
screen, so you would need to press the Clear key to continue viewing

```
listfile
ALL        BACKUP    A1
ALL        NOTEBOOK  A0
ALL        NOTEINDX  A0
ANSICODE   TXT       A1
BOB        SCRIPT    A1
BOB        TEST      A1
BOB        TEST1     A1
BUZZ       EXEC      A2
C_ATTACH   EXEC      A1
CLOOP      C         A1
CLOOP      TEXT      A1
CMDLIST    TXT       A0
CMS        EXEC      A1
CMS        TXT       A1
COMBINE    XEDIT     A1
DIR        EXEC      A1
DOWNLOAD   EXEC      A1
EMPLOYEE   DATA      A1
EMPLOYEE   INDEX     A1
GRAPH      DATA      A1
GRAPH      EXEC      A1


                                          MORE...
```

Figure 19.2 Using the listfile command.

them (or wait 60 seconds between each screenful). Don't forget the HT command described in Section 18.1.3.2, "Aborting screen output"; it can be handy here.

As explained in Section 18.2.1, "Wildcards," the LISTFILE (and FILELIST) commands give you the most flexibility of any of the commands that allow the use of wildcards. (For more information on FILELIST, see Section 21.4, "The FILELIST Program.") To list only the files with a filetype of EXEC, use the asterisk to mean "any filename." For example, when you enter

```
L * EXEC
```

CMS displays output similar to this:

```
BUZZ       EXEC    A2
C_ATTACH   EXEC    A1
CC         EXEC    A1
CMS        EXEC    A1
CRITBETA   EXEC    A1
DIR        EXEC    A1
DOWNLOAD   EXEC    A1
EMPATTCH   EXEC    A1
FIND       EXEC    A1
GRAPH      EXEC    A1
HTRACK     EXEC    A1
INFONT     EXEC    A1
IOBETA     EXEC    A1
MARY       EXEC    A1
P          EXEC    A1
PROFILE    EXEC    A1
SERVER     EXEC    A1
```

```
STAFF     EXEC     A1
TEST1     EXEC     A1
TEST4     EXEC     A1
TUTOR     EXEC     A1
```

Although the default filemode of listed files is A, using the asterisk to denote a filemode with the LISTFILE command tells the system to list file IDs on any minidisk that match the filename and filetype given. For example, to list all the SCRIPT files (text files with IBM formatting codes) on any minidisk that are accessible to your user ID, enter the following:

```
L * SCRIPT *
```

This command means "list the IDs of files with any filename, a filetype of SCRIPT, and any filemode." The output looks like this:

```
DOCCHAP1  SCRIPT   A1
DOCCHAP2  SCRIPT   A1
DOCCHAP3  SCRIPT   A1
DOCCHAP4  SCRIPT   A1
DOCCHAP5  SCRIPT   A1
DOCCHAP6  SCRIPT   A1
DOCCHAP7  SCRIPT   A1
GCC024    SCRIPT   Y2
GCC025    SCRIPT   Y2
GCC029    SCRIPT   Y2
GCC311    SCRIPT   Y2
GCC312    SCRIPT   Y2
```

If someone tells you that your system has a report menu program that you start up by typing RPTMENU, you could check out the program's filetype and minidisk location by typing this:

```
L RPTMENU * *
```

If the output was something along the lines of

```
RPTMENU EXEC      Y2
RPTMENU HELPCMS   Y2
```

you would know that the RPTMENU program was an EXEC file (a CMS command file) that you can probably look at with the TYPE command or the XEDIT text editor now that you know the file's full name. (You'll learn how to write your own EXECs in Section 21.2, "Command Files.") The other file listed probably stores HELP information that RPTMENU EXEC uses if someone presses PF1 while using the RPTMENU program.

19.1.3.1 Listing more than filenames.   The LABEL option specifies that you want to see much more than the files' names. Enter

```
LISTFILE * EXEC (LABEL
```

and CMS displays a screen similar to this:

```
FILENAME   FILETYPE   FM    FORMAT   LRECL   RECS   BLOCKS     DATE       TIME      LABEL
BUZZ       EXEC       A2    V          70      36      1     8/17/92    17:54:44   DSK191
C_ATTACH   EXEC       A1    F          80       2      1     1/30/92    16:48:41   DSK191
CRITBETA   EXEC       A1    V          19       4      1     1/21/94    11:23:18   DSK191
DIR        EXEC       A1    V          24       1      1     1/29/92    16:27:20   DSK191
DOWNLOAD   EXEC       A1    V          73      31      1     2/02/92    11:01:21   DSK191
HTRACK     EXEC       A1    V          24       2      1     7/27/92    13:17:05   DSK191
INFONT     EXEC       A1    V          19       2      1    12/10/92    13:30:28   DSK191
IOBETA     EXEC       A1    V          19       4      1     1/07/94    12:34:47   DSK191
MBAILEY    EXEC       A1    V          22       1      1     1/30/92    16:49:02   DSK191
PROFILE    EXEC       A1    V          29       8      1     1/18/94    12:47:00   DSK191
TEST1      EXEC       A1    V          27       9      1     2/02/92    10:53:40   DSK191
TEST4      EXEC       A1    V          18       8      1     8/21/92    10:20:19   DSK191
TUTOR      EXEC       A1    V           7       1      1     9/23/93    16:16:57   DSK191
Ready; T = 0.01/0.01 10:18:00
```

The screen shows the following information about the files:

FILENAME	The first part of a file ID's three parts. See Section 18.2, "Filenames," for more on this.
FILETYPE	The second of a file ID's three parts. The filetype shows the type of file on that line.
FM	The filemode, or the third of a file ID's three parts. The file-mode is the letter that represents the minidisk where the file is located. Section 18.3, "How Files Are Organized," describes its role more fully.
FORMAT	A format (or "record format") of V means that a file's records have variable length. "Records" here means "lines." The terms were once fairly synonymous, but as the science of dealing with databases advanced, the term "record" took on a more specific meaning.) In other words, the lines aren't all the same length. A format of F means that they have fixed length. If any lines seem shorter than others, spaces are in-serted to make their lengths equal.
LRECL	The Logical RECord Length (pronounced "ell-rekkul," with the accent on the first syllable). For a fixed format file, this shows each line's length; otherwise, this shows the longest line's length.
RECS	The number of records, or lines.
BLOCKS	How many blocks, or units of hard disk space, the file takes up.
DATE	The date the file was last modified.
TIME	The time of day the file was last modified.
LABEL	A name used to identify the actual physical disk where the file is located (as opposed to the virtual disk, which is repre-sented by the filemode).

The most important information that you ever need to know about a file (besides its name) is its size and when it was last modified. So RECS, DATE, and TIME are the most important columns here. You may need to worry about FORMAT and LRECL if an application program expects a file to have one format but it actually has another. We'll see in Section 19.1.5, "Copying files," that when you copy a file, you can specify the copy's FORMAT and LRECL and make a copy that doesn't cause you trouble if the original did not cooperate with the application that tried to use it.

Forget about BLOCKS and LABEL. Part of the point of RECS and filemodes are to keep you from worrying about these.

19.1.4 Displaying a text file's contents

The command to type out a file's contents on the screen is simple: TYPE. For example, if you want to see what's in a file called PHONLIST TXT, type the following:

```
TYPE PHONLIST TXT
```

CMS displays the file's contents on your screen:

```
Frank x5388
Kate x3325
Jim x0543
Kevin x5453
Tastee Deli 874-5342
Messenger Service 878-0775
Mary 878-3431
Mary @ work 874-5363
Cinema 123 874-6543
```

If the file's contents take up more than one screen, you may end up pressing the Clear key repeatedly, so don't forget about the HT command described in Section 18.1.3.2, "Aborting screen output." If you don't know how long a file is, you might want to check it out before displaying it with the TYPE command by using the LISTFILE command's LABEL option. For example, if you entered the command

```
LISTFILE PHONLIST TXT (LABEL
```

and CMS told you something like

```
FILENAME  FILETYPE  FM  FORMAT  LRECL  RECS  BLOCKS    DATE      TIME     LABEL
PHONLIST  TXT       A2    V        70  1046       1  8/17/92  17:54:44  DSK191
```

you would know that, with 1046 lines, using the TYPE command with this file could keep you pressing that Clear key for a while. It's better to use the XEDIT text editor to look at such a file.

19.1.5 Copying files

The command to copy a file is COPY. (The full name is actually COPYFILE, but you only need the first four letters.) You simply tell

CMS the name of the file you want to copy and the name that you want to give to the copy. The only tough part to remember is that unlike many other CMS commands, you must include the filemode in both file IDs. It's easy to make this mistake, because so many CMS commands don't require you to specify the filemode for files that have a filemode of A.

Let's say you want to make a copy of the file PHONLIST TXT and call it PHONLIST BACKUP. This is the correct syntax:

```
COPY PHONLIST TXT A PHONLIST BACKUP A
```

If you entered

```
COPY PHONLIST TXT PHONLIST BACKUP
```

CMS would tell you:

```
DMSCPY054E Incomplete fileid specified
```

as if to tell you, "If you want to copy this file PHONLIST TXT P (it ignores any character after the first in a filemode, unless it's a number designating the file's access rights), you need to give the copy a full three-part name, not just BACKUP." If you try to make a copy with the same name as an existing file, CMS displays the following error message:

```
DMSCPY024E File PHONLIST BACKUP A1 already exists; specify REPLACE
option
```

If you look at the detailed help for COPY, you will see that REPLACE is one of its many possible options. (Don't forget the left parenthesis before you add an option.) If included, it means "Make a copy of file1 and call it file2, even if a file named 'file2' already exists." Section 19.1.5.1, "Changing a file's format," describes other options for the COPY command.

Using the equal sign can reduce the amount of typing necessary for the COPY command if any part of the copy's file ID is the same as that of the source file. For example, instead of typing

```
COPY SCHEDULE TXT A SCHEDULE BACKUP A
```

you could type

```
COPY SCHEDULE TXT A = BACKUP =
```

and the copy would have the same filename and filemode as the original.

You can use the asterisk as a wildcard in the COPY command, but not in combination with other letters. It must be used to represent an entire filename, filetype, or filemode. For example, to make copies of all your files that have a filetype of TXT so that all the copies have a filetype of BACKUP, you could type this:

```
COPY * TXT A = BACKUP =
```

19.1.5.1 Changing a file's format. Sometimes a file might not have the right record format for your needs. For example, if you use a telecommunications program like Kermit to copy a file from a PC to a VM/CMS system, the VM copy will probably have a variable record format (a V shows up as the FORMAT for that file when you list its name with the LABEL option). If this is a data file for use by some CMS application, the application might not read it, claiming that it's in the wrong format.

Instead of actually changing its format, it's better to make a copy of it with a different format. This is safer in case it takes more than one try, because you leave your original intact. To specify the copy's format, use the RECFM and LRECL options:

```
COPY fn1 ft1 fm1 fn2 ft2 fm2 (RECFM F LRECL xx
```

where fn1, ft1, and fm1 are the filename, filetype, and filemode, respectively, of the file you're copying and fn2, ft2, and fm2 are the copy's filename, filetype, and filemode. xx is the length of the lines in the fixed format copy.

How do you determine what this number should be? Eighty is always popular, being the number of characters that fit on one line of a character-based display screen (as well as the number of characters that fit on the ancestor of one of these lines, a punch card). The value listed under LRECL for your source file provides another clue. This shows the length of the longest line. If you pick a smaller value for the record length of your fixed-format copy, you will cut off the longer lines and lose data.

If you enter the command

```
COPY PHONLIST TXT A PHONTEST TXT A (RECFM F LRECL 80
```

and then type

```
LISTFILE PHON* TXT (LABEL
```

to check on the results of your copy command, CMS displays something like this:

FILENAME	FILETYPE	FM	FORMAT	LRECL	RECS	BLOCKS	DATE	TIME	LABEL
PHONLIST	TXT	A1	V	78	1046	1	10/11/92	15:36:15	DSK191
PHONTEST	TXT	A1	F	80	1046	1	1/24/94	9:35:13	DSK191

The best clue for the LRECL value for your data file is found by looking at any other data files used by the application that rejected your file in the first place. They'll probably all have the same filetype, since they all serve the same purpose.

For example, say you've used the PC version of the UpRiteBase database program to create a data file called ADDRESS.UPR. You use Kermit to move it to the mainframe and rename it ADDRESS UPRITE so that it has the same filetype as other data files used by the CMS version of UpRiteBase. The CMS version still doesn't accept it as a data file, so you enter the command

```
LIST * UPRITE (LABEL
```

and CMS shows you the following:

FILENAME	FILETYPE	FM	FORMAT	LRECL	RECS	BLOCKS	DATE	TIME	LABEL
ADDRESS	UPRITE	A1	V	78	342	1	10/11/94	15:36:15	DSK191
INVENTRY	UPRITE	A1	F	80	1046	1	10/10/94	9:35:13	DSK191
EMPLOYEE	UPRITE	A1	F	80	214	1	9/24/94	12:34:42	DSK191

It looks like the other CMS UpRiteBase data files have a fixed format and an LRECL of 80, so you need to change ADDRESS UPRITE to have these attributes. You copy it with the following command:

```
COPY ADDRESS UPRITE A ADDRESS1 = = (RECFM F LRECL 80
```

If the CMS version of UpRiteBase accepts ADDRESS1 UPRITE as a proper UpRiteBase data file, then you can erase ADDRESS UPRITE and rename ADDRESS1 UPRITE with that name.

Whatever you try, make sure that there are no problems with your copy being accepted by the program that will use it before you erase your original file and rename the copy to have the same name as the original. If your LRECL value shortens any lines, you should keep your original as a backup to check for the lost data.

Changing the format can work the other way, if you need to make a variable length copy of a fixed format file. Use the following syntax:

```
COPY fn1 ft1 fm1 fn2 ft2 fm2 (RECFM V
```

Note that the command includes no LRECL value. The system automatically figures it out. It's not hard to guess, if your original file had fixed format records: the length of those records will be the length of the lines in the copy.

19.1.6 Renaming files

The syntax for renaming a file is nearly identical to the syntax for copying a file:

```
RENAME oldfn oldft oldfm newfn newft newfm
```

where `oldfn`, `oldft`, and `oldfm` are the filename, filetype, and file-mode, respectively, of the file to rename and `newfn`, `newft`, and `newfm` are the three parts of the new file ID. Don't forget the file-modes.

Since you rarely change all three parts of a file's ID when renaming it, the equal sign mentioned in Section 19.1.5 ("Copying files") is handy when renaming files. For example, to rename the file PROPOSED SCHEDULE as APRIL SCHEDULE, entering

```
RENAME PROPOSED SCHEDULE A APRIL = =
```

requires less typing than entering this:

```
RENAME PROPOSED SCHEDULE A APRIL SCHEDULE A
```

You can also use the asterisk the same way that you use it when copying files. To rename all the files with a filetype of SCHEDULE so that they have a filetype of OLDSCHED, type:

```
RENAME * SCHEDULE A = OLDSCHED =
```

19.1.7 Deleting files

It's better to remember this as "erasing" files instead of "deleting" them, because it makes it easier to remember the command:

```
ERASE filename filetype
```

If you leave off the filemode, CMS assumes that you mean a filemode of A. You may never need to specify the filemode when you erase a file, because you may never have permission to erase any files other than those on your own A minidisk.

You can use the asterisk with the ERASE command the same way you use it with the COPY or RENAME commands, but be careful. If you decide that you want to erase all the files that you don't need with the command

```
ERASE * BACKUP
```

then you might want to use the same file ID specification with the LIST command first:

```
LIST * BACKUP
```

This shows you the names of the files that fit this description, so you can be sure that you don't erase more files than you had planned.

19.2 Sharing Files between Users

IBM mainframes have always made security a high priority. Poking around the hard disk to see what else is on the system is not nearly as easy as it is with UNIX or VMS. There is a way, however, to gain access to minidisks assigned to other user IDs. And remember, each user ID doesn't necessarily represent a user, because some programs get assigned their own user ID when they are installed onto the system. To run these programs, you need access to the disk where they are stored.

There are two steps to gaining access to another minidisk:

- Telling CP about the disk to access with the LINK command
- Telling CMS what to call this new minidisk with the ACCESS command

The QUERY DISK command (first mentioned in Section 18.3, "How Files Are Organized") gives you some good background information that is useful to check before you tell the LINK and ACCESS commands what they need to know. This was the output we saw before from the QUERY DISK command:

```
LABEL   VDEV  M    STAT  CYL  TYPE  BLKSIZE  FILES  BLKS USED-(%)  BLKS LEFT  BLK TOTAL
DSK191  191   A    R/W     2  3390  4096       110       202-56         158        360
65Y-XA  19F   F    R/O    32  3380  4096       727      3915-82         885       4800
MNT190  190   S    R/O    70  3380  4096       279      6547-62        3953      10500
CMSLIB  19E   Y/S  R/O    45  3380  4096       670      6163-91         587       6750
```

In addition to the M column that shows the letters assigned to the minidisks, note the VDEV column that shows the three-digit hexadecimal number that CMS uses to keep track of each disk. (Hexadecimal numbers have 16 possible digits going from 0 through 9 and then A through F, so you occasionally see the first six letters of the alphabet showing up as a digit. The buzzword version of the term is "hex numbers," a variation whose voodoo numerology overtones make it one of the more evocative terms in computer science.) If someone wants to access your A disk, they need to know that your copy of CMS treats it as device number 191. Almost everyone's A disk has a device number of 191.

When you gain access to someone else's minidisk, you add it to your list of accessible minidisks, so you must assign it a letter and a device number. You can use any letter of the alphabet that's not already assigned to a minidisk in your list, and you can use just about any number that's not currently assigned to a minidisk. Let's say we need access to the minidisk of Mary Jones' MJONES user ID, and we're going to call it disk B and give it the device number 192.

First issue the LINK command. Use the following syntax:

```
LINK userid devnumber1 devnumber2 mode password
```

where:

userid	Is the user ID of the person whose minidisk you're going to link to.
devnumber1	Is the virtual device number used by that ID for that disk. (In other words, the number that the ID uses to keep track of which piece of hardware it is.) A user's A disk is usually 191; if not, they have to tell you. They can't expect you to guess it.
devnumber2	Is the device number that your ID will use for the disk. You can pick just about any number you like, as long as it doesn't show up in the VDEV column when you enter the command QUERY DISK, because those numbers show the ones that are already taken. The upper limit on allowable numbers varies from system to system; keep it under 300 and you'll be safe.
mode	Shows whether you want read and/or write access to the disk, and whether it matters to you if someone else is currently using it. The safest value to put here is r, which means you want read access, and only if no one else is currently using the disk. A mode of rr means you want read access even if someone is currently using the disk. This means that you can read files currently in the process of being changed, which can lead to trouble.
password	Is the password required to link to the disk. This is not the same as the password that the other user logs on with; they must have a specific password known as the "read password" for someone to link to their disk to read their files. Another password known as the "write password" is necessary if other users are going to link to their disk to change or add files. CMS has no direct command for setting this password; each installation buys a special program like DIRMAINT or VMSECURE. You start either of these programs by typing its name, and then a series of menus leads you through the necessary steps.

If you link to a disk with software that everyone's allowed to use, there might not even be a password. If you leave it out when you should have included it, the system will ask you for it.

Instead of having people use read and write passwords, the system administrator may assign a set of rules determining who can link to where to do what. People in the same group might get permission to link to each other's disks for read permission, but nothing else. If you try to link to a disk using a mode that a rule prevents you from using, CMS displays an error message telling you that a rule prevents you from making the requested link.

Just because you lack write access to a particular disk doesn't mean you lack read access; because write access leads to trouble more easily, system administrators often withhold this permission when they grant read access.

Now it's time to link to Mary's disk. The QUERY DISK command showed that no disk is using the number 192, and Mary said that her read password is READTHIS. So we enter this:

```
LINK MJONES 191 192 R READTHIS
```

If the system displays no error messages, it worked.

CP now knows that you can use Mary's disk, but you must still tell CMS. We do this with the ACCESS command, which has the following syntax:

```
ACCESS devnumber2 diskletter
```

where devnumber2 is the same number you used when you issued the LINK command—the number you said you would use to refer to this hardware device. The diskletter is the letter of the alphabet that you will use to refer to it in CMS commands. In other words, it's the filemode of any files that you will use from that disk. You can use any letter that didn't show up in the M column when you entered QUERY DISK, because those letters are taken. We now enter

```
ACCESS 192 B
```

and then another QUERY DISK to see what happened:

LABEL	VDEV	M	STAT	CYL	TYPE	BLKSIZE	FILES	BLKS USED-(%)	BLKS LEFT	BLK TOTAL
DSK191	191	A	R/W	2	3390	4096	110	202-56	158	360
MKTJXS	192	B	R/O	45	3390	4096	355	883-70	377	1260
65Y-XA	19F	F	R/O	32	3380	4096	727	3915-82	885	4800
MNT190	190	S	R/O	70	3380	4096	279	6547-62	3953	10500
CMSLIB	19E	Y/S	R/O	45	3380	4096	670	6163-91	587	6750

And there it is, labeled "MKTJXS." The STAT column for the B disk says "R/O" to show that you have "Read Only" access.

19.2.1 Unlinking the disk

The system automatically unlinks these disks when you log off, but you may need to undo these two steps without logging off (for example, if your link prevents someone else from linking). You can unlink in two steps, but it can also be done in one with the following syntax:

```
RELEASE devnumber2 (DETACH
```

These terms each play the following roles:

RELEASE   Undoes the ACCESS command

devnumber2   Is the device number you've been using to refer to the disk
                 since you accessed it

(DETACH   Shows that you want to detach as well as release the disk

You'll probably want to do a QUERY DISK again just to make sure that it worked correctly.

19.2.2 Other ways to link

Because LINK and ACCESS are used together so often, many sites have an EXEC command file available that automates these two steps. It might be called something like ATTACH. (Don't be surprised if many users at that site aren't even aware that ATTACH—or whatever the EXEC is called—isn't even a real CMS command. This is the beauty of command files, that creating them is like adding a new command to an operating system.) Just ask if they use LINK and ACCESS to gain access to other disks, or if they use something else. If the terms LINK and ACCESS inspire a blank stare, you can be sure that a system administrator at that site has put together an EXEC for them to use. This won't prevent you from using LINK and ACCESS; in fact, the EXEC that they call will be using it.

20

The VM/CMS XEDIT Text Editor

XEDIT (pronounced "eks-edit") is a powerful text editor with plenty for the beginner and even more for the expert. It is popular enough that a DOS version called KEDIT has been developed for PCs. It features extensive on-line help, and you can easily create files called macros that are like command files for the text editor. When you tell XEDIT to execute a certain macro, it executes the series of commands in that file as if the file was a program.

20.1 Entering XEDIT

To invoke XEDIT, you only need its first letter. Enter X followed by the name of the file you want to edit. If it exists, XEDIT displays its first 18 lines on the screen. If the file doesn't exist, XEDIT creates an empty file with that name. For example, if you don't have a file named KUBLA KHAN and you enter

```
X KUBLA KHAN
```

XEDIT displays a screen similar to the one shown in Figure 20.1.

Across the top line, XEDIT displays various details about the file. (For more on these details, see Section 19.1.3.1, "Listing more than filenames.")

KUBLA	The file's filename.
KHAN	The file's filetype.
A1	The file's filemode.
F	The file's record format: either Fixed or Variable.
80	The length of these fixed-length records (lines of text).
Trunc = 80	XEDIT truncates any characters after the 80th.

```
 KUBLA      KHAN       A1   F 80   Trunc=80 Size=0 Line=0 Col=1 Alt=0

===== * * * Top of File * * *
===== * * * End of File * * *













====>
                                                       X E D I T   1 File
```

Figure 20.1 Opening XEDIT screen for a new file.

Size = 0	The number of records in the file.
Line = 0	The current line number.
Col = 1	The column location of a string found using certain advanced commands.
Alt = 0	The number of alterations since the last autosave. See Section 20.2, "Customizing Your XEDIT Environment" for more on this.

The next two lines show the file's top and bottom. You enter data between these lines. To their left, the five equal signs show the prefix area, where you enter commands to insert, delete, copy, and move lines. At the bottom of the screen, the arrow (==== >) shows the command-line, where you enter commands, and the message X E D I T 1 File shows that XEDIT is currently editing one file. (It is capable of editing several at once.)

20.2 Customizing Your XEDIT Environment

Your screen may look slightly different from this. For example, your command line might be at the top of the screen, your prefix area may show up as sequential numbers (00000, 00001, 00002, etc.). Your prefix area might not be there at all. You can control these details with the XEDIT SET command. For now, type in the following SET commands manually at the XEDIT command line; you'll see in Section 20.7.2, "The automatic startup macro," how to make them execute automatically whenever you start up XEDIT.

To move your cursor to the command line, just press your Enter key.

If you don't see a prefix area, enter

```
SET PREFIX ON
```

at the command line and press Enter to display it. If the prefix area displays as numbers instead of equal signs, it won't affect the way you use it. `SET NUMBER ON` and `SET NUMBER OFF` control whether it displays as numbers.

Because old-fashioned terminals could only deal with uppercase letters, sometimes XEDIT translates everything you type to uppercase. This can be annoying when you type a paragraph, press Enter to move your cursor to the command line, and the whole paragraph gets translated to uppercase. To tell XEDIT to preserve a mix of upper- and lowercase letters, enter

```
SET CASE MIXED
```

at the command line. When writing a program in a language like FORTRAN, which expects all uppercase letters, entering the command

```
SET CASE UPPER
```

translates every new line of text to all uppercase letters each time you press Enter.

XEDIT has a great feature called "autosave." You can set it to periodically save your work in a backup file automatically. The backup frequency is determined by how often you press the Enter key. If you like, you can set it to back up your file every time you press Enter, but the extra second or two it takes to save can make this annoying. Setting it to back up your file every fifth time you press Enter is a good interval. Enter the command

```
SET AUTOSAVE 5
```

to do this. As you edit your file, the `Alt =` message at the top of your screen shows how many alterations since the last save. When it reaches 5, XEDIT displays a message similar to the following:

```
DMSXSU510I AUTOSAVED as 100005 AUTOSAVE A1
```

The number used for the filename may vary, but the filetype is always `AUTOSAVE` and the filemode is A1.

Note that it doesn't save your file with the same name that you originally gave it. This leaves you the option of aborting your changes if you like. If the system does crash or you lose your connection, you probably will have forgotten your autosaved file's filename, so you can enter

```
LISTFILE * AUTOSAVE (LABEL
```

to see what autosave files you have and when they were created. Don't worry about these autosave files cluttering up your A disk—if your editing session goes without incident and you save your file or abort the session without interruption, the system automatically gets rid of any autosave files.

XEDIT has many other SET commands to customize your session. Section 20.7.1, "XEDIT on-line help," tells how you can find out about more of them.

20.3 Prefix Commands

In addition to command-line commands, many XEDIT operations are performed with prefix commands. You can add, delete, copy, and move lines by entering one- or two-character commands in the prefix area and pressing the Enter key. (MVS and AS/400 users who find that the screen looks similar to the ISPF or SEU editor screens will be familiar with line commands; prefix commands are those editors' counterpart to this.)

Prefix commands are not limited to the prefix area of the contents of your file; you can also enter them in the prefix area of the Top of File and End of File lines. (If you couldn't do this, it would be pretty tough to add your first blank line.)

You can enter a prefix command anywhere on the prefix. For example, if you enter 2d, the command to delete two lines, like this

```
2d===
```

or like this

```
===2d
```

it still works the same. Likewise, if you issue the SET NUMBER ON command so that your prefixes appear as numbers, it doesn't matter whether you enter the 2d as

```
2d001
```

or

```
0002d
```

```
KUBLA     KHAN      A1  F 80  Trunc=80 Size=0 Line=0 Col=1 Alt=0

==a== * * * Top of File * * *
===== * * * End of File * * *
```
Figure 20.2 Entering the a prefix command to add a new line in XEDIT.

although it can obviously lead to confusion if you enter prefix commands that use numbers (like 2d) on a prefix area that is displayed as numbers instead of as equal signs.

If you ever enter a prefix command and then realize, before you press Enter, that you didn't mean to enter that prefix command there, just type spaces over it. The next time you press Enter, XEDIT puts back whatever was there before you entered the prefix command—either equal signs or, if the prefix area took the form of numbers, the appropriate prefix numbers.

20.3.1 Adding new lines

Before you can type any text into your file, you must add some blank lines. To add one blank line, move your cursor to the prefix of the line that says * * * Top of File * * * and type the letter a anywhere on the prefix. Figure 20.2 shows where to enter the a.

Press Enter, and XEDIT adds a new line below the one where you entered the prefix command, as shown in Figure 20.3.

To add multiple lines, you don't need to do this over and over. Instead, most prefix commands let you put a number before or after them to say "perform this command this many times." If you enter

```
==a7=
```

or

```
==7a=
```

and then press Enter, XEDIT adds seven blank lines below the line where you entered the command.

20.3.2 Moving your cursor around

Your up, down, left, and right cursor keys move the cursor in the direction in which they point.

```
KUBLA     KHAN      A1  F 80  Trunc=80 Size=0 Line=0 Col=1 Alt=0

===== * * * Top of File * * *
=====
===== * * * End of File * * *
```
Figure 20.3 Result of the a prefix command entered in Figure 20.2.

The Tab key helps you move around more quickly. To move your cursor to the beginning of the previous line, use the Backtab key (if you're using a PC that is emulating a mainframe terminal, press the Shift key and the Tab key simultaneously). If your XEDIT prefix area is displayed and your cursor is on a line of text, Tab and Backtab jump your cursor to the prefix area. If your cursor is on the prefix area, pressing either key jumps your cursor to the beginning of the appropriate line.

20.3.3 Inserting, deleting, and typing over words and characters

To add text to blank lines, just move your cursor to the line and type. When you need to move your cursor back to the command line, press Enter; if XEDIT turns all your text into uppercase, you'll need the SET CASED MIXED command described in Section 20.2, "Customizing Your XEDIT Environment."

To delete an individual character, move your cursor there and press your Delete key. On a 3270 terminal, the delete key has a lowercase "a" with a proofreader's symbol for deletion: a line through it that forms a loop. When emulating a 3270 terminal, your emulation software probably has your PC's Delete key doing this job.

To type over existing text, just move your cursor where you want the new text and type.

To insert text, move your cursor to the place where you want to insert it and press the Insert key. On a 3270 terminal, this key has the letter "a" with a caret symbol (^) over it. When you press it, a carat symbol should appear at the bottom of your screen to indicate that you are in insert mode. (When emulating a 3270, your cursor may change shape.) Text that you type in moves any text currently to the right of the cursor further to the right. If the last character gets moved to the column indicated by the TRUNC = value at the top of your screen, XEDIT beeps at you to indicate that you can't insert more characters on that line.

To return to overstrike mode while using a 3270 terminal, press the key marked "Reset." The carat symbol should disappear, and newly typed text takes the place of the characters at the cursor. (When your keyboard "locks up," or refuses to accept input, the Reset key is also useful for freeing up the keyboard.) On most PCs emulating a 3270, the Insert key does the job of the 3270 keyboard's Insert key and the Escape key serves as the Reset key. Check you emulation program's documentation to make sure.

20.3.4 Duplicating lines

Use the double quotation mark, sometimes called the "ditto" symbol (") to duplicate a line of text. Suppose you entered it next to the line "A stately pleasure-dome decree" as shown in Figure 20.4.

```
KUBLA    KHAN     A1  F 80  Trunc=80 Size=8 Line=0 Col=1 Alt=0

===== * * * Top of File * * *
===== In Xanadu did Kubla Khan
="=== A stately pleasure-dome decree
===== Where Alph, the sacred river, ran
===== Through caverns measureless to man
===== Down to a sunless sea.
=====
=====
```
Figure 20.4 Entering the " prefix command for line duplication in XEDIT.

```
KUBLA    KHAN     A1  F 80  Trunc=80 Size=8 Line=0 Col=1 Alt=0

===== * * * Top of File * * *
===== In Xanadu did Kubla Khan
===== A stately pleasure-dome decree
===== A stately pleasure-dome decree
===== Where Alph, the sacred river, ran
===== Through caverns measureless to man
===== Down to a sunless sea.
=====
```
Figure 20.5 Result of the " prefix command entered in Figure 20.4.

```
KUBLA    KHAN     A1  F 80  Trunc=80 Size=8 Line=0 Col=1 Alt=0

===== * * * Top of File * * *
===== In Xanadu did Kubla Khan
===== A stately pleasure-dome decree
===== A stately pleasure-dome decree
===== A stately pleasure-dome decree
===== A stately pleasure-dome decree
===== A stately pleasure-dome decree
===== A stately pleasure-dome decree
===== Where Alph, the sacred river, ran
===== Through caverns measureless to man
===== Down to a sunless sea.
=====
```
Figure 20.6 Result of using the 5" prefix command to duplicate a line five times.

After pressing Enter, the line is duplicated; Figure 20.5 shows the result.

If you put a number immediately before or after the ditto symbol, XEDIT duplicates the line that many times. Figure 20.6 shows what would have happened if you had entered 5" instead of just " as in Figure 20.4.

This command is handy when you need to type something repetitive. You just type it once, make as many copies as you need, and edit the copies.

```
KUBLA     KHAN      A1  F 80  Trunc=80 Size=8 Line=0 Col=1 Alt=0

===== * * * Top of File * * *
===== In Xanadu did Kubla Khan
=2d== A stately pleasure-dome decree
===== Where Alph, the sacred river, ran
===== Through caverns measureless to man
===== Down to a sunless sea.
=====
=====
```
Figure 20.7 Entering the 2d prefix command to delete two lines in XEDIT.

```
KUBLA     KHAN      A1  F 80  Trunc=80 Size=8 Line=0 Col=1 Alt=0

===== * * * Top of File * * *
===== In Xanadu did Kubla Khan
===== Through caverns measureless to man
===== Down to a sunless sea.
=====
=====
=====
=====
```
Figure 20.8 Result of the 2d prefix command entered in Figure 20.7.

```
KUBLA     KHAN      A1  F 80  Trunc=80 Size=8 Line=0 Col=1 Alt=0

===== * * * Top of File * * *
===== In Xanadu did Kubla Khan
=dd== A stately pleasure-dome decree
===== Where Alph, the sacred river, ran
===dd Through caverns measureless to man
===== Down to a sunless sea.
=====
=====
```
Figure 20.9 Entering the dd prefix command to delete a block of lines in XEDIT.

20.3.5 Deleting lines

The letter d in a line's prefix deletes that line the next time you press
Enter. A number immediately preceding or following it tells XEDIT to
delete that many lines, starting with the line where the command is
entered. In Figure 20.7, two lines are about to be deleted.

After you press Enter, they're gone. Figure 20.8 shows the result.

Put the letter d twice in a prefix without any number to indicate
that the line begins or ends a block that you want to delete. If you
press Enter while only one line has the dd, XEDIT leaves it there
until it has a partner. In Figure 20.9, XEDIT is ready to delete all but
the first and last lines of text the next time you press Enter.

This is particularly useful when the beginning and end of the block
that you want to delete are not on the same screen, because the alter-

```
KUBLA    KHAN      A1  F 80  Trunc=80 Size=8 Line=0 Col=1 Alt=0

===== * * * Top of File * * *
====p In Xanadu did Kubla Khan
===== A stately pleasure-dome decree
cc=== Where Alph, the sacred river, ran
===== Through caverns measureless to man
===cc Down to a sunless sea.
=====
=====
```
Figure 20.10   Using the cc and p prefix commands to copy a block in XEDIT.

native (counting the number of lines to delete so that you can put a number after a single d) is a lot of trouble.

20.3.6 Copying lines

Copying is similar to deletion except that you use the letter c to indicate the line or lines to copy and you must indicate a destination for the copied text. XEDIT gives you three options for indicating the text to copy:

- Enter a single c in a line's prefix if you only need to copy that one line.
- Enter a single c preceded or followed by a number to indicate how many lines to copy.
- Enter cc at the first and last lines of the block to copy.

In addition to indicating the line or lines to copy, you must indicate where to copy them. Two prefix commands make this possible:

p   When Enter is pressed, copy the block to the line preceding this one.

f   When Enter is pressed, copy the block to the line following this one.

In Figure 20.10, the third, fourth, and fifth lines are about to get copied above the first line, to the beginning of the file.

Figure 20.11 shows how it looks after you press Enter.

```
KUBLA    KHAN      A1  F 80  Trunc=80 Size=8 Line=0 Col=1 Alt=0

===== * * * Top of File * * *
===== Where Alph, the sacred river, ran
===== Through caverns measureless to man
===== Down to a sunless sea.
===== In Xanadu did Kubla Khan
===== A stately pleasure-dome decree
===== Where Alph, the sacred river, ran
===== Through caverns measureless to man
===== Down to a sunless sea.
=====
=====
```
Figure 20.11   Result of the cc and p prefix commands entered in Figure 20.10.

20.3.7 Moving lines

Moving is similar to copying, except that after you press Enter, the original lines are no longer there—they're moved to their new location. As with copying, there are three ways to specify the block to move, but these use the letter m:

- Enter a single m in a line's prefix if you only need to move that one line.

- Enter a single m preceded or followed by a number to indicate how many lines to move.

- Enter mm at the first and last lines of the block to move.

To specify the destination of the block to move, use the letters p or f the same way you do to specify the destination of a block to copy.

20.4 Searching for Text

To search for a particular string of text, use the following command:

```
LOCATE /string
```

where string is the string you want to find. Actually, you don't really need the LOCATE part. If you enter the command

```
/ALPH
```

and press Enter, XEDIT scrolls forward to make the the line with "Alph" in it the first line on the screen, as shown in Figure 20.12.

Note that although we were searching for "ALPH" it found "Alph." The search is not case-sensitive.

When XEDIT searches, it searches forward. If you now try the command

```
/kubla
```

XEDIT skips to the bottom and tells you "Target not found." To jump to the top of the file before the next search, enter this command:

```
KUBLA     KHAN     A1  F 80  Trunc=80 Size=8 Line=3 Col=1 Alt=1

===== Where Alph, the sacred river, ran
===== Through caverns measureless to man
===== Down to a sunless sea on 10/12/94.
=====
=====
=====
===== * * * End of File * * *
```

Figure 20.12 Result of searching for the string "ALPH" with the command /ALPH

```
  KUBLA    KHAN     A1  F 80   Trunc=80 Size=8 Line=3 Col=1 Alt=1
===== Down to a sunless sea on 10/12/94.
=====
=====
=====
===== * * * End of File * * *
```
Figure 20.13   Result of searching for the string "10/12/94" with the command #10/12/94

```
        TOP
```

BOTTOM is an equally valid command.

You can use another character instead of the slash to show where your search target begins, but then you must include the LOCATE command. This is useful when searching for something that contains a slash, like a date. If you enter

```
LOCATE #10/12/94
```

at the XEDIT command line and press return, XEDIT jumps to the next occurrence of that string, as shown in Figure 20.13.

20.5 Saving Your Changes

In Section 20.2, "Customizing Your XEDIT Environment," we saw how SET AUTOSAVE 5 tells XEDIT to automatically back up your file with a special name every fifth time you press the Enter key. To save your file with its normal name, just enter SAVE at the command line.

To save a copy with a different file ID, enter the new file ID after the SAVE command. For example, entering

```
SAVE CHAKA KHAN
```

saves the file in its current state under the name CHAKA KHAN.

20.6 Quitting XEDIT

To quit out of XEDIT, type QUIT at the command line. If you made any edits to the file and have not saved it since you made the most recent edit, XEDIT tells you

```
DMSXSU577E File has been changed; type QQUIT to quit anyway
```

The extra "Q" means "Quit no matter what, I don't want to save the changes I've made."

20.7 Other Useful XEDIT Features

XEDIT is one of the most powerful, full-featured text editors that you'll ever find included as part of an operating system's basic tools. We can't leave it without mentioning a few additional features that, without being absolutely essential, can make your life much easier.

20.7.1 XEDIT on-line help

XEDIT's built-in help works almost identically to the CMS help. Type HELP by itself at the XEDIT command line, and you'll see a menu of XEDIT commands. You can move your cursor to one and press Enter to find out more about that command. (You won't see all of them; press PF8 to page down for the complete list.)

As with help from the CMS command line, you can also enter the command HELP followed by a command name if you want help about that command. For example

```
HELP LOCATE
```

displays the on-line help for the LOCATE command. And, while viewing help information, the PF1 key toggles between brief and detailed help just like it does with CMS help.

20.7.2 The automatic startup macro

You can store a series of XEDIT commands in a file called a macro and then instruct XEDIT to execute that macro. All XEDIT macros have XEDIT as a filetype, and one has a special filename: PROFILE. Whenever you start XEDIT, it looks for this PROFILE XEDIT file and if it exists, executes it automatically. We saw in Section 20.2, "Customizing Your XEDIT Environment," that certain commands are useful enough to run every time you start XEDIT. Let's see how to create a profile macro with them.

Start up XEDIT with the command

```
X PROFILE XEDIT A
```

to create this file (or edit the existing one, if it's there). You need to include the A filemode because if you leave it off and XEDIT doesn't find the specified file ID on the current A disk, it looks for a file with that filename and filetype on other disks that your user ID has access to, and you'll be looking at some system default PROFILE XEDIT. You're not allowed to edit one from another disk, so make sure to include the filemode of A so that XEDIT knows to create a PROFILE XEDIT for you if no PROFILE XEDIT A exists.

Use the a3 prefix command to add three blank lines to your file,

```
PROFILE  XEDIT    A1  V 80  Trunc=80 Size=3 Line=0 Col=1 Alt=0

===== * * * Top of File * * *
===== SET CASE M
===== SET PREFIX ON
===== SET AUTOSAVE 5
===== * * * End of File * * *
```

Figure 20.14 Sample PROFILE XEDIT file.

```
===== In Xanadu did Kubla Khan_
===== A stately pleasure-dome decree
===== Where Alph, the sacred river, ran
===== Through caverns measureless to man
===== Down to a sunless sea.
```

Figure 20.15 Cursor position just before pressing PF11 to join two lines.

```
===== In Xanadu did Kubla KhanA stately pleasure-dome decree
===== Where Alph, the sacred river, ran
===== Through caverns measureless to man
===== Down to a sunless sea.
```

Figure 20.16 XEDIT file from Figure 20.15 after pressing PF11 to join two lines.

```
===== In Xanadu did_Kubla KhanA stately pleasure-dome decree
===== Where Alph, the sacred river, ran
===== Through caverns measureless to man
===== Down to a sunless sea.
```

Figure 20.17 Cursor position just before pressing PF11 to split a line.

and type in the commands covered in Section 20.2 so that your screen ends up looking like Figure 20.14.

After you save this file, every time you start up XEDIT it automatically executes these three commands.

If you already have a PROFILE XEDIT file, see if any of these commands are there before you add them. Now you know what they do.

20.7.3 The Split/Join key

One annoying thing about an editor that deals with text almost exclusively in lines is the effect when you delete words from a line, making it too short, or add words to a line, making it too long. PF11, the Split/Join key, can fix this for a line or pair of lines.

If your cursor is at the end of a line, pressing PF11 joins the following line to the one with the cursor. In Figure 20.15, the cursor is right after the "n" in "Khan."

Pressing PF11 moves the beginning of the following line to the cursor's location, as shown in Figure 20.16.

```
===== In Xanadu did
=====   Kubla KhanA stately pleasure-dome decree
===== Where Alph, the sacred river, ran
===== Through caverns measureless to man
===== Down to a sunless sea.
```

**Figure 20.18   XEDIT file from Figure 20.17 after pressing PF11
to split a line.**

If PF11 is not at the end of a line, pressing it splits the line into two at the cursor's location. With the cursor after the word "did" this time, as shown in Figure 20.17, pressing PF11 moves everything beginning at the cursor's location (including the character at the cursor—in this case, a space) to a new line underneath the one where the cursor is located, as shown in Figure 20.18.

21

Using a VM/CMS System

21.1 Printing Text Files

Printing a text file is simple. Just enter

```
PRINT fn ft fm
```

at the `Ready;` prompt, where `fn`, `ft`, and `fm` show the filename, filetype, and filemode, respectively, of the file you wish to print. If you leave off the filemode, the system assumes that the file is on your `A` minidisk. For example, to print a file named `SEPT1294 MEMO A`, just type this:

```
PRINT SEPT1294 MEMO
```

You'll need to ask where the printer is located in your office. There are probably multiple printers attached to the system, with a particular one specified as your default printer. Ask your system administrator which one your user ID is configured to print on.

21.1.1 Checking the print queue

To display a list of the jobs waiting to print, enter the following command:

```
QUERY PRINTER ALL
```

Your output will look similar to this:

```
ORIGINID   FILE  CLASS   RECORDS  CPY  HOLD   DATE   TIME       NAME      TYPE  DIST
ACCLEN     0098  K PRT   000832   001  NONE   10/18  12:24:43   SALES     DATA  RM234
ACCLEN     0099  K PRT   000110   001  NONE   10/18  12:25:08   MEETING   DATA  RM234
JOEUSER    0103  K PRT   000110   001  NONE   10/18  12:25:12   SEPT1294  MEMO  RM101
MJONES     0112  K PRT   000359   001  NONE   10/18  12:26:23   SETUP     EXEC  RM112
```

The NAME and TYPE of each waiting file shows its file ID. The TIME shows when it was added to the print queue, and the RECORDS column shows the length of each file. This is important because it can let you know if there's a huge job ahead of yours in the queue.

The ORIGINID column shows who sent each waiting job, and the FILE column shows the number, or "spoolid" (pronounced "spool ID") that the printing program uses to refer to the print job. This number is important if you want to cancel the print job.

21.1.2 Canceling your print job

Canceling your print job is known as "purging" because of the command used to do it. Use the following syntax:

```
PURGE PRINTER spoolid
```

where spoolid is the number that shows up in the FILE column when you issue the QUERY PRINTER ALL command. (If your file doesn't show up when you query the print queue, either it already printed—a likely possibility, if it was a small file and no other files were ahead of it in the print queue—or it never got into the queue in the first place.) You must include the word PRINTER because the PURGE command can be used to purge other temporary storage areas, like your reader. (Section 21.3, "Communicating with Other Users," covers some uses of the reader.)

If Joe User wants to purge the SEPT1294 MEMO file from the print queue shown above, he enters the following:

```
PURGE PRINTER 0103
```

If he wants to purge the SALES DATA file to speed up the printing of his own file, it's too bad. That file belongs to the ACCLEN user ID, and only a system administrator can purge other people's files.

21.2 Command Files

Command files in CMS are called EXECs (pronounced "egg-zeks") after their filetype, which is short for "executable." Creating and using them is simple; just use XEDIT to create a file with a file type of EXEC that has a valid CMS or CP command on each line. To run the EXEC, type in the file's filename.

Nearly all IBM operating systems (with the notable exception of PC/DOS, thanks to the Byzantine politics of IBM's relationship with Microsoft) include some version of a programming language called REXX that is a superset of the EXEC command language. In other words, REXX has all the same commands as EXEC, plus more. Once you learn it on any computer, you can transfer that knowledge (and maybe even the REXX program) to other IBM computers. You can tell a REXX program from an EXEC program by its first line: if it begins with a slash and an asterisk (/*) and ends with an asterisk and a slash (*/), then it's a REXX program. Anything between these asterisks is considered a comment to the program, so the system ignores it. It doesn't really matter what you put there, but it's best to put a line describing the title and purpose of the program.

You should begin all EXECs (except for the PROFILE EXEC described in Section 21.2.1, "The automatic logon command file") with this so that you can indicate the purpose of your program and have access to the REXX commands. I've written EXECs that didn't work until I added this first line, so I always add it now.

For example, let's say that you often need to link to a particular minidisk on your system so that you can run a program called MAINMENU that displays the main menu of available reports for you to run. It would make your life easier to have a command file that performs the following steps:

- Link to the RPTPROG user ID, which has a virtual address of 192
- Access the disk as your B disk
- Type MAINMENU to run the program

If you want to call your program RPTMENU, you use XEDIT to create a file with a filename of RPTMENU and a filetype of EXEC. Enter the following at the Ready; prompt:

```
X RPTMENU EXEC
```

Once in XEDIT, you add these four lines:

```
/* RPTMENU EXEC link to the RPTPROG disk and start the MAINMENU */
/* program */
LINK RPTPROG 192 193
ACCESS 193 B
MAINMENU
```

Note how the first line describes the purpose of the program. Save it and quit out of XEDIT. From then on you only need to type RPTMENU to use the MAINMENU program instead of the three commands you needed to type before.

In Section 18.4.2 ("Help menus") we saw that entering HELP by itself at the Ready; prompt displays a menu of various types of information for which help is available. One of the menu choices was the following:

```
STATEMTS - Show statements for REXX, EXEC2, and EXEC
```

Choose this to learn more about EXEC, EXEC2 (a variation on the EXEC command language), and REXX programming.

21.2.1 The automatic logon command file

Whenever you log on to your CMS account, the system looks for a special EXEC called `PROFILE EXEC` and executes it if found. If there's any command that you want executed every time you log on, use XEDIT to add a line with that command to your `PROFILE EXEC` file. If you don't have one, create it as you would create any other EXEC.

Many systems are set up to give a default `PROFILE EXEC` to each new user. In other words, you may have one the first time you log on without even knowing it. If so, take a good look at it; if your system doesn't seem to behave the way this book describes, it's probably because of something in your PROFILE. (For example, if a function key acts differently than I've described or if the system automatically displays a menu when you log on.)

21.3 Communicating with Other Users

Sending mail or files to another user means putting a copy of it into their "reader," which is like a mailbox. It's actually a software simulation of the machine that was once used to read punch cards. The sidebar "This is the Nineties. Why Do I Need a Card Puncher or a Punch Card Reader?" in Section 18.1.3.2 ("Aborting screen output") explains why we still use the term "reader" even though the hardware being simulated is so archaic.

All CMS systems have the NOTE program to send electronic mail to other users. NOTE gets the job done, but it's limited enough that many sites purchase a fancier program. On my first CMS system, I was unaware of the existence of NOTE because of a program that we used called `MAIL`. Keep your eye out for a more full-featured alternative to NOTE.

Sending a note is simple: type

```
NOTE userid
```

where `userid` is the ID of your note's recipient. The recipient doesn't need to be logged on. If not, the next time he or she logs on a message will appear telling them that something is in their reader.

If Joe User wants to send a note to Mary Jones at her MJONES user ID, he enters this:

```
NOTE MJONES
```

CMS then displays the note editing screen, as shown in Figure 21.1.

It looks a lot like the XEDIT screen when you're creating a new file, except that it automatically added a header to your message. The "at

```
 JOEUSER   NOTE       A0  V 132   Trunc=132 Size=9 Line=9 Col=1 Alt=0

* * * Top of File * * *
OPTIONS: NOACK     LOG      SHORT      NOTEBOOK ALL




Date: 6 February 94, 19:20:11 EST
From: Joe User                  212/930-3342 x4288    JOEUSER  at JUPITER
To:    MJONES

* * * End of File * * *





1= Help       2= Add line  3= Quit    4= Tab     5= Send      6= ?
7= Backward  8= Forward    9= =      10= Rgtleft 11= Spltjoin 12= Power input

====>
```

Figure 21.1 Screen for entering a note to another user.

JUPITER" part shows that Joe's particular VM system is named
JUPITER. The system name is necessary when multiple systems are
connected and someone on one wants to send mail to a user ID on another.

All the XEDIT commands described in this book are valid here. You
can start with SET PREFIX ON and then use the a prefix command to
add some blank lines on which to type your message.

Two function keys speed the creation and delivery of your message:

- Press PF2 to add blank lines to your message. Move your cursor to
  any line above "End of File," (for a start, put it on the line that says
  "To:") and press PF2 to add a new blank line under the line with
  the cursor.

- Use PF5, the "Send" key, to show that you have completed your
  note. When you press it, the NOTE program sends your message to
  the recipient's reader.

It also saves a copy in a file on your A disk called ALL NOTEBOOK.
This is handy when you want to see exactly what you sent to someone.

21.3.1 Sending files

The SENDFILE command makes it easy to send an existing file to
someone's reader. At the Ready; prompt, enter

SENDFILE fn ft fm userid

```
                ---------------  SENDFILE  ---------------
File(s) to be sent     (use * for Filename, Filetype and/or Filemode
                                 to select from a list of files)
Enter filename :
      filetype :
      filemode :

Send files to  :

Type over 1 for YES or 0 for NO to change the options:

   0     Request acknowledgement when the file has been received?

   1     Make a log entry when the file has been sent?

   1     Display the file name when the file has been sent?

   0     This file is actually a list of files to be sent?

   1= Help           3= Quit            5= Send            12= Cursor

====>
                                                      Macro-read 1 File
```

Figure 21.2 SENDFILE screen for sending a file to another user.

where `fn`, `ft`, and `fm` show the ID of the file to send and `userid` shows the ID of the user who gets the file. If CMS does not find a single letter as the third parameter here (in other words, if you leave out the filemode and just say `SENDFILE fn ft userid`), it assumes that `fn ft` represents a file on your A minidisk. Make sure to type all eight letters of the `SENDFILE` command; CMS has a separate, unrelated command called `SEND`.

If you enter `SENDFILE` by itself, you will see a screen similar to Figure 21.2.

In addition to filling out the file ID and recipient's name, you can set the options shown in the bottom half of the screen. Most of them are self-explanatory. For example, the "log entry" means that SEND-FILE adds a line describing what you sent, when, and to whom to a file called `userid NETLOG`, where `userid` is your user ID name.

When you are done with this screen, press PF5 to send the file whose ID you entered or PF3 to abort the SENDFILE program.

21.3.2 Receiving mail and files

When you first log on, you may see a message similar to this:

```
FILES: 0003 RDR, NO PRT, NO PUN
```

This shows that your reader has three files. To get them out, you could use the `RECEIVE` command, which people originally used to read real punch cards and turn their information into a disk file.

```
JOEUSER   RDRLIST   A0   V 108   Trunc=108 Size=2 Line=1 Col=1 Alt=0
Cmd    Filename Filetype Class User  at Node     Hold  Records  Date     Time
       MJONES   NOTE     PUN A MJONES   JUPITER  NONE      14  10/16   09:30:59
       ACCLEN   NOTE     PUN A ACCLEN   JUPITER  NONE       4  10/16   13:01:44
       SALES    DATA     PUN A ACCLEN   JUPITER  NONE     832  10/16   13:02:45




1= Help      2= Refresh  3= Quit     4= Sort(type) 5= Sort(date) 6= Sort(user)
7= Backward  8= Forward  9= Receive  10=           11= Peek      12= Cursor

====>
                                                     X E D I T   1 File
```

Figure 21.3 RDRLIST screen for viewing files in the reader.

However, the RDRLIST program makes it much easier. (If your reader is empty and you want to play with the RDRLIST program for practice, use the NOTE and SENDFILE commands to send a few things to your own ID's reader.)

Enter RDRLIST at the Ready; prompt, and you see a screen similar to Figure 21.3.

RDRLIST is a specialized version of FILELIST, which is explained in the next section. Most of the columns of information here are similar to the information displayed when you enter the LISTFILE command with the (LABEL option, but with two important new columns: the User column shows who sent the file, and the Cmd column provides a place where you can enter commands to act on the file named on a given line. You can also move your cursor to the line with a particular file's name and press function keys to perform actions on that file. (See Section 19.1.3.1, "Listing more than filenames," for more on the (LABEL option to the LISTFILE command.)

The three most important things that you want to do to a file in your reader are:

- Look at it while it's still in the reader.
- Pull it out of the reader and save it as a disk file.
- Delete it from the reader.

21.3.2.1 Looking at a file in the reader. Unless someone told you exactly what they sent you, you'll want to look at each file first, so that you

```
   0023      PEEK      A0  V 132  Trunc=132 Size=12 Line=0 Col=1 Alt=0
Note from ACCLEN at JUPITER Format is NETDATA
* * * Top of File * * *
Date: 16 October 94, 11:43:24 EST
From: Larry Niven            212/930-3342 x3277    ACCLEN   at Jupiter
To:    JOEUSER

Joe -

I can't make lunch with you today.  Preparing for the sales meeting Monday
looks like a lot more work than I had originally thought.  A lot of the
figures still aren't in yet.  How about Monday after the meeting for lunch?

- Larry
* * * End of File * * *




1= Help       2= Add line  3= Quit     4= Tab      5= Clocate    6= ?/Change
7= Backward   8= Forward   9= Receive  10= Rgtleft 11= Spltjoin  12= Cursor

====>

                                                    X E D I T   1 File
```

Figure 21.4 Sample received note.

can decide whether to keep it. Use the Peek function key for this. Move your cursor to anywhere on the line showing the file you want to peek at and press PF11. For example, let's say Joe recognizes the ACCLEN user ID as that of Larry Niven, his friend in Accounting. If Joe moves his cursor to the ACCLEN NOTE line and presses PF11 to see the note that Larry sent him, he might see something like the screen shown in Figure 21.4.

It looks like an XEDIT screen because it is. The RDRLIST program uses XEDIT to display the received message. As the function key list at the bottom shows, pressing PF3 quits out of this display and returns you to the list of files in your reader.

21.3.2.2 Saving a file from the reader.

PF9 "receives" the file, or takes it out of the reader and saves it as a disk file. If someone sent it to you with the NOTE command, receiving it appends it onto your ALL NOTEBOOK file. If someone sent it to you with the SENDFILE command, receiving it saves it on your disk with the file ID specified in the Filename and Filetype columns—in other words, the name it had before it was sent to you. PF9 also sends a brief message to the message's sender telling them that you've received it. (This brings up one advantage of PF11, the Peek function key: you can look at a received file, but the sender never knows that you saw it.)

Note how the function key lists on the RDRLIST screen and on the screen used to peek at files both show that PF9 receives the file. At the RDRLIST screen, your cursor must be on the same line as the file you want to receive when you press PF9, so that the system knows which file to receive. At the PEEK screen, your cursor's location doesn't matter, because the file you're peeking at is obviously the one you want to receive.

PF9 is a shortcut to use instead of typing out the RECEIVE command. It won't handle special situations, like receiving a file that has the same name as an existing file. To do this you need to type RECEIVE at the PEEK screen command line or in the RDRLIST screen's Cmd column so that you can take advantage of one of its options.

Although the Cmd column isn't very wide, you can type longer commands that begin there, even if this means typing over the Filename and Filetype columns. When you press Enter, the system knows what you mean.

To receive a file that is displayed on the PEEK screen and assign it a new name, enter the RECEIVE command at the PEEK screen prompt followed by the file ID. For example, to save a displayed file and give it the name LNIVEN 101694, enter

```
RECEIVE LNIVEN 101694
```

at the command line. To receive a file that is displayed on the PEEK screen and have it replace your existing file that has the same name, enter

```
RECEIVE (REPLACE
```

at the PEEK screen command line.

These commands have the same effect when you type them in the RDRLIST screen's Cmd column, except that you must put a slash character after the RECEIVE command to stand in for the name of the file being received. For example, to save the file with the name LNIVEN 101694 type

```
RECEIVE / LNIVEN 101694
```

over the beginning of the line that describes that file, as shown in Figure 21.5.

After you press Enter, the system acknowledges your command with a message similar to the one in Figure 21.6.

Similarly, you type RECEIVE / (REPLACE in the same place to pull it out of the reader and store it on your disk with its original name regardless of whether you already had a file with that name.

```
JOEUSER  RDRLIST  A0   V 108   Trunc=108 Size=2 Line=1 Col=1 Alt=0
Cmd    Filename Filetype Class User  at Node    Hold  Records  Date      Time
       MJONES    NOTE     PUN A MJONES  JUPITER  NONE       14 10/16   09:30:59
RECEIVE /LNIVEN 101694    PUN A ACCLEN  JUPITER  NONE        4 10/16   13:01:44
       SALES     DATA     PUN A ACCLEN  JUPITER  NONE      832 10/16   13:02:45
```

Figure 21.5 Receiving a file from the reader.

```
JOEUSER  RDRLIST  A0   V 108   Trunc=108 Size=2 Line=1 Col=1 Alt=0
Cmd    Filename Filetype  Class User   at Node      Hold  Records  Date
       MJONES   NOTE      PUN A MJONES    JUPITER   NONE      14 10/16
  *    LNIVEN   101694    received from ACCLEN at JUPITER
       SALES    DATA      PUN A ACCLEN    JUPITER   NONE     832 10/16
```

Figure 21.6 System acknowledgement of receipt of file from the reader.

21.3.2.3 Discard a file from the reader. Don't think of it as "deleting" a file from the reader, but as "discarding" it. After all, you'll remember the command more easily: DISCARD. You can type it at the PEEK screen command line or on the RDRLIST screen beginning in the Cmd column. No parameters are necessary. Either way, when you press Enter, RDRLIST displays the words "has been discarded" after the file ID.

21.4 The FILELIST Program

Many people find the FILELIST program useful to carry out basic operations on files. It displays a list of file IDs and you enter commands next to the names of the files that you want to manipulate. In fact, the RDRLIST's interface is based on FILELIST.

Entering FILELIST by itself lists your A disk's files on a screen similar to the RDRLIST screen. You can also enter wildcards to show that you only want to see certain files listed in FILELIST. For example, if you type

```
FILELIST * EXEC
```

FILELIST starts up and displays a screen similar to the one shown in Figure 21.7.

```
DOCBED    FILELIST A0   V 108   Trunc=108 Size=126 Line=1 Col=1 Alt=0
Cmd    Filename Filetype Fm Format Lrecl  Records  Blocks    Date      Time
       BUZZ     EXEC     A2 V         70      36       1   8/17/92 17:54:44 DSK191
       C_ATTACH EXEC     A1 F         80       2       1   1/30/92 16:48:41 DSK191
       CRITBETA EXEC     A1 V         19       4       1   1/21/94 11:23:18 DSK191
       DIR      EXEC     A1 V         24       1       1   1/29/92 16:27:20 DSK191
       DOWNLOAD EXEC     A1 V         73      31       1   2/02/92 11:01:21 DSK191
       HTRACK   EXEC     A1 V         24       2       1   7/27/92 13:17:05 DSK191
       INFONT   EXEC     A1 V         19       2       1  12/10/92 13:30:28 DSK191
       IOBETA   EXEC     A1 V         19       4       1   1/07/94 12:34:47 DSK191
       MBAILEY  EXEC     A1 V         22       1       1   1/30/92 16:49:02 DSK191
       PROFILE  EXEC     A1 V         29       8       1   1/16/94 12:47:00 DSK191
       TEST1    EXEC     A1 V         27       9       1   2/02/92 10:53:40 DSK191
       TEST4    EXEC     A1 V         18       8       1   8/21/92 16:20:19 DSK191
       TUTOR    EXEC     A1 V          7       1       1   9/23/93 16:16:57 DSK191
1= Help        2= Refresh  3= Quit   4= Sort(type)  5= Sort(date)  6= Sort(size)
7= Backward    8= Forward  9= FL /n 10=             11= XEDIT       12= Cursor

====>
                                                         X E D I T   1 File
```

Figure 21.7 FILELIST screen listing EXEC files.

```
DOCBED    FILELIST A0   V 108   Trunc=108 Size=126 Line=1 Col=1 Alt=0
Cmd   Filename Filetype Fm Format Lrecl  Records   Blocks   Date     Time
      BUZZ     EXEC     A2 V        70      36       1  8/17/92 17:54:44 DSK191
      C_ATTACH EXEC     A1 F        80       2       1  1/30/92 16:48:41 DSK191
      CRITBETA EXEC     A1 V        19       4       1  1/21/94 11:23:18 DSK191
copy / test5 exec a     A1 V        24       1       1  1/29/92 16:27:20 DSK191
      DOWNLOAD EXEC     A1 V        73      31       1  2/02/92 11:01:21 DSK191
      HTRACK   EXEC     A1 V        24       2       1  7/27/92 13:17:05 DSK191
      INFONT   EXEC     A1 V        19       2       1 12/10/92 13:30:28 DSK191
      IOBETA   EXEC     A1 V        19       4       1  1/07/94 12:34:47 DSK191
      MBAILEY  EXEC     A1 V        22       1       1  1/30/92 16:49:02 DSK191
      PROFILE  EXEC     A1 V        29       8       1  1/16/94 12:47:00 DSK191
      TEST1    EXEC     A1 V        27       9       1  2/02/92 10:53:40 DSK191
      TEST4    EXEC     A1 V        18       8       1  8/21/92 16:20:19 DSK191
      TUTOR    EXEC     A1 V         7       1       1  9/23/93 16:16:57 DSK191
1= Help       2= Refresh  3= Quit    4= Sort(type)  5= Sort(date)  6= Sort(size)
7= Backward   8= Forward  9= FL /n 10=             11= XEDIT      12= Cursor

====>
                                        X E D I T   1 File
```

Figure 21.8 Copying a file using FILELIST.

As with RDRLIST, you enter a command that acts on a file in the Cmd column on the line listing that file. Unlike the commands you enter at the Ready; prompt, you don't need to indicate the file that you want to act on, because FILELIST can tell from your cursor's position. Instead, enter the slash character where you would have put the file's name.

21.4.1 Copying files

To make a copy of a file and call it TEST5 EXEC A, enter

```
COPY / TEST5 EXEC A
```

right on the line with the file you want to copy. It doesn't matter whether you enter it in upper- or lowercase. Figure 21.8 shows a FILELIST screen with this command entered.

When you press Enter, FILELIST executes the command. (Or commands—you can enter multiple commands on multiple lines before you press Enter.) Make sure to include the file's mode (a in Figure 21.8) or FILELIST will display an error message.

21.4.2 Renaming files

Renaming is similar to copying. To rename a file as TEST5 EXEC A, enter the command

```
RENAME / TEST5 EXEC A
```

beginning in the Cmd column on the line with the file you want to copy. After you press Enter, FILELIST displays the message

```
** Discarded, Renamed, or Relocated **
```

on that line.

21.4.3 Deleting files

Deleting a file is like deleting it from the reader: enter the DISCARD command, beginning in the Cmd column, on the line with the file you want to delete. After you press Enter, FILELIST displays the same message that it displays when you rename a file, showing you that the file no longer exists.

21.4.4 Displaying a text file's contents

Displaying a file's contents in FILELIST is similar to doing it from the Ready; prompt, except that you don't have to enter the file ID. Move your cursor to the Cmd column next to the file whose contents you want to view, enter the TYPE command, and press Enter. Use the Clear key and HT command just as you would when using the TYPE command from the Ready; prompt. When you are done, you will be back at the FILELIST screen.

21.4.5 Editing a file

Note how the bottom of the FILELIST screen shows that pressing PF11 invokes XEDIT. To edit a file whose name is displayed by the FILELIST program, move your cursor to that file's line and press PF11. When you finish editing it, CMS returns you to the FILELIST screen.

21.4.6 Printing a file

By now, you can probably guess how to do this: move your cursor to the Cmd column next to the name of the file you want to print, enter PRINT, and press Enter. This has the same effect as when you enter

```
PRINT filename filetype
```

at the Ready; prompt.

21.5 A Sample VM/CMS Session

One morning you log on and the system displays the following message, which shows that your reader has two files:

```
FILES: 0002 RDR, NO PRT, NO PUN
```

You enter RDRLIST at the command prompt, and the RDRLIST program shows you information about the two files in your reader, as shown in Figure 21.9.

```
 JOEUSER  RDRLIST  A0  V 108  Trunc=108 Size=2 Line=1 Col=1 Alt=0
Cmd   Filename Filetype Class User  at Node      Hold Records  Date     Time
      ACCLEN   NOTE     PUN A ACCLEN   JUPITER   NONE       4 10/16   13:01:44
      SALES    DATA     PUN A ACCLEN   JUPITER   NONE     148 10/16   13:02:45
```

Figure 21.9 Sample reader contents.

```
 0023     PEEK     A0  V 132  Trunc=132 Size=12 Line=0 Col=1 Alt=0
Note from ACCLEN at JUPITER Format is NETDATA
* * * Top of File * * *
Date: 16 October 94, 13:01:44 EST
From: Larry Niven           212/930-3342 x3277    ACCLEN   at Jupiter
To:   JOEUSER

Joe -

I'm sending the SALES DATA file to your reader for you to look over.  Don't
read the whole thing (you probably won't have time) but look over the
monthly totals before the meeting Monday.  Sorry to do this to you on a
Friday!

- Larry
* * * End of File * * *
```

Figure 21.10 Sample message to you from Larry.

It looks like the user with user ID ACCLEN (your good pal Larry in accounting) sent you a note and a medium-sized file. You move your cursor to the ACCLEN NOTE file and press PF11 to peek at the file, and RDRLIST displays the screen shown in Figure 21.10.

So now you know what that other file is. You save the note from Larry by entering RECEIVE at the PEEK screen's command line. The system returns you to the RDRLIST screen, which shows you that the ACCLEN NOTE file has been "added to ALL NOTEBOOK A0." Now you know the name of the file in which to find this note if you need to refer to it again.

While viewing the RDRLIST screen, you pull the SALES DATA file out of the reader by moving your cursor to that line and pressing PF9. Then, you quit the RDRLIST program by pressing PF3.

Next, you take a quick look at this SALES DATA file that Larry mentioned. You enter

```
TYPE SALES DATA
```

at the Ready; prompt and see the screen shown in Figure 21.11.

You press the Clear key, and see the screen shown in Figure 21.12.

You get the pattern, and don't need to do this for the whole file, so you type HT to Halt the Typing, press Enter so that the HT takes effect, and then press Clear one more time.

If Larry said that you should only bother with the monthly totals, it might be a good idea to consolidate those figures by making a copy of the SALES DATA file and editing out the details. You enter

```
Page 01                   O'Rourke Enterprises              10/16/94
                       Monthly Sales Figures by Region


JANUARY                 Gross      Net
                        ------    ------
Northeast               77,423   12,756
Mid-Atlantic            65,812   11,447
Southeast               58,222    8,800
Southwest               42,342    5,663
Midwest                 73,242   12,000
Northwest               14,433    1,500
West Coast              68,443    7,445
                        ------    ------
JANUARY TOTAL          399,917   59,611

FEBRUARY                Gross      Net
                        ------    ------
Northeast               75,732   11,890
Mid-Atlantic            69,348   11,008


                                              MORE...
```

Figure 21.11 Beginning of SALES DATA file.

```
Southeast               61,835    8,890
Southwest               42,445    5,556
Midwest                 70,762   12,934
Northwest               14,242    1,634
West Coast              65,447    7,556
                        ------    ------
FEBRUARY TOTAL         399,811   39,468

MARCH                   Gross      Net
                        ------    ------
Northeast               76,788   12,020
Mid-Atlantic            67,789   11,003
Southeast               62,640    9,126
Southwest               40,400    4,900
Midwest                 69,730   11,500
Northwest               13,554    1,330
West Coast              73,354    8,020
                        ------    ------
MARCH TOTAL            399,811   59,468

APRIL                   Gross      Net
                        ------    ------


                                              MORE...
```

Figure 21.12 Second screen of SALES DATA file.

```
             COPY SALES DATA A TOTALS DATA A
```

and then call up the TOTALS DATA file with XEDIT:

```
    X TOTALS DATA
```

```
SALES    DATA    A1  F 80   Trunc=80 Size=148 Line=0 Col=1 Alt=0

===== * * * Top of File * * *
===== Page 01                    O'Rourke Enterprises            10/16/94
=====                     Monthly Sales Figures by Region
=====
=====
=dd== JANUARY                 Gross    Net
=====                        ------   ------
===== Northeast              77,423   12,756
===== Mid-Atlantic          65,812   11,447
===== Southeast              58,222    8,800
===== Southwest              42,342    5,663
===== Midwest               73,242   12,000
===== Northwest             14,433    1,500
===== West Coast            68,443    7,445
===dd                        ------   ------
===== JANUARY TOTAL        399,917   59,611
=====
===== FEBRUARY                Gross    Net
=====                        ------   ------
===== Northeast              75,732   11,890
====>
                                             X E D I T  1 File
```

Figure 21.13 Deleting a block from the SALES DATA file.

With the beginning of the file displayed in XEDIT, you enter the XEDIT prefix command dd at the beginning and end of the first block to get rid of in the file, as shown in Figure 21.13.

After pressing Enter, you indicate the next block to get rid of with the same command, as shown in Figure 21.14.

```
SALES    DATA    A1  F 80   Trunc=80 Size=139 Line=0 Col=1 Alt=1

===== * * * Top of File * * *
===== Page 01                    O'Rourke Enterprises            10/16/94
=====                     Monthly Sales Figures by Region
=====
=====
===== JANUARY TOTAL        399,917   59,611
=dd==
===== FEBRUARY                Gross    Net
=====                        ------   ------
===== Northeast              75,732   11,890
===== Mid-Atlantic          69,348   11,008
===== Southeast              61,835    8,890
===== Southwest              42,445    5,556
===== Midwest               70,762   12,934
===== Northwest             14,242    1,634
===== West Coast            65,447    7,556
===dd                        ------   ------
===== FEBRUARY TOTAL       399,811   39,468
=====
===== MARCH                   Gross    Net
====>
                                             X E D I T  1 File
```

Figure 21.14 Deleting another block from the SALES DATA file.

You press Enter and continue this until it is a one-page file that only shows the header and the monthly totals. As you do this, you periodically enter XEDIT's SAVE command; when you are finished, you enter SAVE one last time and quit out of XEDIT with the QUIT command.

To print, you enter

```
PRINT TOTALS DATA
```

at the Ready; prompt. It's a short file, so a minute later the system displays a message that tells you that it has printed your file. You're done with your CMS session for now, so you enter

```
LOGOFF
```

to log off.

MVS: An Introduction

MVS is the primary operating system on the IBM 370 series of mainframes. (You may hear people use various initials and four-digit numbers when referring to IBM mainframes, such as 3033, 3090, or ES9000, but they are all considered hardware models of the 370 series.) MVS is the 18-wheeler of operating systems. People don't use it for flash and speed; they use it to bear large, heavy loads steadily and dependably.

When we talk about the tremendous processing power of a mainframe running MVS, we're talking about a power different from that of supercomputers. Supercomputers do complicated calculations at very high speeds. Designing them for the best possible calculation speed often means sacrificing I/O (input/output) speed; the scientists who use them are more likely to give them a complex math problem and say "grind away at this equation all night" than they are to say "read in these 300,000 records of data, do 8 calculations on each, and then output 300,000 separate reports."

Reading and writing a tremendous amount of data and doing relatively simple calculations with it (for example, calculating interest payments, as opposed to calculating a boat hull's optimum shape) is the province of mainframes running MVS. An insurance company keeping track of its accounts, a chain of stores keeping track of its inventory, or any large company keeping track of its employees and payroll would use MVS. Because it's a multiuser operating system, MVS lets many different users use the same programs and data at once.

Personal computer users like to make fun of big computers running MVS, calling them "dinosaurs." While the interface may seem primitive, MVS has had many features since its introduction in 1974 that people are only now trying to shoehorn into the operating systems that control PC networks. MVS includes built-in recovery routines for dealing with faulty hardware like tape drives or even (in a multiprocessor environment) faulty processors. A system running MVS can support thousands of users at once. The security of one user's data against tampering by others is an integral part of the system, designed into it from the ground up. (How often do you hear of a virus or a worm breaking into an MVS system?)

The primitive interface isn't the only thing that give people the wrong idea about MVS. A given MVS installation is highly customizable, and so is the way that each user uses it. Many different parameters can be set when doing virtually anything, and MVS doesn't always have the default settings that we take for granted on other systems. The most efficient settings are left to individual system administrators to figure out. Since many settings and details are site-specific, a new user on a particular system—no matter how much MVS experience he or she brings to that system—can't be expected to know the best way to approach that system. Don't be embarrassed to ask questions when faced with an unfamiliar MVS installation.

22.1 Batch Jobs

The name "MVS," which stands for "Multiple Virtual Storage," comes from the technique it uses to manage memory. It lets any user work with huge amounts of memory at once, making MVS ideal for batch processing.

Running a job in batch mode is the opposite of running it interactively. Instead of starting a program, typing in some input, waiting for the response, typing some more, and continuing this cycle, you specify what needs to be done at the outset. You tell the system the program to run, the data to use, and what to do with the output. Preparing a company's payroll or feeding in thousands of inventory transactions are typical of jobs that should be run as batch jobs. (A batch job is also known as a "background" job—you can instruct the computer to start running it and then do something else interactively while your batch job runs in the background.)

In the early days of computers, no one else could use the computer once it began a batch job. Modern multitasking computers let people run other programs while a batch job runs. This makes MVS ideal for doing huge jobs involving lots of I/O.

Two acronyms that come up when people discuss batch jobs are JES2 and JES3. These are two versions of the Job Entry Subsystem, the part of MVS that deals with the scheduling of batch jobs. You need not worry about JES, but you may hear people refer to it.

See the sidebar "JCL: Job Control Language" for an explanation of how we give the system instructions for running a batch job.

JCL: Job Control Language

JCL is a language for telling a mainframe system how to deal with a batch job. You use it to indicate the job's size, priority, output destination or destinations, and files, printers, processor time, and disk space to use.

Many mainframe users use JCL regularly without ever knowing anything about the language. How can they do this? JCL statements are often inserted at the beginning and end of a file holding the program or data to submit. While doing data entry on a CMS system years ago (although it comes up more often on MVS systems, the batch capability of VM/CMS means that JCL is used there as well) I knew of a file of JCL code that I had to add to the beginning of my file and another to add to the end of my file before I submitted that file as a job to run. I didn't know what any of the JCL code did; I only knew that I had to add the JCL files to my data file before I typed the command that told the computer to process the data file. This sort of arrangement is not uncommon. Often, a more hardcore programmer writes a couple of chunks of reusable JCL for less sophisticated end users who know enough about the text editor to insert these chunks into the appropriate places in their files.

JCL code looks strange and intimidating because it uses so many abbreviations. Since part of its job is to specify the treatment of certain files, you will discover that several MVS TSO commands have JCL equivalents, especially `ALLOCATE`.

Once you have a good handle on the different parts of a mainframe system, you can learn how they are represented in JCL and then start writing (or at least modifying) JCL yourself. It's valuable job skill.

22.2 Interacting with MVS

MVS offers several ways to interact with it: TSO, ISPF, and CICS.

22.2.1 TSO

TSO stands for Time Sharing Option. It's the part of MVS that lets you use the system interactively; you type commands at a command line and see the response on your screen. In addition to the commands that all operating systems have to copy, rename, and delete files, TSO also has commands to submit batch jobs and to check on their progress. Most of the next couple of chapters show you various TSO commands for dealing with MVS basics.

When IBM first introduced TSO in 1969, interactive computing was a hot new feature that required a huge portion of the computer's memory. This is where the "O" in its name comes from: when all jobs were batch jobs, IBM made this interactive component of MVS optional. Today, it is part of all MVS systems.

22.2.2 ISPF

ISPF stands for Interactive System Productive Facility. Some refer to it by its older name, SPF, or by its full name of ISPF/PDF. This alternative to TSO lets you carry out most basic functions by making menu selections and filling out forms called "panels" on your screen. The menus vary from system to system, but you will find the same important choices available at all MVS installations.

Since ISPF often makes things easier, it has become more popular than TSO as a way to get work done in MVS. TSO, however, offers more speed and flexibility; typing out a command that indicates what you want to do takes less time than going through a series of menus, and the command may have options that are unavailable to you when doing the same thing from an ISPF menu. Also, some terminals and hardware connections to an MVS system may not provide everything necessary to run ISPF, so you should still know the basic TSO commands. (For more information on terminal connections and the use of TSO versus ISPF, see Section 23.1.1, "VTAM.")

22.2.3 CICS

Developers use the Customer Information Control System (CICS) to ease the development of end-user applications. Programmers write applications in a traditional mainframe programming language, usually COBOL, and include sections consisting of CICS commands. Before compiling the program, they run a program called a CICS preprocessor, which finds each CICS statement in the program and converts it into the appropriate series of commands for the programming language being used.

What do the CICS commands do? Usually they accomplish tasks that are difficult in a language like COBOL. For example, if you want to write a series of COBOL commands that display a form to fill out on the end user's screen, you must worry about the different makes and models of terminals that the user might have. If you let CICS worry about this for you, you can describe and display your input form with a minimum of commands and let the the CICS processor turn them into the appropriate COBOL commands. CICS commands also simplify the use of data files and the relationship between an end user's activity and the contents of the files.

22.2.4 Other MVS components

MVS is made up of many parts. Like TSO, many started as optional features, but eventually became standard issue at MVS installations. Some components became obsolete and are no longer offered; others, especially those that take advantage of the extra power of more recent versions of MVS (like MVS/ESA) are optional now.

Many popular MVS programs, useful enough to seem like part of the operating system instead of being a separate application used for a specific purpose, don't even come from IBM. The existence of these and IBM's optional MVS features mean that the list of software tools available at one MVS site may not be the same as those available at another. You can, however, take for granted that TSO and ISPF are always available, which is why this book covers them.

22.3 History

The history of MVS must begin with its lineage. It is descended from the forefather of modern operating systems: OS. IBM introduced OS, which stands for "Operating System," in 1964 when it announced the 360 series of computers. (For more on this, see the sidebar "IBM's 360 Series of Mainframes" in the Introduction.)

The history of operating systems over the next few years is really the history of IBM's improvements to OS, as it introduced versions that allowed more users the ability to simultaneously run more programs and to let each of these programs use more memory. IBM called successive versions MFT (Multiprogramming with a Fixed number of Tasks), MVT (Multiprogramming with a Variable number of Tasks), SVS in 1972 (Single Virtual Storage), and MVS/XA (Multiple Virtual Storage/Extended Architecture) in 1974.

In 1988, IBM introduced its ESA/370 mainframes, and a new version of MVS known as MVS/ESA (Extended System Architecture) to take advantage of the increased power of the new hardware. The version of MVS that you use has no effect on any of the basic commands explained in this book; improvements to the operating system usually involve additional power for users pushing the outer limits of the system.

23

Getting Started with MVS

23.1 Starting Up

Logging on to an MVS system consists of two basic steps: entering
your user ID and entering your password. Before you reach the point
where you log on, however, you may need to go through an MVS component known as VTAM.

23.1.1 VTAM

VTAM (pronounced "vee-tam") stands for "Virtual Telecommunications
Access Method." The phrase "access method" comes up often in MVS.
An *access method* is a collection of programs that acts as an interme-
diary between you and something that would otherwise be difficult
and complicated to gain access to.

VTAM is essentially a telecommunications program. When you connect to the MVS system, you might really be connecting to some hardware running VTAM, which then enables you to connect to the MVS
system. If you see a screen that lists several possible commands to
type and one of them is DIAL, then DIAL VTAM will probably connect
you to the MVS system.

Sometimes you can choose between logging on to TSO directly or
logging on to VTAM and using that to access the MVS TSO system.
(For example, in addition to the DIAL command, the screen mentioned above might offer TSO userid as a choice.) Going through
VTAM might offer better control of your terminal than a direct connection to TSO. This increased control might be reflected in the ability to run ISPF: displaying menus and forms on your screen to fill out
requires a more sophisticated relationship between a computer and a
terminal than the ability to just scroll lines of text from the bottom of
the screen to the top. Trying to start up ISPF at the TSO prompt after

connecting directly to TSO (and bypassing VTAM) might produce an error message similar to this:

```
INVALID TERMINAL ACCESS METHOD, ISPF VERSION 3 REQUIRES ACF/VTAM.
```

In other words, the connection made allows the primitive screen control necessary to let you enter TSO commands and watch the system's responses scroll up the screen, but not the screen control necessary to display menus and forms that you would fill out by moving your cursor from place to place.

23.1.2 Logging on

When you first connect to an MVS system, there are several ways to tell it that you want to log on. The simplest is to just type the following:

```
logon
```

The system responds by asking you for your user ID:

```
IKJ56700A ENTER USERID -
```

Type in the ID that you were assigned when you received the account. If the system does not recognize a user ID of "JOEUSER," it displays a message similar to this:

```
IKJ56420I Userid JOEUSER not authorized to use TSO
```

An alternate way to log on at some sites uses menus that offer you the choice of connecting to several different systems. This screen will let you know the syntax for logging on to the system you want. Joe User would use a command similar to this to log on to MVS's TSO component directly:

```
tso joeuser
```

Regardless of how you typed in your user ID, once the system knows it, it then prompts you for the password that goes with that ID:

```
ENTER CURRENT PASSWORD FOR JOEUSER-
```

When you type the characters of your password, they will probably not appear on your screen. This security feature prevents someone from learning your password by watching you log on.

Instead of prompting you for the password as above, the system may display a form to complete with the USERID field already filled

```
----------------------------- TSO/E  LOGON -----------------------------------


    ENTER LOGON PARAMETERS BELOW:            RACF LOGON PARAMETERS:

    USERID   ===> JOEUSER

    PASSWORD ===> _                          NEW PASSWORD ===>

    PROCEDURE ===>                           GROUP IDENT  ===>

    ACCT NMBR ===>

    SIZE     ===>

    PERFORM  ===>

    COMMAND  ===>


    ENTER AN 'S' BEFORE EACH OPTION DESIRED BELOW:

          -NOMAIL        -NONOTICE       -RECONNECT      -OIDCARD
```

Figure 23.1 TSO logon form.

```
ICH70001I JOEUSER  LAST ACCESS AT 18:31:55 ON MONDAY, JANUARY 11, 1994
JOEUSER LOGON IN PROGRESS AT 09:09:30 ON JANUARY 12, 1994
**********************************************************************
*                    O'Rourke Enterprises MVS/XA                    *
**********************************************************************
*   Use CLASS=T for all server batch JOBs or they may be cancelled. *
**********************************************************************
*   Please report any problems to the Help Desk at 878-4531.        *
**********************************************************************
***                        N e w s :                             ***
**********************************************************************
*   Due to a possible security breach, all users must change their  *
*   passwords by Thursday, January 14.                              *
**********************************************************************
You have no messages or data sets to receive.
**** NATIVE TSO READY ****
READY
```

Figure 23.2 Typical opening series of messages upon logon.

out and the cursor waiting at the PASSWORD field for your response.
Figure 23.1 shows an example.

Don't worry about the other fields; type in your password (again,
the characters do not display as you type) and press Enter.

Once you enter a valid ID and password, MVS displays some logon
messages and the TSO READY prompt. Figure 23.2 shows a typical series of messages. (Because the system administrator can change the
default prompt, it might be something other than the word "READY."
Also, the system may automatically start up ISPF instead of display-

ing the TSO prompt; if not, we'll soon see how to start it up manually.)

The messages appearing in uppercase letters are from the system, telling you some statistics about this logon and the same user ID's last logon. The rest of the messages are from the system administrator, to keep you abreast of news about the system. The last line, READY, is the TSO command-line prompt. It means that the system is ready for you to type in TSO commands.

23.1.2.1 Reconnecting. Let's say you're accidentally disconnected from the system and you try to log on again. It may tell you this

```
IKJ56425I LOGON REJECTED, USERID JOEUSER IN USE
IKJ56400A ENTER LOGON OR LOGOFF-
```

because you didn't log off properly. This isn't a problem; MVS provides the RECON option to the LOGON command, which means "reconnect me to my earlier session." If you respond to the above message with

```
logon joeuser recon
```

the system prompts you for your password and reconnects you, displaying the same screen you were viewing when you were disconnected.

If you log on by filling out the form displayed in Figure 23.1, note the line at the bottom that says, "ENTER AN 'S' BEFORE EACH OPTION DESIRED BELOW." (The "S" stands for "Select.") One of the options is "RECONNECT," so after you enter your password and before you press Enter, move your cursor to the RECONNECT option by repeatedly pressing the Tab key. If you type the letter "S" there and press Enter, the system reacts as if you had entered

```
logon joeuser recon
```

at the TSO prompt.

23.1.3 Entering commands

When you start your session, and at any time throughout, the READY prompt shows that the system is ready for you to type in a TSO command.

When you type a command, it appears on the line under the READY prompt. After you press Enter, the command's output appears under the typed command. If there is too much to fit on the screen, asterisks appear on the last line to tell you that there is more to see. For example, the LISTCAT command lists file names (they're really called data

```
ICH70001I JOEUSER  LAST ACCESS AT 18:31:55 ON MONDAY, JANUARY 11, 1994
JOEUSER LOGON IN PROGRESS AT 09:09:30 ON JANUARY 12, 1994
***********************************************************************
*    Use CLASS=T for all server batch JOBs or they may be cancelled.  *
***********************************************************************
*    Please report any problems to the Help Desk at 878-4531.         *
***********************************************************************
***                        N e w s :                               ***
***********************************************************************
*    Due to a recent security breach, all users must change their     *
*    passwords by Thursday, January 14.                               *
***********************************************************************
You have no messages or data sets to receive.
**** NATIVE TSO READY ****
READY
listcat
 IN CATALOG:SYS1.BGCCTLG
 JOEUSER.ACCNTING.CLIST
 JOEUSER.ACCNTING.COBOL
 JOEUSER.APL.ASM
 JOEUSER.CICS.CNTL
 JOEUSER.ERRORS.DATA
 JOEUSER.FMU.DATA
 JOEUSER.HLIPRINT.DATA
 JOEUSER.HLIPRINT.FOCUS
 JOEUSER.INVENTRY.DATA
 ***
```

Figure 23.3 Beginning of LISTCAT output when remainder doesn't fit on screen.

sets; more on this later). Figure 23.3 shows the LISTCAT command entered when there isn't enough room for all of its output on the screen.

When you press Enter, more of the command's output appears. If the remaining output doesn't fit on the second screen, the asterisks will appear at the bottom again, waiting for you to press Enter. When you do reach the end, the READY prompt reappears, as shown in Figure 23.4.

```
JOEUSER.INVENTRY.COBOL
JOEUSER.ACCNTING.COBOL.BACKUP
JOEUSER.ISPF.ISPPROF
JOEUSER.JU.ASM
JOEUSER.JU.CLIST
JOEUSER.LOG.MISC
JOEUSER.MASTER.DATA
JOEUSER.OFFLINE.DATA
JOEUSER.PROD.PROCLIB
JOEUSER.RDBAPP.DATA
JOEUSER.RDBAPP.OBJ
JOEUSER.RDBAPP.REXX
JOEUSER.TEST.CNTL
JOEUSER.TEST.ASM
READY
```

Figure 23.4 End of LISTCAT output.

23.1.3.1 Aborting screen output.   If you find yourself repeatedly pressing Enter and regretting that you entered the command that produced so much output, you have an alternative to pressing Enter: the PA1 key. Pressing it puts you right back at the TSO `READY` prompt after it clears the screen, aborting the output of any command currently putting information on the screen. (When using a PC with a terminal emulation program instead of an actual mainframe terminal, check the emulation program's documentation to see which key acts as PA1.)

23.1.3.2 Command parameters.   Many commands need some information from you in order to do their job. For instance, when you type the `COPY` command, the system needs to know the name of the data set you want to copy and the name you want to assign to your new copy. As you'll see in the section on this command, you could type

```
copy old.dsname new.dsname
```

but if you just type

```
copy
```

by itself, MVS turns out to be fairly user-friendly about this abbreviated syntax—it prompts you for the information it needs:

```
copy
ENTER 'FROM' DATA SET NAME -
jan13.memo
ENTER 'TO' DATA SET NAME -
jan13.memo.backup
READY
```

(VMS also does this, although MVS and VMS are completely different operating systems from completely different companies. IBM's VM and Wang's VS add to the name confusion—the fact that MVS, VS, VMS, and VM are four unrelated operating systems from three different companies is a big part of what makes the mini and mainframe world so confusing.)

23.1.3.3 Long commands.   Complicated commands may take up more than one whole line of your screen. If this happens, you can indicate that your command continues on the next line with the plus (+) or minus (-) sign. For example, listing the contents of the `TESTSEQ1.DATA` data set by entering

```
list +
testseq1.data
```

has the same effect as entering

```
list testseq1.data
```

Of course, there wouldn't be much point to breaking up a command this short over more than one line.

23.1.3.4 Case sensitivity.   TSO maps all entered commands to uppercase, so it doesn't matter whether you type

```
LIST TESTSEQ1.DATA
```

or

```
LIST testseq1.data
```

or

```
list testseq1.data
```

at the READY prompt. They all list the contents of the data set called TESTSEQ1.DATA. In the TSO examples in this book, entered commands are shown in lowercase to make it easier for you to distinguish between lines that the user types and lines that the system displays, which almost always appear in uppercase.

23.1.3.5 Command-line options.   IBM's on-line help and literature about TSO refer to command-line options as "operands." You don't need any special character to indicate that something you add to the command line is an operand for that command. For example, the LIST command's NONUM option indicates that you don't want line numbers listed with a data set's contents. You add it onto the command just as it is, with no "-" (as in UNIX) or "/" (as in VMS) or "(" (as in CMS) to indicate that it is a special option for the LIST command:

```
list testseq1.data nonum
```

Certain TSO commands have options that need extra information from you. This information is enclosed in parentheses right after the option's name. For example, the ALLOCATE command, which creates a new data set or indicates an existing data set for a program to use, sometimes takes the following form:

```
allocate dataset(dsname)
```

In this example, dsname represents the name of the data set to allocate. You would substitute a data set name between the parentheses.

Whether you enter an existing data set name or a new one depends on your purpose in entering the ALLOCATE command. We'll see more about this in Section 24.1.7, "Allocating data sets." We'll also see that this command can take many more options than this—enough to give you practice at using the "+" character to spread your ALLOCATE command over two lines, as described in Section 23.1.3.3, "Long commands."

23.1.4 Finishing your MVS session

Logging off is simple: just type

```
logoff
```

at the TSO READY prompt. The system then displays a message telling you the user ID being logged off, the time, and the date.

23.2 Filenames

Files in MVS are known as *data sets*. Although most books on MVS tell you that "data set" is the term used for a file, keep in mind that the terms are not completely interchangeable. The word "file" has a specific meaning in MVS: when you use the ALLOCATE command to indicate a data set that a particular program will use, FILE is a synonym for DDNAME, or "data definition name." The program uses the ddname to refer to the data set. For example, if a database program saves report output in a data set instead of displaying it on the screen, it might expect the data set to have a DDNAME of RPTOUT. If you wanted the data saved in a data set called JOEUSER.SUMRPT.TEXT, you would allocate this data set with a DDNAME of RPTOUT. For more on this, see Section 24.1.7, "Allocating data sets."

23.2.1 Sequential and partitioned data sets

There are two kinds of data sets: sequential and partitioned. (Actually, there's a third called VSAM—pronounced "vee-sam"—used to store data for database applications, but that's a more advanced topic.) A sequential data set is like a regular file in other operating systems; a partitioned data set (also known as a PDS, or a "library") is like a group of files under one name. Each one of the files, or "members" of a PDS, is basically the same as a sequential data set. In fact, we'll see with the COPY command how easily you can take an existing sequential data set and make it a member of an existing partitioned data set.

Because a partitioned data set is a collection of "files," it's tempting to compare it to a directory or folder on another operating system. In practice, however, MVS users do not really use partitioned data sets this way. A single PDS usually holds a group of files that all serve the same purpose within their respective contexts and that all have the same characteristics (for example, record length, maximum size, and the units in which their size is defined). In VM/CMS, this would be like grouping together a collection of files with the same filetype; in other operating systems, it would be like grouping files with the same extension. For example, one PDS might hold several CLISTs (TSO command procedures). Another could hold the data files used by a certain database management program, and another could hold a collection of report specifications for using data from that program.

Section 23.3, "How Files Are Organized," describes the role of partitioned data sets in greater detail.

23.2.2 Line numbers and data sets

You may have seen text editors on some operating systems that include line numbers next to the text. The two text editors used in MVS also do this, but there's an important difference when compared with other operating systems: MVS editors save the numbers with the data sets. If this ever presents a problem, most TSO commands offer an operand that lets you omit the line numbers—for example, when you print or copy a numbered data set.

23.2.3 Naming data sets

The rules for naming sequential and partitioned data sets are the same. (As we'll see, referring to a particular member of a PDS requires something extra added to the PDS name.)

A data set name is composed of pieces called qualifiers. A period separates each qualifier. For data sets that you create, MVS adds your user ID as the first, or "high-level" qualifier. For Joe User, the full name (or, in MVS parlance, the "fully qualified data set name") of a data set that he named `MYFILE.TEXT` would be `JOEUSER.MYFILE.TEXT`.

Some MVS users call this high-level qualifier the data set's "prefix." It's not always the user ID of the person who created it; it could be the name of the application that uses it or something else assigned by the system. The data sets that you create, however, nearly always have your user ID as their high-level qualifier.

When you refer to a data set, you rarely include the high-level qualifier in its name. The system assumes that your user ID is it. If you are including the high-level qualifier when specifying a data set name and don't want TSO to automatically add one, enclose the data set name in apostrophes. For a user ID of JOEUSER, this tells the system that you've added the "JOEUSER" yourself, as in the following:

```
'joeuser.myfile.text'
```

MVS users refer to the apostrophe as a "tick" and the period as a "dot," so if you were reading the above data set name out loud to someone you would say "tick joeuser dot myfile dot text tick."

You enclose a data set name in "ticks" to refer to a data set that is not your own, such as a data set that another user told you to use. Remember, all data sets have a high-level qualifier; if you enclose a data set name in apostrophes and leave out the high-level qualifier, or use an invalid one, MVS rejects it.

A fully qualified data set name can have as many parts (that is, qualifiers) as you want, as long as the total number of characters (including the periods that separate the qualifiers) does not exceed 44 and no qualifier has more than eight characters. If Joe User's user ID is JOEUSER, this leaves him with 36 characters for the rest of his fully qualified data set names, because MVS automatically adds his seven-character user ID and a period to the beginning of any data set he creates.

Qualifiers can contain letters and numbers, and must begin with a letter. The only other allowable characters are @, $, and #. (Note that the underscore, which is OK on most operating systems, cannot be used in MVS.) The case of alphabetical characters doesn't matter, since lowercase letters are converted to uppercase.

Although your data set name could have over a dozen qualifiers, three is the most popular number. ISPF makes life easier for people who use data set names with three qualifiers; it even has a name for each of the three:

project	The user ID, or high-level qualifier
group	The name that you make up to distinguish this data set from others with the same project and type
type	The type of the data set—much like the concept of a file's type in VMS, its filetype in CMS, or its extension in DOS or UNIX

For example, if Joe User had written three programs in the COBOL programming language, he might store them in data sets named JOEUSER.INPUT.COBOL, JOEUSER.SUMRPT.COBOL, and JOEUSER.DETRPT.COBOL. He could have named the last one JOEUSER.DETAIL.REPORT.VER1.COBOL, but the three-part name is more conventional.

Some MVS users call the type the "low-level qualifier." This applies not only to three-part data set names, but to all data set names with two or more parts—in other words, all data set names. The last part, the part that identifies what kind of data set it is, is always considered the low-level qualifier. (In the previous paragraph, all the data set names listed as examples have a low-level qualifier of COBOL—even JOEUSER.DETAIL.REPORT.VER1.COBOL.) We call the qualifiers in between *intermediate qualifiers*.

23.2.3.1 The members of a partitioned data set.   The rules for naming a partitioned data set are the same as those for naming a sequential data set. Since a PDS is actually a collection of data sets, we also need a way to refer to a particular member of the PDS.

A member name goes right after the PDS name in parentheses. For example, if Joe User keeps his COBOL programs as members of a partitioned data set called JOEUSER.SOURCE.COBOL, the member SUMRPT actually has the full name JOEUSER.SOURCE.COBOL (SUMRPT). Joe refers to it as SOURCE.COBOL(SUMRPT), knowing that the system adds the JOEUSER part for him. If he wants to refer to the fully qualified name by enclosing it in apostrophes, he calls it 'JOEUSER.SOURCE.COBOL(SUMRPT)'.

Member names must follow the same rules as qualifier names: they can be up to eight characters long, they can contain letters, numbers and the @, $, and # symbols, and they must begin with a letter of the alphabet.

The limit of 44 characters on a data set name does not include the characters of a member name. A PDS with a 44-character name can still have members with 8-character names.

23.2.4 Wildcards

The only wildcard in TSO is the asterisk (*). You can use it to represent any single qualifier in a data set name. For example, the LISTCAT command can use the ENTRIES operand to list information about a single data set, as with the following:

```
listcat entries(dept.data)
```

Substituting an asterisk for one of the qualifiers means "perform this command on any data set that matches the other qualifiers, with anything in the asterisk's position." The following tells TSO to list the names of the data sets with "DEPT" as the second qualifier (remember, "JOEUSER" is the first) and anything as the third:

```
listcat entries(dept.*)
```

When you write out the data set name, you cannot make the asterisk the first part of the data set name. For example, to list all the data sets having "DATA" as their last qualifier, you could not enter this:

```
listcat entries(*.data)
```

To get around this, use fully qualified data set names. Don't forget the apostrophes:

```
listcat entries('joeuser.*.data')
```

Remember, the use of the asterisk as a wildcard is not restricted to the LISTCAT command. Others, including COPY, RENAME, and DELETE can also use it.

23.3 How Files Are Organized

MVS keeps track of data sets in lists of their names and locations called catalogs. The system's master catalog stores a list of the names and locations of the user ID catalogs, and your ID's catalog is the list of your data sets. (Note that the command for listing data set names is LISTCAT; you're asking the system to list the contents of a catalog.)

The actual storage device that holds a particular data set is identified by a unique number called a Volume Serial Number, or VOLSER (pronounced "voll-sear"). Part of the purpose of the catalog system is to keep you from worrying about VOLSERs. On some ISPF screens where you enter a data set name, one line asks you to enter the "VOLUME SERIAL (IF NOT CATALOGUED)." In other words, it only needs to know this information if the data set is not in any catalog. (To see the VOLSER of your data sets when you list their names, add the VOLUME operand to the LISTCAT command. See Section 24.1.2, "Listing data set names," for more on LISTCAT.)

A related term is VTOC, the Volume Table of Contents, a special data set that serves as the table of contents for a particular storage device. As with the VOLSER, advanced users sometimes use the VTOC to access their data more directly, but the use of catalogs relieves beginners from the need to worry about VTOCs. If it comes up in conversation, remember to pronounce it "vee-tok" and people will assume you know what you're talking about.

23.4 Available On-Line Help

TSO's on-line is neither terrific nor terrible. Help information appears in all uppercase letters, which is rather primitive, but it gives you syntax and a description for any command that you can name.

If you don't know command names, you can use the on-line help to find them. Typing HELP all by itself at the TSO READY prompt displays a list of TSO commands, with a brief description of each one's purpose. Figure 23.5 shows the first of these screens displayed.

For more detailed help about a specific command, enter the command's name as an operand to the HELP command. Figure 23.6 shows the HELP command being entered with LISTCAT as an operand, and the beginning of the HELP command's output.

Again, the asterisks at the bottom show that you're only looking at the first screen of a fairly extensive description of the command. The

```
READY
help
LANGUAGE PROCESSING COMMANDS:

ASM         INVOKE ASSEMBLER PROMPTER AND ASSEMBLER F COMPILER.
CALC        INVOKE ITF:PL/1 PROCESSOR FOR DESK CALCULATOR MODE.
COBOL       INVOKE COBOL PROMPTER AND ANS COBOL COMPILER.
FORT        INVOKE FORTRAN PROMPTER AND FORTRAN IV G1 COMPILER.

PROGRAM CONTROL COMMANDS:

CALL        LOAD AND EXECUTE THE SPECIFIED LOAD MODULE.
LINK        INVOKE LINK PROMPTER AND LINKAGE EDITOR.
LOADGO      LOAD AND EXECUTE PROGRAM.
RUN         COMPILE, LOAD, AND EXECUTE PROGRAM.
TEST        TEST USER PROGRAM.
TESTAUTH    TEST APF AUTHORIZED PROGRAMS.

DATA MANAGEMENT COMMANDS:

ALLOCATE    ALLOCATE A DATA SET WITH OR WITHOUT AN ATTRIBUTE
            LIST OF DCB PARAMETERS.
ALTLIB      DEFINE OPTIONAL, USER-LEVEL OR APPLICATION-LEVEL SETS OF
***
```

Figure 23.5 First TSO help screen.

```
help listcat

  FUNCTION -
    THE LISTCAT COMMAND LISTS ENTRIES FROM EITHER THE MASTER CATALOG OR
    A USER CATALOG.

  SYNTAX -
          LISTCAT    CATALOG('CATNAME/PASSWORD')
                     FILE('DNAME')
                     OUTFILE('DNAME')
                     LEVEL('LEVEL') | ENTRIES('ENTRYNAME/PASSWORD' ...)
                     CREATION('NNNN')
                     EXPIRATION('NNNN')
                     NOTUSABLE
                     CLUSTER  DATA  INDEX  ALIAS  SPACE  NONVSAM
                        USERCATALOG  GENERATIONDATAGROUP  PAGESPACE
                        ALTERNATEINDEX  PATH
                     ALL | NAME | HISTORY | VOLUME | ALLOCATION
    REQUIRED - NONE
    DEFAULTS - NAME
    ABBREVIATIONS -
          NOTE - IN ADDITION TO NORMAL TSO SHORT FORMS, THESE ARE ACCEPTED.
   ***
```

Figure 23.6 Command and output for help about LISTCAT.

```
OPERANDS -
  CATALOG('CATNAME/PASSWORD')
            - SPECIFIES THE NAME OF THE CATALOG CONTAINING THE ENTRIES
              TO BE LISTED.
   'CATNAME'
            - NAME OF THE CATALOG CONTAINING THE ENTRIES TO BE
              LISTED.
   'PASSWORD'
            - PASSWORD OF THE CATALOG CONTAINING THE ENTRIES TO BE
              LISTED.
  REQUIRED - 'CATNAME'
  FILE('DNAME')
            - IDENTIFIES THE VOLUMES THAT CONTAIN THE CATALOG
              ENTRIES TO BE LISTED.
   'DNAME'  - NAME OF THE DD STATEMENT THAT IDENTIFIES THE VOLUMES
              CONTAINING CATALOG ENTRIES TO BE LISTED.
  OUTFILE('DNAME')
            - IDENTIFIES THE ALTERNATE OUTPUT DATA SET.
   'DNAME'  - NAME OF THE JCL STATEMENT THAT IDENTIFIES THE
              ALTERNATE OUTPUT DATA SET.
  LEVEL('LEVEL')
            - SPECIFIES THE LEVEL OF ENTRY NAMES TO BE LISTED.
   'LEVEL'  - LEVEL OF ENTRY NAMES TO BE LISTED.
***
```

Figure 23.7   More help for LISTCAT.

list of possible syntax variations alone take up almost the entire screen.

The separate lines show options that you may add after the `LISTCAT` command. When you see several options listed on the same line, such as

```
ALL | NAME | HISTORY | VOLUME | ALLOCATION
```

in Figure 23.6, that means you can choose one of these, but not more than one.

So what do all these options mean? This is revealed after the syntax. For example, Figure 23.7 shows some later help material for the `LISTCAT` command; each option has at least one line describing it.

Using Files in MVS

24.1 The Seven Most Important Commands

The seven most important TSO commands in MVS are:

`LISTCAT`	Lists the data sets in a catalog
`LISTDS`	Lists the members in a partitioned data set
`LIST`	Displays the contents of data sets
`COPY`	Copies data sets and data set members
`RENAME`	Renames data sets and data set members
`DELETE`	Deletes data sets and data set members
`ALLOCATE`	Creates and provides access to data sets

Remember, in addition to performing these functions with TSO commands, you can use ISPF. TSO, however, gives you more flexibility. In other words, if you see a lot of potential options when you enter "HELP" followed by the name of one of the commands in this section, ISPF won't necessarily have an equivalent to all of those options.

Nearly all of the commands described here require you to name the data set you wish to act on. The examples leave out the high-level qualifier, but they all work the same way if you include the high-level qualifier—as long as you remember to put it between apostrophes. For example, when logged on to Joe User's ID, there's no difference between entering

```
delete memos.text
```

and

```
delete 'joeuser.memos.text'
```

24.1.1 Common error messages

The simplest mistake to make at the TSO command line is typing in the name of a "command" that doesn't exist at the READY prompt. If you type in such a command, like

```
hlep listcat
```

when you meant to type help listcat, TSO tells you

```
COMMAND HLEP NOT FOUND
```

In other words, TSO has no command called HLEP.

A classic mistake on many systems is entering a command that expects command-line parameters without entering as many parameters as it expects. (For example, entering the COPY command without saying what you want to copy and what to call the copy.) When using TSO, this is not a mistake; as we saw in Section 23.1.3.2, "Command parameters," TSO prompts you for the rest of the necessary information.

If you try to perform a command on a nonexistent data set, you will find that TSO has a variety of ways to tell you that there's a problem. Trying to rename a nonexistent data set called MYNOTES.TEXT gives you the following error message

```
DATA SET MYNOTES.TEXT NOT IN CATALOG OR AMOUNT OF DATASETS EXCEEDS
WORKAREA FOR GENERIC RENAME
```

while trying to copy the same nonexistent data set gives you a much terser error message:

```
COPY ENDED DUE TO ERROR
```

The justification for this disparity in error message information goes something like this: real TSO commands, like RENAME, get reasonable error messages, but COPY is not a real TSO command. It's actually a TSO utility program, but it's so useful that it's installed wherever TSO is installed—sort of like ISPF.

Another error message is worth examining because of its use of MVS terminology. Try to delete a nonexistent data set called MYNOTES.TXT and you see

```
ERROR QUALIFYING JOEUSER.MYNOTES.TEXT
```

The system first adds the high-level qualifier (the user's ID) so that it has the complete data set name, and then it uses this name to find the data set. Obviously, it fails; there's no such data set in the JOEUSER catalog. (You'll get the same error message for a data set that seems to exist, but isn't part of your catalog. See Section 24.1.8, "Adding a data set to a catalog," for more on this.)

If you try to do something to a data set and leave off the last qualifier, TSO displays the final qualifiers for data sets that begin with whatever you entered. For example, if you have data sets named APRIL.MEMOS.SENT and APRIL.MEMOS.RECEIVED and you enter the command

```
delete april.memos
```

TSO responds like this:

```
QUALIFIERS FOR DATA SET APRIL.MEMOS ARE
SENT RECEIVED
ENTER QUALIFIER-
```

You then enter the final qualifier of the data set that you want to delete and press Enter.

TSO reacts similarly when it understands a command name, but not one of its operands. For example, Section 24.1.2.2, "Listing a partitioned data set's members," shows how you can list a partitioned data set's members by adding the MEM operand to the LISTDS command after the data set's name. If you misspelled it as in the following

```
listds setup.clist mom
```

TSO responds with this:

```
INVALID KEYWORD, MOM
REENTER THIS OPERAND -
```

This gives you the chance to enter the wrong part again. If you really thought that MOM was right and you're not sure what to enter now, enter a question mark and TSO responds with a description of the proper syntax for the command you entered:

```
?
SYNTAX -
        LISTDS 'DSLIST' STATUS HISTORY MEMBERS LABEL
                CATALOG('CAT.NAME') LEVEL
REQUIRED - 'DSLIST'
DEFAULTS - NONE
```

24.1.2 Listing data set names

TSO users use two commands to list data set names: LISTCAT lists the names of data sets in a catalog, and LISTDS lists a partitioned data set's members.

```
listc
 IN CATALOG:SYS1.BGCCTLG
 JOEUSER.ACCNTING.CLIST
 JOEUSER.ACCNTING.COBOL
 JOEUSER.APL.ASM
 JOEUSER.CICS.CNTL
 JOEUSER.ERRORS.DATA
 JOEUSER.FMU.DATA
 JOEUSER.HLIPRINT.DATA
 JOEUSER.HLIPRINT.FOCUS
 JOEUSER.INVENTRY.DATA
 JOEUSER.INVENTRY.COBOL
 JOEUSER.INVENTRY.COBOL.BACKUP
 JOEUSER.ISPF.ISPPROF
 JOEUSER.JU.ASM
 JOEUSER.JU.CLIST
 JOEUSER.JU.CLIST1A
 JOEUSER.JU.CNTL
 JOEUSER.JU.COBOL
 JOEUSER.JU.DATA
 JOEUSER.JU.DS14
 JOEUSER.JU.LOAD
 ***
```

Figure 24.1 Sample output of the LISTCAT command.

24.1.2.1 Listing a catalog's data sets. If you enter the LISTCAT command without any operands, it lists the names of data sets in your user ID's catalog, as shown in Figure 24.1.

(The three asterisks on the last line show that TSO is only displaying the first screenful of names, not the entire list.) Note how only the first five letters of "LISTCAT" were entered. This abbreviation is all you need.

Two operands to the LISTCAT command let you narrow down the list of data set names to display. The ENTRIES operand takes a data set name as an argument, in parentheses, and lists the name of the data set and the name of the catalog that holds information about the data set. The following command

```
listc entries(inventry.cobol)
```

produces the following output:

```
NONVSAM ------- JOEUSER.INVENTRY.COBOL
IN-CAT --- SYS1.BGCCTLG
```

The ENTRIES operand is more useful when you use an asterisk as a wildcard in the data set name included in the parentheses. Substituting an asterisk for one (and only one) of the data set name qualifiers causes the LISTCAT command to list all the data set names that have any qualifier in the asterisk's position, and whose other qualifiers match the corresponding ones in the data set name between the parentheses. See Section 23.2.4, "Wildcards," for examples.

The LEVEL operand tells the LISTCAT command to list data set names that begin with the qualifier (or qualifiers) entered as a parameter. For example, entering

```
listc level(joeuser.inventry)
```

produces the following output:

```
JOEUSER.INVENTRY.DATA
JOEUSER.INVENTRY.COBOL
JOEUSER.INVENTRY.COBOL.BACKUP
```

You can use the LEVEL operand to list the data set names in another user ID. For example, entering

```
listc level(mjones)
```

lists all the data set names in the MJONES catalog—if you have permission to list them. Either Mary Jones must authorize you to list them, or you must be in her group. MVS's high priority on data security means that your default access to the list of another user's data sets is no access. For an extra touch of heavy security, a warning message may be mailed to Mary telling her that you tried to list the names of her data sets.

24.1.2.2 Listing a partitioned data set's members.   Use the LISTDS command to determine if a data set is sequential or partitioned, and if it is partitioned, the names of its members.

When you enter this command with one data set name as a parameter, like this

```
listds errors.data
```

you'll see output similar to this:

```
--RECFM-LRECL-BLKSIZE-DSORG
   FB    80    23200   PO
--VOLUMES--
   USERMB
```

The most important part of this right now is the data set organization, designated by "DSORG." The "PO" means that INVENTRY.COBOL is a partitioned data set; if it was sequential, the DSORG value would be PS. Other values may show up here, for things like specific types of database data sets, but PO and PS are the DSORG values that you will see most often for data sets in your user ID.

To list the members of a partitioned data set, add the MEMBERS (or just MEM) operand to the LISTDS commands. Figure 24.2 shows an example.

Adding the MEM operand when using LISTDS with a sequential data set has no effect—the command lists information about the data set as if you hadn't included the MEM operand. Figure 24.3 shows an example.

As with the ENTRIES operand of the LISTCAT command, you can substitute the asterisk wildcard for one of the qualifiers in the speci-

```
listds inventry.cobol mem
 JOEUSER.INVENTRY.COBOL
 --RECFM-LRECL-BLKSIZE-DSORG
    FB    80    23200    PO
 --VOLUMES--
    USERMB
 --MEMBERS--
    SETUP
    ADDNEW
    DELETE
    SUMRPT
```

Figure 24.2 Listing a data set's members by adding MEM to the LISTDS command.

```
listds autoexec.bat mem
 JOEUSER.AUTOEXEC.BAT
 --RECFM-LRECL-BLKSIZE-DSORG
    VB    84    6233    PS
 --VOLUMES--
    USERMC
```

Figure 24.3 Adding MEM to LISTDS with a sequential data set.

fied data set name. This lets you list information about more than one data set, but only if their names have several qualifiers in common.

24.1.3 Looking at data sets

Use the LIST command to display the contents of a data set. Like the COPY command, LIST is technically a utility and not part of TSO. It's so basic and useful, however, that you can almost take for granted that it is installed on the system you're using.

Using LIST is simple: just add the name of the data set you want to display. For example, typing

```
list schedule.text
```

displays the contents of the data set SCHEDULE.TEXT:

```
SCHEDULE.TEXT

00010 APRIL 7
00020 10 AM meet Mary Ann in conference room about new office space
00030 1 PM Lunch with Jimmy
00040 3:30 meet Frank in his office. Bring budget notes.
READY
```

The LIST command is a good example of how you can treat a partitioned data set's individual members like sequential data sets. To view the contents of the APRIL6 member of the MEMOS.TEXT partitioned data set, type the following:

```
list memos.text(april6)
```

The system displays the contents of that member:

```
MEMOS.TEXT(APRIL6)
    Joe -
    Can you come to my office tomorrow at 3:30 to discuss
    the proposed budget? If not, let me know as soon as
    possible so that I can find another time that is
    convenient for Jack and Mary.
    - Frank
```

If you try to list a partitioned data set without specifying a member name, MVS looks for a member named TEMPNAME in that PDS and lists it if found. Otherwise, it tells you that it couldn't find it:

```
MEMBER TEMPNAME NOT IN DATA SET MEMOS.TEXT+
```

24.1.4 Copying data sets

In its simplest form, copying data sets is similar to copying files on most other operating systems. Entering

```
copy schedule.text schedule.text.backup
```

instructs the system to make a copy of SCHEDULE.TEXT called SCHEDULE.TEXT.BACKUP. If a data set named SCHEDULE.TEXT.BACK-UP already exists, TSO copies SCHEDULE.TEXT right on top of it without displaying any warning message, assuming that the two data sets have a compatible data set organization (DSORG).

Some data sets include line numbers and some don't. The default action of COPY is to include the line numbers, and if the source data set has none, you might see the following error message:

```
COPY TERMINATED, RENUMBERING ERROR+
```

If this happens, enter the copy operation again, but include the operand that instructs TSO not to bother with any line numbers in the source data set:

```
copy schedule.text schedule.text.backup nonum
```

24.1.4.1 Copying and partitioned data sets. Copying an entire PDS uses the same syntax as copying a sequential data set. To copy a specific member of a PDS, you can substitute the name of a PDS member for either or both of the data sets in the COPY syntax shown above. For example, the following makes a copy of the APRIL6 member of the MEMOS.TEXT PDS. The copy is a sequential data set called FRANK.TEXT:

```
copy memos.text(april6) frank.text
```

Similarly, you could add a copy of an existing sequential data set to a partitioned data set as a new member of that PDS with a command like this:

```
copy joan.text memos.text(april7)
```

When copying a member from one PDS to another, it's not enough to enter the name of the destination PDS. If you enter

```
copy memos.text(april6) memos1994.text
```

you'll get the following error message:

```
DATA SET ORGANIZATIONS ARE NOT COMPATIBLE+
```

Your source data set here is the functional equivalent of a sequential data set, and your destination is a partitioned data set—that's why they're incompatible. To indicate that you want APRIL6 added as a member of the PDS MEMOS1994.TEXT, enter the following:

```
copy memos.text(april6) memos1994.text(april6)
```

Of course, you can call this new member of MEMOS1994.TEXT anything you want; it doesn't have to have the same name as the original.

There a couple of points to keep in mind about copying data sets:

- If you enter the above command and the PDS MEMOS1994.TEXT doesn't exist, TSO creates it for you before adding APRIL6 as its only member.

- If you specify a partitioned data set as the source of your copy and a nonexistent PDS as the destination, TSO makes a copy of the whole PDS.

- You will see in Section 24.1.7, "Allocating data sets," that when data sets are created, one characteristic specified about them is whether its records (lines) are of fixed or variable length. You can copy a fixed-length member to a PDS with variable-length records, but you can't copy from a PDS with variable-length records to a destination with fixed-length records.

Section 24.1.7 also describes how creating a new data set means specifying its maximum size in directory blocks. If a PDS gets too big and runs out of directory blocks, copying it somewhere else is the first step toward fixing the problem. After you make a copy, you can reallocate it and then copy the temporary copy back onto the original.

24.1.5 Renaming data sets

Using the RENAME command is simple. Just indicate the data set (or PDS member) to rename and its new name. The following renames

the data set FRANK.TEXT, giving it the new name
FRANK.AUG23.TEXT:

```
rename frank.text frank.aug23.text
```

Renaming a member of a partitioned data set uses similar syntax:

```
rename memos.text(april6) memos.text(fbapril6)
```

A renamed member is still in the same data set, so MVS doesn't allow
you to change any of the qualifiers that make up the member's PDS
name.

Renaming a whole PDS and leaving its members' names alone has
the same syntax as renaming a sequential data set:

```
rename memos.text oldmemos.text
```

You can rename multiple data sets if their names are all the same except for one qualifier in the same position in each data set. For example,
to rename MEMOS.JAN.TEXT, MEMOS.FEB.TEXT, and MEMOS.MAR.TEXT
to the names MEMOS.JAN.TEXTBAK, MEMOS.FEB.TEXTBAK, and
MEMOS.MAR.TEXTBAK enter the following:

```
rename memos.*.text memos.*.textbak
```

24.1.6 Deleting data sets

To delete a data set, just type the DELETE command followed by the
name of the data set you want to delete:

```
delete memos.jan.text
```

After deleting the data set, TSO confirms the deletion:

```
ENTRY (A) JOEUSER.MEMOS.JAN.TEXT DELETED
```

To delete a single member of a data set, just specify the member
name with its data set:

```
delete memos.text(apr6)
```

As with the RENAME command, you can enter an asterisk instead of
one of the qualifiers to delete multiple data sets at once. The following command deletes all data sets with a first qualifier of MEMOS
(after the high-level qualifier of the user's ID), a low-level qualifier of
TEXT, and any second qualifier:

```
delete memos.*.text
```

To delete multiple data sets with completely different names, you don't have to enter the DELETE command multiple times; just list the names of each data set between parentheses:

```
delete (apl.asm test.data memos.text)
```

TSO responds with messages about the deletion of each data set:

```
ENTRY (A) JOEUSER.APL.ASM DELETED
ENTRY (A) JOEUSER.TEST.DATA DELETED
ENTRY (A) JOEUSER.MEMOS.TEXT DELETED
```

24.1.7 Allocating data sets

There are two kinds of allocation:

- Allocation of an existing data set usually sets it up for use by a particular program
- Allocation of a nonexistent data set is how you create new data sets

If you have used other operating systems but are new to MVS, data set allocation is the most difficult concept to get used to, because it has no direct equivalent in other operating systems. (VM/CMS, being another IBM mainframe operating system, has a related command called FILEDEF, but it's not as crucial to survival as ALLOCATE is to MVS users.) With most operating systems, telling the text editor to edit a nonexistent file creates a file by that name; in MVS, however, you must explicitly create a new data set by allocating it before you can do anything with it.

Allocation requests access to a data set, whether it already exists or not. There are various levels of access, and if you try to allocate a data set so that you can modify its contents while someone else currently has it allocated for modification, MVS won't let you. This is part of the point: more than one user trying to modify the same data set could result in the loss of one user's work. This doesn't mean that multiple users can't edit the same data set; they just need to use software—for example, a database management system—that coordinates their actions so that no user's work destroys another's.

24.1.7.1 Allocating existing data sets. There are several possible reasons to allocate an existing data set:

- Specifying the data sets that will be needed by an application program you're about to use
- Telling the system where to find things like your command procedures (CLISTs), error list partitioned data sets, and startup procedures

- Redirecting output from a program to a new destination, like the printer, a data set, or your terminal

The first of these is the most important for now. An application program often refers to a data set that it uses by a data definition name, or "ddname." The documentation for that program tells you the ddnames it expects to find already assigned to the data sets it needs. Before starting the program, you assign these names with the following syntax:

```
allocate dataset(dataset.name) ddname(ddname) [old/shr/mod]
```

The order of these three operands does not matter. Also, you can abbreviate the keyword DATASET to DSNAME or even just DA, and DDNAME can be written as FILE, FI, or just F. This is why you must be careful about using the terms "data set" and "file" interchangeably: MVS users sometimes use the term "file" to mean "ddname," which is quite distinct from a data set name. Like a data set qualifier, a ddname can have no more than eight characters.

The final operand in the syntax above shows the status, or the kind of access to the data set that you want:

OLD   Requests exclusive access to the data set. If you or the program that needs to use the data set will modify its contents, you need this type of access. This is the default.

SHR   Requests sharable access to the data set. If you or the program will only read the data (for example for running a report), you don't need to prevent others from using it by requesting OLD or MOD access.

MOD   Requests access allowing the appending of data onto the end of the data set. Unlike OLD, which requests access to edit data currently existing in the data set, we use MOD to add new data—for example, to perform data entry with a database.

Again, when you need this command, the chances are slim that you will need to figure out all the syntax elements yourself. Part of the job of the documentation for MVS application programs that require specific data set allocations is to explain the details of these allocations. Just remember to recognize the various alternatives to the keywords DATASET (DSNAME, DA) and DDNAME (FILE, FI, or F) when it tells you the necessary allocations.

For example, the documentation for the UpRiteBase database system might tell you that it expects data files to have the ddname "urdata" associated with them, and that you would allocate the data for your inventory data file with the following command (note that ALLOCATE only needs its first five letters included):

```
alloc da(inventry.data) fi(urdata) old
```

This has exactly the same effect as entering this:

```
allocate dataset(inventry.data) ddname(urdata) old
```

Since you may need to allocate more than one data set, and a typo in the ddname could cause trouble, you'll want the ability to list out the allocations made in your session. See Section 24.1.7.4, "Finding out a data set's allocation status," for more on this.

24.1.7.2 Allocating new data sets. When creating a new data set, the system needs to know much more about it than just its name—whether it's sequential or partitioned, how much space to set aside for it, the length of its lines, and several other details that few users completely understand. This brings us back to the high degree of customization possible with MVS: allocating data sets with the best possible settings for your site boosts the efficiency of the system. (And there's the converse: doing it badly, on a large scale, can slow down the machine.)

Fortunately, there's a way to tell TSO to allocate a new data set with a particular name and to copy all of its other attributes from an existing data set: the LIKE operand. For example, to create a new data set called PROJECT2.COBOL and model its attributes after PROJECT1.COBOL, enter this:

```
allocate dataset(project2.cobol) like(project1.cobol)
```

By using a fully qualified data set name for the model, you can easily copy the details from someone else's data set:

```
allocate dataset(project2.cobol) like('mjones.project1.cobol')
```

If you want to model your new data set after an existing one in all details except certain ones, you can specify those extra details after the LIKE operand. For example, if you know that Mary Jones' PROJECT1.COBOL data set is a partitioned data set with room for 18 members, but you want to allow more room in yours, include the DIR operand, which specifies how many directory blocks to set aside for a new PDS:

```
allocate dataset(project2.cobol) like('mjones.project1.cobol') dir(6)
```

Since each block holds about six members (although this varies from installation to installation—ask about the figure at your site), this leaves room for 36 members.

If you don't model a new data set after an existing one, a new data set requires you to at least specify the following:

- Its name

- How much space to set aside for it
- Whether it's a sequential or partitioned data set

We've already seen that the DATASET operand specifies the name. We also saw earlier that the LISTDS command produces output in which one of the headings, DSORG, shows a data set's organization. It is usually either sequential (PS) or partitioned (PO). Specifying this with the ALLOCATE command uses the same abbreviations: you add the DSORG() operand with either PS or PO between the parentheses. (Other values are possible, but most data sets will be one of these two.) If you do specify PO as the data set organization, don't forget to also include the DIR operand to indicate the maximum number of members that may be stored in the partitioned data set.

When you specify the space to set aside for your new data set, you must first decide on the units you will use to indicate this space. You have a choice of TRACKS, CYLINDERS, or BLOCKS. Most typical data sets are just a handful of blocks or tracks. Only very large data sets are allocated in terms of cylinders.

To understand tracks and cylinders, picture a mainframe's storage device as a stack of 15 or so hard disks. A typical individual disk has 2600 tracks arranged as concentric rings. Each track holds about 47 kilobytes of data. A cylinder is a collection of tracks represented by the same track on each disk in the pack; a typical size for a cylinder is 15 times 47 kilobytes, or 705 kilobytes.

A *block* is a unit of storage whose size you specify with the BLK-SIZE or BLOCK operand. The best possible size depends on the particular model of storage device that your system uses; typical values are 2160, 3600, and 6160. Fortunately, we've already seen the command to check an existing data set's block size: the LISTDS command. Along with the data set organization (DSORG), which tells you whether a data set is partitioned or not, LISTDS displays BLKSIZE as one of the headings describing a data set. Investigating the block size of existing data sets gives you an idea of how to set this parameter if you choose to allocate your new data set in units of blocks instead of tracks or cylinders.

Once you decide on the units of storage, you must choose how many of these units to set aside with the SPACE operand. SPACE takes two arguments: the primary allocation, which indicates how much space you expect the data set to need, and the secondary allocation, a backup amount that the system provides if the data set grows beyond the primary amount. The figure for the secondary amount is usually half of the primary amount.

The following command allocates a sequential data set called MYTEST.TEXT and sets aside 10 tracks of space for it, with 5 tracks as the amount of secondary space to add on if 10 isn't enough:

```
allocate dataset(mytest.text) dsorg(ps) tracks space(10 5)
```

The next command creates a partitioned data set named INVENTRY.COBOL with room for 10 members. Its total space is ten 8000-byte blocks, with five blocks set aside as the secondary storage if necessary. Note that the command won't fit on one line; as Section 23.1.3 ("Entering commands") explains, we add a plus sign at the end of one line to show that the next typed line is a continuation of the first one.

```
allocate dataset(inventry.cobol) block(8000) space(10 5) +
dsorg(po) dir(10)
```

Another common operand shows the disposition of the data set, or what happens to it when it is unallocated (see Section 24.1.7.3, "Unallocating data sets," for information on how this happens.) There are three possible operands for the data set's disposition:

CATALOG   Add the new data set to the master catalog, because you plan to keep this data set around. This is the default, so you don't need to add it to your ALLOCATE command if you choose it for your data set.

DELETE   Delete the data set as soon as it is unallocated. Use this for temporary data sets.

KEEP   Don't delete it, but don't add it to the catalog. Leave this option to the experts. Part of the point of the catalog is to make it unnecessary for you to know the physical details of the data set's storage; accessing an uncataloged data set requires you to know more than you want to about your data set.

The following command allocates a sequential data set that MVS deletes as soon as the data set is unallocated:

```
allocate dataset(temp.tmp) ddname(tempfile) dsorg(ps) tracks +
space(10 5) delete
```

The last two important ALLOCATE operands to be aware of are RECFM, for Record Format, and LRECL, or Logical Record Length.

A record format of V means that a data set's records have variable length. ("Records" here means "lines." The terms were once fairly synonymous, but as the science of dealing with databases advanced, the term "record" took on a much more specific meaning.) In other words, the lines aren't all the same length. A format of F means that they have fixed length. If any lines seem shorter than others, the system inserts spaces to make their lengths equal.

When you indicate the record format, you also indicate whether to use blocked records by including (or leaving out) a comma and the letter "B." For example, RECFM(F,B) tells MVS to make them fixed length, blocked records; RECFM(V) means variable-length, unblocked records. Generally, you'll want blocked records unless you're told specifically otherwise. For example, if a program's documentation tells you about data sets to create for that program's use, it tells you how it expects RECFM to be set for these data sets.

If the records have a fixed length, you must set this length—in other words, you must indicate how long the records are. For variable length records, you must indicate the longest possible length. Use the LRECL, or Logical Record Length operand, for this. A setting of LRECL(80) is pretty common.

The following command allocates a data set called HEYJOE.TEXT as a fixed-length, blocked data set with a record length of 80. Note how the BLOCK operand is an even multiple of 80 (1760/80 = 22). This way, when the system reads or writes a block of data, it never includes a partial record, so input and output are more efficient.

```
allocate dataset(heyjoe.text) space(10 5) tracks dsorg(ps) +
recfm(f,b) lrecl(80) block(1760)
```

The ALLOCATE command actually has over 50 possible operands. If you're curious to see them all, enter HELP ALLOCATE to display further information. I guarantee that you'll be using that PA1 key ("Aborting screen output," Section 23.1.3.1) before you've seen them all!

24.1.7.3 Unallocating data sets.

When you log off, the system automatically unallocates any allocated data sets. You may want to unallocate one or more data sets before logging off if someone else needs to use one that you've been using and you're not ready to log off yet. You also may want to unallocate a data set if you've allocated it with some of the wrong details, like its disposition, and you want to redo it. MVS won't let you allocate a data set that's already been allocated, so you must unallocate it first.

The FREE command makes this possible. The only operand it really needs is the name of the data set to unallocate. For example, to free up the TEMP.TMP data set mentioned above, enter

```
free dataset(temp.tmp)
```

Because the allocation of TEMP.TMP in Section 24.1.7.2 included a disposition of DELETE, unallocating it deletes it.

You also have the option of unallocating it by specifying the ddname used to allocate it. Since each allocated data set must have a unique ddname, MVS knows which data set you want to unallocate. Given the allocation of TEMP.TMP shown earlier, the following command has the same effect as the previous one:

```
free dataset(tempfile)
```

Both the DATASET and DDNAME operands of the FREE command can take multiple arguments. For example, if you had allocated the data sets MAYMEMOS.TEXT, JUNMEMOS.TEXT, and JULMEMOS.TXT with the ddnames MAY, JUNE, and JULY you could free all three with either the command

```
free dataset(maymemos.txt junmemos.txt julmemos.txt)
```

or with this:

```
free ddname(may june july)
```

You can unallocate all the data sets you've allocated with the following command:

```
free all
```

Note that this frees up all the data sets that you personally allocated, not all the allocated ones you may use. The system automatically allocates some, as you'll see in the next section, and it takes care of unallocating them.

24.1.7.4 Finding out a data set's allocation status.   Two commands show you a data set's allocation status. You already know one; the LISTDS command, described in Section 24.1.2.2 ("Listing a partitioned data set's members"), can take an additional operand that shows a data set's ddname and disposition along with its block size and data set organization: STATUS. The command

```
listds dept.data status
```

produces the following output:

```
--RECFM-LRECL-BLKSIZE-DSORG--DDNAME---DISP
  FB    80    3120    PO     SYS00002 KEEP
--VOLUMES--
  USERME
```

It's a partitioned data set, the ddname looks like something the system assigned, and it's a keeper.

Instead of listing a particular data set's allocation status, you might want to list the names of all of the allocated data sets. Use the LISTALC command for this. Figure 24.4 shows some sample output from typing LISTA (you only need the first five letters) with no operands.

The asterisks at the bottom show that this is only the first screen of names. You don't have to allocate over 23 data sets to see output like Figure 24.4; the system automatically allocates quite a few data sets on its own, and their names are mixed in.

```
DSN220.DSNLOAD
SYS1.DFQLLIB
EDC.V2R1M0.SEDCCOMP
EDC.V2R1M0.SEDCLINK
SYS1.V2R3M0.SIBMLINK
IPO1.CMDPROC
EDC.V2R1M0.SEDCLIST
ISR.V3R2M0.ISRCLIB
UBU0.CLIST
UBU1.CLIST
DSN220.DSNCLIST
SYS1.SBLSCLI0
ISR.V3R2M0.ISRCLIB
ISP.V3R2M0.ISPEXEC
SYS1.SBLSCLI0
DSN220.DSNSPFP
EDC.V2R1M0.SEDCPNLS
ISP.V3R2M0.ISPPENU
ISR.V3R2M0.ISRPENU
ISF.V1R3M1.ISFPLIB
SYS1.SBLSPNL0
SYS1.DFQPLIB
ISP.V3R2M0.ISPMENU
***
```

**Figure 24.4 Listing allocated data
sets with LISTALC (or LISTA).**

```
--DDNAME---DISP--
DSN220.DSNLOAD
   STEPLIB   KEEP
SYS1.DFQLLIB
   ISPLLIB   KEEP
EDC.V2R1M0.SEDCCOMP
             KEEP
EDC.V2R1M0.SEDCLINK
             KEEP
SYS1.V2R3M0.SIBMLINK
             KEEP
IPO1.CMDPROC
   SYSPROC   KEEP
EDC.V2R1M0.SEDCLIST
             KEEP
ISR.V3R2M0.ISRCLIB
             KEEP
UBU0.CLIST
             KEEP
UBU1.CLIST
             KEEP
DSN220.DSNCLIST
             KEEP
SYS1.SBLSCLI0
***
```

**Figure 24.5 Listing the ddname
and status of allocated data sets by
adding STATUS to the LISTALC
command.**

As with the LISTDS command, you can add the STATUS operand to the LISTALC command to find out the ddname and status of the allocated data sets. Figure 24.5 shows a sample.

The first one listed, DSN220.DSNLOAD, has a ddname of STEPLIB and a status of KEEP. Most others on the list don't have ddnames. Ours is not to question why; it's the system's job to worry about these things.

24.1.8 Adding a data set to a catalog

There's no specific command for adding a data set to a catalog, but as I mentioned in Section 24.1.7.3, "Unallocating data sets," the ability to unallocate lets you reallocate a data set with different operands. This makes it possible to take an existing data set that doesn't belong to a catalog and add it to one.

The following series of commands and responses shows an attempt to take a data set called MEMOS.TXT and add it to the user's catalog. At first, the system won't allow this because it's already allocated and not part of a catalog. After the data set is freed up, the same allocation command works the second time and adds the data set to the catalog.

```
allocate dataset(memos.text) tracks space(4 2) catalog
DATA SET JOEUSER.MEMOS.TEXT NOT ALLOCATED, REQUESTED AS NEW BUT
CURRENTLY ALLOCATED
READY
free dataset(memos.text)
READY
allocate dataset(memos.text) tracks space(4 2) catalog
READY
```

The lack of an error message after the second attempt shows that it worked.

The MVS ISPF Text Editor

25.1 The ISPF Text Editor

Editing data sets is one of the few places in MVS where ISPF gives you far more power and flexibility than TSO. Given the choice between the ISPF text editor and the TSO EDIT text editor, virtually everyone chooses the former. If the lack of a proper system connection limits you to using TSO without access to ISPF, see Section 25.8, "TSO's EDIT Text Editor," for the basics of editing data sets with the more primitive editor. (In fairness, I should mention one advantage of EDIT over the ISPF editor: you can get in and out of it much faster. The lack of menus and panels to fill out make it more efficient for quickly creating small data sets or performing simple edits to short data sets.)

25.2 Entering the ISPF Editor

To get into the ISPF editor, you must first enter ISPF by typing

```
ispf
```

at the TSO command prompt. This displays the ISPF main (or "primary") menu screen shown in Figure 25.1. (An MVS system administrator can customize the ISPF menu screens, so your main menu may not look exactly the same.)

Your cursor appears next to the OPTION ===> prompt, waiting for you to enter the number of one of the menu choices. On the menu shown in Figure 25.1, entering 2 brings you to the entry panel shown in Figure 25.2, where you enter the name of the data set that you will edit. (Here's a nice shortcut: if you enter ISPF 2 at the TSO prompt, you jump right to this screen.)

Each arrow (===>) points at a field of the entry panel to fill out. To move your cursor forward from field to field, press your Tab key. To move your cursor in the other direction, press Backtab. (On most

```
----------------------- ISPF/PDF PRIMARY OPTION MENU -----------------------
OPTION  ===>  _
                                                        USERID   -JOEUSER
     0   ISPF PARMS  - Specify terminal and user parameters   TIME     - 09:24
     1   BROWSE      - Display source data or output listings  TERMINAL - 3278
     2   EDIT        - Create or change source data            PF KEYS  - 24
     3   UTILITIES   - Perform utility functions
     4   FOREGROUND  - Invoke language processors in foreground
     5   BATCH       - Submit job for language processing
     6   COMMAND     - Enter TSO Command, CLIST, or REXX exec
     7   DIALOG TEST - Perform dialog testing
     8   LM UTILITIES- Perform library administrator utility functions
     9   IBM PRODUCTS- Additional IBM program development products
    10   SCLM        - Software Configuration and Library Manager
     D   DB2         - DB2 Facilities
     H   HSM         - DFHSM Facilities
     C   CHANGES     - Display summary of changes for this release
     S   SDSF        - System Display and Search Facility
    SO   DFSORT      - DFSORT Facility
     T   TUTORIAL    - Display information about ISPF/PDF
     X   EXIT        - Terminate ISPF using log and list defaults
   F1=HELP      F2=SPLIT     F3=END      F4=RETURN    F5=RFIND     F6=RCHANGE
   F7=UP        F8=DOWN      F9=SWAP     F10=LEFT     F11=RIGHT    F12=RETRIEVE
```

Figure 25.1 The ISPF primary menu.

```
-------------------------- EDIT - ENTRY PANEL ------------------------------
COMMAND ===>

ISPF LIBRARY:
   PROJECT ===>
   GROUP   ===>           ===>           ===>           ===>
   TYPE    ===>
   MEMBER  ===>                (Blank or pattern for member selection list)

OTHER PARTITIONED OR SEQUENTIAL DATA SET:
   DATA SET NAME  ===>
   VOLUME SERIAL  ===>        (If not cataloged)

DATA SET PASSWORD ===>        (If password protected)

PROFILE NAME    ===>          (Blank defaults to data set type)

INITIAL MACRO   ===>          LMF LOCK   ===> YES    (YES, NO or NEVER)

FORMAT NAME     ===>          MIXED MODE ===> NO     (YES or NO)


   F1=HELP      F2=SPLIT     F3=END      F4=RETURN    F5=RFIND     F6=RCHANGE
   F7=UP        F8=DOWN      F9=SWAP     F10=LEFT     F11=RIGHT    F12=RETRIEVE
```

Figure 25.2 Entry panel for naming the data set to edit.

```
ISPF LIBRARY:
   PROJECT ===> JOEUSER
   GROUP   ===> INVENTRY  ===>              ===>              ===>
   TYPE    ===> COBOL
   MEMBER  ===>                     (Blank or pattern for member selection list)

OTHER PARTITIONED OR SEQUENTIAL DATA SET:
   DATA SET NAME   ===>
   VOLUME SERIAL   ===>              (If not cataloged)
```

Figure 25.3 Sample entries in the ISPF LIBRARY section of the EDIT entry panel to edit INVENTRY.COBOL.

PC keyboards, this means pressing the Shift key and the Tab key together; on a mainframe keyboard, Backtab has its own key.)

The only really crucial fields on this entry panel are the ones that you use to enter the name of the data set that you want to edit. (The other fields on the Edit entry panel are used for more advanced features like password protection and stored collections of settings known as edit profiles. If you don't know what to do with any of these other fields, leave them alone. Blank is a good default in ISPF.) As explained in Section 23.2.3, "Naming data sets," fully qualified data set names often have a total of three qualifiers, and ISPF refers to the three as the data set's project, group, and type. Figure 25.3 shows how Joe User fills out the ISPF LIBRARY section of the entry panel to edit the data set INVENTRY.COBOL.

To edit a member of a partitioned data set, enter the three parts of the PDS name in the PROJECT, GROUP, and TYPE fields, and then the member name in the MEMBER field.

If your full data set name does not have three qualifiers, enter its name at the DATA SET NAME field under the line "OTHER PARTITIONED OR SEQUENTIAL DATA SET." You don't need the high-level qualifier; ISPF assumes that it's your user ID. If you don't want it to automatically add this, do the same thing that you do when entering the data set name as part of a command on the TSO command line: enclose it in apostrophes. (You really only need the first one.)

Figure 25.4 shows how Joe fills out the DATA SET NAME field to enter the same data set name in the panel.

```
ISPF LIBRARY:
   PROJECT ===>
   GROUP   ===>              ===>              ===>              ===>
   TYPE    ===>
   MEMBER  ===>                     (Blank or pattern for member selection list)

OTHER PARTITIONED OR SEQUENTIAL DATA SET:
   DATA SET NAME   ===> INVENTRY.COBOL
   VOLUME SERIAL   ===>              (If not cataloged)
```

Figure 25.4 Sample entries in the DATA SET NAME section of the EDIT entry panel to edit INVENTRY.COBOL.

You don't always have to fill out the data set name; once you've entered a data set's qualifiers in the PROJECT, GROUP, and TYPE fields, the ISPF editor redisplays the qualifier names you typed there the next time you use this entry panel. To edit that data set again, just call up that panel and press the Enter key. To edit a data set with a similar name, you only need to change the appropriate fields. (However, if you entered the name at the DATA SET NAME field, ISPF will not remember what you typed there.)

One way or another, some existing data set's name must be entered. With many text editors included with other operating systems, telling the editor to edit a data set that doesn't exist causes it to create a file with that name. The ISPF editor, however, expects the data set to already exist, even if it's empty. If you want to create a new data set, you must allocate it first with the ALLOCATE command. (For more on this, see Section 24.1.7.2, "Allocating new data sets.")

Once you tell ISPF the data set that you want to edit press Enter. ISPF displays the editing screen, as shown in Figure 25.5.

Besides showing that you're using the ISPF EDIT program, the top line of the screen shows the name of the data set being edited and which columns of this data set are being displayed. The second line has the prompt where you enter editing commands and, to the right of where it says SCROLL ===>, a message telling you how far you will scroll when you press the PF7 or PF8 keys to move up or down in your data set.

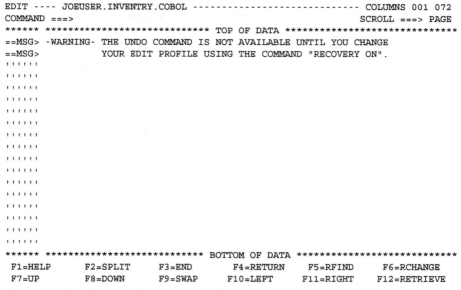

```
EDIT ---- JOEUSER.INVENTRY.COBOL --------------------------- COLUMNS 001 072
COMMAND ===>                                                   SCROLL ===> PAGE
****** *************************** TOP OF DATA *******************************
==MSG> -WARNING- THE UNDO COMMAND IS NOT AVAILABLE UNTIL YOU CHANGE
==MSG>           YOUR EDIT PROFILE USING THE COMMAND "RECOVERY ON".
''''''
''''''
''''''
''''''
''''''
''''''
''''''
''''''
''''''
''''''
''''''
''''''
''''''
''''''
''''''
****** *************************** BOTTOM OF DATA ***************************
   F1=HELP      F2=SPLIT     F3=END      F4=RETURN    F5=RFIND    F6=RCHANGE
   F7=UP        F8=DOWN      F9=SWAP     F10=LEFT     F11=RIGHT   F12=RETRIEVE
```

Figure 25.5 ISPF editor screen for an empty new data set.

The left side of the screen shows the numbers automatically added to the lines of your data set. Where no lines of data exist, the editor shows six apostrophes (' ' ' ' ' ') instead.

The main blank space on the screen is where you enter your text. When editing an existing data set, this is where it appears. As Figure 25.5 shows, other kinds of information can also appear there. The column on the left identifies the type of this information. For example, ==MSG> means that the line shows a message from the editor to you. The message shown in the example tells the user that the UNDO command is unavailable until a certain change is made to the edit profile. (For more on edit profiles, see the following section.)

25.2.1 Customizing your editor's environment

There are several commands that you can type at the editor's command line to customize the editor's behavior. (If your cursor is not already at the command line, press the Home key to move it up there.)

Because some programming languages expect everything to be in uppercase, the ISPF editor sometimes translates everything you type to uppercase. This is annoying when you type a paragraph, press Enter, and the whole paragraph gets converted. If you want the editor to respect a mix of upper- and lowercase letters, enter

```
caps off
```

at the command line. When writing a program in a language like FORTRAN, which requires uppercase letters, entering the command

```
caps on          .
```

translates every new line of text to all uppercase letters each time you press Enter.

Another setting that can cause confusing behavior is NULLS. You set it on by typing

```
nulls on
```

at the editor's command line and set it off by typing OFF instead of ON in the same command.

When set to OFF, the editor automatically puts blanks everywhere on a line where you didn't type anything else (between each word and throughout the remainder of the line after the last word) as if you had moved to each of these places and pressed the space bar to insert the blank character. This fills up each line, and causes problems when you want to insert new characters on a line. As with any text editor, inserted characters move existing characters on the right of the cursor further to the right; if the blank character fills all the space that looks empty, then the editor has nowhere to move the existing characters when you insert new characters. Trying to do so locks the keyboard, and you must press the Reset key to continue. (For more detailed information on inserting new characters, see Section 25.4, "Inserting, Deleting, and Typing over Words and Characters.")

If setting NULLS to ON avoids this problem, there must be a disadvantage to setting it ON. Otherwise, the editor wouldn't offer you two different settings, right? Many books describing the ISPF editor describe the following "problem": sometimes you want a space inserted where you didn't actually press the space bar, and with NULLS set to ON, pressing Enter resets the typed line, squeezing out all the places where nothing was typed. If you type "how are you" on a line and use your cursor-right key instead of the space bar for the spaces between the words, pressing Enter turns the phrase into "howareyou."

When editing a simple text data set, it makes more sense to set NULLS to ON. Setting it to OFF only provides an advantage when the ISPF editor is used to fill out a data entry form, in which the screen displays named fields of fixed lengths. In this case, use the Erase EOF (erase to end of field) key to clear any characters in the field from the cursor's position to the end of the field.

To sum up: if you have problems inserting, set NULLS to ON so the editor will not automatically fill in the remainder of a line after the last word with blanks.

Once you've set various parameters to customize your editing environment, many editors provide a way to save these settings for future use in a collection called an edit profile. The ISPF editor does this for you automatically, and it goes a step further than many other editors: it saves different collections of settings based on the TYPE of the data set. This way, if you set CAPS to ON when writing a program in FORTRAN (e.g, a data set called `MAINMENU.FORT`), then CAPS will always be ON for any data set you edit with a type of FORT, whether it's called `RPTMENU.FORT`, `SUMRPT.FORT`, or `MAINMENU.FORT`. If you set CAPS to OFF when editing a data set called `MAY6MEMO.TEXT`, it remains set to OFF every time you edit a data set with that type. If you alternately edit TEXT and FORT data sets, you won't have to reset CAPS every time, because the editor remembers how you set CAPS and all the other settings for each data set type.

25.3 Line Commands

In addition to the kind of commands that you enter at the command line at the top of your screen (described in Section 25.2.1, "Customizing your editor's environment,") the ISPF editor has another category of commands called "line commands." (These will be familiar to users of the AS/400's SEU editor. Also, CMS users who find that the screen resembles the XEDIT text editor's screen will find that line commands are the ISPF editor's counterpart to XEDIT prefix commands.) You can add, delete, copy, and move lines by entering one- or two-character commands in the line command area and pressing the Enter key. You can enter line command commands in the column to the left of the TOP OF DATA and BOTTOM OF DATA lines as well; if you couldn't, it would be pretty tough to add your first line.

You can enter a line command command anywhere on the line command area. For example, if you enter d2, the command to delete two lines, on the line command area like this

```
d2000
```

or like this

```
000d2
```

it still works the same. If you enter a command with a number in it, make sure that your cursor is right after the number when you press Enter, because the system treats every character up to the character preceding the cursor as part of the number you meant to type. For example, when you enter your 2d on the line command area for line number 11400 like this

```
d2400
```

and press Enter with your cursor at the 4, the editor deletes two lines. If your cursor was on the second zero when you pressed Enter, the system would think that you wanted to delete 240 lines!

25.3.1 Adding new lines

Use the line command i (for "insert") to add new lines on which to type. Figure 25.6 shows an example.

When you press Enter, the editor adds a new blank line after the line where you entered the command and positions your cursor at the beginning of the new line, waiting for you to type in text, as shown in Figure 25.7.

The new line isn't really a part of your data set until you add something there. After you type some text and press Enter, the editor as-

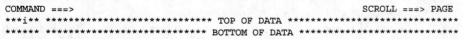

```
COMMAND ===>                                              SCROLL ===> PAGE
***i** *************************** TOP OF DATA ******************************
****** *************************** BOTTOM OF DATA ***************************
```

Figure 25.6 Adding the i line command to insert a new blank line.

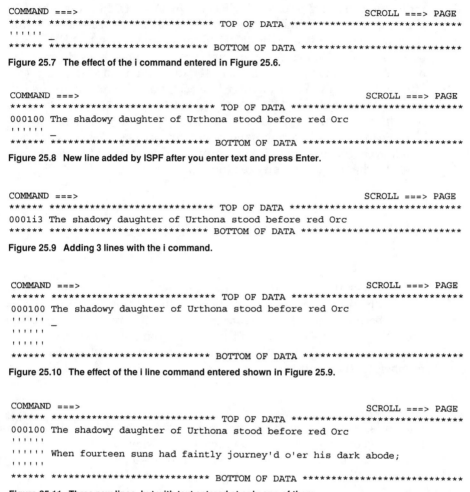

```
COMMAND ===>                                                    SCROLL ===> PAGE
****** *************************** TOP OF DATA ******************************
'''''''   _
****** *************************** BOTTOM OF DATA ****************************
```
Figure 25.7   The effect of the i command entered in Figure 25.6.

```
COMMAND ===>                                                    SCROLL ===> PAGE
****** *************************** TOP OF DATA ******************************
000100 The shadowy daughter of Urthona stood before red Orc
''''''   _
****** *************************** BOTTOM OF DATA ****************************
```
Figure 25.8   New line added by ISPF after you enter text and press Enter.

```
COMMAND ===>                                                    SCROLL ===> PAGE
****** *************************** TOP OF DATA ******************************
0001i3 The shadowy daughter of Urthona stood before red Orc
****** *************************** BOTTOM OF DATA ****************************
```
Figure 25.9   Adding 3 lines with the i command.

```
COMMAND ===>                                                    SCROLL ===> PAGE
****** *************************** TOP OF DATA ******************************
000100 The shadowy daughter of Urthona stood before red Orc
''''''
''''''   _
''''''
****** *************************** BOTTOM OF DATA ****************************
```
Figure 25.10   The effect of the i line command entered shown in Figure 25.9.

```
COMMAND ===>                                                    SCROLL ===> PAGE
****** *************************** TOP OF DATA ******************************
000100 The shadowy daughter of Urthona stood before red Orc
''''''
'''''' When fourteen suns had faintly journey'd o'er his dark abode;
''''''
****** *************************** BOTTOM OF DATA ****************************
```
Figure 25.11   Three new lines, but with text entered at only one of them.

signs a number to the line, creates a new blank line under it, and positions your cursor at the beginning of the new one. Figure 25.8 shows an example.

If the editor converts your entered text to all uppercase, but you didn't want it to, you'll need the CAPS OFF command to change this. See Section 25.2.1, "Customizing your editor's environment," for more information.

Adding a number after the i command tells the editor to add that many lines. In Figure 25.9, three lines are about to be added; Figure 25.10 shows the effect of this command.

If any of these new lines have no text when you press Enter, the editor removes them and only assigns numbers to the new lines with text. Figure 25.11 shows three new blank lines with text entered at

```
COMMAND ===>                                        SCROLL ===> PAGE
****** *************************** TOP OF DATA ******************************
000100 The shadowy daughter of Urthona stood before red Orc
000200 When fourteen suns had faintly journey'd o'er his dark abode;
****** *************************** BOTTOM OF DATA ***************************
```

Figure 25.12 The effect of pressing Enter when viewing Figure 25.11.

only one of them, and Figure 25.12 shows how this looks after pressing Enter.

If you do want a blank line to remain in your data set, use your space bar to type at least one space there.

25.3.2 Moving your cursor around

Your up, down, left, and right cursor keys move the cursor in the direction in which they point.

The Tab key moves your cursor around more quickly. To move your cursor to the beginning of the previous line, use the Backtab key (with a PC that is emulating a mainframe terminal, press the Shift key and the Tab key simultaneously). If your cursor is on a line of text, Tab and Backtab jump your cursor to the line command area; if your cursor is on the line command area, pressing either key jumps your cursor to the beginning of the appropriate line.

Some mainframe terminals have a Return key that is separate from the Enter key. It might have an arrow pointing down and then left, or it might say "New Line" on it. When using the editor, pressing this key jumps your cursor to the beginning of the next line.

Use the commands UP, DOWN, LEFT, and RIGHT at the command line to scroll the text in one of those four directions. For example,

```
down 10
```

scrolls the text down ten lines, and

```
right 20
```

scrolls to the right 20 positions.

25.4 Inserting, Deleting, and Typing over Words and Characters

To delete an individual character, move your cursor there and press your Delete key. On a 3270 terminal, the delete key has a lowercase "a" with a proofreader's symbol for deletion: a line through it that forms a loop. When emulating a 3270 terminal, your emulation software probably has your PC's Delete key doing this job.

To type over existing text, just move your cursor where you want the new text and type.

To insert text, move your cursor to the place where you want to insert it and press the Insert key. On a 3270 terminal, this key has the letter "a" with a carat symbol (^) over it. When you press it, a carat symbol should appear at the bottom of your screen to indicate that you are in insert mode. (When emulating a 3270, your cursor may change shape.) Text that you type in moves any text currently on the right of the cursor further to the right.

If the last character gets moved too far to the right, the ISPF editor beeps at you to indicate that you can't insert more characters on that line. When you first allocate a data set, the LRECL operand (described in Section 24.1.7.2, "Allocating new data sets") sets its width and the maximum length of any lines.

To return to overstrike mode while using a 3270 terminal, press the key marked "Reset." The carat symbol disappears, and newly typed text then takes the place of the characters at the cursor. (When your keyboard "locks up," or refuses to accept input, the Reset key is also useful for freeing up the keyboard.) On most PCs emulating a 3270, the Insert key does the job of the 3270 keyboard's Insert key and the Escape key serves as the Reset key. Check you emulation program's documentation to make sure.

25.4.1 Duplicating lines

When duplicating lines, think of it as "repeating" lines. This makes it easier to remember the line command: r. Enter r by itself in the line command area and press Enter to make a single copy of a line. For example, if you enter r on the third line in the text shown in Figure 25.13, and then press Enter, you get the result shown in Figure 25.14.

```
COMMAND ===>                                          SCROLL ===> PAGE
****** *************************** TOP OF DATA ***************************
000100 The shadowy daughter of Urthona stood before red Orc
000200 When fourteen suns had faintly journey'd o'er his dark abode;
0r0300 His food she brought in iron baskets, his drink in cups of iron
000400 Crown'd with a helmet & dark hair the nameless female stood.
000500 A quiver with its burning stores, a bow like that of night
****** *************************** BOTTOM OF DATA ***************************
```

Figure 25.13 Entering the r line command to repeat a line.

```
COMMAND ===>                                          SCROLL ===> PAGE
****** *************************** TOP OF DATA ***************************
000100 The shadowy daughter of Urthona stood before red Orc
000200 When fourteen suns had faintly journey'd o'er his dark abode;
000300 His food she brought in iron baskets, his drink in cups of iron
000400 His food she brought in iron baskets, his drink in cups of iron
000500 Crown'd with a helmet & dark hair the nameless female stood.
000600 A quiver with its burning stores, a bow like that of night
****** *************************** BOTTOM OF DATA ***************************
```

Figure 25.14 The effect of pressing Enter after entering the r line command shown in Figure 25.13.

```
COMMAND ===>                                                SCROLL ===> PAGE
****** ************************** TOP OF DATA ******************************
000100 The shadowy daughter of Urthona stood before red Orc
r40200 When fourteen suns had faintly journey'd o'er his dark abode;
000300 His food she brought in iron baskets, his drink in cups of iron
000400 Crown'd with a helmet & dark hair the nameless female stood.
000500 A quiver with its burning stores, a bow like that of night
****** ************************** BOTTOM OF DATA ***************************
```

Figure 25.15   Entering the r line command with a 4 to repeat the line 4 times.

```
COMMAND ===>                                                SCROLL ===> PAGE
****** ************************** TOP OF DATA ******************************
000100 The shadowy daughter of Urthona stood before red Orc
000200 When fourteen suns had faintly journey'd o'er his dark abode;
000300 When fourteen suns had faintly journey'd o'er his dark abode;
000400 When fourteen suns had faintly journey'd o'er his dark abode;
000500 When fourteen suns had faintly journey'd o'er his dark abode;
000600 When fourteen suns had faintly journey'd o'er his dark abode;
000700 His food she brought in iron baskets, his drink in cups of iron
000800 Crown'd with a helmet & dark hair the nameless female stood.
000900 A quiver with its burning stores, a bow like that of night
****** ************************** BOTTOM OF DATA ***************************
```

Figure 25.16   The effect of pressing Enter after entering the r4 line command shown in Figure 25.15.

Notice how the editor renumbered the line (or if applicable, lines) after the new one.

Following the r command with a number tells the editor to add that many repetitions of the line with the command. Pressing Enter after entering the command shown on line 200 in Figure 25.15 repeats that line four times, as shown in Figure 25.16.

25.4.2 Deleting lines

Delete lines with the d line command. Entering d by itself in the line command area and then pressing Enter deletes the line where you entered the command; adding a number after the d command deletes a total of that many lines, beginning with the line where you entered the command.

You can also delete multiple lines by indicating the beginning and end of a block to delete. Enter dd at the first and last line of the block to delete and the editor will delete all of those lines, including the ones where you entered the dd commands, when you press Enter. For example, after entering dd at lines 200 and 700 in Figure 25.17, pressing Enter deletes those lines and the lines between them, as shown in Figure 25.18.

You will find this particularly handy when you want to delete a block that doesn't begin and end on the same screen, because the alternative (counting the number of lines so that you can put a number after a single d) is a lot of trouble.

```
000100 The shadowy daughter of Urthona stood before red Orc
dd0200 When fourteen suns had faintly journey'd o'er his dark abode;
000300 When fourteen suns had faintly journey'd o'er his dark abode;
000400 When fourteen suns had faintly journey'd o'er his dark abode;
000500 When fourteen suns had faintly journey'd o'er his dark abode;
000600 When fourteen suns had faintly journey'd o'er his dark abode;
0dd700 His food she brought in iron baskets, his drink in cups of iron
000800 Crown'd with a helmet & dark hair the nameless female stood.
000900 A quiver with its burning stores, a bow like that of night
****** ************************** BOTTOM OF DATA ****************************
```

Figure 25.17 Entering the dd line commands to delete 6 lines.

```
COMMAND ===>                                              SCROLL ===> PAGE
****** ************************** TOP OF DATA ****************************
000100 The shadowy daughter of Urthona stood before red Orc
000200 Crown'd with a helmet & dark hair the nameless female stood.
000300 A quiver with its burning stores, a bow like that of night
****** ************************** BOTTOM OF DATA ****************************
```

Figure 25.18 The effect of pressing Enter after entering the dd line commands shown in Figure 25.17.

```
COMMAND ===>                                              SCROLL ===> PAGE
****** ************************** TOP OF DATA ****************************
0b0100 The shadowy daughter of Urthona stood before red Orc
cc0200 When fourteen suns had faintly journey'd o'er his dark abode;
000300 His food she brought in iron baskets, his drink in cups of iron
0cc400 Crown'd with a helmet & dark hair the nameless female stood.
000500 A quiver with its burning stores, a bow like that of night
****** ************************** BOTTOM OF DATA ****************************
```

Figure 25.19 Entering the cc line commands to copy 3 lines above the first line.

25.4.3 Copying lines

Copying is similar to deletion except that you use the letter c to indicate the line or lines to copy and you must indicate a destination for the copied text. The ISPF editor gives you three options for indicating the text to copy:

- Enter a single c in a line's command area if you only need to copy that one line.

- Enter a single c followed by a number to indicate how many lines to copy.

- Enter cc at the first and last lines of the block to copy.

In addition to indicating the line or lines to copy, you must indicate where to copy them. Two line commands make this possible:

b   When Enter is pressed, copy the block to the line before this one.

a   When Enter is pressed, copy the block to the line after this one.

In Figure 25.19, Joe User is about to copy the second, third, and fourth lines above the first line, to the beginning of the data set.

```
COMMAND ===>                                                      SCROLL ===> PAGE
****** *************************** TOP OF DATA ******************************
000100 When fourteen suns had faintly journey'd o'er his dark abode;
000200 His food she brought in iron baskets, his drink in cups of iron
000300 Crown'd with a helmet & dark hair the nameless female stood.
000400 The shadowy daughter of Urthona stood before red Orc
000500 When fourteen suns had faintly journey'd o'er his dark abode;
000600 His food she brought in iron baskets, his drink in cups of iron
000700 Crown'd with a helmet & dark hair the nameless female stood.
000800 A quiver with its burning stores, a bow like that of night
****** *************************** BOTTOM OF DATA ****************************
```

Figure 25.20 The effect of pressing Enter after entering the cc line commands shown in Figure 25.19.

Figure 25.20 shows the effect of pressing Enter after he enters these commands.

25.4.4 Moving lines

Moving is similar to copying, except that after pressing Enter, the original lines are no longer there—they're at their new location. As with copying, there are three ways to specify the block to move, but these use the letter m:

- Enter a single m in a line's command area if you only need to move that one line.
- Enter a single m followed by a number to indicate how many lines to move.
- Enter mm at the first and last lines of the block to move.

To specify the destination of the block to move, use the letters b or a the same way you do to specify the destination of a block to copy.

25.5 Searching for Text

If you think of searching for text in the ISPF editor as "finding" it, you'll remember the command: the letter "F" entered at the command line. Figure 25.21 shows this command entered to find the word "his," and Figure 25.22 shows the result.

The cursor jumps to the first occurrence, and a message in the upper right of the screen shows the characters that it found.

```
EDIT ---- JOEUSER.BLAKE.TEXT ------------------------------ COLUMNS 001 072
COMMAND ===> f his                                               SCROLL ===> PAGE
****** ***************************** TOP OF DATA ******************************
000001 The shadowy daughter of Urthona stood before red Orc
000002 When fourteen suns had faintly journey'd o'er his dark abode;
000003 His food she brought in iron baskets, his drink in cups of iron;
000004 Crown'd with a helmet & dark hair the nameless female stood.
000005 A quiver with its burning stores, a bow like that of night
****** ***************************** BOTTOM OF DATA ****************************
```

Figure 25.21 Using the find command to look for the word "his."

```
EDIT ---- JOEUSER.BLAKE.TEXT ---------------------------- CHARS 'his' FOUND
COMMAND ===>                                              SCROLL ===> PAGE
****** **************************** TOP OF DATA ********************************
000001 The shadowy daughter of Urthona stood before red Orc
000002 When fourteen suns had faintly journey'd o'er his dark abode;
000003 His food she brought in iron baskets, his drink in cups of iron;
000004 Crown'd with a helmet & dark hair the nameless female stood.
000005 A quiver with its burning stores, a bow like that of night
****** ************************** BOTTOM OF DATA ******************************




F1=HELP       F2=SPLIT      F3=END        F4=RETURN     F5=RFIND      F6=RCHANGE
F7=UP         F8=DOWN       F9=SWAP       F10=LEFT      F11=RIGHT     F12=RETRIEVE
```

Figure 25.22 The effect of pressing Enter after entering the find command shown in Figure 25.21.

```
EDIT ---- JOEUSER.BLAKE.TEXT ---------------------------- CHARS 'His' FOUND
COMMAND ===>                                              SCROLL ===> PAGE
****** **************************** TOP OF DATA ********************************
000001 The shadowy daughter of Urthona stood before red Orc
000002 When fourteen suns had faintly journey'd o'er his dark abode;
000003 His food she brought in iron baskets, his drink in cups of iron;
000004 Crown'd with a helmet & dark hair the nameless female stood.
000005 A quiver with its burning stores, a bow like that of night
****** ************************** BOTTOM OF DATA ******************************
```

Figure 25.23 Finding "his" a second time by pressing the F5 key.

If your search target has a blank in it (for example if you want to search for the string "his drink") enclose the string in apostrophes, like this:

```
f 'his drink'
```

Note at the bottom of the screen in Figure 25.22 how the F5 key means RFIND, or "repeat find." Press it, and the cursor jumps to the next occurrence of the string "his." Figure 25.23 shows the effect of pressing F5 when viewing the screen shown in Figure 25.22.

What happens if the search target isn't found? Figure 25.24 shows what happens after pressing F5 a third time, when there are no more occurrences. As the message in the upper right of Figure 25.24 shows, it searched from the cursor location to the bottom of the data, and didn't find the string.

```
EDIT ---- JOEUSER.BLAKE.TEXT ----------------------- *BOTTOM OF DATA REACHED*
COMMAND ===>                                          SCROLL ===> PAGE
****** *************************** TOP OF DATA ******************************
000001 The shadowy daughter of Urthona stood before red Orc
000002 When fourteen suns had faintly journey'd o'er his dark abode;
000003 His food she brought in iron baskets, his drink in cups of iron;
000004 Crown'd with a helmet & dark hair the nameless female stood.
000005 A quiver with its burning stores, a bow like that of night
****** *************************** BOTTOM OF DATA ******************************
```

Figure 25.24 The result of an unsuccessful search for a string.

Searching is not case-sensitive; although we were searching for "his," it also found "His." To do an exact-case search, put the letter "C" just before your search target. (Whether the target has a blank in it or not, you need to enclose it in apostrophes to separate it from the "C.") The following shows an example:

```
f c'his'
```

The f command always searches from the cursor location, unless you tell it otherwise with the word "first." Typing the following

```
f first his
```

tells the system, "search for the word 'his' starting at the first line of the data set."

Combining these features is no problem; entering

```
f first c'his'
```

tells the editor to do an exact-case search for the string "his" starting at the beginning of the data set.

25.6 Saving Your Changes

To save your edits, enter SAVE at the command line and press Enter. You can then continue editing. To abort any edits made since the last time you saved your work, enter CANCEL at the command line. The editor returns you to the Edit Entry Panel where you first entered the name of the data set to edit.

The next section shows a shortcut for saving your work and quitting all at once.

25.7 Quitting the ISPF Editor

As the bottom of the screen shows, F3 is the END key. Pressing this saves your work and returns you to the Edit Entry Panel, where you

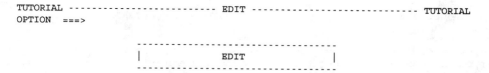

```
TUTORIAL ------------------------- EDIT ---------------------------- TUTORIAL
OPTION  ===>

                    -----------------------------------
                    |                 EDIT            |
                    -----------------------------------

     Edit allows you to create or change source data.

The following topics are presented in sequence, or may be selected by number:
   0 - General introduction              8 - Display modes (CAPS/HEX/NULLS)
   1 - Types of data sets                9 - Tabbing (hardware/software/logical)
   2 - Edit entry panel                 10 - Automatic recovery
   3 - SCLM edit entry panel            11 - Edit profiles
   4 - Member selection list           12 - Edit line commands
   5 - Display screen format           13 - Edit primary commands
   6 - Scrolling data                  14 - Labels and line ranges
   7 - Sequence numbering              15 - Ending an edit session

The following topics will be presented only if selected by number:
  16 - Interaction between LMF and SCLM
  17 - Edit models
  F1=HELP       F2=SPLIT     F3=END       F4=RETURN    F5=RFIND      F6=RCHANGE
  F7=UP         F8=DOWN      F9=SWAP      F10=LEFT     F11=RIGHT     F12=RETRIEVE
```

Figure 25.25 Main help menu for ISPF editor.

can enter the name of another data set to edit or quit back to the main ISPF menu.

If you are done editing your data set and know that you don't want to edit any other data sets, press F4, the RETURN key (not to be confused with the Return key on the right side of your keyboard). This saves your data set, quits out of the editor, and skips the Edit Entry Panel, returning you directly to the ISPF main menu. To exit this menu and return to the TSO prompt, select the EXIT menu choice.

25.7.1 On-line help in the editor

While using the editor, you can access on-line help in two ways:

- Typing HELP at the command line
- Pressing F1

Either way, the system displays the main help menu for the editor, as shown in Figure 25.25.

As with any other help screen, pressing F1 again gives you help about the available help—in other words, it tells you how to use the help system. Using it is pretty simple: at the OPTION ===> prompt, enter the number of the menu choice about which you want to learn more. Help about a complicated topic may lead to another menu that lets you choose a subtopic. When you are done, press F3 or F4 to return to the editing screen.

25.8 TSO's EDIT Text Editor

If you can't use the ISPF editor, you can still use the TSO EDIT text editor. Some PC users who used DOS before Release 5.0 endured a similar situation: when they needed a text editor but lacked a decent one, they had to use the dreaded EDLIN, which came with the operating system.

As a matter of fact, anyone with experience with EDLIN will find the TSO EDIT editor familiar. It has a command mode and an input mode, and everything you enter and everything that the system displays scrolls up the screen a line a time.

25.8.1 Starting the editor

In its simplest form, you can tell the editor that you want to edit a particular data set by entering EDIT followed by the data set name. However, as you will see in Section 25.8.16, "On-line help and the TSO editor," typing HELP EDIT at the TSO prompt reveals quite a few possible operands that you can add. Many of these tell the editor what kind of data set you are editing—for example, whether it's a text data set or source code for a FORTRAN or COBOL program—if the editor can't figure it out from the data set name.

For example, if you enter

```
edit blake.text
```

it knows that you are editing a data set consisting of simple text. If, on the other hand, you enter

```
edit jan3bc.memo
```

then TSO asks you to

```
ENTER DATA SET TYPE-
```

and you enter "text" in response to this. If the data set type is not obvious from the low-level qualifier, you can add it as an operand, like this

```
edit jan3bc.memo text
```

and the editor doesn't prompt you to enter the type of the data set.

25.8.2 Creating a new data set

The TSO editor does have one significant advantage over the ISPF editor: if you tell it to edit a nonexistent data set, it allocates and creates the data set for you instead of just telling you that it doesn't exist. For example, if you enter

```
edit test.text
```

the TSO editor responds with

```
DATA SET OR MEMBER NOT FOUND, ASSUMED TO BE NEW
```

Because the details of the allocation vary from installation to installation, try creating a data set this way and then using the LISTDS command to learn the allocation parameters used. (Section 24.1.7.4, "Finding out a data set's allocation status," explains more about the LISTDS command.)

After creating a new data set, the editor displays the line number for the data set's first line and puts you in input mode. The following section explains more about using input mode.

25.8.3 Line numbering and the EDIT editor

Data sets may be numbered or unnumbered, which affects how you use the EDIT editor. Like the programs that enable you to write programs in BASIC on older computers, you can use these numbers to indicate which lines should be affected by each command. Also, when editing a numbered data set, you can tell more easily when you are in input mode, because EDIT displays the number of the line being added.

25.8.4 Input mode and edit mode

The EDIT program is always waiting for you to type something in. While in input mode (see Section 25.8.7, "Adding new lines," for more on input mode) each line you type becomes a new line of the data set. In edit mode, the editor interprets each line you type as a command ("command mode" would have been a better name than "edit mode") and executes it, if possible, or gives you an error message if not. The two classic mistakes are the following:

- Entering a command when you're really in input mode, which adds a line to your data set consisting of the command you thought you were entering

- Entering what you think is a new line of text when it's really in edit mode, so that the editor tries to interpret the text as a command and tells you something along the lines of "'Dear Mom' is an unrecognized editor command"

When editing a numbered data set, this won't happen too easily, because the editor displays the number of the line you are entering when you are in input mode. In the following example, after Joe User entered each line and pressed Enter, the next line number appeared, waiting for a new line. For the third line, instead of entering anything, he pressed Enter immediately. This told the editor that he was done with input mode, so it went back to edit mode.

```
INPUT
00010 Lo, a shadow of horror is risen
00020 In Eternity! Unknown, unprolific?
00030
EDIT
Self-closd, all-repelling: what Demon
INVALID SUBCOMMAND
input
INPUT
00030 Self-closd, all-repelling: what Demon
00040
```

Joe then typed the third line, but the editor thought he was typing a command (a subcommand, actually, since EDIT is the command to start the editor, and commands within the editor are considered subcommands). It displayed an error message saying that it couldn't find a subcommand called "SELF-CLOSD." Joe then entered the command INPUT to return to input mode, the line number appeared, waiting for his text, and he entered it without a problem.

When editing an unnumbered data set, the lack of line numbers requires you to pay closer attention to which mode you're in. The following example shows the same steps as the previous one, only with an unnumbered data set.

```
INPUT
Lo, a shadow of horror is risen
In Eternity! Unknown, unprolific?
EDIT
Self-closd, all-repelling: what Demon
INVALID SUBCOMMAND
input
INPUT
Self-closd, all-repelling: what Demon
EDIT
INPUT
EDIT
```

Although no line number appeared after Joe typed the second line, pressing Enter without typing anything on the third line produced the same effect: it put him in edit mode. The same "Self-closd" mistake caused the same error message, and entering the INPUT command put him back into input mode.

After inputting the "Self-closd" line properly, Joe pressed the Enter key a few more times. Note how it shifted him between edit and input mode as long as he didn't enter anything at the command line. This shows that pressing Enter once or twice is a good way to switch between modes and to double-check which mode you're in.

When in input mode or edit mode, you can use all the same keys that you use to edit any TSO command line: cursor left and right, insert, and delete.

25.8.5 Displaying the data set's current contents

Enter LIST to see the contents of the data set that you are editing. (This command is easy to remember because it's the same as the TSO command to do the same thing.) If it has too many lines to fit on the screen, you can enter beginning and ending line numbers. For example, if you enter

```
list 20 30
```

while editing the numbered data set shown above, the editor responds with this:

```
00020 In Eternity! Unknown, unprolific?
00030 Self-closd, all-repelling: what Demon
```

If you try this with an unnumbered data set, the editor responds with an error message telling you that it can't list lines 20 and 30 because the data set is unnumbered. When editing an unnumbered data set, you must list either the whole data set or just the current line.

25.8.6 The current line

At any given time, the editor treats one line of your data set as the "current" line. It's important to be aware of which line is current because certain commands (like DELETE) have a default action of only acting on the current line.

With a command whose default action is to act on the whole data set, like LIST, you can add a line number to refer to a specific line or an asterisk to refer to the current line. For example, to list just the current line, enter this:

```
list *
```

You'll probably enter this command often, because it's the best way to check on which line is current.

The commands UP and DOWN let you change the current line. For example, if the fifth line is current, entering

```
up 2
```

makes the third line current. If you enter a number that's too big, like

```
up 1000
```

you won't get an error message; the editor just makes the first line current. DOWN works the same way: entering it with a number greater than the number of lines in your data set makes the last line current. (For a simpler way to jump to the top or bottom of your data set, enter the commands TOP or BOTTOM.)

Be careful when using the LIST command to view the whole data set. After viewing the data set, the last listed line becomes the current one regardless of which line was current before you entered the command. Try this by entering LIST alone, pressing Enter, and then entering LIST * to see which is the new current line.

25.8.7 Adding new lines

The examples in Section 25.8.4, "Input Mode and Edit Mode," show how to use the INPUT command to add new lines. Remember, once in input mode, you remain there until you enter a line with nothing on it by pressing Enter when the editor is waiting for you to type in a new line.

If you enter INPUT with no operands in edit mode, the editor puts you in edit mode and appends each new line that you enter to the end of your data set. Adding new lines between existing lines depends on whether you are editing a numbered or unnumbered data set.

When editing a numbered data set, you have a little more flexibility for entering new lines. The simplest way is to enter the new line number followed by the new line while in edit mode.

If you enter

```
25 (You gotta love this Blake guy)
```

and press the Enter key, the editor adds the line and returns you to edit mode. If you then enter the LIST command to see how the data set looks, you'll see this:

```
00010 Lo, a shadow of horror is risen
00020 In Eternity! Unknown, unprolific?
00025 (You gotta love this Blake guy)
00030 Self-closd, all-repelling: what Demon
```

If you want to enter more than one new line, use the INPUT command, but with two operands: the number of the line after which you want to begin and the increment to increase the line number. If you omit the second operand, the editor assumes a default of 10. This default value could cause a problem; for the data set above, if you enter

```
INPUT 20
```

then the new line after line 20 would be line 30. As it already has a line 30, it gives you an error message saying

```
INPUT TERMINATED, NEXT LINE NUMBER IS 30
```

If, on the other hand, you entered

```
INPUT 20 2
```

then you would be in input mode to enter line 22, then 24, and so forth until you entered line 28. After 28, you would get the same error message, because 30 comes after 28. For subsequent INPUT commands in that editing session, it will assume an increment of 2 until you reset it with a similar command.

After squeezing new lines between the existing ones, you might want to occasionally set all the line numbers back to multiples of 10 by entering the command RENUM in Edit mode.

To input new lines between existing lines in an unnumbered data set, use the asterisk denoting "current line" with the INPUT command. First, use the UP, DOWN, and LIST * commands to find the line just before the place where you want to insert new lines. For example, let's say Joe User is editing the following data set

```
The shadowy daughter of Urthona stood before red Orc
When fourteen suns had faintly journey'd o'er his dark abode;
His food she brought in iron baskets, his drink in cups of iron;
Crown'd with a helmet & dark hair the nameless female stood.
```

He makes the second line current and enters LIST * to make sure it's current. It displays by itself, so he knows that he's in the right place. He enters

```
INPUT *
```

and then, underneath it,

```
(Fourteen suns? What a wildman!)
```

and then presses Enter twice to show that he only wants to input that one line. When he enters LIST again to see the whole data set, he sees this:

```
The shadowy daughter of Urthona stood before red Orc
When fourteen suns had faintly journey'd o'er his dark abode;
(Fourteen suns? What a wildman!)
His food she brought in iron baskets, his drink in cups of iron;
Crown'd with a helmet & dark hair the nameless female stood.
```

25.8.8 Editing existing lines

To edit a string in the current line, use the CHANGE command. Its operands are the string to replace and the new one to put there, both enclosed in apostrophes. For example, if the current line is

```
His food she brought in iron baskets, his drink in cups of iron;
```

and you enter

```
change 'cups of iron' 'a plaid Thermos'
```

then entering `LIST *` shows that the line now reads:

```
His food she brought in iron baskets, his drink in a plaid Thermos;
```

To replace the entire current line, you can enter an asterisk followed by the new line while in edit mode, like this:

```
* Here is text for a new line
```

Both of these tricks for editing existing lines work for numbered and unnumbered data sets. You can take the last trick a step further for numbered data sets; if the line you want to replace is not the current line, but you know its number, enter its number followed by the new contents of the line. (Replacing the current line by entering an asterisk and the new text is actually a variation on this; remember, the asterisk acts as a substitute for the current line's line number.)

25.8.9 Deleting lines

Entering `DELETE` by itself deletes the current line. To delete a range of lines from a numbered data set, enter `DELETE` followed by the line numbers of the first and last lines to delete. For example, entering

```
DELETE 40 90
```

deletes lines 40, 90, and all the lines between them.

To delete multiple lines from an unnumbered data set, first make the first line to delete the current line. Then, enter the command to delete the current line, followed by the total number of lines you want to delete. For example, entering

```
DELETE * 5
```

deletes the current line and the four lines following it.

25.8.10 Copying lines

Whether you are copying lines in a numbered or unnumbered data set, the syntax for specifying the lines to copy is just like the syntax for indicating lines to delete. The `COPY` command takes one more parameter: a number telling you where to put the copy.

To copy lines in a numbered data set, you need three parameters after the `COPY` command: the first of the lines to copy, the last of the lines to copy, and the line number where the copy should start. For example, the command

```
COPY 20 50 95
```

means "make a copy of lines 20 through 50 and start it at line 95." If line 95 exists, it starts the copy right after it.

With an unnumbered data set, you must first make the first of the lines to copy your current line. As with deleting lines in an unnumbered data set, your first parameter is the asterisk and the second is the number of lines you want to copy. The third parameter is the position of the line just before where you want to put your copy. If you picture the data set being numbered in increments of one (as opposed to the increments of 10 more popular in numbered data sets), then this would be the line number of the target line. For example, in the following data set

```
The shadowy daughter of Urthona stood before red Orc
When fourteen suns had faintly journey'd o'er his dark abode;
His food she brought in iron baskets, his drink in cups of iron;
Crown'd with a helmet & dark hair the nameless female stood.
A quiver with its burning stores, a bow like that of night
When pestilence is shot from heaven—no other arms she need:
```

we want to copy the lines beginning "Crown'd with a helmet," "A quiver with" and "When pestilence" and put the copy after the line "When fourteen suns." First, make the line "Crown'd with a helmet" the first line; then, the command

```
COPY * 3 2
```

tells the editor "copy three lines, beginning with the current one (represented by the asterisk) and put the copy after the second line."

25.8.11 Duplicating lines

Duplicating the current line of your data set involves using the COPY command with the asterisk. Section 25.8.10, "Copying lines," shows that when you copy a line or lines, you indicate the lines to copy and the line after which to put the copy. Using the asterisk to indicate the current line as both of these parameters, you can type

```
COPY * *
```

to tell the editor, "Make a copy of the current line, and put the copy right after itself."

25.8.12 Moving lines

Move lines with the MOVE command. For numbered and unnumbered data sets, the syntax is the same as when copying. The only difference is, after you've executed the command, the original won't exist anymore—it will be in the location specified by the third parameter of either of the following commands:

```
MOVE firstline lastline destination
```

for numbered data sets or

```
MOVE * lines destination
```

for unnumbered data sets.

25.8.13 Searching for text

The `FIND` command does a case-sensitive search for the string entered as its operand. Enclose the string in apostrophes. For example, entering

```
find 'helmet'
```

when the first of the earlier passage's lines is current makes the fourth line the current line because it has the phrase "Crown'd with a helmet." Entering

```
find 'potrzebie'
```

causes the editor to look for, but not find this string, and it gives you the message `TEXT NOT FOUND`. Entering `find 'helmet'` twice in a row displays the `TEXT NOT FOUND` message the second time, because the search always begins at the current line and the passage has no more occurrences of the word "helmet" after it finds it the first time.

If you want to search for something with an apostrophe in it, you can enclose your search string in quotation marks. For example, when searching from the top of the passage, you could enter

```
find "o'er"
```

to find the line with the phrase "journey'd o'er his dark abode." That line then becomes the current line.

25.8.14 Saving your changes

To save your changes, simply enter `SAVE` while in edit mode. See the next section for information on quitting and saving in one command.

25.8.15 Quitting the TSO editor

The `END` command tells the editor that you want to return to the TSO prompt. If you have any unsaved changes, it tells you:

```
NOTHING SAVED
ENTER SAVE OR END-
```

At this point, enter `END` to quit without saving your changes or `SAVE` to save them. If you enter `SAVE`, it returns you to edit mode, waiting for another command. (You'll probably want to enter END again; this time, it won't give you the message about unsaved changes.)

To save your work and quit with one command, enter the following:

```
END SAVE
```

The editor saves your data set and return you to the TSO prompt. To quit without saving your changes, enter this:

```
END NOSAVE
```

25.8.16 On-line help and the TSO editor

Entering HELP EDIT at the TSO prompt gives you several screens of information about the EDIT program. Most of it is information about the command-line parameters that you can add when starting up the EDIT program, and not help about actions you can take within the EDIT program, but this is what the TSO help does: it tells you about the syntax of commands typed at the TSO prompt.

The first part of the information displayed by HELP EDIT is a section called SUBCOMMANDS that lists the commands that you can use in edit mode. Including the ones described in this section, the editor has over 30 of these subcommands. One of them is HELP, which shows that you can get help from within the editor.

If you enter HELP by itself in the editor's edit mode, it lists the subcommands and tells you this:

```
FOR MORE INFORMATION ENTER HELP SUBCOMMANDNAME OR HELP HELP
```

In other words, you can enter HELP followed by one of the subcommand names to find out more about that particular subcommand. This includes the HELP subcommand itself—entering HELP HELP tells you more about the use of the HELP command within the text editor.

26

Using an MVS System

26.1 Printing Data Sets

There are several ways to print data sets. Many involve printing the result of a batch job; in a case like this, you add certain commands to the JCL part of the job telling it to route output to a particular printer.

The simplest way to print a data set uses the PRINTDS or DSPRINT programs, whichever is available on your system. At their most basic level, both of these commands require the same information from you:

- The data set you want to print

- The name of the printer to which you want to send the data set

The main difference between the two is that DSPRINT assumes that the first operand is the data set to print and the second identifies the printer. With PRINTDS, you can enter them in any order, but you must include the words DATASET and DEST (for "destination"), putting the appropriate information in parentheses.

For example, to use PRINTDS to send the data set BLAKE.TEXT to the printer called ACCTNG, enter this:

```
printds dataset(blake.text) dest(acctng)
```

With the DSPRINT command, you enter this:

```
dsprint blake.text acctng
```

Ask about the name of the closest mainframe printer, which each site's system administrator assigns.

Other differences between PRINTDS and DSPRINT lie in the additional operands available to control their print output. One that you will find useful with both is NONUM. It tells the command, "If the data set is numbered, don't print the numbers." The TSO on-line help tells you more about other operands for these commands.

26.2 Command Files

A CLIST (pronounced "see-list") is a program written in the TSO command language. In other words, it's a data set consisting of a series of TSO commands. CLISTs can be complex, but simple ones consisting of the TSO commands that you already know can be useful.

CLISTs are usually stored as members of a partitioned data set called either CLIST or whatever.CLIST, where whatever is a name you supply.

There are two ways to execute a particular CLIST. The first uses the EXEC command. To execute a CLIST in MYCLISTS.CLIST with a member name of MYTEST, enter the following:

```
exec myclists(mytest)
```

If you stored MYTEST in a partitioned data set called only CLIST, execute it with this command:

```
exec (mytest)
```

You can execute a CLIST by just entering its name. To execute MYTEST, type

```
mytest
```

at the TSO prompt. How will the system know the partitioned data set in which to find it? It looks for a special ddname of SYSPROC. This means that you must allocate the partitioned data set that holds your CLISTs with a ddname of SYSPROC by entering a command like this:

```
allocate dataset(myclists.clist) ddname(sysproc)
```

If you want to let others use the MYCLISTS CLISTs while you use them, add the SHR parameter to this allocation command.

People often use CLISTs to allocate several data sets at once. Many application programs require you to do several allocations before starting them up; creating a new member of a CLIST partitioned data set with the required ALLOCATE commands means that you only have to type that member's name to do all those allocations.

For example, let's say the MVS version of the UpRiteBase database program requires you to allocate the partitioned data set holding your data files with the ddname URDATA and the PDS holding the command procedures to use with that data as URPROC. You store your data as members of the `MYDATA.DAT` PDS and your procedures in the `MYPROCS.PRC` PDS, and you start UpRiteBase by entering `URBASE`. You can automate the allocations and the `URBASE` part by creating a new member of the partitioned data set holding your CLISTs called `UR` with the following commands in it:

```
/* UR: allocate procedure and database files for UpRiteBase, */
/* then start up UpRiteBase. 2/23/94 Joe User */
FREE DD(URPROC URBASE)
ALLOCATE DS(MYDATA.PRC) DD(URPROC) SHR
ALLOCATE DS(MYPROCS.DAT) DD(URBASE) SHR
URBASE
```

Note three things about this CLIST:

- The first two lines begin with `/*` and end with `*/`. TSO ignores everything between the asterisks, so they are used to demarcate comments describing the purpose of the CLIST. Among other things, the comments shows that this member of the CLISTs PDS is called `UR`.

- The `FREE` command frees up the ddnames before the subsequent lines allocate the data sets, just in case these ddnames are already allocated.

- The CLIST finishes by starting up UpRiteBase for you with the `URBASE` command.

Using this CLIST, you only have to type "UR" and TSO performs all these tasks for you. In addition to TSO commands, CLISTs can contain REXX commands. In their attempt to make a command language that is portable from one operating system to another, IBM made the basic rules of REXX the same on MVS systems as on CMS systems. See Section 21.1 (VM/CMS "Command files") for more on REXX.

26.2.1 The automatic logon command file

When you log on to your MVS account, TSO looks for a sequential data set named `LOGON.CLIST`. If it finds it, it automatically executes it. You will find this useful for automating actions that you want performed every time you log on. For example, if you keep your other CLISTs in a partitioned data set called `MYCLISTS.CLIST`, you could put the line

```
ALLOCATE DATASET(MYCLISTS.CLIST) DDNAME(SYSPROC)
```

in your `LOGON.CLIST` data set so that you could then invoke any one of your CLISTs by typing its name at the TSO prompt. A `LOGON.CLIST` that ends with the command `ISPF` automatically starts up ISPF for you when you log on.

26.3 Communicating with Other Users

MVS offers no built-in mail facility. Many companies buy mail programs to run on their MVS system; check to see whether your site has one installed.

You can use the SEND command to send a one-line message to someone else's terminal. (Most operating systems have some equivalent command; it seems a little more important in MVS because of the lack of a built-in mail facility.) To send the message "Are we still on for lunch?" to Mary Jones' MJONES user ID, Joe User would enter

```
send 'Are we still on for lunch?' user(mjones)
```

If Mary is logged on, the message appears on her screen followed by the user ID of the person who sent it:

```
Are we still on for lunch? JOEUSER
```

If Mary is not logged on when Joe enters the SEND command asking her about lunch, he will see a message like this:

```
USER(S) MJONES NOT LOGGED ON OR TERMINAL DISCONNECTED, MESSAGE
CANCELLED
```

He could then type the command again, adding the SAVE operand at the end. This tells TSO to display the message the next time Mary logs on. But an even better alternative exists: he could have added the operand LOGON when he first typed the command:

```
send 'Are we still on for lunch?' user(mjones) logon
```

This tells the system, "If Mary is logged on now, display this on her screen right away; otherwise, display it the next time she logs on."

You may have noticed that the message is enclosed in apostrophes. If you want one displayed in your message, enter two where you want it to appear. For example, entering

```
send 'Looks like I''ll have to work through lunch' user(mjones)
```

displays the following on Mary's screen:

```
Looks like I'll have to work through lunch JOEUSER
```

Another way to send a message to appear on someone's screen is with the MSGDATASET option of the TRANSMIT command. For more on this, see Section 26.3.1, "Sending files."

26.3.1 Sending files

Data sets are sent from one ID to another with the TRANSMIT command and received with the RECEIVE command. You have two options when you send a data set with TRANSMIT:

- If you send a data set as a regular data set, RECEIVE stores it with the recipient's other data sets.
- If you send it as a message, RECEIVE displays it on the screen for them.

It's not unusual to send two data sets this way simultaneously. One might be a data file, and the other, a memo about the first.

The simplest form of TRANSMIT just includes the name given to the recipient's system, the user ID, and the data set to send. To send the BLAKE.TEXT data set to the MJONES ID on an MVS system called SATURN, the command is:

```
transmit saturn.mjones dataset(blake.text)
```

After you press the Enter key, TSO displays a message telling you whether it sent the data set successfully and if not, why.

To send a message stored in the data set YOMARY.TEXT along with BLAKE.TEXT so that the RECEIVE command displays the message on Mary's screen when she uses RECEIVE to pull in BLAKE.TEXT, enter this:

```
transmit saturn.mjones dataset(blake.text) msgdataset(yomary.text)
```

You can't store the message in just any data set; it must meet the following requirements:

- It must be either a sequential data set or a specific member of a partitioned data set.
- It must be allocated with a fixed, blocked record format: RECFM(F,B).
- It must have a logical record length of 80: LRECL(80).

If you try to send a data set that doesn't meet these requirements, you'll get an error message saying that the message data set "contains attributes that are not valid."

The data set sent with the DATASET operand doesn't have to be sequential, but part of this command's flexibility may become a limitation when you try to send a partitioned data set. The flexibility lies in the capability to send data sets to other, non-MVS systems: if your MVS system's company or university site has other systems connected to it through a network, you can send data sets to them using the same syntax. For example, if you want to send the `BLAKE.TEXT` data set to Mary's MJONES ID on a VAX system called NEPTUNE, enter this:

```
transmit neptune.mjones dataset(blake.text)
```

Although `TRANSMIT` can send partitioned data sets as well as sequential data sets, remember that the concept of a PDS is peculiar to MVS—sending one to a machine running another operating system doesn't mean that the other operating system can do anything with it.

You can, however, send a particular member of a PDS and instruct `TRANSMIT` to treat it as a sequential data set by adding the `SEQ` operand. For example, the following command sends the `TUTORIAL` member of the `REXX.CLIST` PDS:

```
transmit neptune.mjones dataset(rexx.clist(tutorial)) seq
```

What happens if you just enter `TRANSMIT` and a user ID, without specifying anything to send? The `TRANSMIT` command assumes you want to send a message, not an existing data set. After prompting you to enter your message's recipient it displays an editor to allow you to enter that message, as shown in Figure 26.1.

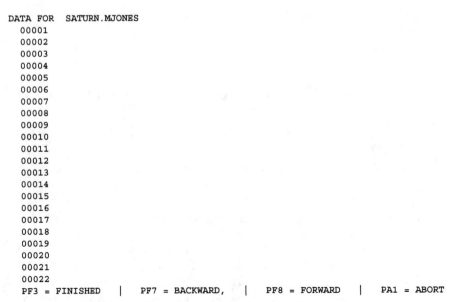

```
DATA FOR   SATURN.MJONES
  00001
  00002
  00003
  00004
  00005
  00006
  00007
  00008
  00009
  00010
  00011
  00012
  00013
  00014
  00015
  00016
  00017
  00018
  00019
  00020
  00021
  00022
  PF3 = FINISHED   |   PF7 = BACKWARD,   |   PF8 = FORWARD   |   PA1 = ABORT
```

Figure 26.1 Data entry screen for a message sent with TRANSMIT.

The editor is a simplified version of the ISPF editor. As the bottom line shows, PF7 and PF8 scroll backward and forward a page at a time if you enter more than 22 lines of text, PF3 tells the editor that you are finished, and PA1 indicates that you want to abort this message.

26.3.2 Receiving mail and data sets

The `TRANSMIT` command doesn't automatically add data sets to the recipient's disk space. They wait in a special area until they are pulled in with the `RECEIVE` command. If you enter `RECEIVE` when no data sets or messages are waiting for you to pull them in, TSO displays a message similar to this:

```
You have no messages or data sets to receive.
```

If there are one or more data sets waiting for you, it displays either the first message sent, a prompt asking you about a data set that was sent to you, or both if the message was sent with the data set. The prompt tells you the name of the data set, who sent it, and what system they sent it from. For example, let's say Mary Jones sent the data set `STATS.TEXT` to the JOEUSER ID from her ID on an MVS system identified as SATURN. When Joe enters the `RECEIVE` command, the system responds with a message like this:

```
Dataset MJONES.STATS.TEXT from MJONES on SATURN
Enter restore parameters or 'DELETE' or 'END' +
```

Although the prompt only offers two choices to respond with, you actually have several. Pressing Enter without entering anything is the equivalent of typing the word `RESTORE` as a response. It means "put this data set, as is, with the rest of my data sets." If Mary named it `MJONES.STATS.TEXT` before she sent it and your ID is JOEUSER, `RECEIVE` stores it as `JOEUSER.STATS.TEXT`.

Responding with `DELETE` means "I don't want that data set; delete it." Responding with `END` tells the `RECEIVE` program to leave off where it was and return to the TSO prompt. The next time you start up `RECEIVE`, it gives you the same prompt about the data set where you left off.

To restore the data set with a name that differs from the one shown in the message, enter the word "DATASET" followed by parentheses surrounding the new name. For example, if the `RECEIVE` program displayed the message above and you want to save the `STATS.TEXT` data set as `STATSFEB.TEXT`, respond by entering this:

```
dataset(statsfeb.text)
```

Of course, since you probably don't know the names of all your current data sets, you may not notice that an incoming data set has the same name as one already in your collection. If you press Enter to tell RECEIVE to recover the data set and you already have one with that name, RECEIVE displays a message like this:

```
Dataset 'JOEUSER.STATS.TEXT' already exists. Reply 'R' to replace it. +
```

As the message tells you, entering an "R" and pressing Enter replaces the existing STATS.TEXT data set with the one being recovered. You can also respond with an alternate name, the same way you can respond to the "Enter restore parameters" prompt with dataset(new.dsname). When you press Enter, RECEIVE saves the incoming data set with the new name. You can also respond to the "already exists" prompt by typing "END," which returns you to the TSO prompt. In fact, this is the default action, so pressing Enter without typing anything also returns you to the TSO prompt, leaving any unrecovered data sets for you to deal with later.

Most other potential responses to the "Enter restore parameters" prompt let you specify allocation details of the data set to recover, if you want to change them. To see them before recovering the data set, enter a question mark (?) in response to the prompt.

If you never respond with END, the RECEIVE program goes through the waiting messages and data sets one a time, giving the same information and asking the same question with each. When none are left, it tells you

```
No more files remain for the receive command to process.
```

Many users want to check whether data sets are waiting for them every time they log on. Your ID may be set up to invoke the RECEIVE command each time you log on; if not, you can easily add it to (or create) a LOGON.CLIST data set. (Section 26.2.1, "The automatic logon command file," covers LOGON.CLIST in more detail.)

26.4 ISPF

Chapter 25, "The MVS ISPF Text Editor," showed how to start ISPF, pick the appropriate choice from the main (or "primary") menu to edit a data set, and fill out the entry panel to indicate the data set you want to edit. Most of the important things that you do with ISPF begin with similar steps: selecting a menu choice and then filling out a panel to indicate the data set that you want to act on.

As you go from menu to menu in ISPF, you may display a menu that you didn't mean to. As the bottom of the screen shows you, the PF3 key ("END") ends the display of the current menu—in other

```
----------------------- ISPF/PDF PRIMARY OPTION MENU -----------------------
OPTION  ===>  _
                                               USERID   -JOEUSER
    0  ISPF PARMS  - Specify terminal and user parameters   TIME    - 09:24
    1  BROWSE      - Display source data or output listings  TERMINAL - 3278
    2  EDIT        - Create or change source data            PF KEYS  - 24
    3  UTILITIES   - Perform utility functions
    4  FOREGROUND  - Invoke language processors in foreground
    5  BATCH       - Submit job for language processing
    6  COMMAND     - Enter TSO Command, CLIST, or REXX exec
    7  DIALOG TEST - Perform dialog testing
    8  LM UTILITIES- Perform library administrator utility functions
    9  IBM PRODUCTS- Additional IBM program development products
   10  SCLM        - Software Configuration and Library Manager
    D  DB2         - DB2 Facilities
    H  HSM         - DFHSM Facilities
    C  CHANGES     - Display summary of changes for this release
    S  SDSF        - System Display and Search Facility
   SO  DFSORT      - DFSORT Facility
    T  TUTORIAL    - Display information about ISPF/PDF
    X  EXIT        - Terminate ISPF using log and list defaults
F1=HELP      F2=SPLIT     F3=END      F4=RETURN    F5=RFIND     F6=RCHANGE
F7=UP        F8=DOWN      F9=SWAP     F10=LEFT     F11=RIGHT    F12=RETRIEVE
```

Figure 26.2 ISPF primary option menu.

words, it backs out of that menu to the previous one. To leave the main menu, note how the last menu choice has an "X" instead of a number preceding it, as shown in Figure 26.2. This means that entering X at the OPTION ===> prompt returns you to the TSO prompt.

If you do anything more than browse around the menus in ISPF, like running programs or copying, renaming, editing or deleting data sets, then ISPF may keep a log of your activity. This log lists the date, time, and nature of each transaction. When you exit from the main menu, you may see a screen asking what you want to do with that log; Figure 26.3 shows an example.

The four "VALID PROCESS OPTIONS" are fairly self-explanatory; you'll probably want to choose D most of the time to delete the log so that it doesn't take up space. You might want to try entering K at the Process Option prompt some time to see what the log looks like. When ISPF returns you to the TSO prompt, it displays a message similar to this:

```
JOEUSER.SPFLOG1.LIST HAS BEEN KEPT.
READY
```

Now you know the name of the data set where the system stored this log. You can then use the LIST command to look at it.

If you choose K, ISPF continues to use this data set to log transactions the next time you use ISPF. If you choose KN, ISPF saves your transactions but create a new log data set the next time you use ISPF.

```
------------------- SPECIFY DISPOSITION OF LOG DATA SET -------------------
COMMAND ===>

LOG DATA SET DISPOSITION                    LIST DATA SET OPTIONS NOT AVAILABLE
-------------------------                   ----------------------------------
Process option   ===>
SYSOUT class     ===> A
Local printer ID ===>

VALID PROCESS OPTIONS:
    PD - Print data set and delete
    D  - Delete data set without printing
    K  - Keep data set (allocate same data set in next session)
    KN - Keep data set and allocate new data set in next session

  Press ENTER key to complete ISPF termination.
  Enter END command to return to the primary option menu.

JOB STATEMENT INFORMATION:   (Required for system printer)
   ===> //JOEUSERA  JOB   (ACCOUNT),'NAME'
   ===> //*
   ===> //*
```
Figure 26.3 Entry panel for dealing with ISPF log.

```
----------------------- UTILITY SELECTION MENU ----------------------------
OPTION  ===>

    1   LIBRARY    - Compress or print data set.  Print index listing.
                       Print, rename, delete, or browse members
    2   DATASET    - Allocate, rename, delete, catalog, uncatalog, or
                       display information of an entire data set
    3   MOVE/COPY  - Move, copy, or promote members or data sets
    4   DSLIST     - Print or display (to process) list of data set names
                       Print or display VTOC information
    5   RESET      - Reset statistics for members of ISPF library
    6   HARDCOPY   - Initiate hardcopy output
    8   OUTLIST    - Display, delete, or print held job output
    9   COMMANDS   - Create/change an application command table
   10   CONVERT    - Convert old format menus/messages to new format
   11   FORMAT     - Format definition for formatted data Edit/Browse
   12   SUPERC     - Compare data sets (Standard dialog)
   13   SUPERCE    - Compare data sets (Extended dialog)
   14   SEARCH-FOR - Search data sets for strings of data
```
Figure 26.4 ISPF Utility menu.

26.4.1 Allocating data sets

Selecting UTILITIES from the main ISPF menu displays a new menu that looks similar to the one shown in Figure 26.4. As the description of the DATASET choice tells you, choosing it allows you to allocate data sets. Selecting DATASET displays a menu similar to the one shown in Figure 26.5.

Enter the letter "A" at the OPTION ===> prompt and the name of the data set to allocate in the ISPF LIBRARY section of the panel.

```
--------------------------- DATA SET UTILITY -------------------------------
OPTION  ===>

   A - Allocate new data set              C - Catalog data set
   R - Rename entire data set             U - Uncatalog data set
   D - Delete entire data set             S - Data set information (short)
   blank - Data set information

ISPF LIBRARY:
   PROJECT ===> JOEUSER
   GROUP   ===> FIELDING
   TYPE    ===> TEXT

OTHER PARTITIONED OR SEQUENTIAL DATA SET:
   DATA SET NAME   ===>
   VOLUME SERIAL   ===>            (If not cataloged, required for option "C")

DATA SET PASSWORD ===>            (If password protected)
```

Figure 26.5 ISPF data set utility menu.

```
------------------------- ALLOCATE NEW DATA SET -----------------------------
COMMAND ===>

DATA SET NAME: JOEUSER.FIELDING.TEXT

   VOLUME SERIAL       ===> USERMD     (Blank for authorized default volume) *
   GENERIC UNIT        ===>            (Generic group name or unit address) *
   SPACE UNITS         ===> TRACK      (BLKS, TRKS, or CYLS)
   PRIMARY QUANTITY    ===> 2          (In above units)
   SECONDARY QUANTITY  ===> 2          (In above units)
   DIRECTORY BLOCKS    ===> 0          (Zero for sequential data set)
   RECORD FORMAT       ===> FB
   RECORD LENGTH       ===> 80
   BLOCK SIZE          ===> 27920
   EXPIRATION DATE     ===>            (YY/MM/DD, YYYY/MM/DD
                                       YY.DDD, YYYY.DDD in Julian form
                                       DDDD for retention period in days
                                       or blank)

 ( * Only one of these fields may be specified)
```

Figure 26.6 Data set allocation screen.

When you press Enter, ISPF displays ALLOCATE NEW DATA SET screen, where you enter the details of how you want your data set allocated. As you can see in Figure 26.6, this screen includes the data set name you entered on the DATA SET UTILITY screen. The crucial fields on the ALLOCATE NEW DATA SET screen are covered in Section 24.1.7, "Allocating data sets."

It's still a lot of trouble, dealing with all those allocation parameters; luckily, ISPF offers you a way to model a new data set's allocation parameters on those of an existing data set. On the DATA SET UTILITY screen, if you enter an existing data set's name and press the Enter key without entering anything at the OPTION ===> prompt (note how the OPTION choices include "blank - Data set in-

```
------------------------- DATA SET INFORMATION  ----------------------------
COMMAND ===>

DATA SET NAME: JOEUSER.BLAKE.TEXT

GENERAL DATA:                           CURRENT ALLOCATION:
    Volume serial:        USERMC            Allocated Tracks:          1
    Device type:          3390              Allocated extents:         1
    Organization:         PS
    Record format:        VB
    Record length:        84
    Block size:           6233          CURRENT UTILIZATION:
    1st extent Tracks:    1                 Used Tracks:               1
    Secondary Tracks:     5                 Used extents:              1

    Creation date:        1994/06/04
    Expiration date:      ***NONE***
```

Figure 26.7 Data set allocation information.

formation") ISPF displays allocation information about the data set whose name you entered. Figure 26.7 shows an example of the displayed information.

When you leave this screen and go through the steps of allocating a new data set, the next time you reach the ALLOCATE NEW DATA SET screen, ISPF fills out the allocation parameters of the new data set with those of the existing data set about which you just inquired. Since you entered the name of the new data set that you want to allocate in order to reach the ALLOCATE NEW DATA SET screen, all that remains when viewing that screen is to press Enter to allocate the new data set with the parameters of the existing data set.

26.4.2 Copying data sets

Copying a data set in TSO or a file in another operating system usually means "make me a new file that is a copy of this data set, and give the copy the following name." When you do this in ISPF, there's a catch: the data set specified as the destination of the copy operation must already exist. In other words, you must allocate it before you begin the copy operation. The best way to do this is to allocate the copy with the same allocation parameters as the data set being copied, as explained in Section 24.4.1, "Allocating data sets."

Once it's allocated, you can perform the copy operation. We saw in the last section that after selecting UTILITIES from the main ISPF menu, selecting DATASET from the UTILITIES menu makes it possible to allocate data sets. Another choice on the UTILITIES menu is MOVE/COPY. Selecting it displays the panel shown in Figure 26.8 for you to fill out.

To copy a data set, enter "C" at the OPTION ===> prompt and the name of the data set to copy in the FROM ISPF LIBRARY section of the panel. When you press Enter, ISPF displays a screen

```
-------------------------- MOVE/COPY UTILITY --------------------------------
OPTION  ===>

     C - Copy data set or member(s)          CP - Copy and print
     M - Move data set or member(s)          MP - Move and print
     L - Copy and LMF lock member(s)         LP - Copy, LMF lock, and print
     P - LMF Promote data set or member(s)   PP - LMF Promote and print

SPECIFY "FROM" DATA SET BELOW, THEN PRESS ENTER KEY

FROM ISPF LIBRARY:           ------ Options C, CP, L, and LP only -------
     PROJECT ===> JOEUSER   |                                         |
     GROUP   ===> BLAKE    ===>         ===>          ===>
     TYPE    ===> TEXT
     MEMBER  ===>            (Blank or pattern for member selection list,
                              '*' for all members)


FROM OTHER PARTITIONED OR SEQUENTIAL DATA SET:
     DATA SET NAME   ===>
     VOLUME SERIAL   ===>          (If not cataloged)

DATA SET PASSWORD ===>          (If password protected)
```

Figure 26.8 ISPF screen for moving or copying data sets.

```
COPY --- FROM JOEUSER.BLAKE.TEXT ------------------------------------------------
COMMAND ===>

SPECIFY "TO" DATA SET BELOW.

TO ISPF LIBRARY:
     PROJECT ===> JOEUSER
     GROUP   ===>
     TYPE    ===>
     MEMBER  ===>

TO OTHER PARTITIONED OR SEQUENTIAL DATA SET:
     DATA SET NAME   ===>
     VOLUME SERIAL   ===>          (If not cataloged)

DATA SET PASSWORD ===>          (If password protected)

"TO" DATA SET OPTIONS:
     IF PARTITIONED, REPLACE LIKE-NAMED MEMBERS ===>       (YES or NO)
     IF SEQUENTIAL, "TO" DATA SET DISPOSITION   ===>       (OLD or MOD)
     SPECIFY PACK OPTION FOR "TO" DATA SET      ===>       (YES, NO or blank)
```

Figure 26.9 ISPF screen prompting for destination of copy operation.

similar to the one shown in Figure 26.9 to find out the name of your copy.

In the TO ISPF LIBRARY section, enter the name of the data set to which you want to copy your "FROM" data set. Press Enter, and ISPF makes the copy and returns you to the MOVE/COPY UTILITY screen, with the message "DATA SET COPIED" displayed in the upper right.

```
-------------------------------  LIBRARY UTILITY  ---------------------------
OPTION  ===>

    blank - Display member list        B - Browse member
    C - Compress data set              P - Print member
    X - Print index listing            R - Rename member
    L - Print entire data set          D - Delete member
    I - Data set information            S - Data set information (short)

ISPF LIBRARY:
    PROJECT ===> JOEUSER
    GROUP   ===> URBASE      ===>            ===>            ===>
    TYPE    ===> CLIST
    MEMBER  ===> URTEST          (If "P", "R", "D", "B", or blank selected)
    NEWNAME ===> UR              (If "R" selected)

OTHER PARTITIONED OR SEQUENTIAL DATA SET:
    DATA SET NAME   ===>
    VOLUME SERIAL   ===>         (If not cataloged)

DATA SET PASSWORD ===>           (If password protected)
```

Figure 26.10   The ISPF library utility screen.

26.4.3 Renaming data sets

We've already seen (Figure 26.4) the menu that appears when you select UTILITIES from the main ISPF menu. On this menu, the LIBRARY choice offers you utilities for dealing with members of partitioned data sets, and the DATASET choice offers you utilities for dealing with sequential data sets. So, to rename (or delete) a member of a PDS, select LIBRARY; to rename or delete a sequential data set, select DATASET.

When you select LIBRARY, ISPF displays a panel similar to the one shown in Figure 26.10. At the OPTION ===> prompt, enter an "R" and use your Tab key to move to the ISPF LIBRARY part of the panel so that you can specify the data set member to rename. In the PROJECT, GROUP, and TYPE fields, enter the name of the partitioned data set containing the member you want to rename. In the MEMBER field, enter the member's name, and in the NEWNAME field, enter its new name. (When renaming a member of a PDS you can't change any part of the PDS name; whatever the member's name becomes, it's still part of the same PDS.) When you press Enter, ISPF renames the data set and displays a message in the upper right of the screen telling you that it did so.

If Joe User pressed the Enter key after filling out the panel as shown in Figure 26.10, he would rename the URTEST member of the URBASE.CLIST partitioned data set with a new name of UR. After he pressed Enter, ISPF would display the message MEMBER URTEST RENAMED in the upper right of the screen.

To rename a sequential data set or an entire partitioned data set (as opposed to just renaming one of the members of a PDS), you'll use

```
----------------------------- RENAME DATA SET  --------------------------------
COMMAND ===>

DATA SET NAME: JOEUSER.BLAKE.TEXT
VOLUME:        USERME

ENTER NEW NAME BELOW:      (The data set will be recataloged.)

ISPF LIBRARY:
   PROJECT ===> JOEUSER
   GROUP   ===> BLAKE
   TYPE    ===> BACKUP

OTHER PARTITIONED OR SEQUENTIAL DATA SET:
   DATA SET NAME  ===>
```
Figure 26.11 ISPF screen prompting you for the new name of your renamed data set.

the same panel you used to allocate a data set: the DATA SET UTILI-
TY screen (Figure 24.5). Display it by selecting DATASET from the
UTILITIES menu.

Enter "R" at the OPTION ===> prompt and the name of the data
set to rename in the ISPF LIBRARY section of the panel. Press
Enter, and ISPF displays a panel similar to the one shown in Figure
26.11 to learn the new name you want to give this data set.

The DATA SET NAME field at the top of this panel shows the
name of the data set that you said you wanted to rename. Now you
only need to fill out the new name in the GROUP and TYPE fields. After
you do this and press Enter, ISPF displays the message "DATA SET
RENAMED" in the upper right of the screen.

26.4.4 Deleting data sets

You may have noticed that the LIBRARY UTILITY and DATA SET
UTILITY screens used to rename data set members or entire data
sets offered "D" as an alternative command to enter at the
OPTION ===> prompt. When you enter this and enter a data set
member name on the LIBRARY UTILITY screen, you delete that
member from the specified partitioned data set, leaving the PDS otherwise intact.

When you enter a "D" at the OPTION ===> prompt of the
DATASET screen and a data set name in the ISPF LIBRARY section,
you delete the whole data set, whether sequential or partitioned.
When you press Enter, ISPF displays a screen similar to the one
shown in Figure 26.12 to make sure that you really want to delete the
specified data set.

Press Enter to follow through and delete the data set or enter
"END" at the COMMAND ===> prompt to cancel the deletion. Either
way, you return to the DATA SET UTILITY screen, which will have a
message in the upper right telling you either "DATA SET DELETED"
or "DATA SET NOT DELETED."

```
----------------------------- CONFIRM DELETE  -----------------------------------
COMMAND ===>

DATA SET NAME: JOEUSER.BLAKE.TEXT
VOLUME:        USERME
CREATION DATE: 1994/06/20


INSTRUCTIONS:

    Press ENTER key to confirm delete request.
        (The data set will be deleted and uncataloged.)

    Enter END command to cancel delete request.
```

Figure 26.12   ISPF screen confirming a request to delete a data set.

26.4.5 Displaying a data set's contents

Because ISPF takes better advantage of your terminal than TSO, it has no direct equivalent to the LIST command to put a data set's contents on your screen one screenful at a time from beginning to end. Instead, ISPF has a utility called BROWSE that gives you more flexibility when viewing a data set. Basically, it's just like the ISPF editor, but it won't let you change a data set's contents.

All of the editor's commands for moving around and searching for text work the same when you browse a data set. This means that when looking at the middle or end of a data set, you can go backward and look at the text before the currently displayed text, which you can't do when you use LIST at the TSO command line.

To browse a data set, select BROWSE from the ISPF main menu. On the next screen, enter the name of a sequential data set or a member of a partitioned data set and press Enter. ISPF starts the BROWSE program with the beginning of your data set displayed on the screen.

26.4.6 Printing a data set

Print a data set or a member of a partitioned data set with the same LIBRARY UTILITY panel (accessible by selecting LIBRARY from the UTILITIES menu) that you used to rename a member of a PDS (Figure 26.10). Instead of entering "R" for "rename," you enter either "L" to print a sequential data set or "P" to print a member of a PDS. Type the sequential data set or PDS member's name in the ISPF LIBRARY section of the panel, press Enter, and you're done.

26.5 A Sample MVS Session

One morning you log on to your JOEUSER ID, and you see the screen shown in Figure 26.13.

```
ICH70001I JOEUSER   LAST ACCESS AT 14:40:39 ON MONDAY, JANUARY 18, 1994
JOEUSER LOGON IN PROGRESS AT 14:42:38 ON JANUARY 18, 1994
***********************************************************************
*     The system will be unavailable from 12:01 AM to 10 AM          *
*     Sunday January 24th for maintenance.                           *
***********************************************************************
 Are those CLISTs ready or what? Give me whatever you have. LNIVEN
You have no messages or data sets to receive.
**** NATIVE TSO READY ****
READY
```

Figure 26.13 Joe User's logon messages one morning.

The message from the system administrator doesn't concern you, because you had no plans to log on Sunday morning. The other message, from your friend Larry Niven, is more urgent; you had promised to write him several CLISTs to use with the inventory database system he is developing.

You may as well send him what you've done so far, but you want to see what you have first. They're in a partitioned data set called INVEN.CLIST. You you list out the members of this data set by entering the LISTDS command with the MEM operand and see the output shown in Figure 26.14.

The TESTING one was for playing with some of the CLIST commands. You delete it from the PDS, because you don't need to send that one to Larry:

```
delete inven.clist(testing)
```

The other CLISTs were pretty good, but the UPDATE one is still giving you some problems. No use putting off Larry further; you'll send him the whole PDS of CLISTs, but warn him about the UPDATE CLIST in a separate message.

You type the message into a data set called FORLARRY.TEXT. The TRANSMIT command can be picky about how these message data sets are allocated, so you allocate it by copying the allocation details from the data set FORMARY.TEXT, which you sent to Mary Jones last week:

```
listds inven.clist mem
 JOEUSER.INVEN.CLIST
 --RECFM-LRECL-BLKSIZE-DSORG
   FB    80    3120     PO
 --VOLUMES--
   USERMD
 --MEMBERS--
   ADD
   DELETE
   UPDATE
   REPORT
   TESTING
```

Figure 26.14 List of members in INVEN.CLIST.

```
EDIT ---- JOEUSER.FORLARRY.TEXT ---------------------------- COLUMNS 001 072
COMMAND ===>                                              SCROLL ===> PAGE
****** *************************** TOP OF DATA *****************************
000100 Larry -
000200 I'm sending you INVEN.CLIST, which has the CLISTs.  Most of them
000300 work fine, but the UPDATE one is still a little flaky.  Let me
000400 know if you have any questions.
****** ************************* BOTTOM OF DATA ***************************
```

Figure 26.15 Joe's message to be sent to Larry.

```
allocate dataset(forlarry.text) like(formary.text)
```

You enter text into FORLARRY.TEXT with the ISPF editor. Because
the editor is the second choice on the ISPF main menu, you jump
right to the editor by including a "2" on the command line when you
start up ISPF:

```
ispf 2
```

After indicating the data set you want to edit on the EDIT ENTRY
PANEL, you type in your message. Figure 26.15 shows how it might
look when you are done.

After writing the message, you press PF4 to show that you've finished editing. (If you had wanted to edit another data set, you would
have pressed PF3, which would return you to the screen where you
enter the name of the data set to edit. This time, however, you no
longer need the editing program.)

When you return to the TSO prompt, you are ready to send the
CLISTs and their accompanying message to Larry on the SATURN
system. You can do this with one command. It's a long one, though;
after you enter the first part, you type a plus sign to show TSO that
you haven't finished entering the command.

```
transmit saturn.lniven dataset(inven.clist) +
```

Then, you press Enter, finish typing the command,

```
msgdataset(forlarry.text)
```

and press Enter again. TSO displays a message showing you that it
successfully transmitted the CLIST partitioned data set and the accompanying message.

You'd better straighten out the UPDATE CLIST as soon as possible.
It would be a good idea to print out a hard copy so that you can sit
down with a cup of coffee and write some notes on it. Since the accounting department's mainframe printer is near the coffee machine,
you'll send the printout there so that you can pick it up and get your
coffee in one trip. You enter the command to print it:

```
printds dataset(inven.clist(update)) dest(acctng)
```

You're not even going to try to fix the UPDATE CLIST until you've had a good hard look at the printout. You log off by typing

```
LOGOFF
```

and head for the printer and coffee machine.

Index

| (pipe symbol), 48, 73
*CMD object type, 151
*FILE object type, 151, 152
*LIB object type, 150
*LIBL predefined value, 163
*PGM object type, 151, 208
*PRINT predefined value, 199
.login script, 72
.profile script, 72
3033 mainframes, 295
3090 mainframes, 295
3270 terminal:
    emulation and SEU text editor, 191
    ISPF editor, 341
    OS/400 and, 148
    VM/CMS and, 270
360 series of IBM mainframes, 8, 299
370 series of IBM mainframes, 8, 295

Aborting edits:
    EVE editor, 118
    ISPF editor, 347
    SEU editor, 196
    vi editor, 65
    XEDIT editor, 275
Aborting screen output:
    MVS, 306
    OpenVMS, 87
    VM/CMS, 232
ACCESS command (VM/CMS), 238
Access methods (MVS), 301
Adding lines:
    EVE editor, 116
    ISPF editor, 339
    SEU editor, 188
    TSO EDIT editor, 353
    vi editor, 63

AIX operating system, 9, 27, 137
ALL-IN-1, 82
ALLOCATE command (MVS), 297, 307, 308
    BLKSIZE operand, 327
    BLOCK operand, 327
    CATALOG operand, 328
    DA operand, 325
    DATASET operand, 325
    DDNAME operand, 325
    DELETE operand, 328
    DIR operand, 326
    DSNAME operand, 325
    FI operand, 325
    FILE operand, 325
    KEEP operand, 328
    LIKE operand, 326
    LRECL operand, 329
    MOD operand, 325
    OLD operand, 325
    RECFM operand, 328
    SHR operand, 325
    SPACE operand, 327
Allocating data sets, 324
    CLIST data set, 360
    with ISPF, 368
Alpha processor, 81
Amiga, 14, 22, 27
AmigaDOS, 3, 28, 34
ANSI, 12
AS/400, 7, 82, 133
    as database server, 136
    IBM publications, 159
    system problems, 160
ASCII characters, 12
ASSIST menu (OS/400), 209
Asterisk and:
    COPY command (VM/CMS), 256
    MVS, 304, 311

Asterisk and (*cont.*):
OpenVMS, 89
OS/400, 145, 149
TSO EDIT editor, 352
UNIX, 33
VM/CMS, 236
AT&T, 26, 27
Atari-ST, 22
Attribute, 151
Audience path, 162
Automatic login/logon command procedure:
MVS, 361
OpenVMS, 124
OS/400, 208
UNIX, 71
VM/CMS, 282
Automatic startup macro (XEDIT editor), 276
AUX operating system, 27

Back end, 6
Background job, 296
Backspace key (OpenVMS), 86
Backtab key (SEU), 191
Bang (as buzzword), 65
Batch jobs, 296
BEGIN command (VM/CMS), 230
Bell Labs, 26
Big iron (as buzzword), 6
Binary files, 20
text files and, 12
Blocked records, 328
Blocks, 103
VM/CMS, 254
Blue shop (as buzzword), 135
BOTTOM command:
TSO EDIT editor, 352
XEDIT text editor, 275
Bourne shell, 39, 71
Box (as buzzword), 32
Brief help, 239, 244
BROWSE utility (ISPF), 374
Buzzwords:
bang, 65
big iron, 6
blue shop, 135
box, 32
client/server, 4
DASD, 7
downsize, 2
enterprise, 6
full screen, 19
gen, 38

Buzzwords (*cont.*):
string, 14
The Labs, 26
Vaxen, 83
virtual, 224

C programming language, 137
OS/400 and, 133, 152
C shell, 39, 72
C++, 137
CALL command (OS/400), 208
CANCEL command (ISPF text editor), 347
Cancel function key, 148, 156
Cancelling your print job:
OpenVMS, 122
OS/400, 203
UNIX, 70
VM/CMS, 280
Card reader, 234, 284
Case sensitivity:
EVE text editor, 117
ISPF editor, 347
MVS, 307
OpenVMS, 88
OS/400, 145, 149
SEU editor, 195
VM/CMS, 234
cat command (UNIX), 48
CATALOG data set disposition, 328
Catalogs, 312
adding data sets to, 332
cd command (UNIX), 37, 51
CHANGE command (TSO EDIT editor), 354
Change Direction key (EVE text editor), 117
Change Profile command (OS/400), 144
CHGCURLIB command (OS/400), 153, 183
CHGLIBL command (OS/400), 180
CHGPRF command (OS/400), 144, 202, 208
Child directory, UNIX, 36
chmod command (UNIX), 55, 71
CICS, 298
CL commands, 141
CL programs, 141, 203
compiling, 207
Client, 4
Client/server:
as buzzword, 4
computing, 79
OS/400 and, 136, 137
CLISTs, 309, 324
Clocate command (VM/CMS), 245
CMS, 14, 223, 224, 234

COBOL:
   CICS and, 298
   OS/400 and, 133, 152
   TSO EDIT editor and, 349
Colon (:) prompt (vi text editor), 64
Command procedures, 12
   automatic login:
      OpenVMS, 124
      UNIX, 71
   automatic logon:
      MVS, 361
      VM/CMS, 280
   automatic signon, 208
   MVS, 324, 360
   OpenVMS, 122
   OS/400, 203
   UNIX, 70
   VM/CMS, 280
Command line, 3
   editing (OS/400), 148
   help (EVE editor), 119
   help (VM/CMS), 244
   options:
      MVS, 307
      VM/CMS, 249
Command mode (vi text editor), 62
Command parameters:
   MVS, 306
   OS/400, 142
Command prompt:
   EVE, 114
   UNIX, 32
Command prompt display, 143, 148, 167
Communicating with other users:
   OpenVMS, 125
   UNIX, 72
Compiler, 12
CompuServe, 23
CONTINUE command (OpenVMS), 87
Controlling access to a file:
   OpenVMS, 108
   UNIX, 55, 71
COPY command:
   MVS, 308, 312, 316
   TSO EDIT editor, 355
   VM/CMS, 255
COPYFILE command (VM/CMS), 255
Copying data sets, with ISPF, 370
Copying files:
   OpenVMS, 104
   OS/400, 174
   to other directories (OpenVMS), 105
   to other directories (UNIX), 50

Copying files (cont.):
   UNIX, 50
   VM/CMS, 255
   with FILELIST (VM/CMS), 289
Copying lines:
   ISPF editor, 344
   SEU editor, 193
   TSO EDIT editor, 355
   XEDIT editor, 273
Copying members, 176
Corrupted data, 21
CP (Control Program), 234
CP (VM Control Program), 225, 229
   directory, 227
cp command (UNIX), 50
   read privileges and, 51
CPYF command (OS/400), 174
CPYSRCF command (OS/400), 176
   printing with, 199
CREATE command (OpenVMS)
      /DIRECTORY qualifier, 110
Creating a new data set, with the TSO EDIT
      editor, 349
Creating directories:
   OpenVMS, 110
   UNIX, 57
Creating files (OS/400), 204
CRTCLPGM command (OS/400), 207
CRTDUPOBJ command (OS/400), 174
CRTLIB command (OS/400), 183
CRTSRCPF command (OS/400), 204
CTSS, 223
Cuckoo's Egg, 25
Current directory:
      Default directory vs. (OpenVMS), 93
      UNIX, 35, 36, 51, 53
Current folder, 127
Current library, 140, 152, 153
Current line, TSO EDIT editor, 352
Cursor movement, vi editor, 66

DASD (as buzzword), 7
Data definition name, 308, 325
Data Definition Specification, 206
Data File Utility, 136
Data security, MVS, 319
Data sets, 308
   adding to a catalog, 332
   allocating, 324
   CATALOG disposition, 328
   copying, 321
   DELETE disposition, 328

Data sets (*cont.*):
  deleting, 323
  disposition, 328
  files vs., 325
  finding out allocation status, 330
  KEEP disposition, 328
  looking at, 320
  modifying, 325
  names, 309
  organization (DSORG), 319, 321
  renaming, 322
  sharing, 325
  size, 327
  temporary, 328
  too big, 322
  unallocating, 329
Database data, 152
Database server, 4
DCL, 82
  command procedures, 83
DDNAME, 308, 324, 325, 360
DDS, 206
DEC, 79, 134
  DECstation, 29
  PDP-7, 26
  server, 9
  VT220, 113
Default directory
  current directory vs. (OpenVMS), 93
  OpenVMS, 92, 101, 105
  UNIX, 35
DELETE command:
  /ENTRY qualifier in OpenVMS, 122
  MVS, 238, 323
  OpenVMS, 89, 110
  TSO EDIT editor, 355
DELETE data set disposition, 328
Delete key (OpenVMS), 85, 86
Delete protection (OpenVMS), 108
Deleting data sets (MVS), 316, 323
Deleting files:
  OpenVMS, 107
  OS/400, 179
  UNIX, 53
  VM/CMS, 259
  wildcards and, 17
  with FILELIST (VM/CMS), 290
Deleting lines:
  SEU editor, 192
  XEDIT editor, 272
Deleting members, OS/400, 179
Deleting programs, 179
Deleting text:
  EVE editor, 116

Deleting text (*cont.*):
  ISPF editor, 343
  TSO EDIT editor, 355
  vi editor, 63
Detailed help, 239, 244
Device, 7
  OpenVMS, 90
DFU, 136
Digital Equipment Corporation (DEC), 4, 79
  (*See also* DEC)
DIR command (OpenVMS MAIL), 127
  /FOLDER qualifier, 127
DIR command (OpenVMS), 101
Directories:
  creating (UNIX), 47
  moving between (OpenVMS), 92
  OpenVMS, 90, 91
  removing (UNIX), 58
  renaming in OpenVMS, 107
  UNIX, 34
DIRECTORY command (OpenVMS), 89, 94,
    99, 101
  /DATE qualifier, 103
  /PROTECTION qualifier, 108
  /SIZE qualifier, 102
  /VERSION qualifier, 103
DISCARD command (VM/CMS), 288, 290
Disk space, querying:
  OpenVMS, 94
  VM/CMS, 238
Displaying a data set's contents, 312, 318
  with ISPF, 374
Displaying a text file's contents:
  OpenVMS, 103
  OS/400, 172
  UNIX, 48
  VM/CMS, 255
  with FILELIST (VM/CMS), 290
Distributed systems, 7
DLTF command (OS/400), 179
DLTLIB command (OS/400), 184
DLTPGM command (OS/400), 179
Do key (EVE editor), 117
DOS, 11, 14, 22, 28, 34, 82, 90
  current directory, 93
DOS/VSE, 7
  VM and, 223
Dot, 310
DOWN command:
  ISPF editor, 341
  TSO EDIT editor, 352
Downsize (as buzzword), 2
DSNAME, 325
DSORG, 319, 321

DSPFD command (OS/400), 169, 172
DSPKBDMAP command (OS/400), 163
DSPLIB command (OS/400), 168
DSPLIBL command (OS/400), 180
DSPMSG command (OS/400), 211
DSPPFM command (OS/400), 152, 172, 200
DSPRINT command (MVS), 359
DSRI, 82
Duplicating lines:
  ISPF editor, 342
  SEU editor, 191
  TSO EDIT editor, 356
  XEDIT editor, 270
Duplicating objects, 174
DYNIX operating system, 27

E-mail, 13
  MVS, 362
  OpenVMS, 125
  OS/400, 209
  UNIX, 29, 72
  VM/CMS, 282
ed text editor (UNIX), 61, 64
Edit mode, TSO text editor, 350
Edit profiles, ISPF editor, 335
Edit protection, OpenVMS, 108
Editing a file, from FILELIST (VM/CMS), 290
EDLIN, TSO EDIT editor and, 349
EDT line editor (OpenVMS), 113, 114
EDTLIBL command (OS/400), 180
Electronic Customer Support, 160
Electronic mail (*see* E-mail)
END command (TSO EDIT editor), 357
Enlarge function key, 157
Enter key:
  OpenVMS, 87
  Return key vs., 341
Enterprise (as buzzword), 6
Entry display, on-line help, 153
Equal sign, VM/CMS, 256
ERASE command (VM/CMS), 236, 259
Error messages:
  OpenVMS, 100
  OS/400, 165, 209
  UNIX, 40
  VM/CMS, 250
ES9000 mainframes, 295
ESA/370, 299
Escape key, vi editor, 62, 63
Ethernet, OS/400 and, 136
EVE text editor (OpenVMS), 113
ex text editor (UNIX), 61, 64

Exclamation point (!), 65
EXEC command (MVS), 360
EXEC language, 83
Execution:
  privileges, 71
  rights, 44
EXIT command:
  EVE text editor, 118
  OpenVMS MAIL, 129
Exit function key, 147, 156
Extended:
  attribute, 151
  help, 154
Extensible VAX Editor (EVE), 113
EXTRACT command (OpenVMS MAIL), 129

F command (ISPF text editor), 345
Field Exit key, 140
Field help, 153, 156
FILE command (OpenVMS MAIL), 128
File:
  format, changing, 257
  label (VM/CMS), 234
  mode (UNIX), 44, 54
  organization, 10
  organization (OpenVMS), 90
  organization (UNIX), 34
  protection (OpenVMS), 108
  server, 4
  specification (OpenVMS), 90
  system, 3
  transfer, 22
  type (OpenVMS), 88
  versions (OpenVMS), 89
FILEDEF (VM/CMS), 324
Fileid, 234
Filemode (VM/CMS), 235
Filenames, 9, 14
  MVS, 309
  OpenVMS, 88, 91
  OS/400, 149
  UNIX, 32
  VM/CMS, 234
Files, 10
  Data sets vs., 325
  MVS (data sets), 308
  OS/400, 151
  sending to another user:
    OpenVMS, 126
    UNIX, 73
    VM/CMS, 283
Filespec, OpenVMS, 90

FIND command:
  ISPF text editor, 345
  TSO EDIT editor, 357
Fixed-length records:
  MVS, 328
  VM/CMS, 254
Flavors of UNIX, 27, 43
Folders (OpenVMS MAIL):
  creating messages, 128
  deleting, 129
  moving messages between, 128
FORTRAN, 267
  ISPF editor and, 337
  TSO EDIT editor and, 349
FREE command (MVS), 329
Front end, 6
Full screen (as buzzword), 19
Fully qualified data set name, 309
Function keys, OS/400, 147

Gen (as buzzword), 38
Generic object names, 145, 149
GO command (OS/400), 150
Gold key, 114
Group (MVS qualifier), 310
Group protection category, 108

Halt Type command (VM/CMS), 232
Help:
  brief (VM/CMS), 239
  command-line:
    OpenVMS, 97
    VM/CMS, 244
  detailed (VM/CMS), 239
  function keys (VM/CMS), 240
  UNIX, 37
HELP command:
  OpenVMS MAIL, 130
  XEDIT text editor, 276
Help key:
  EVE editor, 118
  OS/400, 147, 153
Help menus, VM/CMS, 242
Hewlett-Packard, 137
Hexadecimal numbers, 260
Hidden files, 71
High-level qualifier, 309, 315
HOLDING message, 232
Home directory, 35
HT command (VM/CMS), 232
Hypertext links, 160

Hyphen character (-):
  OpenVMS, 92, 100
  UNIX, 40

IBM, 8, 9, 80, 223, 280
IDDU, 136, 206
ILE (Integrated Language Environment), 133
Informational messages, 209, 212
INPUT command (TSO EDIT editor), 353
Input mode, TSO text editor, 350
Inquiry messages, 209, 212
  responding to, 212
Insert mode:
  EVE editor, 116, 117
  MVS, 342
  SEU editor, 191
  vi editor, 63
  VM/CMS, 270
Interactive Data Definition Utility (*see* IDDU)
Interrupt key, 87
IPL (Initial Program Load), 229
ISDN and OS/400, 136
ISPF, 297, 301, 366
  activity log, 367
  data set names, 335
  qualifiers, 310
  starting, 303
  TSO vs., 315
ISPF text editor, 333
  case sensitivity, 337, 347
  environment, 337
  line commands, 338
  NULLS, 337
  SEU text editor and, 187
ISPF/PDF, 297

JCL (Job Control Language), 297
  printing and, 359
JES2, JES3, 296
Job Control Language (*see* JCL)
Job log, 160
Joe User, 13

KEDIT, 19, 265
KEEP data set disposition, 328
Kermit, 23, 257
Kernel, 39
Keyboard help (OS/400), 163
Keyboard locked up:
  MVS, 342

Keyboard locked up (*cont.*):
  OS/400, 149
  VM/CMS, 270

Labels in CL programs, 205
Labs, The (as buzzword), 26
LEFT command (ISPF editor), 341
Lexical functions, 124
LF file attribute, 152
Libraries (OS/400), 150
  changing the current, 183
  creating, 183
  deleting, 183
  renaming, 178
  system, 183
Library, MVS, 308
Library list (OS/400), 151, 152, 168
  displaying, 180
  editing, 180
  user part, 180
Licensed Program Product, 171
Line commands:
  ISPF editor, 338
  SEU editor, 186, 187
Line numbers, 321
  data sets and, 309
  MVS, 360
Lines and records, 254
LINK command (VM/CMS), 260
LIST command (MVS), 320
List display, 146
  on-line help, 154
  option column, 146
LISTALC command (MVS), 330
  STATUS operand, 331
LISTCAT command (MVS), 312, 318
  ENTRIES operand, 311, 318
  LEVEL operand, 318
  VOLUME operand, 312
LISTDS command (MVS), 350
  MEMBERS operand, 319
  STATUS operand, 330
LISTFILE command (VM/CMS), 236, 251
Listing a file's members, 169
Listing filenames:
  OpenVMS, 101
  OS/400, 168
  UNIX, 43
  VM/CMS, 251
Listing more than filenames:
  OpenVMS, 102
  UNIX, 43

Listing more than filenames (*cont.*):
  VM/CMS, 254
LOCATE command (XEDIT text
    editor), 274
Logging in/on, 9
  MVS, 302, 361
  OpenVMS, 85, 124
  OS/400, 139
  UNIX, 31, 71
  VM/CMS, 227, 282
Logging out/off, 9
  MVS, 308
  OpenVMS, 86
  OS/400, 141
  UNIX, 32
  VM/CMS, 234
Logical file, 152
Logical record length, 254
  MVS, 329
LOGIN.COM file, 123
LOGON command (MVS), 302
  RECON operand, 304
LOGON.CLIST data set, 361
Looking at text files, 20
Low-level qualifier, 310
lp command (UNIX), 69
lpstat command (UNIX), 69
LRECL, 254, 257
  ISPF text editor and, 342
  MVS, 329
ls command (UNIX), 41, 70

MACH operating system, 27
Macintosh, 14, 22, 27, 82
Mail, 13
  testing, 18
Major Commands function key, 148
man command (UNIX), 38
Members (MVS), 308
  editing, 335
  listing, 319
  naming, 311
Members (OS/400), 151
  copying with the PDM, 176
  deleting, 179
  deleting with the PDM, 179
  displaying with the PDM, 174
  listing, 169
  listing with the PDM, 171
  renaming, 178
  renaming with the PDM, 179
Menu display, on-line help, 153

Menus:
  initial (OS/400), 209
  OS/400, 140
Message queue, 209
Message type field, 212
Messages (OS/400):
  informational, 209, 212
  inquiry, 209, 212
MFT, 299
Microsoft, 7, 280
Minidisks, 235, 238
MINIX, 28
Minus character (−):
  MVS, 306
  UNIX, 55
mkdir command (UNIX), 57
MOD access to data sets, 325
more command (UNIX), 48, 70
More Keys function key, 148
MORE... message, 231
Mouse, 39
MOVE command:
  OpenVMS MAIL, 128
  TSO EDIT editor, 356
Moving between directories:
  OpenVMS, 92
  UNIX, 36
Moving files:
  OpenVMS, 107
  UNIX, 52
Moving lines:
  ISPF editor, 345
  SEU editor, 194
  TSO EDIT editor, 356
  XEDIT editor, 274
MS-DOS, 7
MULTICS, 26
  VM and, 223
mv command (UNIX), 52
MVS, 14, 295
  disconnecting from, 304
  VM and, 223
MVS/ESA, 298, 299
MVS/XA, 299
MVT, 299

NetWare, OS/400 and, 136
NEWMAIL mail folder, 126
NeXT, 27
Node, 90
NOT ACCEPTED message, 232
NOTE command (VM/CMS), 282, 285
Novell, 9

Object (OS/400):
  size, 169
  type, 150, 175
OfficeVision, 137
OLD access to data sets, 325
On-line help, 10
  EVE editor, 118
  expanding help windows (OS/400), 156
  from command line (OS/400), 159
  hypertext links (OS/400), 160
  ISPF editor, 348
  MVS, 312
  OpenVMS, 94
  OpenVMS MAIL program, 130
  OS/400, 153
  SEU editor, 196
  TSO EDIT editor, 358
  UNIX, 37
  VM/CMS, 239, 249, 250
  XEDIT editor, 276
  (See also Help)
On-line tutorials, OS/400, 160
OpenVMS, 9, 11, 14, 79
Operands, MVS, 307
Operating system (defined), 3
Operational Assistant, 163, 200,
  209, 212
Option column of list display, 146
OS, 299
OS/2, 82, 133, 136
OS/400, 133
  Command Language, 141
OSI, OS/400 and, 136
Overstrike mode:
  EVE editor, 116, 117
  ISPF editor, 342
  SEU editor, 148
  vi editor, 64
  XEDIT, 270
Owner protection category, 108

PA1 key, MVS, 306
Page up, page down keys, 148
Panels, 297
Partitioned data sets, 152, 308
  copying, 321
Passwords, 9
  MVS, 302
  OS/400, 140
  UNIX, 31
Pathname, UNIX, 34, 50
Pathworks, 82
PC Support package, 136

PC/DOS, 7
  VM and, 223
PDM (*see* Program Development Manager)
PDP-1, 4, 134
PDP-8, 5
PDS (partitioned data set), 308
Peek function key, 286
Peer-to-peer communications, 79
  OS/400, 137
Percent sign (%):
  OpenVMS, 90, 100
  VM/CMS, 237
Period character (.):
  in UNIX pathnames, 36
  OpenVMS, 92
PF file attribute, 152
pg command (UNIX), 48
Physical file, 152
Pipe symbol (|):
  UNIX, 48, 73
Plus character (+):
  in CL programs, 206
  MVS, 306
  UNIX, 55
Positional parameters, 144, 175
POSIX, 27
Predefined value, 146, 149
Prefix:
  area (VM/CMS), 266
  commands (XEDIT text editor), 268
PREFIX command (XEDIT text editor), 267
Prefix of MVS dataset, 309
PRINT command (OpenVMS), 121
  /QUEUE qualifier, 121
PRINT command (VM/CMS), 290
Print job, cancelling:
  OpenVMS, 122
  OS/400, 203
  UNIX, 70
  VM/CMS, 280
Print queue:
  OpenVMS, 121
  OS/400, 202
  UNIX, 69
  VM/CMS, 279
Print spooler, 199
PRINTDS command (MVS), 359
Printer writer, 199
Printers, assigning in OS/400, 200
Printing, 12, 20
Printing data sets, MVS, 359
Printing text files:
  from FILELIST (VM/CMS), 290
  OpenVMS, 121

Printing text files (*cont.*):
  OS/400, 199, 200
  UNIX, 69
  VM/CMS, 279
PROFILE EXEC file, 282
PROFILE XEDIT file, 276
Program Development Manager (OS/400):
  availability, 171, 172
  copying members with, 176
  deleting members with, 179
  displaying a file's members with, 174
  listing a file's members with, 171
  printing a file member with, 202
  renaming members with, 179
  starting SEU from, 187
Programs (OS/400):
  deleting, 179
  renaming, 178
Project (MVS qualifier), 310
Prompt key, 143, 148
PS/2, 136
Punch cards, 234
PURGE command (OpenVMS), 108
PURGE PRINTER command (VM/CMS), 280
Purging old versions of your files, 108
pwd command (UNIX), 37, 57

QCLSRC file, 204, 207
QQUIT command (XEDIT text editor), 275
QSYS library, 150
Qualified object name, 151, 172
Qualifiers, 99, 309
QUERY DISK command (VM/CMS), 238
QUERY PRINTER command (VM/CMS), 279
Question mark (?):
  in CL programs, 208
  in UNIX mail program, 73
  OS/400, 143
  UNIX, 33
QUIT command:
  EVE, 118
  OpenVMS MAIL, 129
  XEDIT text editor, 275
Quitting:
  EVE editor, 118
  ISPF editor, 347
  SEU text editor, 196
  TSO TEXT editor, 357
  vi editor, 65
  XEDIT editor, 275

Rdb, 82
RDO, 82

RDRLIST command (VM/CMS), 285
Read access:
    OpenVMS, 108
    UNIX, 45
    VM/CMS, 261
READ command (OpenVMS Mail), 128
READ message, 232
Read password, 261
Read permission, UNIX, 55, 65
Reader, 284
Reading and writing, 21
READY prompt, 303, 304
Ready; prompt, 229, 230
RECEIVE command:
    MVS, 363, 365
    VM/CMS, 287
Receiving a file, OS/400, 216
Receiving mail, UNIX, 73
RECFM, 257
Reconnecting:
    MVS, 304
    OpenVMS, 86
Record format:
    MVS, 328
    VM/CMS, 254
Records and lines, 254
Redraw command (vi text editor), 67
Relative pathnames, 35, 37, 57
RELEASE command (VM/CMS), 263
Removing directories:
    OpenVMS, 110
    UNIX, 55, 58
RENAME command:
    MVS, 312, 316, 322
    VM/CMS, 258
Renaming data sets, with ISPF, 372
Renaming directories, OpenVMS, 107
Renaming files:
    and objects (OS/400), 177
    OpenVMS, 106
    UNIX, 52
    VM/CMS, 258
    with FILELIST (VM/CMS), 289
Renaming members, 178
Request id, 69
Reset key:
    ISPF editor, 342
    OS/400, 148
    SEU text editor and, 191
    VM/CMS, 232, 270
RESUME command (TSO EDIT editor), 354
Retrieve function key, 148
Retrieving previous commands, 87, 107

Return key:
    Enter key vs., 341
    OpenVMS, 87
REXX, 83, 280
RIGHT command (ISPF editor), 341
Rightsizing, 2
RISC System, 137
rm command (UNIX), 53
rmdir command (UNIX), 57, 58
RNMM command (OS/400), 178
RNMOBJ command (OS/400), 177
Root directory:
    OpenVMS, 91
    UNIX, 34
RPG, OS/400 and, 133, 206
RS computers, RS/6000:
    AIX operating system, 27
    AS/400 and, 137
RUNNING message, 232

SAVE command:
    ISPF text editor, 347
    SEU text editor, 196
    TSO EDIT editor, 357
    XEDIT text editor, 275
SAVE FILE (EVE command), 117
Saving a message in a text file, OpenVMS, 129
Saving edits:
    EVE editor, 117
    ISPF editor, 347
    TSO EDIT editor, 357
    vi editor, 64
    XEDIT editor, 275
SCRIPT files, 253
Scroll up, scroll down keys, 148
Search index, 154, 159
Search path, 71
Searching for text:
    ISPF editor, 345
    OS/400, 174
    SEU editor, 194
    TSO EDIT editor, 357
    vi editor, 64
    VM/CMS help, 245
    XEDIT editor, 274
Security, VM/CMS, 260
SELECT command (OpenVMS MAIL), 127, 130
SEND command:
    MVS, 362
    OpenVMS MAIL, 125
    VM/CMS, 284
SENDFILE command (VM/CMS), 283, 285

Sending a file:
  OpenVMS, 126
  OS/400, 215
  UNIX, 72
  UNIX to AS/400, 215
  VM to AS/400, 215
  VM/CMS, 283
Sending messages:
  MVS, 362
  OpenVMS, 125
  OS/400, 209
  UNIX, 72
  VM/CMS, 282
Sequential data sets, 308
Server, 4
SET (OpenVMS):
  DEFAULT, 92
  PROTECTION, 108, 109, 110
SET (XEDIT text editor):
  AUTOSAVE, 267, 275
  CASE, 267
  NUMBER, 267, 268
  PREFIX, 267
SET FIND CASE (EVE command), 117
SET MATCH command (SEU text editor), 195
SEU text editor, 137, 152, 185, 339
  command files and, 203
  command line, 186
  on-line help, 196
  printing a file member with, 202
  starting from the Program Development
    Manager, 187
Sharing files between users, VM/CMS, 260
Shell scripts, 49, 70
Shell, shell commands, 39
Shop (as buzzword), 135
SHOW (OpenVMS):
  DEFAULT, 92
  PROTECTION, 109
  QUEUE, 121, 122
  QUOTA, 94
SHR access to data sets, 325
Signing on, 9
  OS/400, 208
SIGNOFF command (OS/400), 141
Silicone Graphics, 137
Slash character (/):
  OpenVMS, 99
  UNIX, 34, 36
  vi editor, 64
  VM/CMS, 287, 289
  XEDIT, 274
SNA, OS/400 and, 136

SNDMSG command (OS/400), 209
SNDNETF command (OS/400), 215, 216
Source physical file, 152
  creating, 204
SPF, 297
Split/join key (XEDIT text editor), 277
SQL, 82
Stoll, Clifford, 25
STREDU command (OS/400), 161
String (as buzzword), 14
STRSCHIDX command (OS/400), 154
STRSEU command (OS/400), 185
Structured Query Language, 82
Subdirectories:
  maximum levels, 110
  OpenVMS, 91
  UNIX, 34
Subsystem, 139
Sun Microsystems, 27, 29, 137
Sun workstations, 3, 9, 39
SunOS operating system, 27
Supercomputers, 295
SVS, 299
Switches, 40
Symbols, 122
Syntax prompting, 197
System name, OS/400, 215
System protection category, 108
System/3, 134
System/32, 34, 36, 38 134
System/3X, 134, 137

Tab key:
  in ISPF editor, 341
  in SEU, 191
TCP/IP and OS/400, 136
Teletypewriters, 19
Terminal emulation, 23
  EVE editor, 118
  MVS, 306
  OpenVMS, 86, 87
  OS/400, 148, 149, 163
  SEU text editor and, 191
  vi text editor and, 61, 66, 67
  VM/CMS, 227, 232
Text editors, 3, 11
  MVS, 309
  OpenVMS, 113
  OS/400, 185
  testing, 18
  UNIX, 61
  VM/CMS, 265

Text files, 20
    binary files and, 12
Text Processing Utility (OpenVMS), 114
Tick, 309
TOP command:
    TSO EDIT editor, 352
    XEDIT text editor, 274
TPU, 114
TRANSMIT command (MVS), 363
TSO, 297, 301
    command language, 360
    ISPF vs., 315
    prompt, 304
    text editor, 333, 349
TTY mode, 19
Tutorial System Support, 160, 161
Tutorial, on-line, OS/400, 161
Type (MVS qualifier), 310
TYPE command (OpenVMS), 103
    /PAGE qualifier, 104
TYPE command (VM/CMS), 255, 290

UIC, 94
ULTRIX operating system, 27
Unallocating data sets, 332
Undeleting mail messages, 129
UNIX, 3, 9, 11, 80, 91
    current directory vs. VMS default directory,
        93
    flavors, 27, 43
    UNIX International, 27
    VM and, 223
    VMS vs., 81
Unlinking accessed disks, 262
UP command:
    ISPF editor, 341
    TSO EDIT editor, 352
UpRiteBase, 14
USENET, 29
User Identification Code, 94
User profile, 140
    changing, 202, 208
User Support and Education menu, 158
User Support function key, 148
usr/group, 26, 27

Variable-length records, MVS, 328
VAX, 79, 137
    11/780, 80
    VAX, 9000, 79

VAX (*cont.*):
    VAXcluster, 80, 91
    Vaxen (as buzzword), 83
    VAXstation VLC, 79
Version numbers, 89, 91, 105, 107
vi text editor, 61
    on OpenVMS, 113
Viewed Topics function key, 160
Virtual (as buzzword), 224
Virtual Machine, 223
VM, 223
    administrator, 227
    VM/370, VM/ESA, VM/IS, VM/SP, VM/XA,
        225
VM READ message, 232
VM/CMS, 8, 9, 209, 324
VMS, 79, 82
    MVS and, 306
    UNIX vs., 81
VOLSER, 312
VSAM data sets, 308
VT terminals, 86
VTAM, 301
VTOC, 312

WASTEBASKET mail folder, 126, 129
Wildcards, 15
    MVS, 311
    OpenVMS, 89, 102, 107, 109
    OS/400, 145, 149
    UNIX, 33, 43
    VM/CMS, 235
Workstations, 29, 137
World protection category, 108
WRITE (EVE command), 117
Write:
    access (UNIX), 57
    password (VM/CMS), 261
    permission (UNIX), 54, 55
    protection (OpenVMS), 108
Writing and reading, 21
WRKMBRPDM command (OS/400), 149, 171
WRKNETF command (OS/400), 216
WRKSPLF command (OS/400), 199

XEDIT text editor, 265, 282, 286, 338
    SEU text editor and, 187
XENIX operating system, 27
XINU operating system, 28